Analysis of the Institutes of the Christian Religion of John Calvin

Analysis of the Institutes of the Christian Religion of John Calvin

FORD LEWIS BATTLES
ASSISTED BY JOHN WALCHENBACH

BAKER BOOK HOUSE
Grand Rapids, Michigan

ISBN: 0-8010-0766-6
Library of Congress Catalog Card Number: 79-57385
Printed in the United States of America

Foreword

One of the popular courses at Pittsburgh Theological Seminary during the late sixties and through the seventies was a seminar on Calvin's *Institutes of the Christian Religion*, taught by Dr. Ford Lewis Battles. The seminar not only afforded students the opportunity to rub shoulders with one of the world's foremost Calvin scholars, but equipped students to think historically, systematically, and, in the best sense of the word, pastorally.

When students were informed at the beginning of the course that one of the requirements was to read the entire 1559 edition of the *Institutes*, several questioned the wisdom of signing up for this elective. How could one treat all the theological *loci* contained in Calvin's definitive work? Yet those who fought the good fight and persisted to the end came away with a perceptive overview of Calvin's thought, which is so essential in understanding any single doctrine.

As chapters of this *Analysis* emerged, many students in the Calvin seminar and related courses requested reprints, and found them to be of assistance as they made their way through the *Institutes*. Clergy and laypersons have also found the *Analysis* extremely helpful. It is a pleasure to see this work in print so that all those who wish to delve into the roots of the Reformation may have a guide and, as it were, a road map.

If Ford Lewis Battles could have seen the final publication of this work, it certainly would have pleased his heart. With the death of Dr. Battles on Thanksgiving Day, 1979, the world of scholarship and the World Church lost a man at the heart of both. I know that I speak for a generation of students who were privileged to come under his tutelage, to teach under his guidance, and engage in research under his rigorous honesty, in expressing gratitude to God for the gift of his life.

One of Ford Lewis Battles' favorite expressions, and indeed admonitions to all of us, was, "Ad Fontes." Back to the Sources! If this

Analysis of Calvin's monumental work is of assistance in returning even a few people to one of the primary sources of Reformed thought, then the labors here represented will be well rewarded.

John R. Walchenbach
Easter, 1980

Contents

Analysis of the Institutes of the Christian Religion of John Calvin

ERRATA

Four lines of type following the text on page 11 were incorrectly placed at the top of page 14. To maintain continuity, read those four lines before continuing with text on page 12.

Introduction

Another Summary of the *Institutes*?

Praise be to any man who saves us from having to depend upon compendiums of the great classics![1]

In his introduction to the Library of Christian Classics edition of Calvin's *Institutes of the Christian Religion* (Philadelphia: The Westminster Press, 1960), John T. McNeill has traced the complex literary history, not only of full editions in various languages of that work, but also that of the numerous epitomes or abridgments which began to appear shortly after Calvin's death (LCC 20. xlviii-l).[2] Most of these writings are either abridgments of the original or condensations into a number of aphorisms of the thought of Calvin's work. Sometimes these compendia are accompanied by tables which attempt to set out graphically the logical structure which the compendiarist divines in Calvin's work.

The present book, however, does not fall strictly into any of these earlier categories. It is simply a detailed analytical outline of the text of the *Institutes* as Calvin wrote it. The *Analysis* took its origin from my seminar on the *Institutes*, begun at the Hartford Seminary Foundation in 1953, continued at Pittsburgh Theological Seminary in 1967, and at Calvin Theological Seminary (1978–79). In that seminar the entire *Institutes of the Christian Religion* has been read and discussed in the course of a single semester or term.

This is indeed a large assignment, but nothing less than a reading of the full text will afford an accurate picture of Calvin's thought. To attain that, however, some guide is needed. This is the intended function of the *Analysis*, providing as it does a synoptic view of what Dr. McNeill picturesquely called "the cumbrous bulk" of the *Institutes*. The *Analysis* most certainly is not a substitute for reading the whole; it

---

1. H. Hailperin, *Rashi and the Christian Scholars* (Pittsburgh: University of Pittsburgh Press, 1963), p. 27.
2. The Library of Christian Classics edition of Calvin's *Institutes*, volumes 20 and 21 of Westminster's series, will be noted as LCC 20 and LCC 21.

task; it could never have been completed apart from the patient collaboration of John Walchenbach, my sometime teaching assistant at Pittsburgh, now Executive Secretary for Program, the Reformed Church in America. He is responsible for the work in chapters 6, 9, 10, and 11 of Book Two and 11, 12, 13, 14, 16, 17, 18, and 25 of Book Three, as well as 7–17 of Book Four. A. C. Burfeind worked on chapters 3 and 4 of Book Four. The use of the *Analysis* by colleagues in other institutions has also been a source of encouragement to me.

The Life Story of a Book (1536–1559): from Six to Eighty Chapters

The history of the Christian church tells of two kinds of theologians—those whose thought undergoes constant change and development during their lifetime, and those who seem to have grasped at the outset of their theological career a shape that remains thereafter firm and constant. The frankness of Augustine's *Retractations* bespeaks the first sort of theologian. Calvin is usually pointed to as exemplifying the second.

There is a sense in which Calvin's theology is, at beginning and end, one and the same. For unlike Augustine, he needed no book of *Retractations* to explain the contradictions between earlier writings and later ones. Yet, with all its sense of firmness and constancy, the *Institutes of the Christian Religion* did undergo change during the course of its literary history. And that change was in dynamic response to the incessant theological debate of the time. If the source and inspiration of the *Institutes* was Scripture, viewed both in its origins and its long exegetical history, then the matrix was the times in which Calvin lived.

With Augustine, Luther, and many others, Calvin saw the Christian life not as a leap, after conversion, into perfection, but as a gradual, often painful, growth toward the blessed consummation which can come only at death.[3] Thus, when in his "Letter to the Reader" that introduces the final Latin edition of the *Institutes*, Calvin states, "Although I did not regret the labor spent, I was never satisfied until the work had been arranged in the order now set forth" (LCC 20.3), he is saying in effect: Here in these successive editions of my *magnum opus* is the story of my own gradual growth in the Christian life. As we read the *Institutes* we must never wander far from this personal testimony of its author.

The literary history of the *Institutes* has been chronicled many

3. See John Calvin, *The Piety of John Calvin*, trans. and ed. by Ford Lewis Battles (Grand Rapids: Baker, 1978), pp. 55, 84 n.275.

times, and this is not the place to repeat an oft-told tale. What is needful here is a sketch of some of the decisive factors that shaped that quarter-century leading from a small, concise outline of the faith to a full and sustained essay on the Christian religion.

First, Calvin grew greatly as he continued his reading in the Fathers, in Scripture, and in the history of its exegesis. A sound but limited grasp of Augustine marks the 1536 edition. A large increment of Augustinian material enters the 1539 edition for the first time. Still more is appropriated in the third Latin edition of 1543. We see how Calvin's further labor on Christian anthropology and ecclesiology beyond the first edition owes much to Augustine. The second most important church father, John Chrysostom, is virtually absent from the first edition; his influence begins to show itself in 1539, and of course greatly in the New Testament *Commentaries* whose preparation paralleled that of the *Institutes*. Calvin's balanced handling of Scripture texts rests, at least in part, on his highly personal amalgam of Augustine's dogmatics and Chrysostom's exegetics. One could trace as well the lesser, but significant, impact of other church fathers upon Calvin's theological growth.

Second, as Calvin came to know Martin Bucer, both through his writings and through the Strasbourg period of collaboration, he was profoundly influenced. Already dependent on Bucer through the *Enarrationes* on the Gospels (1530) for much of his understanding of prayer,[4] Calvin (under Bucer's tutelage) came to a deeper understanding of predestination. The reading of Bucer's *Metaphrases* on Romans (1536) first is felt in the *Catechism* of 1537/38 (steppingstone as it is between the first and second editions of the *Institutes*[5]); then is fully seen in the 1539 *Institutes* and in Calvin's Romans *Commentary* published the following year.

Third, the "pastoral interlude" of 1538–41, when Calvin was pastor of the small emigré French congregation at Strasbourg, bore fruit in the rich ecclesiastical additions to the 1543 edition. Calvinism would be a poor, or at least inadequate, theological system for the church indeed were it deprived of the significant insight into the life and discipline of the worshiping congregation set down in 1543. Calvin's exposition of the nature of the church and its discipline must be coupled with his not-to-be-forgotten contribution to Christian worship and song.[6] The "Letter to the Reader" that heads *The Form of Church Prayers and Songs* (1542), again, witnesses to Calvin's growth in the faith.

---

4. *Institution 1536*, trans. and ed. by Ford Lewis Battles (Atlanta: John Knox Press, 1975), ch. 3 and notes.
5. See *Catechism 1538*, trans. and ed. by Ford Lewis Battles, 1972, intro.; also sect. 13.
6. See *Piety*, ch. 6.

can be a road-map for the journey; and it can serve as a useful means of review as well.

The *Analysis* could not have been conceived without the help of many students who, by their questions and reflections, drew me to the

Calvin's opponents, as much as his friends, may be singled out as a fourth factor in the growth of the book. From Pierre Caroli, who unsuccessfully challenged Calvin's trinitarian orthodoxy, through Michael Servetus, who endeavored to destroy the doctrine of the Trinity and to break the living bond between the Old and the New Testaments, the stimulation of often acrimonious debate deepened Calvin's theology in a positive way. As he threaded his way through the maze of conflicting eucharistic positions, Calvin's perceptive response to his adversaries gave an ever deeper root to a position already correctly intuited in 1536. There is not a page of the *Institutes* where the ongoing debate with one worthy or another is not evident.

Last, we may set out in a general way a factor of incalculable import in the shaping of the *Institutes*: Geneva itself. Calvin's long struggle to provide workable legal and administrative structures for his adopted city, and to make them work; his day-to-day pastoral round in the church, in the *consistoire*, in the school; his wide correspondence beyond the limits of that city—these activities insured that the *Institutes* would increasingly become, from beginning to end, a work of truly pastoral theology.

By way of summary, two diagrams are offered on pp. 15-16. The first traces the shift and additions of material in the five chief Latin editions of the *Institutes*; the second outlines the literary relationship of the 1536 *Institutes*, the 1538 *Catechism*, and the 1539 *Institutes*.[7]

Spiritual Biography in Systematic Form

The attitude we bring to reading classic works of the faith for the first time is very often crucial in determining what benefit we obtain from it. If we come to Calvin's *Institutes* as a source book for systematic theology, as many have done, it will afford us valuable insights indeed. But in such a reading we come to know but half the man. Suppose, even before we open to the first page, we are told: You are about to share in one of the classic experiences of Christian history; on the deceptively orderly and seemingly dispassionate pages that follow are imprinted one man's passionate responses to the call of Christ. If we keep ever before us that autobiographical character of this book, the whole man will speak to us in very truth.

Calvin tells us that in his *Institutes* he has "paved a road" to the

7. I have discussed these relationships in greater detail elsewhere. See my *Calculus Fidei*. Paper delivered at the International Congress on Calvin Research, Amsterdam (1978).

SHIFTS AND ADDITIONS OF MATERIAL IN THE FIVE CHIEF LATIN EDITIONS OF THE *INSTITUTIO*

(Boxes indicate new material; only main editorial blocs are shown)

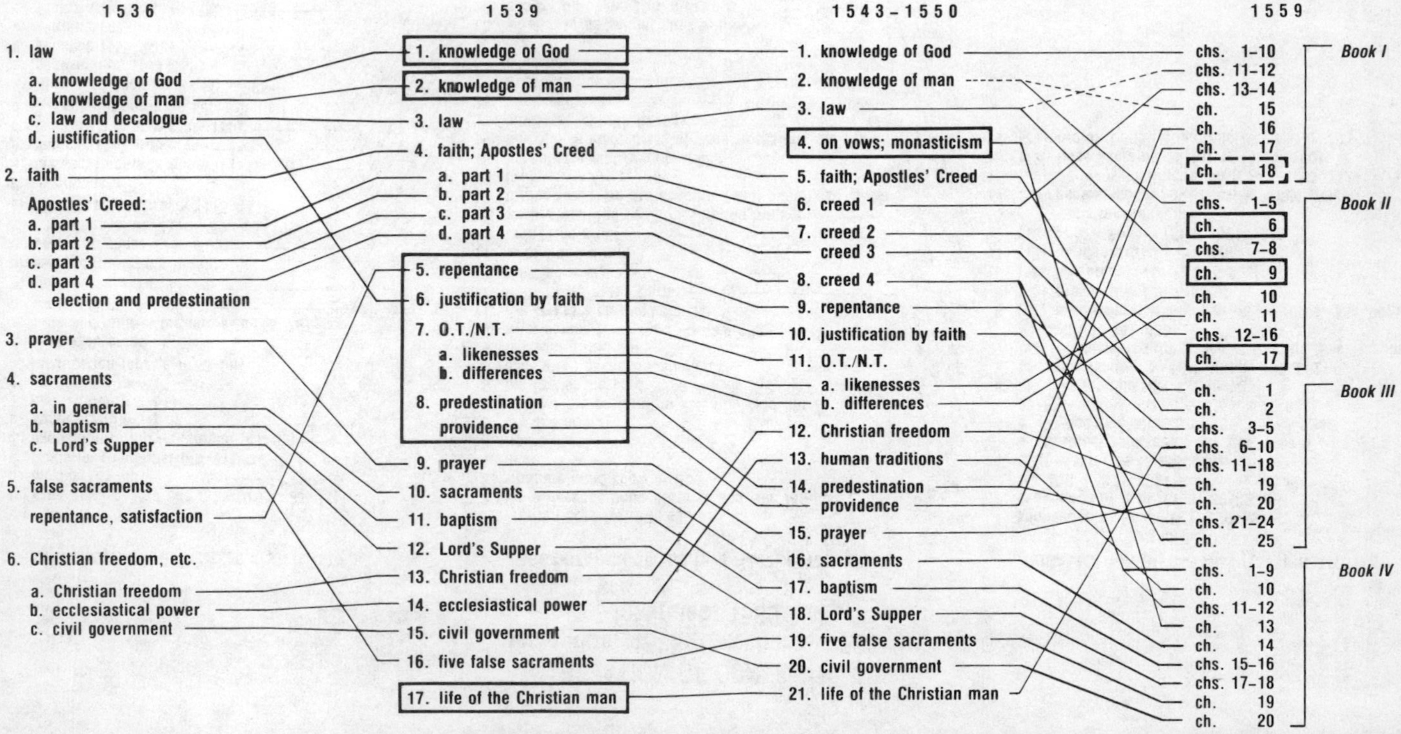

1536

1. law
   - a. knowledge of God
   - b. knowledge of man
   - c. law and decalogue
   - d. justification
2. faith
   - Apostles' Creed:
   - a. part 1
   - b. part 2
   - c. part 3
   - d. part 4
   - election and predestination
3. prayer
4. sacraments
   - a. in general
   - b. baptism
   - c. Lord's Supper
5. false sacraments
   - repentance, satisfaction
6. Christian freedom, etc.
   - a. Christian freedom
   - b. ecclesiastical power
   - c. civil government

1539

1. knowledge of God
2. knowledge of man
3. law
4. faith; Apostles' Creed
   - a. part 1
   - b. part 2
   - c. part 3
   - d. part 4
5. repentance
6. justification by faith
7. O.T./N.T.
   - a. likenesses
   - b. differences
8. predestination
   - providence
9. prayer
10. sacraments
11. baptism
12. Lord's Supper
13. Christian freedom
14. ecclesiastical power
15. civil government
16. five false sacraments
17. life of the Christian man

1543–1550

1. knowledge of God
2. knowledge of man
3. law
4. on vows; monasticism
5. faith; Apostles' Creed
6. creed 1
7. creed 2
   - creed 3
8. creed 4
9. repentance
10. justification by faith
11. O.T./N.T.
    - a. likenesses
    - b. differences
12. Christian freedom
13. human traditions
14. predestination
    - providence
15. prayer
16. sacraments
17. baptism
18. Lord's Supper
19. five false sacraments
20. civil government
21. life of the Christian man

1559

Book I
- chs. 1–10
- chs. 11–12
- chs. 13–14
- ch. 15
- ch. 16
- ch. 17
- ch. 18

Book II
- chs. 1–5
- ch. 6
- chs. 7–8
- ch. 9
- ch. 10
- ch. 11
- chs. 12–16
- ch. 17

Book III
- ch. 1
- ch. 2
- chs. 3–5
- chs. 6–10
- chs. 11–18
- ch. 19
- ch. 20
- chs. 21–24
- ch. 25

Book IV
- chs. 1–9
- ch. 10
- chs. 11–12
- ch. 13
- ch. 14
- chs. 15–16
- chs. 17–18
- ch. 19
- ch. 20

RELATION OF CONTENTS
Institution, 1536; Catechism, 1538; Institutes, 1539

ORGANIZATION OF THE 1536 INSTITUTION

1. the law
   a. knowledge of God and man (OS 1. 37–38)[2]
   b. the law (38–40)
   c. God's love in Christ (40–41)
   d. exposition of the Decalogue (41–53)
   e. summary (53–54)
   f. justification (54–61)
   g. uses of the law (61–63)
   h. justification (cont'd.) (63–68)
2. faith and the creed
   a. faith and faith in the one God (68–75)
   b. creed (75–93)
   c. faith, hope, love (93–96)
3. prayer and the Lord's Prayer
   a. prayer in general (96–105)
   b. exposition of the Lord's Prayer (105–115)
   c. the practice of prayer (115–117)
4. the sacraments
   a. the sacraments in general (118–127)
   b. baptism (127–136)
   c. the Lord's Supper (136–160)
   d. administration of the sacraments (160–162)
5. the five false sacraments (162–223)[3]
   a. confirmation (163–169)
   b. penance (169–202)
   c. extreme unction (202–205)
   d. ecclesiastical orders (205–220)
   e. marriage (220–223)
6. Christian freedom, etc.
   a. Christian freedom (223–233)[4]
   b. ecclesiastical power (233–258)
   c. civil government (258–286)

ORGANIZATION OF THE 1538 (1537) CATECHISM[1]

1. all men born for religion
2. the difference between false and true religion
3. what we must know of God
4. man
5. free will
6. sin and death
7. how we are restored to salvation and life
8. the law of the Lord
   exposition of the Decalogue
9. the sum of the law
10. what comes to us from the law alone
11. the law is a step toward Christ
12. by faith we grasp Christ
13. election and predestination
14. what true faith is
15. faith, God's gift
16. we are justified in Christ through faith
17. through faith we are sanctified into obedience to the law[5]
18. repentance and regeneration[5]
19. how the righteousness of good works and the righteousness of faith fit together
20. the creed
    exposition of the creed
21. what hope is
22. prayer
23. what is to be sought after in prayer
24. exposition of the Lord's Prayer
25. perseverance in prayer
26. the sacraments
27. what a sacrament is
28. baptism
29. the Lord's Supper
30. the pastors of the church and their power
31. human traditions
32. excommunication
33. magistracy

ORGANIZATION OF THE 1539 (1543) INSTITUTES

1. knowledge of God (CR 1. 279–304)[6]
2. knowledge of man (CR 1. 305–372)
3. law (CR 1. 371–438)
4. a. (5) faith (CR 1. 453–476)
   b. (6) Apostles' Creed,[1] (Cr 1. 477–514)
   c. (7) Apostles' Creed,[2–3] (CR 1. 513–538)
   d. (8) Apostles' Creed,[4] (CR 1. 537–686)
5. (9) repentance (CR 1. 685–736)
6. (10) justification by faith (CR 1. 737–802)
7. (11) likeness and difference of Old and New Testaments (CR 1. 801–830)
8. (14) predestination and providence (CR 1. 861–902)
9. (15) prayer (CR 1.901–938)
10. (16) sacraments (Cr 1. 937–958)
11. (17) baptism (CR 1. 957–990)
12. (18) Lord's Supper (CR 1. 991–1038)
13. Christian freedom[4]
14. (13) ecclesiastical power (CR 1. 1039–1066)[3]
15. (20) political administration (CR 1. 1099–1124)
16. (19) false sacraments (CR 1. 1065–1100)
17. (21) life of the Christian man (CR 1. 1123–1152)

---

1. For fuller details of the relation of 1536, 1538, and 1539, see textual notes, *John Calvin, Catechism or Institution of the Christian Religion, 1538*, ET, F.L. Battles (1972).
2. P. Barth and W. Niesel, *Calvini Opera Selecta*. Noted OS.
3. Ch. 5 (five false sacraments, 1536) carried over to ch. 14, 1539.
4. Ch. 6a (Christian freedom, 1536) carried over to ch. 13, 1539.
5. Sects. 17–18 (sanctification, repentance, and regeneration, 1538) scattered to various chapters of 1539.
6. *Corpus Reformatorum: Johannis Calvini Opera quae super sunt omnia.* Noted CR.

understanding of Scripture for students beginning its study ("To the Reader," LCC 20.4f.). Yet he teaches that the understanding of Scripture depends upon the Holy Spirit's illumination of the reader (1:7; 3:2). It is to be expected, then, that his exegesis strongly enters the personal experience of biblical characters, in whom he finds a reflection of his own. In the Psalms of David he finds "an anatomy of all the states of the soul."

Here is an "experiential" approach to biblical exegesis through biographical identification with Old Testament personages strikingly similar to that of Martin Luther[8] and not unrecognized by all authentic preachers. Elsewhere[9] I have discussed the "imitatio Davidis," so frequently met with in Calvin's writings—especially in the *Institutes* and in the *Commentary on the Psalms*. Frequently he prefers to let David speak for his own spiritual condition. Two essays examine this autobiographical employment of David by Calvin, one by R. A. Hasler[10] and a longer one by J. R. Walchenbach.[11] Of the New Testament personages, Paul comes closest to mirroring Calvin's *status animae*. In his *Answer to Balduin's Insults* (1561), he says:

> True it is, that I am not elevated by the greatness of the revelations granted me, as if I were a Paul; still I acknowledge that I have this in common with the Apostle, that a messenger of Satan has been sent by God to buffet me in the face, and that I am thus taught to humble myself. But as we must at all times pray to God to drive back the devil and his angels, it is our duty to oppose their reviling lest the truth should be injured by the falsehoods which they thus promulgate.

The reader armed with Calvin's laconic account of his conversion and later growth as set forth in the preface to the *Commentary on the Psalms* (1555/7) will march with firmer step through the unfolding paths of the *Institutes*.[12] He will perhaps sense the crucial place Romans 1:18–25 (especially verses 18 and 25) probably had in Calvin's conversion and in his pursuit of the Christian life in the years that followed.[13] Surely, Calvin's contraposition of truth and falsehood and his postulation of the two knowledges—of God and of self—stem from this passage particularly.

What is at the heart of the *Institutes*, read in this personal, experien-

---

8. C. W. Hovland, "Anfechtung in Luther's Biblical Exegesis," in Franklin H. Littell, ed., *Reformation Studies* (Atlanta: John Knox Press, 1962).
9. *Piety*, p. 39.
10. R. A. Hasler, "The Influence of David and the Psalms upon Calvin's Life and Thought," *Hartford Quarterly*, vol. 5, no. 2, pp. 7–8.
11. J. R. Walchenbach, *The Influence of David and the Psalms on the Life and Thought of John Calvin*, unpublished Th. M. thesis, Pittsburgh Theological Seminary, 1967.
12. See *Piety*, ch. 2.
13. *Inst. 1536*, pp. xvi–xvii; *Calculus Fidei*, Assumption 1.

tial way? For man, it is a handbook of piety. But what is it toward God? *The Institutes of the Christian Religion* is a bold effort truly to crown God as King of His people (3.20.43). That God may rule among the nations—is this not the central theme of Calvin's theology?[14] God is King. Calvin never speaks literally of the "sovereignty of God," a pale abstraction that cuts away the essential, biblical, royal imagery. This explains the "political frame" of the *Institutes*: it begins with the letter to the French king, Francis I, and ends with the famous chapter on political government (4:20). Calvin's theology lives in the real world and squarely faces it. Calvin's career as writer and as leader was not that of a utopian dreamer or theorist, for in him the study of law and theology meet at the deepest level.

A Book of Antitheses

Calvin's dedicatory epistle to Francis I introduced not only the first edition of the *Institutes* but all subsequent editions as well. This highly important document is, however, omitted by some German translators of the *Institutes* as not of sufficient theological interest!

This epistle holds, in a sense, a further clue to the genesis and growth of the whole book. The young Calvin, addressing his first edition from his Basel refuge both to the sovereign whose repressive regime had led him to flight and exile, and to his beleaguered coreligionists, spells out on those initial pages the two fronts on which his theological campaign is to be waged. On the one hand he rejects the defective Christianity of the Romanist Sorbonne, the theological establishment of the day. On the other, he dissociates himself from the revolutionary, enthusiast party denominated by him as "Catabaptists," and later to be more clearly perceived as a variety of radical tendencies. His message: to assure his sovereign of the catholic character of the party of Reform, more faithful than its Sorbonnist foes to the Scriptural and patristic past claimed by both; to assure his sovereign of the unsubversive, loyal support of the monarchy by the party of Reform, a party to be clearly distinguished from the wild dreams of the Kingdom of Muenster, liquidated only a few months before.

This initial bipolarity of the *Institutes*, imparted by the character of the contemporary political and ecclesial crisis, became the pattern which, with all its elaboration and modification, persisted throughout all subsequent editions. Elsewhere I have examined this technically and in detail.[15] Here one can only speak in descriptive terms that may assist the reader as he threads his way through the book.

---

14. Cf. *Comm. Isaiah*, 2:4.
15. *Calculus Fidei.*

The *Institutes* is, in a sense, a book of antitheses. This is a frustrating feature for the new reader who hopes that each topic dealt with will be thoroughly settled before the next is taken up. It is frustrating, too, for the orderly, tidy, philosophically-minded theological critic who seeks to reduce the whole to its essence. Calvin, it would seem, eludes both. He is a Scriptural theologian first, and a user of philosophy, logic, rhetoric—all human tools of organization—only second. Of these tools he makes good use, but never at the expense of what he deems the manifest word of Scripture, contextually perceived. Always before Calvin's eyes are the chapters of what we today call "salvation history," a history which every Christian must experience for himself, however simply.

I am aware that I run the danger of unfaithfully representing the flow of Calvin's thought through the *Institutes* in offering the following tabular analysis, "The Antithetical Structure of the *Institutes*." For the reader of the *Institutes* who would like to piece together Calvin's search for truth amid falsity, however, it may be of some use.

The Antithetical Structure of the *Institutes*

Book I

A. Knowledge of God the Creator
   1. chs. 1–3/4 } True (Scriptural) vs. false (philosophical) knowl-
   2. ch. 5a/5b[16] } edge of God

B. Revelation
   chs. 6–8/9: Scriptural (true) vs. extra-Scriptural (false: *Schwärmer*) revelation

C. God as Object of Worship
   chs. 10–11/12: idols (false) vs. God (true)

D. The Godhead
   ch. 13a/13b: true vs. false (chiefly Servetus) views of the Trinity

E. Creation: Hexaemeron; Angels; Demons
   ch. 14a/14b: true vs. false views

F. Knowledge of Man (as Created): Soul; Body
   ch. 15a/15b: true (Scriptural) vs. false (philosophical) views of man

G. Providence
   1. ch. 16a/16b: true (Scriptural) vs. false (philosophical) views
   2. ch. 17a/17b: true vs. false attitudes toward providence

16. Note that "a" and "b" here refer not to separate sections of the chapters but to two voices heard antiphonally through a chapter.

3. ch. 18a/18b: true vs. false views of how God's providence works toward the ungodly

Book II

A. The Fall and Degeneration of the Human Race; Condition of the Human Will (Knowledge of Man as Fallen), chiefly against the Roman Catholic view
   1. ch. 1a/1b: true vs. false understanding of man's fallen condition (original sin)
   2. ch. 2a/2b: true vs. false views concerning the human will (bound vs. free)
   3. ch. 3a/3b: total (true) vs. partial (false) corruption of man's nature
   4. ch. 4a/4b: God's dominion (true) vs. human freedom (false)
   5. chs. 1–4/5: will: free (false) vs. unfree (true) (summarizing antithesis)

   (ch. 6: transitional chapter to knowledge of God the Redeemer: Christ)

B. Law and Gospel
   1. Why the Law was given
      ch. 7a/7b: true vs. false views
   2. The Decalogue expounded
      ch. 8a/8b: true vs. false views: in reference to the Law in general and the individual commandments in particular
   3. Christ revealed in Law and Gospel
      ch. 9a/9b: True vs. false views
   4. Relation of Law (Old Testament) and Gospel (New Testament)
      chs. 10–11a/10–11b: true vs. false views (chiefly Servetus)

C. Christ
   1. Necessity of the God-man as mediator
      ch. 12a/12b: true vs. false views (chiefly Osiander)
   2. Incarnation
      ch. 13a/13b: true vs. false views (chiefly Menno Simons)
   3. Unity of the two natures in one person
      ch. 14a/14b: true vs. false views (chiefly Servetus)
   4. The offices and work of Christ on our behalf
      chs. 15–17a/15–17b: true vs. false views

Book III

A. The Working of the Spirit in Men's Hearts (ch. 1): Foundation of Book III

B. Faith
ch. 2a/2b: scholastic (false) vs. true notion of faith

C. Repentance
1. ch. 3a/3b: antitheses between true repentance and false views of repentance (especially the Radical Reformers' insistence on perfectionism)
2. chs. 3/4–5: true repentance vs. scholastic views of repentance (including confession, satisfaction plus indulgences and purgatory)

D. The Christian Life
1. ch. 6a/6b: true vs. false view of Christian life in general
2. chs. 7–8a/8b: true denial of ourselves vs. false patience of the Stoics
3. chs. 9/10: balance between the anticipation of the life to come and the true enjoyment of the present life, fed by it; subsidiary antitheses:
4. ch. 10a/10b: the right attitude toward the present life—poised between the false extremes of strictness and laxity

E. Justification by Faith
1. Justification by faith vs. justification by works and its derived doctrines (merits, supererogation, etc.), the scholastic position: set forth in ch. 11:13–20, but also the chief substance of chs. 12–18
2. Justification by faith in the whole Christ vs. justification by faith in Christ's divine nature alone (the Lutheran Osiander) (ch. 11:5–12)

F. Christian Freedom
ch. 19a/19b: true vs. false views of freedom

G. Prayer (ch. 20)
In the midst of an affirmative interpretation of prayer in general, and the Lord's Prayer in particular, together with related topics, Calvin stresses a course between rejection of prayer as useless and prayer bound to set forms.

H. Predestination
Fundamental antithesis: God's freedom vs. man's freedom, expressed in a series of subordinate antitheses:
1. ch. 22: unconditioned election by a totally free God vs. election dependent on God's foreknowledge of our merits (traditional non-Augustinian Roman Catholic position)
2. ch. 23: incomprehensible nature of predestination vs. efforts

of human reason, going beyond Scriptural boundaries, to fathom it
3. ch. 24: secret decrees of predestination and reprobation vs. various theories which allow some place to the human will

I. Final Resurrection
ch. 25a/25b: immortality of soul plus resurrection of body at last day vs. various opposing views

Book IV

A. Nature and Organization of the Church
1. chs. 1/2: true vs. false church
2. chs. 3–4/5–7: true vs. false officers and government of church

B. Ecclesiastical Power
1. Burdens laid on men by the church
a. ch. 8a/8b: power of church in articles of faith vs. papal practice
b. ch. 9a/9b: true vs. false councils
c. ch. 10a/10b: true church constitutions (in accord with God's Law and human conscience) vs. papal constitutions
d. ch. 11a/11b: right relationship between spiritual and temporal jurisdiction vs. papal usurpation of both
e. ch. 12a/12b: true church discipline (informed by love) vs. false church discipline (excessive laxity or excessive severity)
2. Burdens laid on men by themselves
ch. 13a/13b: simple obedience to God's will vs. human vows (including monasticism) which counterfeit and make impossible true obedience

C. Sacraments
1. The general antithesis: true sacraments (chs. 14–18, summarized at end of ch. 18) vs. false sacraments (ch. 19)
2. Baptism
ch. 15a/15b and 16: true baptism vs. false baptism and false baptismal practices
3. Lord's Supper
a. ch. 17a/17b: a series of antitheses between the "true" doctrine and various false ones (transubstantiation, ubiquity); also between the "true" ad-

ministration and various false ways of administering the Lord's Supper

b. chs. 17/18: true Lord's Supper vs. false Papal Mass

D. Civil Government (ch. 20)

1. sect. 1-2: true view vs. false view of spiritual/civil government
   a. overthrow civil in favor of spiritual
   b. set aside spiritual in favor of civil
2. sects. 3ff. contain a series of subsidiary antitheses against various aspects of false view a; view b is not elaborated (but cf. sect. 9)
3. sects. 10-12: true vs. false view of use of force and war
4. sect. 13: true vs. false view of taxation
5. sects. 14-16: true vs. false view of Mosaic Law in relation to civil government
6. sects. 17-21: true vs. false view of Christian use of law courts
7. sects. 22-32: true vs. false attitudes toward unjust rulers
   a. right of revolution
   b. obedience even when God's will is contravened

On Reading the *Institutes*

How should one undertake to read the *Institutes*? I have a bad habit of reading new books (new to me, that is) by scrutinizing the index, examining the conclusions, savoring the organization, perhaps sampling a few test passages and then asking myself, Is it worth further reading? I would not recommend this approach to reading the *Institutes*. First, you must want to read the book; second, you must set out *from the beginning*; third, you must persist, however long it takes you, until you reach the last page. Do not become a Calvinist of the first five chapters or of the first book. I can generally tell, when people speak of Calvin, whether they know him only by hearsay, have read a few pages, or have sampled him anthologically. They have no clue to the wonderful interconnectedness of Calvin's thought. They ask questions which a fuller reading of the *Institutes* could have answered.

Fourth, do not lament that a question seems to go unanswered, or a loose end seems not to be tied: it will be answered; it will be tied. Be patient. If, after you have read the whole book for the first time, you remain in serious disagreement with Calvin—well, so be it! But what coherent alternative will you have to offer?

Fifth, as you read, think not only of Calvin's time (perhaps reviewed by way of T. H. L. Parker's *Portrait of Calvin* [Philadelphia: Westminster, 1955][17] or W. Monter's *Calvin's Geneva* [New York: Wiley, 1967]) but also of your own. Is Calvin somehow speaking too to the late twentieth century? So speculating, readers of the *Institutes* have sometimes made surprisingly helpful discoveries.

Last, do not hesitate to place this *Analysis* beside you as you read. For some of you who prefer to grasp the structure of the book as a whole before you plunge into it, the *Analysis* can be a help, for it faithfully sets forth the tripartite book, chapter, and section organization of the work. Each section is concisely analyzed into its salient points. The user can, of course, read the book and chapter headings for a quick survey. For a deeper perusal he can scrutinize the sectional topics; at the most detailed level he can study the subordinate categories within each section. Thence he must of course repair to the text itself.[18] Others who wish to approach the book directly without being "briefed" by the *Analysis* may still find the *Analysis* of help. When you seem to lose your way (and we all do in a work of such length and complexity), glance at the analytical outline of what you have just read. It may highlight the points to be kept in mind. And months or years later, as you search your memory for Calvinian insights only partially remembered, this little summary may lead you painlessly to what you are seeking.

These words would be incomplete if Calvin's own call to Scripture were not re-sounded. He wrote the *Institutes* to draw Christians to the Scriptures; he wrote his *Commentaries* to elucidate not so much the larger elements of the faith as the details of the text itself. He proclaimed the Scriptures from the pulpit. The reader of the *Institutes* will find his own understanding and conviction quickened by continuing his study beyond the *Institutes* to the Scriptures that are its source, and to the *Commentaries* and *Sermons* which further expound the biblical faith of John Calvin.

Ford Lewis Battles
Calvin Theological Seminary
April, 1979

17. This earlier, shorter life by Parker is suggested for the neophyte, rather than his more recent, *John Calvin: A Biography* (Philadelphia: Westminster, 1976), a much longer essay.

18. While the *Analysis* has been prepared with my translation of the *Institutes* (LCC 20-21 [1960]) primarily in mind, it can be used with the Allen or Beveridge translation; if either of these two is used, however, the reader will have to cope with differences in the rendering of terms.

Analysis of Calvin's Prefatory Address to Francis I

Analysis of Calvin's Prefatory Address to Francis I

1. Circumstances in which the book was first written
   a. original intention to set forth, especially for French countrymen, certain rudiments to aid the zealous toward godliness
   b. shift in purpose of work due to persecution of and false rumors about the Evangelicals
   c. request for a full and fair inquiry by a truly Christian king

2. The plea for the persecuted Evangelicals
   a. the Evangelicals
      (1) Scriptural faith
      (2) heroic martyrdom
   b. the Romans
      (1) neglect of Scriptural faith
      (2) insistence upon Mass, purgatory, pilgrimages, and like trifles

3. Charges of the antagonists against the Evangelical doctrine refuted
   a. new: God's Holy Word hardly "new"
   b. unknown: true doctrine has long lain buried and forgotten through man's impiety
   c. uncertain: our assurance contrasts with their doubt
   d. lack of supporting miracles: true vs. false miracles

4. Misleading claim that the church fathers oppose the Reformation teaching
   a. the Fathers, like all men, are fallible; the Romanists worship rather their faults and errors than their virtues
   b. "do not transgress the limits" (Prov. 22:28)
      what Fathers said vs. Romanists' practice:
      (1) God does not need gold or silver: lavish rites
      (2) Christian can either eat meat or abstain from it: Lenten fasts

(3) monks must work: idle, licentious monks
(4) no images of Christ or saints: churches crawling with images
(5) after burial of dead let them rest: perpetual solicitude for the dead
(6) bread and wine remain in the eucharist: transubstantiation
(7) all present must partake of Lord's Supper: public and private Masses put grace and merit of Christ up for sale
(8) rash verdicts without basis in Scripture disallowed: jungle of constitutions, canons, etc. not based on God's Word
(9) marriage affirmed for clergy: celibacy enjoined
(10) God's Word to be kept clear of sophistries: speculative theological brawls

5. The appeal to custom is against truth
   a. most custom is the result of the private vices of the majority which become public error and wrongly take on the force of law
   b. in contrast to such public error is the eternal truth of God's kingdom which, in hallowing the Lord of Hosts, we are fearlessly to follow
   c. though the whole world may fall into the same wickedness, strength of numbers does not sanction or excuse it

6. Errors about the nature of the church
   a. the true church eternal, wherein all believing folk worship and adore one God and Christ the Lord as He has always been adored
   b. the points of controversy
      (1) that the form of the church is always observable
      (2) that this form of the church rests in the Roman church and its hierarchy
   c. the true church is marked by pure preaching of God's Word and the lawful administration of the sacraments: this church was often submerged and without visible form during scriptural and post-scriptural ages
      (1) evidence from the Old Testament
      (2) evidence from church history
   d. God's dealing with His church
      (1) punished the unfaithful by a temporary obliteration of the visible image of His true church

    (2) yet preserved His real children from extinction
  e. dangers in judging the church by vain pomp
    (1) exemplified in the Old Testament history
    (2) evidenced in "lawful" council of Basel which led to Eugenius-Amadeus scandal and the abuses in its train
  f. the false doctrine of the visible church deadly for Christian souls

7. Tumults alleged to result from the Reformation preaching
  a. shifting of Satan's strategy
    (1) for centuries Satan kept church asleep in worldly luxury
    (2) but when it started to awaken, he countered with contentions and disagreements by raising up his "Catabaptists" and other rascals
  b. analogy between the experience of the apostles and ourselves (we should therefore possess the same assurance as did the apostles)

8. Let the king beware of acting on false charges: the innocent await divine vindication
  a. the charge that we are seditious is utterly false, for even in exile we pray for your majesty, and our conduct has been exemplary
  b. if in your kingdom any subversives raise tumults under the pretext of the gospel, you have laws and legal penalties to restrain them
  c. you are prejudiced now against us; we hope this appeal will change your attitude; but if it does not we still put our trust in the King of Kings

BOOK ONE

The Knowledge of God the Creator

CHAPTER 1
The Knowledge of God and That of Ourselves Are Connected, and How They Are Interrelated

1. Without knowledge of self there is no knowledge of God
   a. our real wisdom is confined almost entirely to
      (1) knowledge of God
      (2) knowledge of ourselves
   b. our rich blessings, acknowledged as from God, reveal our poverty and ruin which in turn compel us to look Godward
      (1) to seek what we lack
      (2) to learn humility
   c. we cannot seriously aspire to knowledge of God before we begin to become displeased with ourselves

2. Without knowledge of God there is no knowledge of self
   a. if we hypocritically confine our contemplation to ourselves and do not go beyond to contemplate God, we complacently laud our own virtues
   b. but the moment our thoughts rise to God and His excellences, we see our "virtues" as wicked, foolish, and weak

3. Man before God's majesty
   a. scriptural examples of man's painful awareness of his lowly state when confronted by God's majesty: Job, Abraham, Elijah, etc.
   b. proposed order of teaching:
      (1) knowledge of God
      (2) knowledge of ourselves

CHAPTER 2
What It Is to Know God, and to What Purpose the Knowledge of Him Tends

1. The knowledge of God is, in practice, reverence
   a. two aspects of the knowledge of God

- (1) to feel that God our creator sustains and blesses us (the present topic)
- (2) to embrace the reconciliation offered us in Christ (to be dealt with later)

b. the genesis of piety (godliness)

- (1) God not only by His power created and sustains the world, but is the source and cause of all that is good and right
- (2) this awareness of God's excellences teaches us piety, the source of religion
- (3) piety: that reverence joined with love of God which the knowledge of His benefits induces

2. The purpose of the knowledge of God

a. man should not speculate, "What is God?" but should ask, "Of what sort is He? What is consistent with His nature?"

b. the purpose of our knowledge of Him

- (1) to teach us fear and reverence
- (2) to guide us to seek every good from Him and give Him credit when received

c. the attitude of the pious mind toward God is determined by its utter dependence upon Him: "Even if there were no hell, it would still shudder at offending Him"

d. the definition of pure and real religion: faith so joined with an earnest fear of God that this fear also embraces willing reverence, and carries with it such legitimate worship as is prescribed in the law.

CHAPTER 3
The Knowledge of God Has Been Naturally Implanted in the Minds of Men

1. The character of this natural endowment

a. universal

- (1) is in all men by natural instinct
- (2) makes failure to worship God inexcusable
- (3) found even among the most barbarous peoples
- (4) found throughout all times and places

b. idolatry a proof of this universality

- (1) no man willingly humbles himself to something outside himself

(2) worship of wood and stone thus evidence of intense and ineradicable impression of the divine

2. Religion is no arbitrary invention
   a. some charge that religion was arbitrarily invented by subtle unbelieving men to enslave the simple
   b. but this would not have been possible if
      (1) there were no natural awareness of deity in simple men's minds
      (2) the crafty men themselves had no inkling of religion
   c. proofs of religion exist in even the most ungodly
      (1) men turn to religion when under stress or great fear (e.g., Gaius Caligula)
      (2) like drunken or frenzied persons they are fitful in their slumber
      (3) while their awareness of God varies in power, it is never totally absent

3. Actual godlessness is impossible
   a. an ineffaceable sense of divinity is engraved upon men's minds
      (1) even the perversity of the impious demonstrates this
      (2) the awareness of God is our endowment from birth, not a doctrine to be learned at school
   b. the worship of God and the quest to realize likeness to God alone distinguishes man from animals

CHAPTER 4
This Knowledge Is Either Smothered or Corrupted, Partly by Ignorance, Partly by Malice

1. Superstition
   a. real piety and true knowledge of God is absent in the world
      (1) some intentionally revolt from God
      (2) others become lost in superstition
   b. why superstition is not without blame
      (1) it involves pride and obstinacy
      (2) it involves, thus, measuring God by one's own stupid measure, and wildly speculating about His nature and about how He should be worshiped

(3) to sum up, superstition is the result of (a) vain curiosity and (b) inordinate desire for too much knowledge and (c) false confidence, and is thus inexcusable

2. Conscious turning away from God
   a. meaning of Ps. 14:1: "Fools feel in their hearts that there is no God"
      (1) the hardened sinner repels all remembrance of God
      (2) further, they flatly deny God's existence, not in the sense of depriving Him of His being, but in denying His providence and government of the world
      (3) thus they become blind in their obstinacy and deny God
   b. they are compelled to recognize some god but they choose to do so in fashioning a dead and empty idol and denying the true God

3. We cannot conceive of God according to our own whim
   a. vague and erroneous opinions of the divine are ignorance of God
      (1) not just any religion, then, will do, but only true religion
      (2) God is no specter, to be transformed according to anyone's whim
      (3) the true worship of Him is, in superstition, rejected by some in favor of the adoration of mere ravings
      (4) if you forsake God, you have left only an accursed idol
   b. hence, no religion is genuine unless it is joined with truth

4. Hypocrisy
   a. the false religion that results from the slavish, forced fear of God's judgment
      (1) such irreligious men desire to overthrow God and His judgment
      (2) because they realize they cannot do this, out of dread they perform some semblance of religion
      (3) but despite their pretended fear of God, at the same time their lives are vicious and wicked
   b. contrast between true and false godliness
      (1) rebellious at heart, they pretend obedience to God in their paltry sacrifices and trumped-up observances, but their lives are marked by sheer immorality
      (2) their trust is not in God, the Creator, but in themselves, the creatures

(3) the result is spiritual blindness; the innate awareness of the divine, while not lost, is utterly corrupted

(4) to sum up, the sense of deity naturally engraven on human hearts is evidenced by the reluctant and perfunctory prayers extracted from the godless in times of spiritual crisis; yet their stubbornness prevents this sense of deity from leading them to true religion

CHAPTER 5
The Knowledge of God Shines Forth in the Fashioning of the Universe and the Continuing Government of It

1. The clarity of God's self-disclosure strips us of every excuse
   a. like the divinely implanted awareness of deity, the daily disclosure of God in the workmanship of the universe is intended to provide us with the knowledge of God; this is the ultimate goal of the blessed life
   b. while God's essence is incomprehensible to men, the marks of His glory in nature are so obvious that even rude and stupid men have no excuse
   c. as Scripture repeatedly asserts, if you open your eyes upon the vast and beautiful fabric of the universe, you see in a sort of mirror God who is otherwise invisible

2. God's wisdom remains secret to no one
   a. the human arts and sciences, through their close observation of nature, afford men a deeper insight into the mysteries of the divine wisdom
   b. but even for the uneducated, there is more than enough in the natural world to reveal to them the divine wisdom; the structure of the human body will do this

3. Man is the loftiest proof of divine wisdom
   a. man correctly called a *microcosm*; he is a rare example of God's power, goodness, and wisdom
   b. since there is no need to go outside ourselves to find God, we have absolutely no excuse
   c. Scripture and pagan writers alike assert God's fatherhood over men, who as His offspring exhibit His great gifts; we must, then, be drawn to love and worship Him in return

4. But man turns ungratefully against God
   a. despite the divine source of these endowments, men in pride and self-love suppress the impulse to praise God; they take credit for these themselves
   b. the atheists, despite eloquent proofs of God in their very bodies, reject God and substitute "nature" for Him

5. The confusion of creature with creator
   a. some deny the immortality of the soul, on the grounds of nature
      (1) they assert that the soul cannot subsist apart from the body
      (2) on the contrary—in the higher uses of human reason there is no bodily counterpart, and these constitute divinely-imparted signs of immortality
      (3) if, then, man is divine, we are compelled to recognize his Creator, and to see in human arts and crafts their ultimate divine source
   b. some also attribute to nature its own creation
      (1) idle speculation about "universal mind" to be rejected
      (2) nature is not God, but the order prescribed by God
   c. consequently, we must not confuse God with the inferior course of His works

6. The creator reveals His lordship over the creation
   a. God as Lord of creation and giver of every gift wills that we look to Him, direct our faith to Him, and worship and call upon Him
   b. natural phenomena (the works of God within the ordinary course of nature) witness to His power
   c. His power leads us to His eternity
   d. His eternity shows Him as the source and preserver of all things
   e. His creation and preservation of all things are the result of His goodness
   f. His goodness, the sole cause of creation, ought to be more than sufficient to draw us to His love

7. God's government and judgment
   a. in those works of God that occur outside the ordinary course of nature are further clear proofs of God's excellences

b. God shows His mercy in dealing with human society, yet He daily shows His kindness to the godly and His severity to the wicked
c. while the ungodly seem for a time to prosper and the godly to suffer, we must recognize
   (1) that whenever He punishes one sin in this life, He is showing that He hates all sins, and will punish all at judgment
   (2) that by His universal kindness to sinners, He is trying to win them away from their wickedness

8. God's sovereign sway over the life of men
   a. the seemingly chance deliverances of men from danger and tribulation mentioned in the Psalms are proofs of God's providence and fatherly kindness, but most of us are too blind to see this
   b. God's power and wisdom are seen in His destruction of the wicked and of their works, His restoration and elevation of the humble and oppressed—both dealings being timed and tempered to the human situation

9. We ought not to try to penetrate to God's essence, but rather contemplate Him in His works
   a. the knowledge of God to which we are called is not empty speculation, but a sound and fruitful knowledge that takes root in our hearts
   b. the perfect way to seek God:
      (1) not to attempt out of bold curiosity to penetrate to His essence (the object of adoration, not investigation)
      (2) but to contemplate Him in His works by which He familiarly communicates Himself to us

10. The purpose of this knowledge of God
   a. the purpose is twofold:
      (1) to arouse us to worship God
      (2) to encourage us to hope for eternal life
   b. we note that in the present life the examples of His clemency and severity are incomplete, thus assuring us of another life in which iniquity will have its punishment and righteousness its reward
   c. God's works give us in picture form a knowledge of His perfections

d. yet we comprehend their chief purpose, value, and the reason why we should ponder them, only when we descend into ourselves and contemplate:
   (1) His life, wisdom, and virtue in our lives
   (2) His righteousness, goodness, and mercy in His dealing with us

11. The tidings of God that we gain from creation do not achieve their purpose
   a. our response to these bright testimonies in the order of nature is dull
      (1) very few in contemplating heaven and earth think of their maker
      (2) most sit idly by
   b. in regarding those events that take place outside the course of nature, we lean to blind fortune rather than to God's providence as explanation
      (1) when events compel us to entertain some feeling of divinity, we soon subside into our own ravings and imaginings
         (a) each of us forges his own peculiar form of personal error
         (b) but all of us abandon the true God in favor of prodigious trifles (this is even true of such learned men as Plato)
      (2) where the governance of human events reveals providence, we in vanity and error explain it in terms of the blind will of fortune

12. The tidings of God are choked by human superstition and the error of the philosophers
   a. not only nations, but individual men, in the blindness of their minds, came to have their own gods
   b. not only the uneducated, but the learned philosophers themselves, show the shameful variety of men's efforts to penetrate into heaven
      (1) the higher their art and wit, the more camouflaged and lying their idols were
      (2) no mortal ever contrived anything that did not basely corrupt religion; witness the Stoics and the Egyptians
      (3) the inevitable disagreements over these private misconceptions of God led the Epicureans and others impiously to cast out all awareness of God

c. it appears that if men were taught only by nature, they would hold to nothing certain, solid, or clear-cut, but would be so tied to confused principles as to worship an unknown God

13. The Holy Spirit rejects all cults contrived by men
   a. the Holy Spirit pronounces all men who corrupt pure religion by embracing their own opinions to be apostates who substitute demons for God
   b. even the classical notion that religious worship ought to conform to the traditions of a given country or city is too weak and frail a bond of piety to follow in worshiping God
   c. hence, it remains for God Himself to give witness of Himself from heaven

14. Evidences of God in nature speak to us in vain
   a. unaided, these evidences cannot lead us to God
   b. as Paul teaches, our eyes remain blind to them until they are illuminated by the inner revelation of God through faith

15. Our powerlessness is guilt
   a. we cannot pretend ignorance as an excuse for our failure to follow these evidences to a knowledge of God, when even mute and irrational creatures speak forth God's glory
   b. such instruction is insufficient, for we are led from the slight taste of deity it gives, to worship the dreams and specters of our own brains and to defraud God of the praise we owe Him

CHAPTER 6
Scripture Is Needed as Guide and Teacher for Anyone Who Would Attain to God the Creator

1. God bestows the actual knowledge of Himself upon us only in the Scriptures
   a. despite the universal disclosure of God in the brightness of earth and heaven we require another and better help to direct us to its Creator
   b. this help we have in God's Word
      (1) which first kept the Jews from sinking into oblivion, and now keeps Christians in the pure knowledge of Himself
      (2) which disperses our dullness just as spectacles magnify the printed page for weak-sighted readers

c. two stages in the knowledge which Scripture gives us
    (1) knowledge of God as Creator (the present topic): not only that we should worship some God, but that He is the God whom we should worship
    (2) knowledge of God as Redeemer (to be dealt with in Book 2)

d. the plan of treatment
    (1) present topic: how Scripture teaches us that God, the Creator of the universe, can by sure marks be distinguished from the throng of feigned gods
    (2) subsequently we shall proceed to a discussion of redemption in Christ

2. The Word of God as Holy Scripture
    a. the unbroken transmission of truth throughout all ages
        (1) God spoke to the patriarchs through oracles and visions or by the works and ministry of men what they should hand down to posterity
        (2) these oracles were subsequently recorded when the law was published
        (3) still later, prophets were added as interpreters of the law
    b. true religion (both faith and right knowledge) has its origin in heavenly doctrine, which we can know only through the reverent study of Scripture and obedient acceptance of what God has there been pleased to witness of Himself

3. Without Scripture we fall into error
    a. men's powerful tendencies to move away from God made written proof of heavenly doctrine very necessary
    b. the Word truly and vividly describes God to us from His works
    c. if we leave the Scriptural path we will always wander in error and never reach our goal

4. Scripture can communicate to us what revelation in works cannot
    a. David teaches us that, since God in vain calls all people to Himself by the contemplation of heaven and earth, the law constitutes the unique school of God's children
    b. this is also the purport of Jesus' teaching to the Samaritan woman

CHAPTER 7
Scripture Must Be Confirmed by the Witness of the Spirit. Thus Its Authority May Be Established as Certain; and It Is a Wicked Falsehood that Its Credibility Depends on the Judgment of the Church

1. Scripture has its authority from God, not from the church
   a. Scripture has full authority only where men consider it as God's living words sprung from heaven
   b. it is a pernicious error that the authority of Scripture rests upon the determination of the church
   c. this is based upon the absurd notion that the promises of eternal life given in Scripture consist in and solely depend upon human judgment

2. The church is itself grounded upon Scripture
   a. Ephesians 2:20
   b. the claim that the prophetic and apostolic writings remain in doubt until the church decides upon their authenticity is refuted by the fact that the acceptance of Scripture had to precede the founding of the church
   c. Scripture exhibits clear evidence of its own truth and needs no external witness

3. Augustine cannot be cited as counter-evidence
   a. Augustine's statement that he would not believe the gospel if the authority of the church did not move him to do so must be interpreted in the light of its context
      (1) he is here refuting the Manichees who used the gospel as a cloak to promote faith in their Mani
      (2) what leads unbelievers to the gospel? The church by its authority introduces the gospel to unbelievers, but the certainty of the gospel does not depend upon the church
   b. in other words, the authority of the church is an introduction through which we are prepared for faith in the gospel; this interpretation of Augustine's statement is borne out by his teaching in other works

4. The witness of the Holy Spirit: stronger than all "proof"
   a. when we are convinced that God in person speaks in Scrip-

ture, we have the highest proof of the credibility of sacred doctrine

b. this conviction comes to us not from mere human reasons, judgments, or conjectures, but from the secret testimony of the Spirit
c. not rational proofs, but the majesty of God shining forth from Scripture teaches us its heavenly origin
d. supporting Scripture by disputation is doing things backwards, even though skeptical men demand such proofs to avoid foolish or giddy beliefs, for the Spirit's testimony is more excellent than all reason
e. the Word will not find acceptance in men's hearts until it is sealed there by the inner testimony of the Spirit, the same Spirit that spoke through the prophets' lips

5. Scripture bears its own authentication: *αὐτόπιστον*
   a. our conviction that in Scripture we hold the unassailable truth rests upon the testimony of the Spirit in our hearts
   b. "I speak of nothing other than what each one of the faithful experiences within himself . . . "
   c. only the elect of God experience this singular privilege, and they, not the multitude, are granted the capacity to comprehend the mysteries of God

CHAPTER 8
So Far as Human Reason Goes, Sufficiently Firm Proofs Are at Hand to Establish the Credibility of Scripture

1. Scripture is superior to all human wisdom
   a. once we accept the authentication of Scripture by the Spirit, the proofs that before were useless become very useful aids in helping us to understand Scripture
   b. grandeur of subject rather than grace of language draws us to admiration of Scripture
      (1) God wisely expressed great themes in lowly language to remind us that the power of Scripture rests not in human eloquence but in its divine source
      (2) delighted as we are by the elegance of such classical authors as Demosthenes or Cicero, Plato or Aristotle, we

turn from delight in them to the overwhelming power of Scripture which makes their impression vanish

2. Not style but content is decisive
   a. that some of the prophets had an eloquent style shows that the Spirit did not lack eloquence
   b. yet in other prophets, despite their unpolished style, the majesty of God is equally present
   c. Satan imitates even this rude and archaic style to trap souls, but even moderately sensible men detect his imposture
   d. those for whom the prophets are tasteless have no organs of taste

Old Testament Proofs [*3–10*]

3. The great antiquity of Scripture
   a. Egyptian theology and all other religions are far more recent than the age of Moses
   b. Moses was actually reiterating a covenant made 400 years before with Abraham
   c. thus, Scripture surpasses all other writings in antiquity

4. The truthfulness of Scripture shown by Moses' example
   a. no need to refute the Egyptian claim to a history antedating the creation by 6,000 years
   b. Moses' outspokenness concerning Levi, Aaron, and Miriam, which went against the feeling of the flesh, his relegation of his own sons to the lowest social station (excluding them from the priesthood), and other instances, prove the divine origin of what he wrote

5. Miracles strengthen the authority of God's messengers
   a. the miraculous events of the Exodus under Moses demonstrate that Moses was God's undoubted prophet
   b. since all these things were published before the congregation, there was no opportunity for fraud among the eyewitnesses of the events

6. Moses' miracles are incontestable
   a. with miracles are mentioned disagreeable things that would have stirred up the people to hostility if they had not experienced them

b. to counter the irrefutable fact that Moses performed the miracles, Satan has falsely attributed them to magic arts—a charge sufficiently refuted by the many severe tests to which God subjected Moses

7. Prophecies [by Moses] which are fulfilled contrary to all human expectations
   a. the future primacy of Judah: the prophecy looks to the anointing of a lowly herdsman of the tribe of Judah—David
   b. the eventual sharing by the Gentiles in God's covenant: the prophecy looks to events of almost 2,000 years later
   c. in conclusion, the Song of Moses (Deut. 32) is a bright mirror in which God clearly appears

8. God has confirmed the prophet's words
   a. examples from Isaiah
      (1) foretold fall of Jerusalem to the Chaldeans
      (2) also prophesied deliverance by Cyrus (born 100 years after Isaiah's death) from the Chaldeans
   b. examples from Jeremiah and Ezekiel
      (1) prophecy of the 70-year duration of the exile, the return and restoration
      (2) though separated geographically, Jeremiah and Ezekiel agreed in their statements
   c. Daniel, too, prophesied as if he were writing the history of events generally known

9. The transmission of the law is to be trusted
   a. some irrationally question the authenticity of the authorship of Scripture, but unquestioningly accept the genuineness of classic authors
   b. the hand of the divine providence seen in the preservation of the law and its rediscovery by King Josiah after the priests' negligence
   c. the sacred writings were transmitted by the fathers who experienced the events therein described, or heard them from their fathers and kept them fresh in memory

10. God has marvelously preserved the law and the prophets
   a. detractors of Scripture assert that after Antiochus ordered all books to be burned [I Mac. 1:56–57] they were subsequently replaced by forgeries

b. the care which the Lord took to preserve His Word exposes this as a false accusation
   (1) armed priests to preserve the Scriptures with their very lives if need be
   (2) saw to it that the holy books returned to a vastly enhanced place of honor, now translated into Greek and spread throughout the world
   (3) despite the vicissitudes of the Jews, the books were safe and intact
   (4) while the Jews under the Restoration almost lost the Hebrew language, the ancient Hebrew books remained
   (5) God chose the Jews, Christ's most violent enemies, to preserve for us the doctrine of salvation until it might be made manifest in Him

***New Testament Proofs and Those from the History of the Church* [*11–13*]**

11. The heavenly mysteries were transmitted by unlearned men
    a. the first three Evangelists, criticized by some for their lowly style, are actually discoursing on heavenly mysteries above human capacity
    b. this is especially true of John's Gospel; it may also be said of the writings of Paul and Peter
    c. these authors, rude and uneducated men for the most part, suddenly began to speak of heavenly mysteries—proof positive of their instruction by the Spirit

12. Despite opposition, the church in all times and places has clung to Scripture
    a. more than human protection witnessed by the constant obedience to Scripture of men of many times, although Satan and the world have tried their best to overthrow it
    b. divine power seen also in the acceptance of Scripture by many nations, widely scattered and otherwise having nothing in common

13. The blood of martyrs
    a. grounds for assurance in the heroic stand of Christian martyrs
    b. theirs not faith of fanatic excess, but of firm and constant, yet sober, zeal toward God

Summary: All Adduced Proofs Cannot Replace the Witness of the Spirit

a. while eloquent, these proofs are not of themselves strong enough to provide a firm faith
b. until men receive certainty from the inner persuasion of the Spirit, it is useless to try to prove to unbelievers that Scripture is the Word of God

CHAPTER 9
Fanatics, Abandoning Scripture and Flying Over to Revelation, Cast Down All the Principles of Godliness

1. The fanatics wrongly appeal to the Holy Spirit
   a. the Libertines forsake Scripture in favor of the inspiration of the Spirit, feeling that they have freed themselves from "the letter that kills"
   b. the Apostles in the primitive church, illumined by Christ's Spirit, did not on that account treat God's Word with contempt.
      (1) their reverent attitude foretold by Isa. 59:21
      (2) witnessed by Paul, who despite his ecstatic experience (II Cor. 12:2) insists upon knowing the law and prophets
   c. the task of the Spirit is not to dream up a new kind of doctrine that leads away from the gospel

2. The Holy Spirit is recognized in His agreement with Scripture
   a. to benefit from the Spirit of God we must apply ourselves to reading and hearing Scripture
   b. any spirit that foists another doctrine upon us than that in God's Word is vain and lying
   c. the Libertines contend that it is not worthy for the Spirit (to whom all things should be subject) to be subject to Scripture, but this is to judge the Spirit by standards inferior to His own, when He is to be compared solely with Himself
   d. He is the author of Scripture and on Scripture His image is stamped

3. Word and Spirit belong inseparably together
   a. they falsely allege Paul's rejection of "the letter that kills"; this statement does not reject the Scriptures but insists that the

Holy Spirit so inheres in His truth, which He expresses in Scripture, that only when its proper reverence and dignity are given to the Word does He show forth His power

b. certainty of Word and certainty of Spirit joined by a mutual bond
   (1) the light of the Spirit extinguished when prophecies are held in contempt
   (2) contrast between the careless forsaking of God's Word by these haughty enthusiasts and the sobriety of the children of God who rest their assurance upon the illumination of the Holy Spirit and upon His instrument, the Scriptures

CHAPTER 10
Scripture, to Correct All Superstition, Has Set the True God Alone over Against All the Gods of the Heathen

1. The Scriptural doctrine of God the Creator
   a. is the knowledge of God set forth in the created universe consonant with that expressed in the Word?
      (1) this question is too long for a thorough discussion here
      (2) present purpose merely to provide an index of what to look for in Scripture and how to seek it out
   b. limits of the present discussion
      (1) the covenant with Israel eventuating in the coming of the Redeemer will not at present be considered
      (2) rather, those Scriptural passages which describe how God, the Maker of heaven and earth, governs the world—His goodness, His righteous vengeance, and His forbearance—will be pointed out

2. The attributes of God according to Scripture agree with those known in His creatures
   a. scriptural passages show us not as He is in Himself, but as He is toward us: in kindness, goodness, mercy, justice, judgment, and truth
      (1) Exod. 34:6-7
      (2) Ps. 145
      (3) Jer. 9:24 (I Cor. 1:31)
   b. the purpose of this scriptural knowledge of God: fear→trust→true worship→full dependence upon Him

3. Even worshipers of idols knew the unity of God
   a. Scripture rejects all gods of the heathen
   b. polytheists never completely lost the awareness that there was really only one God
      (1) thus their persistence in polytheism is evidence of their own vanity and of Satan's deceptions, and is inexcusable
      (2) all, from the rude multitude to the sophisticated philosophers, have corrupted the truth of God

CHAPTER 11
It Is Unlawful to Attribute a Visible Form to God, and Whoever Sets Up Images Generally Forsakes the True God

Refutation of Those Who Ascribe a Visible Form to God [*1–7*]

1. We are forbidden every pictorial representation of God
   a. all sorts of human speculation about deity, of common folk or of philosophers, are lumped under idolatry by Scripture
   b. in the Ten Commandments the prohibition of idol-making directly follows the insistence upon one God
   c. the universal tendency to attach a visible form to God is utterly repudiated; no admission of degrees of truth among images

2. Every figurative representation of God contradicts His being
   a. Moses, Isaiah, and Paul speak out against visible images of God as dishonorable to His majesty
   b. even enlightened pagans like Seneca condemn this
   c. absurd contention of image-supporters that Jews were forbidden to make images because they inclined to superstition

3. Even direct signs of the divine presence give no justification for images
   a. such direct manifestations of the divine presence as appear in Scripture are intended to restrain men's curiosity, to teach God's invisibility, or to prelude God's future revelation in Christ
   b. the Cherubim of the mercy seat belonged to the pedagogy of

the old Covenant and have no place in our spiritually more mature age

c. Juvenal, a pagan, had more sense than the papists (who support images on the basis of the Old Testament) when he chided the Jews for worshiping mere clouds and the deity of the sky

d. we must recognize our own great inclination to idolatry, a common vice not confined to the Jews

4. Images and pictures are contrary to Scripture
   a. the absurd tendency to make his deity out of dead matter—noted both in Scripture and in the pagan poets—is a thing natural to man
   b. Scripture outspokenly threatens those who fashion their gods with their own hands
   c. the foolish distinction of the Greeks between "graven image" and "likeness" thoroughly refuted by Scripture

5. Scripture rejects images as the "books of the uneducated"
   a. Gregory the Great characterizes images as the books of the uneducated
   b. the prophets teach that anything of God learned from images is futile and false, because the two are unalterably opposed
   c. when we reject the papist's view we are but repeating verbatim the prophets' teaching

6. The doctors of the church also partly reject them
   a. Lactantius, Eusebius, and especially the Council of Elvira are outspoken on this point
   b. Augustine quotes the pagan Varro to telling effect on this also:
      (1) images did not originate, but proliferated, the errors concerning God
      (2) further, they diminished fear of God
   c. let men know God, then, from some other source than images

7. The images of the papists are entirely inappropriate
   a. the "books of the uneducated" idea is refuted by Scripture
   b. the papists indecently represent even the saints and martyrs: let them depict them more modestly if these are to be "books of holiness"

c. there would be no "uneducated" at all if the church had done its duty

The Origin of Idols [*8-11*]

8. The origin rests in man's desire for a tangible deity
   a. Wisd. of Sol. 14:15 suggests that idols arose out of the desire to honor the dead, but Scripture shows that the idol-making penchant antedates this wish to honor the dead
   b. the mind begets an idol; the hand gives it birth
   c. idol-making is an almost universal tendency, seeking a God who may actually be seen

9. Any use of images leads to idolatry
   a. the next step after construction of idols was their adoration
   b. for this reason the Lord forbade the making of images of God
   c. excuses for making idols
      (1) the heathen understood God to be other than stocks and stones: had many more images than gods, and changed likenesses at will
      (2) the vulgar sort held that they were not worshiping a visible object but a presence that dwelt there
      (3) the more refined denied this but asserted that through the physical image they gazed upon the sign of the thing they ought to worship
   d. Jewish and Gentile idolaters were animated by the same desire: they thought that through images the god would be impressed more surely and closely, and ultimately manifest his power in the images; thus they thought they were worshiping a deity in heaven

10. Image worship in the church
    a. the actions of the papists before their images betray their claim that, unlike ancient idolaters, they are not worshiping images
    b. the critique of idolatry of the Old Testament prophets applies just as much to the idolatry of present-day papists

11. Foolish evasions of the papists
    a. the absurd distinction of the papists between *dulia* (idol veneration or service) and *latria* (idol worship)

b. they irrationally assert that they "worship their idols without worship," as the meanings of the two Greek words show
c. thus the papists are just like the ancient idolaters

***Use and Abuse of Images** [**12–16**]*

12. The functions and limits of art
    a. painting and sculpture as gifts of God are to be used lawfully: that is, to depict things which the eyes are capable of seeing, not God who is invisible and who has forbidden any pictorial representation of Himself
    b. such lawful objects of artistic effort include
        (1) histories and events: for teaching and admonition
        (2) images and forms of bodies without historical connection: for pleasure
    c. most images in churches are of the latter type—many of them works of evil and wantonness

13. As long as doctrine was pure and strong, the church rejected images
    a. for the first 500 years the church remained free of images
    b. when the degeneration of the ministry set in, images began to adorn churches
    c. Fathers like Augustine and Jerome warn of the danger of images
    d. rather than dead images, Christians should accept the living images of Baptism and the Lord's Supper
    e. for the Papists, however, images are an incomparable boon

14. The Council of Nicea, friendly toward images, is itself a proof of the terrible distortion of doctrine
    a. the Second Council of Nicea, under the Empress Irene, decreed that images be worshiped; used as proof by the supporters of images
    b. the *Libri Caroli*, an authentic document of Charlemagne's time, reproduce the absurd arguments of the attending bishops in favor of images

15–16. Evidence of the absurdities at Nicea II, continued
    a. Scripture is not only misinterpreted but misquoted

b. the papists' pretense of antiquity of images is sufficiently dispelled by the absurd reasonings of that Council
c. "Where now is the distinction between *latria* and *dulia*, by which they are wont to hoodwink God and men? For the Council accords, without exception, as much to images as to the living God."

CHAPTER 12
God Is Distinguished from Idols, so That He Alone May Be Wholly Worshiped

1. True religion binds us to God as the one and only God
   a. the definition of "religion"
      (1) Scriptural insistence upon *one* God also implies that nothing of His divinity is to be transferred to another
      (2) both *religio* and *eusebia* suggest ordered worship, and the avoidance of confusion
      (3) superstition heaps up a needless mass of inanities
   b. in combatting the universal perversion of religion among men, God shows Himself a jealous God
      (1) law and right worship are combined in God's law to conform man to His will
      (2) thus men are restrained from entering into vicious rites
   c. the proliferation of lesser deities under the supreme God (among Greeks and Jews as well) detracts from God's glory by parceling out his functions
   d. saint worship is nothing but an extension of this tendency

2. The "worship" and "veneration" of idols are the same thing
   a. the distinction between *latria* and *dulia* was invented to allow the transference of divine honors to angels and the dead
   b. in Greek *dulia* means service, *latria* worship; since service is higher than worship, the Papists are actually giving more honor to the saints than to God

3. Idol worship is an attempt to rob God of His being and to appropriate it to the creature
   a. Scriptural usage shows the invalidity of the Romanists' false distinction between *dulia* and *latria*, and denies to men and angels the right to receive the highest worship

b. the genesis of saint worship
   (1) transference of observances of piety to another than the sole God
   (2) divine honors for sun, stars, idols
   (3) ambition: men stole for mortals what was due God—offering sacrifices indiscriminately to tutelary divinities, lesser gods, or dead heroes

CHAPTER 13
In Scripture, from the Creation Onward, We Are Taught One Essence of God, Which Contains Within Itself Three Persons

THE ORTHODOX DOCTRINE OF THE TRINITY [1-20]

The Signification of the Persons [1-6]

1. Transcendence, unity, and spirituality of God
   a. Scriptural teaching about God ought to rule out both vulgar and sophisticated delusions about Him: His spiritual nature emphasized
   b. in Scripture, God accommodates the knowledge of Himself to our slight capacity: this the true explanation for the so-called anthropomorphisms of the Bible

2. The three "persons" in God
   a. three persons; another special mark to distinguish God more precisely from idols
   b. to avoid error we must eliminate wrong notions of "person" and base our understanding of the concept upon Scripture [Heb 1:3ff.]
      (1) one essence or *ousia* in God
      (2) but three persons, *hypostases,* substances, or better, subsistences, each distinct from the other

3. The expressions "trinity" and "person" aid the interpretation of Scripture and are therefore admissable
   a. our conviction, despite pedantic quibbling: one God in three persons, each of which is entirely God
   b. the charge against using "foreign" words
      (1) if terms go against the simplicity of God's Word they are of course to be rejected

(2) however, if they concisely express something in Scripture, they are to be admitted

4. The church has regarded as necessary such expressions as "trinity," "person," etc.
   a. these terms were made necessary in the past as well as in the present by corrupters of true doctrine
   b. Arius confessed Christ to be God and Son of God, but went on to state that Christ was created and had a beginning: the orthodox fathers exposed the man's duplicity by the word *homoousios*
   c. Sabellius, too, looked upon Father, Son, and Spirit as mere names of God, without rank or distinction: the church fathers exposed him by asserting a trinity of persons in a unity

5. Limits and necessity of theological terms
   a. while it would be better to get along without such terms, we should not rashly repudiate them, but recognize that they express the fact that Father, Son, and Holy Spirit are one, yet are differentiated from one another by a certain property
   b. in all humility many of the fathers warn against the limitations of these Greek and Latin terms: we ought to imitate their humility, but at the same time recognize the utility of these terms in discussion

6. The meaning of the most important conception
   a. person—a "subsistence" in God's essence
   b. subsistence—the act of being related by a common bond to the essence, but distinguished from it by a special mark
   c. when *God* is mentioned simply and indefinitely, reference is to the Son and Spirit as well; but where the persons of the Trinity are compared, their special properties distinguish each from the rest
   d. divine economy of the Triune God has no effect on unity of essence

***The Deity of the Son* [*7-13*]**

7. The deity of the "Word"
   a. the "Word" mentioned in the Old Testament as well as the New Testament is not a mere utterance but rather the ever-

lasting wisdom, residing with God, and the source of all prophecies

b. unchangeable, the Word abides everlastingly one and the same with God, and is God Himself

8. The eternity of the Word

a. while not openly depriving the Word of His deity, some men secretly steal His eternity, asserting that He began to be with the creation of the universe

b. on the contrary, the Word, conceived beyond the beginning of time by God, has perpetually resided with Him: whence both His eternity, His true essence, and His deity are proved

9. The deity of Christ in the Old Testament

a. here we are concerned with Old Testament testimonies affirming Christ's deity, not those that proclaim His mediatorial office

b. the Jews force the interpretation of these passages to exclude, for the most part, any application of the titles to Christ

10. The "Angel of the eternal God"

a. the Jews are wrong in not recognizing Jehovah as set forth often in the person of an angel

b. Servetus impiously asserts that God never revealed Himself to Abraham and the other patriarchs, but that they worshiped an angel in His place: from such passages and others, we follow the church fathers in interpreting the Angel as the Word, Christ

c. thus it is proved that Christ is the same God who had always been worshiped among the Jews

11. The deity of Christ in the New Testament: witness of the apostles

a. passages from the Psalms and Isaiah applied by Paul to Christ show that He is that very God whose glory cannot be transferred to another

b. John asserts that the majesty of God seen by Isaiah in his temple vision was actually Christ

c. other passages, too, make this identification, asserting no second god, but proclaiming Christ that sole God, always worshiped

12. The deity of Christ is demonstrated in His works
    a. in the governing of the world
    b. in searching men's hearts and in remitting men's sins

13. The deity of Christ is demonstrated by His miracles
    a. difference between the miracles of prophets and apostles, and those of Christ
        (1) they merely distributed God's gifts by their ministry
        (2) Christ showed forth His own power
    b. true salvation, goodness, justice are of God Himself; Christ has these perfectly in Himself; therefore Christ is God
    c. these evidences show that
        (1) by the Son's intercession come to us those things the Father bestows
        (2) by mutual participation in power the Son Himself is the author of them
    d. better than all rational proofs, though, is the pious mind's perception of the very presence of God: it almost touches Him when it feels itself quickened, preserved, justified, and sanctified

The Deity of the Spirit [*14–15*]

14. The deity of the Spirit is demonstrated in His work
    a. the Spirit's activity seen in the tending of the chaotic mass [Gen. 1:2] and then in the adorning of the universe with order and beauty in creation
    b. the Spirit shared with God the sending of the prophets
    c. not only from Scripture but from our own sure experience of godliness do we learn the Spirit's manifold divine activities
        (1) the cause of essence, life, and growth in created things
        (2) the author of regeneration into incorruptible life, by His very own energy
        (3) the bestower of wisdom and speech
        (4) the giver of justification, power, sanctification, truth, grace, and every good—through Him we enter the fellowship of God to enjoy these
    d. therefore the Spirit shares in God's power and resides hypostatically in God

15. Express testimonies for the deity of the Spirit
    a. by the indwelling Spirit we are temples of God; therefore the Holy Spirit = God
    b. the words which the prophets refer to the Lord of Hosts are referred in the New Testament to the Holy Spirit: therefore the Holy Spirit = God
    c. the heinousness of the "sin against the Holy Spirit" also proves His deity

The Trinity as Oneness and Threeness **[*16–20*]**

16. Oneness
    a. Paul's insistence on *one* God, faith, and baptism and Christ's commission to baptize in the name of Father, Son, and Holy Spirit argue for one essence in God, wherein three persons reside
    b. the folly of the Arians who deny the common essence of Father and Son; and of the Macedonians, that of Father, Son, and Holy Spirit

17. Threeness
    a. while Scripture distinguishes the three persons from one another, we ought to handle such distinctions with great reverence and sobriety, as Gregory of Nazianzus says: "I cannot think on the one without quickly being encircled by the splendor of the three; nor can I discern the three without being straightway carried back to the one."
    b. Father, Son, and Spirit not mere titles but involve a real distinction, not a division
    c. texts of Scripture adduced to show the distinction of Father and Son, and Son and Spirit

18. Difference of Father, Son, and Spirit
    a. the inadequacy of human comparisons
    b. the distinction expressed from Scripture
        (1) Father = beginning of activity; fountain and wellspring of all things
        (2) Son = wisdom, counsel (plan), and ordered dispensation of all things
        (3) Holy Spirit = power and efficacy of that activity

c. a distinction of order, not of time
   (1) no *before* or *after* in eternity
   (2) but human mind naturally contemplates
      (a) God first
      (b) then wisdom coming from Him
      (c) lastly power whereby He executes the decrees of His plan (counsel) [double procession—as seen in Rom. 8]

   } note reverse order to experience of faith

19. The relationship of Father, Son, and Spirit
   a. in each hypostasis the whole nature is to be understood, but to each belongs His special characteristic
   b. as Augustine shows, the diversity of terms for the persons of the Trinity is due to their interrelationships

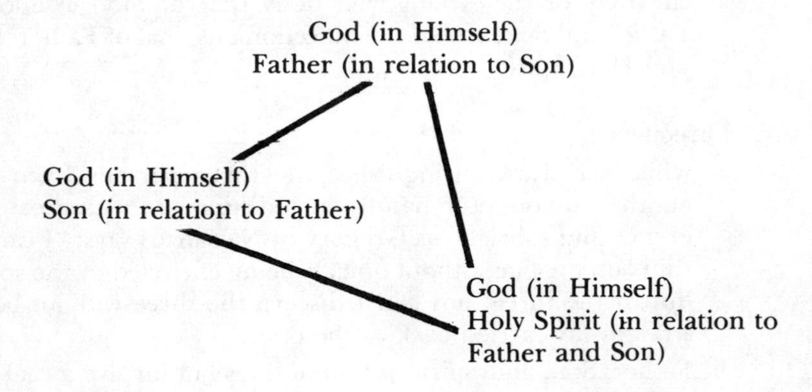

20. The Triune God
   a. belief in God implies a single, simple essence, in which we comprehend three persons or hypostases
   b. uses of the name "God"
      (1) undifferentiated: designates all three persons
      (2) but preeminently the Father as beginning and source, yet without detracting from deity of the Son and Holy Spirit
   c. names "Father," "Son," "Holy Spirit," imply a relationship among the persons
   d. therefore the whole essence of God is spiritual and comprehends Father, Son, and Holy Spirit

REFUTATION OF SOME RECENT HERESIES [*21–29*]

21. The mystery of the Trinity is to be received by a teachable faith and not by subtlety
    a. today as in the past, Satan is stirring up contention over the divine essence of Son and Spirit, and over the distinction of persons: our original intention was to speak to the teachable, but now we are compelled to wrestle with these subverters of doctrine
    b. such discussion calls for soberness because of the manifest limitations of man's mind in the knowledge of God
    c. the task calls not for inordinate curiosity but for an adherence to what God teaches in His Word

22. Servetus' contention against the Trinity
    a. it is useless to catalogue ancient errors and heresies; our task is to assert the unity of essence and distinction of persons against those who confuse these
    b. summary of Servetus' views
        (1) definitions
            (a) Trinity—unthinkable and hostile to notion of God's unity: Deity is tripartite if three persons are said to reside in God's essence
            (b) Persons—certain external ideas which do not truly subsist in God's essence but represent God to us in some sort of appearance; or—visible appearance of the glory of God
        (2) Servetus' "theogony"
            (a) beginning: no distinction in God
            (b) Christ came forth as God from God; the Spirit proceeded from Him as another God
            (c) a part of God is both in the Son and in the Spirit; the Spirit is substantially in us and in the whole creation
            (d) thus Son and Spirit are indiscriminately mingled with created beings generally, and there is substantial deity not only in the soul of man but in other created things

23. The Son is God even as the Father
    a. Gentile, Fazy, and others avoid Servetus' impiety by confessing three persons, but proceed to qualify this affirmation

b. summary of their views
    (1) the Father truly and properly is the sole God, and *essentiator*
    (2) He infused His own deity into the Son and Spirit when He formed them
    (3) thus they make a distinction in essence between the Father, on the one hand, and the Son and Spirit on the other

c. refutation: there must be some mark of differentiation in order that the Father may not be the Son. Those who locate that mark in the essence clearly reduce Christ's true deity to nothing, which without essence, and indeed the whole essence, cannot exist

24. The name "God" in Scripture does not refer to the Father alone
  a. they object that unqualified references to God in Scripture apply to the Father alone on the ground that "unless the Father alone were truly God, He would be His own Father"
  b. on the contrary, from the incarnation onward Christ has been called the Son of God
    (1) as the eternal Word, begotten before all ages from the Father
    (2) as Mediator, come to join us to the Father
  c. other objections in the same vein refuted from Scripture

25. The divine nature is common to all three persons
  a. they divide the divine essence among Father, Son and Holy Spirit, contrary to our teaching and Scripture where it is held that God is one in essence
  b. they falsely attribute to us a "quaternity" (of divine essence plus three persons)
  c. for us the unity lies in the essence, the Trinity in the persons
  d. the end of their absurd and impious error would be that the Trinity becomes the conjunction of one God with two created things

26. The subordination of the incarnate Word to the Father is no counter-evidence
  a. they assert that Christ, if properly God, is wrongly called "Son"
  b. when Christ addresses God in John 17:3 He is speaking as Mediator, but on this account His divinity is in no sense di-

minished, although it is hidden to the world; in the word "God" He includes Himself

c. the highest station of the Father in regard to the Son does not mean the subordination of the Son to a second rank of deity beneath the Father in terms of heavenly glory: but Christ descended to us, to bear us up to the Father and to Himself, too, as He is one with the Father

27. Our adversaries falsely appeal to Irenaeus
    a. Irenaeus had insisted that the Father of Christ was the sole and eternal God of Israel; this they turn against us
    b. remember that Irenaeus was fighting heretics who denied that the Old Testament God and the Father of Christ were one and the same; our contention is against those who deny the same essential deity to Christ as they attribute to God the Father
    c. many passages of Irenaeus prove that he accepted Christ as one and the same God as His Father

28. The appeal to Tertullian also is of no avail
    a. in brief, Tertullian insists upon the essential unity of the Godhead, but sees in the divine economy or dispensation the distinction among the persons
    b. Tertullian's subordination of Son to Father thus is not in the realm of substance or essence but in the realm of the economy

29. All acknowledged doctors of the church confirm the doctrine of the Trinity
    a. in like manner Justin and Hilary are adopted as patrons by our opponents on the same false grounds as Irenaeus
    b. the citation of Ignatius is from a forgery
    c. Augustine, whom our opponents reject, knew the previous fathers, and holds that the name "God" is especially ascribed to the Father, because if the beginning comes not from Him, the simple unity of God cannot be conceived
    d. this refutation is sufficient except to inveterate speculators

CHAPTER 14
Even in the Creation of the World and of All Things, Scripture by Unmistakable Marks Distinguishes the True God from False Gods

THE WORK OF THE SIX DAYS OF CREATION [*1–2*]

1. We cannot and should not go behind God's act of creation in our speculation
   a. God made manifest the history of creation in order that men might not conceive Him as pagans falsely do, or as philosophers ephermerally do as the mind of the universe, but distinctly (as Moses does) as the maker and founder of the universe, and His eternal wisdom and Spirit
   b. the uses of the creation narrative and of history as outlined in Scripture
      (1) to refute Egyptian fables
      (2) to make known the beginning of the universe and thus to set forth more clearly God's eternity, in fact a living likeness of Himself, like spectacles for enfeebled eyes
   c. we must hold our curiosity and speculation within the bounds of the 6,000 years set by God's narrative

2. The work of the six days shows God's goodness toward men
   a. the six days make allowance for our brief attention span and bid our reason contemplate, in obedience of faith and looking to the quiet of the seventh day, the works of God
   b. the six days also show us God's fatherly care in providing for man's every need before man's creation

THE ANGELS [*3–12*]

Importance and Usefulness of This Doctrine [*3–4*]

3. God is Lord over all!
   a. the angels, though not mentioned in the Mosaic hexaemeron, (out of accommodation for rude minds), were not divine but created beings as may be inferred from other Scripture
   b. the Manichaean heresy, that God and the devil are coordinate principles, arose out of the refusal to ascribe to the good God the creation of any evil thing
   c. the mention of the creation of "things invisible" in the Nicene Creed is probably a reflection of this

4. We should not indulge in speculations concerning the angels, but search out the witness of Scripture
   a. the rule of modesty and sobriety: not to speak, or guess, or even to seek to know, concerning obscure matters anything except what has been imparted to us by God's Word; to seek out and meditate upon those things that make for edification
   b. let us not then speculate on which of the six days the angels were created; it is enough to know that they were
   c. let us then eschew the foolish wisdom of Dionysius and his *Celestial Hierarchy*
   d. the theologian's task: not to divert the ears with chatter but to strengthen consciences by teaching things true, sure, profitable

The Ministry of Angels [5–7]

5. The designation of the angels in Scripture
   a. messengers: intermediaries whereby God manifests Himself to men
   b. hosts: analogy of the bodyguards who adorn the majesty of a prince
   c. virtues: set forth the power and strength of God's hand
   d. principalities, powers, dominions: through angels God wields His authority in the world
   e. thrones: in a sense the glory of God resides in them
   f. "gods"; (= Christ)
      (1) they mirror His divinity to us
      (2) they deserve the title far more than princes and governors

6. The angels as protectors and helpers of believers
   a. the Old Testament contains instances of angels protecting men from harm
   b. in the New Testament Christ was ministered to by angels in His tribulations, and His coming and resurrection were announced by them

7. Guardian angels?
   a. it is doubtful whether each man has his own guardian angel; rather, all the angels look after each one of us
   b. there are no grounds for the popular belief in a "good" and "bad" angel for each man

The Life of Angels [*8–9*]

8. The hierarchy, number, and form of the angels
   a. Scripture offers us no details on the number, orders, or form of angels: only general indications
   b. the rest must be among the mysteries to be revealed at the Last Day

9. The angels are not mere ideas but actuality
   a. against the "Libertines" who, like the Sadducees of old, denied the real existence of angels, there are many Scriptural texts in defense of their reality
   b. even Christ, as the prime mediator, is in one place called "angel" [Mal. 3:1]

Against the Worship of Angels [*10–12*]

10. The divine glory does not belong to the angels
    a. because they so reflect God's glory, and dispense God's care to us, men tend to worship angels
    b. Paul warned us against this as a degradation of Christ: angels draws from the same well as we, they simply reflect the splendor of God's majesty

11. God makes use of the angels not for His own sake but for ours
    a. God has no need of angels to carry out His commands; in fact He sometimes disregards them and acts directly
    b. God uses angels to accommodate to our feeble capacity and show us more intimately His loving protection of us: for example, Elisha and his servant [II Kings 6:17]

12. The angels must not divert us from directing our gaze to the Lord alone
    a. angels are intended to lead us to God, not draw us away from Him
    b. Scripture does not allow the Platonic way of seeking access to God through the worship of angels

DEVILS AND DEMONS [13–19]

Activity of Demons [13–15]

13. Scripture forearms us against the adversary
    a. all Scriptural imagery concerning devils is intended solely to warn us and equip us for combat against the adversary
    b. our life is a military service in which we are urged to perseverance, in our weakness and faintheartedness calling upon God for strength and help

14. The realm of wickedness
    a. Scriptural references to devils (in the plural) remind us of the vast host of enemies against us, that we may not slacken our efforts
    b. Scriptural references to Satan (in the singular) set the kingdom of wickedness over against the kingdom of righteousness, the church of the saints over against the faction of the impious

15. An irreconcilable struggle
    a. the picture of the devil presented in Scripture ought to fire us to the defense of God's glory and our own salvation against this implacable enemy
    b. the devil's consummate depravity depicted

Fall of Satan and Demons [16–17]

16. The devil is a degenerate creation of God
    a. devils were first created as angels of God, but by degeneration they ruined themselves and became instruments of ruin for others
    b. this alone is profitable to know; any speculation beyond this about the fall of devils is to no effect

17. The devil stands under God's power
    a. yet Satan can only act with God's permission and sufferance
    b. Satan's actions, however, arise from his own passionate and deliberate opposition to God
    c. hence he carries out only what has been permitted to him, and so willy-nilly obeys his Creator

The Struggle of Believers against Satan *[18]*

18. Assurance of victory!
    a. God never lets Satan vanquish or crush believers, even though they may be sore pressed by him
    b. with the wicked, however, it is different: Satan is permitted to subdue them
    c. this is true corporately as well as individually: believers bear the image of God; the impious are the children of Satan into whose image they have degenerated

Personality of Demons *[19]*

19. Devils are not thoughts, but actualities
    a. [the Libertines] claim the same unreality for devils as they do for angels (sect. 9, above)
    b. this view amply refuted by clear Scriptural testimonies which would be meaningless if devils were nonexistent

THE RIGHT VIEW OF GOD'S WORKS AND THEIR BENEFITS [20-22]

20. Greatness and abundance of creation
    a. let us delight in the works of God which meet us on all sides, and ponder them with pious meditation, even though they are not the chief evidence for faith
    b. out of Gen. 1–2 and the *Hexaemerons* of Basil and Ambrose, we can summarize the following:
        (1) God created heaven and earth out of nothing, and in a wonderful series peopled it with living beings, each in its own place, and, though they are all subject to corruption, each is capable of preserving its species until the Last Day
        (2) from time to time He renews some and by his gift of propagation ensures the continuance of the species in a universe abundantly furnished
        (3) man, at last, is put forth as the most excellent example of God's works

21. How should we view God's works?
    a. we have neither the capacity nor the space to describe how God's attributes shine in the creation of the universe; our task

is rather to teach what it is for God to be Creator of heaven and earth

b. the rule: do not pass over in ungrateful thoughtlessness or forgetfulness those conspicuous powers which God shows forth in His creatures; learn to apply the rule to ourselves so our very hearts are touched

c. "the Hymn to Creation"

22. The contemplation of God's goodness in His creation will lead us to thankfulness and trust

a. expansion of the second part of the "rule" (sect. 21): God's great benefits prepared for us should lead us to call upon Him, praise, love Him

b. to react otherwise toward His liberality would be sheer ingratitude

c. trust in what God will give us; acknowledge every benefit to ourselves as a blessing from Him; study and love and serve Him with all our heart

CHAPTER 15
Discussion of Human Nature as Created, the Faculties of the Soul, of the Image of God, of Free Choice, and of the Original Integrity of Man's Nature

Introduction

1. Man proceeded spotless from God's hand; therefore he may not push the blame for his sins on the Creator

a. why discuss the creation of man?

(1) because man is the noblest example of God's justice, wisdom, and goodness

(2) because knowledge of ourselves is required for us to come to a clear and complete knowledge of God

b. two-fold character of knowledge of self

(1) as man was at creation (present topic)

(2) as man became after the fall (to be discussed later)

c. our intention: to vindicate God's justice of every accusation

NATURE OF THE SOUL [2-5]

2. Diversity of body and soul
   a. definition of soul and spirit
      (1) soul: an immortal yet created essence, man's nobler part
      (2) spirit: a synonym for "soul" except when the two words are used together
   b. common evidences of the divine and immortal character of the soul as essence, apart from the body
      (1) sense of immortality
      (2) conscience: observed in our feelings of guilt, fear, etc.
      (3) great gifts with which the human mind has been endowed
      (4) sleep and dreams
   c. Scriptural evidences of the same

3. God's image and likeness in man
   a. besides the external and physical evidence (upright gait, for example) or man's separateness from animals and likeness to God, we have the more cogent fact that man was created in God's image, in a *spiritual* sense
   b. Osiander's assertion that this image extends to both soul and body is absurd
   c. the question of image/likeness
      (1) there is no difference between these words as some interpreters insist—there is, rather, an evidence of Hebrew literary parallelism
      (2) man, in respect to his soul, is called God's image, although the likeness of God extends to the whole superiority of man over other creatures
      (3) image/likeness expresses the integrity with which Adam was endowed
         (a) right intelligence
         (b) affections kept within bounds of reason
         (c) all senses tempered in right order
         (d) truly referred all gifts to his Maker
   d. although the primary seat of the divine image was in the mind and heart, or in the soul and its powers, yet there was no part of man, not even the body itself, in which some sparks did not shine

4. The true nature of the image of God is to be derived from what Scripture says of its renewal through Christ

a. a full definition of "image" is to be sought in the distinctively human faculties, and especially as they are seen in man restored through Christ, for
    (1) Adam's fall did not involve the total destruction of God's image in man, but its frightful deformity
    (2) thus, we turn to man regenerated in Christ
b. aspects of this renewal, according to Paul
    (1) knowledge
    (2) pure righteousness and holiness
c. God's image is the perfect excellence of human nature which shone in Adam before the fall, but was subsequently so vitiated and almost blotted out that nothing remains after the ruin except what is confused, mutilated, disease-ridden. Therefore in some part it now appears in the elect, insofar as they have been reborn in the spirit; but it will attain its full splendor in heaven
d. to know the parts of this image, we need to discuss the faculties of the soul

5. The soul of man is created by God and is not a sort of emanation of His nature
    a. Servetus has revived the false Manichaean notion that man's soul is a portion of deity; this is refuted by the fact of man's sinful nature and by the unity of God's essence
    b. Osiander believes that the image of God in man consists in the presence of God's essential righteousness there; this too is sheer Manichaeism
    c. Paul teaches that man's soul is like God not in essence but by the power of His Spirit

OPINION OF THE PHILOSOPHERS ON THE SOUL CRITICIZED IN VIEW OF THE FALL OF ADAM [*6–8*]

6. The soul and its faculties
    a. of the philosophers only Plato comes close to an appreciation of the soul's incorporeal nature
    b. the nature of the soul from Scripture
        (1) incorporeal substance
        (2) dwells as the animating principle in the body as in a house
        (3) man's quest after God is a proof that he is divinely endowed with reason
        (4) disagreement within the soul arises not from the exis-

tence of two souls in each man (as some philosophers hold), but from man's fallen nature

c. the faculties of the soul from the philosophers
   (1) Plato via Themistius [see diagram below]
   (2) Aristotle (*Ethics*): division of powers of soul into appetitive (without reason, but obeying it), intellective (through itself participating in reason); three principles of action: sense, understanding, appetite
   (3) these views, while probable, are too complicated for our purpose

7. Understanding and will as the truly fundamental powers
   a. the philosophers, ignorant of man's fall, confuse two very diverse states of man
   b. the human soul consists of two faculties
      (1) understanding: distinguishes between objects to be approved or disapproved—acts as leader and governor of the soul
      (2) will: chooses and follows what the understanding pronounces good and eschews what it disapproves—respects the decision of the understanding and awaits judgment of the understanding in its own desires
   c. equivalent terms: philosophers distinguish between understanding and sense; we include sense under understanding. We also substitute the word "will" for the philosophers' use of "appetite"

8. Free choice and Adam's responsibility
   a. man's faculties before the fall
      (1) mind (understanding) given to man to distinguish good from evil, right from wrong, what should be followed from what should be avoided—*τὸ ἡγεμονικόν*, the "guider"
      (2) will: the seat of free choice
   b. thus [supralapsarian] man had the power, if he so willed, of attaining eternal life; but he was not given the constancy to persevere
   c. this changed with man's fall: man was far different at the first creation from his whole posterity, who, deriving their origin from him in his corrupted state, have contracted from him a hereditary taint
   d. the schemes of the philosophers fail because they do not take into account the fall

FACULTIES OF THE SOUL

SENSE PERCEPTIONS

COGNITIVE FACULTIES

five senses

sensus communis — common sense (receptacle of sense perception)

fantasia — fantasy (distinguishes what has been apprehended by common sense)

ratio — reason (embraces a universal judgment)

intellectus — understanding (quietly contemplates what reason discursively ponders)

desire (*vis concupiscendi*)

anger (*vis irascendi*)

will (*voluntas*)

APPETITIVE FACULTIES

(strive after what the cognitive faculties and common sense present to them)

Calvin *Institutes* 1:15:6, from Themistius *De Anima* II, VII (ed. R. Heinze, pp. 36, 120, 122).

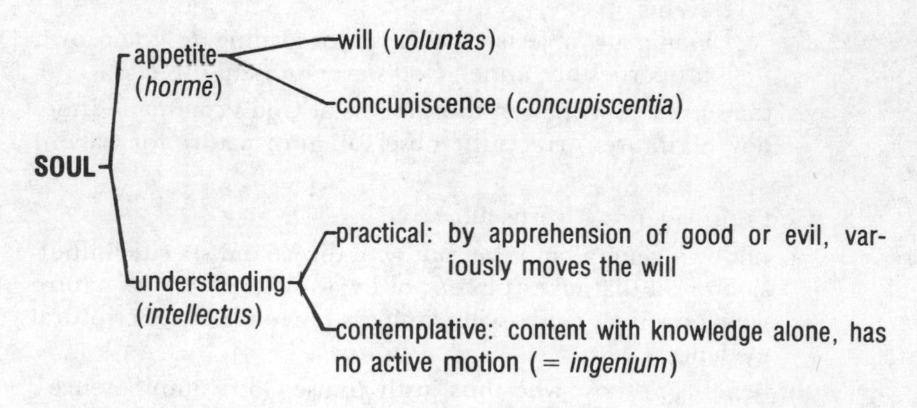

Aristotle, *Nicomachean Ethics* I, 13 (p. 1102 b 30ff.); VI, 2 (p. 1139 a 17); *Themistius* VI, 112–114.

hormē
- obeying reason: *boulēsis*
- disobeying reason: *pathos*→intemperance

CHAPTER 16
God by His Power Nourishes and Maintains the World Created by Him, and Rules Its Several Parts by His Providence

God's Special Providence Asserted, Against the Opinions of Philosophers *[1-4]*

1. Creation and providence inseparably joined
   a. carnal sense can recognize a God who once created all things, and who gives them sufficient energy to carry on by themselves thereafter
   b. but faith, penetrating more deeply, sees the Creator as also governor and preserver of all He has created [doctrine of providence]
      (1) the celestial frame
      (2) all things on earth, including human affairs

2. There is no such thing as fortune or chance
   a. carnal sense (in all ages) has attributed all happenings to fortune or chance, thus beclouding God's providence
   b. but faith, Scripturally based, knows that all things happen in accord with God's will
      (1) events
      (2) inanimate objects, which act according to their own properties but under God's ever-present direction
   c. the sun in all its power and glory is at God's command [note how Scripture corrects the observation of nature for Calvin]

3. God's providence governs all
   a. not by a general impulse, but with direct and specific impulsion of all that takes place; not by a universal law of nature which confines God's will within its narrow limits: Scriptural evidence
   b. benefits to those who thus justly praise God's omnipotence
      (1) His power is ample to do good in heaven and earth and among His creatures attentive and obedient to Him
      (2) He protects us from all harmful things; allays our superstitious fear of whatever threatens us: Scriptural examples

4. The nature of providence
   a. two errors
      (1) not mere foreknowledge but active governance of events
      (2) not general, confused governance of individual creatures (false distinction of God's will and His determination)
   b. "general" and "special" providence
      (1) doctrine of general providence is accepted in the sense that God not only watches over but exercises especial care over each of His works
      (2) some writers obscure God's special providence by restricting it to particular acts alone; we hold that God actively regulates all individual events, so that nothing takes place by chance

Doctrine of Special Providence Supported by the Evidence of Scripture [5–7]

5. God's providence also directs the individual
   a. some assume that God gives general direction to the forces of nature, but that individual things, by themselves or by chance, are impelled by inclination of nature
   b. but while accounting for the progression of the seasons, this does not account for fruitfulness or scarcity of crops, abundance or famine: these are God's blessing or curse: Scriptural examples

6. God's providence especially relates to men
   a. even as the universe was established especially for mankind, so also is this the purpose of His governance of it
   b. no man can act, or even speak, except as God wills
   c. even occurrences that seem quite fortuitous are subject to God's will, as Scripture demonstrates; all things live under God's secret plan

7. God's providence also regulates natural occurrences
   a. examples from Scripture
      (1) wind: no wind ever arises or increases except by God's express command
      (2) power of procreation
      (3) nourishment

b. God's general providence
   (1) continues the order of nature
   (2) is adapted to a definite and proper end

***Discussion of Fortune, Chance, and Seeming Contingency in Events** [8–9]*

8. The doctrine of providence is no Stoic belief in fate!
   a. false charge against Christian providence that it is the Stoic doctrine of fate (cf. Augustine)
      (1) Stoic: necessity lies in a chain of causes
      (2) Christian: eternal decrees of God carried out in His governance of all things
   b. fortune and chance are pagan terms inadmissible to Christians, as Basil and Augustine say

9. The true causes of events are hidden to us
   a. the sluggishness and limits of the human mind see as fortuitous those things which are actually ordered by God's purpose
   b. in this sense "fate" and "fortune" are used in Scripture to explain events seemingly contingent, but known by faith to derive from a secret impulse of God. [God's freedom in directing events may be inferred from his exempting Christ's fragile bones from breaking]

CHAPTER 17
How We May Apply the Doctrine of Providence to Our Greatest Benefit

***Interpretation of Divine Providence with Reference to the Past and the Future** [1–5]*

1. The meaning of God's ways
   a. three things to be noted
      (1) God's providence to be considered with regard to the future as well as the past [discussion in sects. 3–5]
      (2) its works (especially in sect. 9]
         (a) sometimes through an intermediary
         (b) sometimes without an intermediary
         (c) sometimes contrary to an intermediary

(3) through it God reveals His concern for the whole human race, but especially His vigilance in ruling the church [discussed in sects. 6–8]

b. the occasional obscurity of God's providence in His dealing with men should not drive us to attribute all occurrences to blind fortune or to lash out against His hidden judgments

(1) God's providence revealed in the final outcome which shows His purpose even in the harshest events

(2) analogy of the thunderstorm which strikes upon us, while far above the storm serenity reigns

2. God's rule will be observed with respect!

a. the proper attitude toward God's providence is one of fear, reverence, and humility, not the arrogance of some who try to limit God's acts by their own reason

b. Scripture incontrovertibly proves that whatever happens in the universe is governed by God's incomprehensible plan

(1) the will of God as revealed in the law (and gospel) distinguished from His hidden will, called by the Scriptures "abyss" [See 1:18:3 for assertion of the unity of God's will]

(2) testimony of Job, especially, to this

c. let us so assent to God's supreme authority, that His will may be for us the sole rule of righteousness and the truly just cause of all things

(1) it is not an absolute will divorced from His justice (Sorbonne)

(2) but providence, the source of right alone, yet hidden

3. God's providence does not relieve us from responsibility

a. we must not blame our wickedness or adversities upon God as certain pagan poets do

b. the Libertines, too, absurdly argue that providence

(1) makes foolish any precautions against danger or death, because we cannot escape the end God has ordained for us

(2) exonerates us of our own crimes, for God decreed that they would take place, and is thus their cause, we only their instrument

4. God's providence does not excuse us from due prudence

a. God has set limits to our life by his eternal decrees

b. but this does not hinder us from using the means and remedies He has given us for the preservation of our life
c. thus both folly and prudence are instruments of the divine dispensation

5. God's providence does not exculpate our wickedness
 a. the charge: that all past deeds, even those that are evil, take place at the intervention of God's will, and therefore should go unpunished
 b. the answer:
  (1) in His Word, God requires of us only what He commands; if we go against His will, we are obstinate and disobedient; yet He uses even our evil deeds to achieve His good end
  (2) the blame is, however, upon us; for if we do evil our consciences are convicted, but in God there is only the lawful use of our evil intent: analogy of the corpse stinking in the sun; the sun's rays do not therefore stink

Meditating on the Ways of God in Providence: the Happiness of Recognizing Acts of Providence [*6-11*]

6. God's providence as solace of believers
 a. meditation upon God's providence is a fitting and comforting antidote to the above-mentioned critics
 b. testimonies of Scripture to God's particular (not generalized) care of all creatures, especially man, and in a singular manner, His church

7. God's providence in prosperity
 a. testimonies of Scripture show that all men, good or evil, are under God's power; His care is to govern all creatures for their good and safety
 b. the benefits which derive from this knowledge:
  (1) gratitude for prosperity [sect. 7]
  (2) patience in adversity [sect. 8]
  (3) freedom from worry about the future [sects. 10-11]

8. Certainty about God's providence helps us in all adversities
 a. in adversity, let us raise up our hearts to God, thus to receive patience and peaceful moderation of mind

b. as numerous examples in Scripture teach, we should recall our minds to this: "the Lord has willed it; therefore it must be borne, not only because one may not contend against it, but also because He wills nothing but what is just and expedient."
    (1) this true for injustices caused by men
    (2) and for misfortunes which happen without human agency

9. No disregard of intermediate causes!
    a. with respect to past events
        (1) for kindness shown we should be grateful to men, but supremely to God as principal author
        (2) for loss suffered, we should recognize it came about by the Lord's will, but we must also impute it to ourselves
        (3) in all crimes we should contemplate, at one and the same time, God's righteousness and man's wickedness
    b. with respect to future events
        (1) we should avail ourselves of human assistance, but always look upon it as a lawful instrument of divine providence to be put to use
        (2) we should strive to what seems, to our minds, expedient, but rely ultimately upon God's wisdom as the guide to our goal, not upon external helps
    c. thus we will be able to put off rashness and overconfidence and to call continually upon God

10. Without certainty about God's providence life would be unbearable
    a. threat of countless misfortunes meets us at every turn, even though most of them rarely happen, or at least not to all or at the same time
    b. what a miserable life of trepidation would we spend if we were tossed and buffeted about by blind fortune!

11. Certainty about God's providence puts joyous trust toward God in our hearts
    a. divine providence relieves us of fear and anxiety, and gives us comfort and assurance
    b. providence teaches us that even the devil and his angels are fettered to God's service (Scripture examples)
    c. ignorance of providence is the ultimate of all miseries; the knowledge of it is the highest blessedness

Answers to Objections [*12–14*]

12. On God's "repentance"
    a. the "God repents" passages of the Old Testament lead some to state that God has not determined the affairs of men by an eternal decree, but decrees at each moment according as He deems man fair and just
    b. God is no more to be charged with repentance than with ignorance or error or powerlessness
    c. some passages that speak of God's repentance also speak of His unchangeableness above all repentance

13. Scripture speaks of God's "repentance" to make allowance for our understanding
    a. in the limits and weakness of our minds we cannot understand God as He truly is
    b. hence He must represent Himself to us not as He is, but as He seems to us
    c. emotion, change of action and like human qualities involved in repentance are not to be attributed to God who is above all this, but to man who is displeased with himself
    d. hence God's plan and will remain eternally inviolate

14. God firmly executes His plan
    a. the examples of Jonah at Nineveh and of King Hezekiah illustrate not changes of God's plan, but God's threats that men may repent, and thus carry out His will and His decrees
    b. this is also seen in the instance of Abraham and King Abimilech

CHAPTER 18
God So Uses the Works of the Ungodly, and So Bends Their Minds to Carry Out His Judgments, that He Remains Pure from Every Stain

1. No mere "permission"!
    a. the false distinction between "doing" and "permitting"
        (1) intended by carnal [human] sense to "preserve" God from the defilement of committing evil, and from the seeming absurdity of God's punishing men for a God-inflicted blindness
        (2) yet this proposed distinction would suggest that there

are areas of existence over which God has no knowledge or control, or at least acquiesces in a motion not directed by Himself

(3) on the contrary, all the impious are so under God's power that He directs their evil intent to whatever end seems good to Him, and uses their wicked deeds to carry out His judgments—without any defilement or blame on His part

b. examples from Scripture

(1) as Job himself recognizes, not Satan, but God is the source of his trials: men or Satan may instigate something, but God by His key turns their efforts to carry out His judgments

(2) the blinding and insanity of Ahab [I Kings 22:20,22]

(3) the apostles recognize Pilate and the Jews as merely carrying out what God has decreed [Acts 4:28; cf. 2:23, etc.]

(4) Absalom's incest was God's own work [II Sam. 16:22; 12:12]

(5) the Chaldeans' cruelty toward Judah was God's work according to Jeremiah [Jer. 1:15; 7:14; 50:25, etc.]

(6) God's "hissing," the "rod of His anger," and like expressions in Scripture attest the same thing

therefore God does not sit idly in a watchtower awaiting chance events as if His judgments depended upon human will [Epicurean view]

2. How does God's impulse come to pass in men?

a. sundry Scriptural expressions show that "whatever we conceive of in our minds is directed to His own end by God's secret inspiration"; not by divine permission merely but with the active agency of the Spirit

b. this is notably seen in the "hardening of Pharaoh's heart"

(1) it would be absurd to say that Pharaoh hardened his own heart

(2) rather God's will is the cause: man, while he is acted upon by God, yet at the same time himself acts

c. often by Satan's intervention God acts in the wicked, but always with God's impulsion, direction, and limitation

d. this topic will be further discussed under free will in Book Two

therefore "since God's will is said to be the cause of all things, I have made His providence the determinative principle for all human plans and works, not only in order to display its force in the elect, who are ruled by the Holy Spirit, but also to compel the reprobate to obedience"

3. God's will is a unity
   a. the blasphemies of those who reject the open and unambiguous oracles of Scripture
   b. refutation of their first objection that if nothing happens apart from God's will, there are in Him two contrary wills: by His secret plan He decrees what He has openly forbidden by His law
      (1) evidence from Scripture; testimony of Augustine
      (2) only our sluggishness and incapacity of understanding suppose that there is any contradiction in God's will, any variation in Him, any change in His plan, or disagreement with Himself

4. Even when God uses the deeds of the godless for His purposes, He does not suffer reproach
   a. their objection: if God not only uses the work of the ungodly, but also governs their intention:
      (1) He is the author of all wickedness
      (2) men are undeservedly damned if they carry out what God has decreed, because they obey His will
   b. confusion of will and precept in their charge: while God accomplishes through the wicked what He has decreed by His secret judgment, they are not excusable, as if they had obeyed his precept which out of their own lust they deliberately break
   c. examples from Scripture discussed
      (1) the split of Israel and Judah and related Old Testament events seen in the light of God's will and man's wickedness
      (2) Augustine on Judas' betrayal of our Lord
   d. an attitude of humble teachableness and admission of our mental limitations is to be held toward Scripture's teaching in this matter

BOOK TWO

The Knowledge of God the Redeemer in Christ, First Disclosed to the Fathers Under the Law, and Then to Us in the Gospel

CHAPTER 1
By the Fall and Revolt of Adam the Whole Human Race Was Delivered to the Curse, and Degenerated from Its Original Condition; the Doctrine of Original Sin

A True Knowledge of Ourselves Destroys Self-Confidence [1–3]

1. Wrong and right knowledge of self
   a. the ancient proverb: "Know thyself"
   b. its perverted application by certain philosophers who urge man to know himself in order to recognize his own worth and excellence
   c. the elements of true self-knowledge; consider:
      (1) what God gave us at the creation and still gives us: we owe all to Him
      (2) our miserable condition after Adam's fall lost us our original upright nature and leaves us humbled and shamed
   d. the dynamic of Christian life
   primal worthiness→ utter contrast to our fallen condition→ abhorrence and displeasure with ourselves→ humility→ new zeal to seek God→ recover the good things we have lost (immortality)

2. Man by nature inclines to deluded self-admiration
   a. the self-knowledge required is one that strips us of all confidence in our own ability
   b. the pitfalls in giving man credit for excellence
      (1) enhances our innate blind self-love
      (2) even if we concede part to God we leave enough to occasion boasting and overconfidence
   c. in nearly every age men who have extolled human virtues have been popular because they appeal to men's pride
   d. but those confident they can do anything by their own power hurtle, through self-ignorance, to destruction

3. The two chief problems of self-knowledge
   a. how do we acquire self-knowledge?
      (1) carnal judgment suggests that man can know himself very well, can boldly declare war on vices and achieve a good life by his own effort
      (2) but if the standard of divine judgment is used, man is emptied of self-confidence, driven to utter dejection and powerlessness
      (3) yet God drives us thus to meditate on our original nobility and thus to arouse us to yearn after the kingdom of God
   b. the two parts of man's self-knowledge; consider
      (1) the purpose for which he was created and endowed—meditation upon divine worship and the future life [nature of his duty]
      (2) his own lack of abilities—confusion [extent of his capability to carry out this duty]

Adam's Sin Entailed Loss of Man's Original Endowment and Ruin of the Whole Human Race [*4–7*]

4. The history of the fall shows us what sin is [Gen. 3]: unfaithfulness
   a. what kind of sin in Adam's desertion kindled God's vengeance against all mankind?
      (1) it is childish to call it gluttonous intemperance, for all sorts of fruits abounded for Adam's delight
      (2) the enjoining to eat the fruit of the tree of life and the prohibition of the fruit of the tree of the knowledge of good and evil was a test of Adam's faith
      (3) hence it was, as Augustine suggests, *pride* that began all evils
   b. what was the nature of Adam's temptation?
      (1) disobedience was the beginning of the fall (cf. Rom. 5:19) occasioned by:
         (a) Satan's blandishments
         (b) man's own contempt of truth: irreverence toward God's Word
      (2) unfaithfulness was the root of the fall
      (3) this led to ambition and pride plus ungratefulness (toward God's great bounty): apostasy
      (4) ambition led to obstinate disobedience—men threw off fear of God and followed their own lust

c. summary: Adam would never have dared oppose God's authority unless he had disbelieved God's Word

5. The first sin as original sin
   a. presence of the curse, of the contrast between what men are and were created to be, throughout the world is the basis for inferring that the punishment for Adam's sin spread to all his offspring
   b. original sin = the depravation of a nature previously good and pure
   c. attitude of the church fathers toward original sin
      (1) the early fathers dealt with it obscurely because the thought that the guilt of one was made the common sin of all is not the usual view
      (2) Pelagius and Celestius shamelessly denied original sin but Augustine (and others) labored to show that we are corrupted not by derived wickedness but bear an inborn defect from our mother's womb
      (3) Ps. 51:5 the proof text: this confession is not peculiar to David; therefore the common lot of mankind is exemplified in him
   d. summary: descended from impure seed, we are all born infected with the contagion of sin

6. Original sin does not rest upon imitation
   a. the Adam/Christ contrast set in Rom. 5:12–17 is the basis for a belief in original sin by propagation (not imitation as the Pelagians hold), and in righteousness acquired by communication from Christ
   b. Paul's purpose in I Cor. to strengthen the faith of the godly in the resurrection: life lost in Adam is recovered in Christ (I Cor. 15:22)
   c. "We have died in Adam" to be interpreted by the analogy of infection
   [d. all this to heighten our rebirth in Christ]

7. The transmission of sin from one generation to another
   a. not the source of the human soul but the gifts entrusted to Adam and lost in the fall should be our concern
   b. the gifts were given not to one man but assigned to the whole

human race; so when they were taken away from one man, they were withdrawn from all

c. metaphors
  (1) rotten roots produce rotten branches and twigs
  (2) the stream of contagion goes forth not from nature as originally created but as subsequently corrupted

d. children descend not from their parents' spiritual regeneration but from their carnal generation [Augustine versus the Pelagians]

Original Sin Defined as a Depravity of Nature, which Deserves Punishment, but which Is Not from Nature as Created [*8–11*]

8. The nature of original sin
   a. definition: "original sin is a hereditary depravity and corruption of our nature, diffused into all parts of the soul, which first makes us liable to God's wrath then also brings forth in us 'works of the flesh'"
   b. two considerations:
      (1) we are so vitiated and perverted in every part of our nature that we stand justly condemned and convicted before God: all, even infants, are guilty not of another's fault but of their own
      (2) this perversity never ceases in us but continually bears new fruits
         (a) it is not a mere absence of original righteousness, but the presence of active power and energy for evil
         (b) it is not mere concupiscence of one part—the whole man is defiled

9. Sin overturns the whole man
   a. all parts of the soul as well as the body possessed by sin [Paul]
   b. Scriptural descriptions of original sin in terms of renewal
      (1) the whole third chapter of Romans
      (2) Eph. 4:23
      (3) Rom. 12:2; 8:7; 8:6

10. Sin is not our nature, but its derangement
    a. our sin is no reflection upon God's handiwork; distinction is again made between nature as created and nature as corrupted

b. let no one grumble that God could have provided better by forestalling Adam's fall: the secret of predestination is the clue (see 3:21–24, below)
c. not the Author of nature, but our own depravity of nature, is to be charged with our ruin: man alone is responsible

11. "Natural" corruption of the "nature" created by God
   a. our use of the term "natural" has reference here to corrupted nature, not to a substantial property of original nature, and is used to rule out bad conduct as cause of corruption rather than hereditary right
   b. this use of the term "nature" permits us to
      (1) use such phrases as "naturally abominable to God," and "naturally depraved and faulty"
      (2) deny the Manichaean fiction of two creators (which they invented to avoid assigning the cause of evil to the righteous God)

CHAPTER 2
Man Has Now Been Deprived of Freedom of Choice and Bound over to Miserable Servitude

1. Introduction and method
   a. dangers of pride and brazen confidence
   b. one must in humility glorify God

Opinion of "free will" Given by Philosophers and Theologians [*2–9*]

2. The philosophers trust in the power of the understanding

3. In spite of all, the philosophers assert the freedom of the will

4. The views of the ecclesiastical writers in general and in particular
   a. generally show less clarity but tend to accept free will
   b. definition of free will by
      (1) Origen
      (2) Augustine
      (3) Bernard
      (4) Anselm

(5) Peter Lombard
(6) Thomas Aquinas

5. Patristic and scholastic distinctions between freedom of will in temporal and in spiritual matters
   a. patristic distinction of the spheres of human freedom and divine grace
      (1) "intermediate things," not pertaining to God's Kingdom come under man's free counsel
      (2) true righteousness—referred by fathers to God's special grace and spiritual regeneration
   b. three kinds of will (Prosper of Aquitaine, *Calling of the Gentiles*)
      (1) sensual } free endowments of man
      (2) psychic }
      (3) spiritual—work of the Holy Spirit in man
   c. this is not a refutation but an assessment of the opinions of the church fathers
      (1) they are mainly concerned with the relation of will to obedience to divine law
      (2) but we must not neglect its importance for civil or external actions
   d. scholastic distinction of kinds of freedom [Lombard]
      (1) from necessity—still inheres in man
      (2) from sin } lost through sin
      (3) from misery }

6. Mistaken distinction of the Schoolmen
   a. all agree (except the Socinians, who say grace is equally and indiscriminately distributed) that free will will not suffice to enable man to do good works, unless he is helped by special grace (received only by the elect, through regeneration)
   b. but has man been wholly deprived of all power to do good, or does he still have some meager power?
      (1) Augustine says man is wholly deprived
      (2) the earlier Schoolmen (Bernard, Lombard, Fulgentius) think they are following Augustine when they suggest that once man receives initial grace, his free acceptance of it is meritorious [Council of Orange]
      (3) the later Schoolmen (Ockham, Biel, the Sorbonnists) are even further removed from Augustine's thought

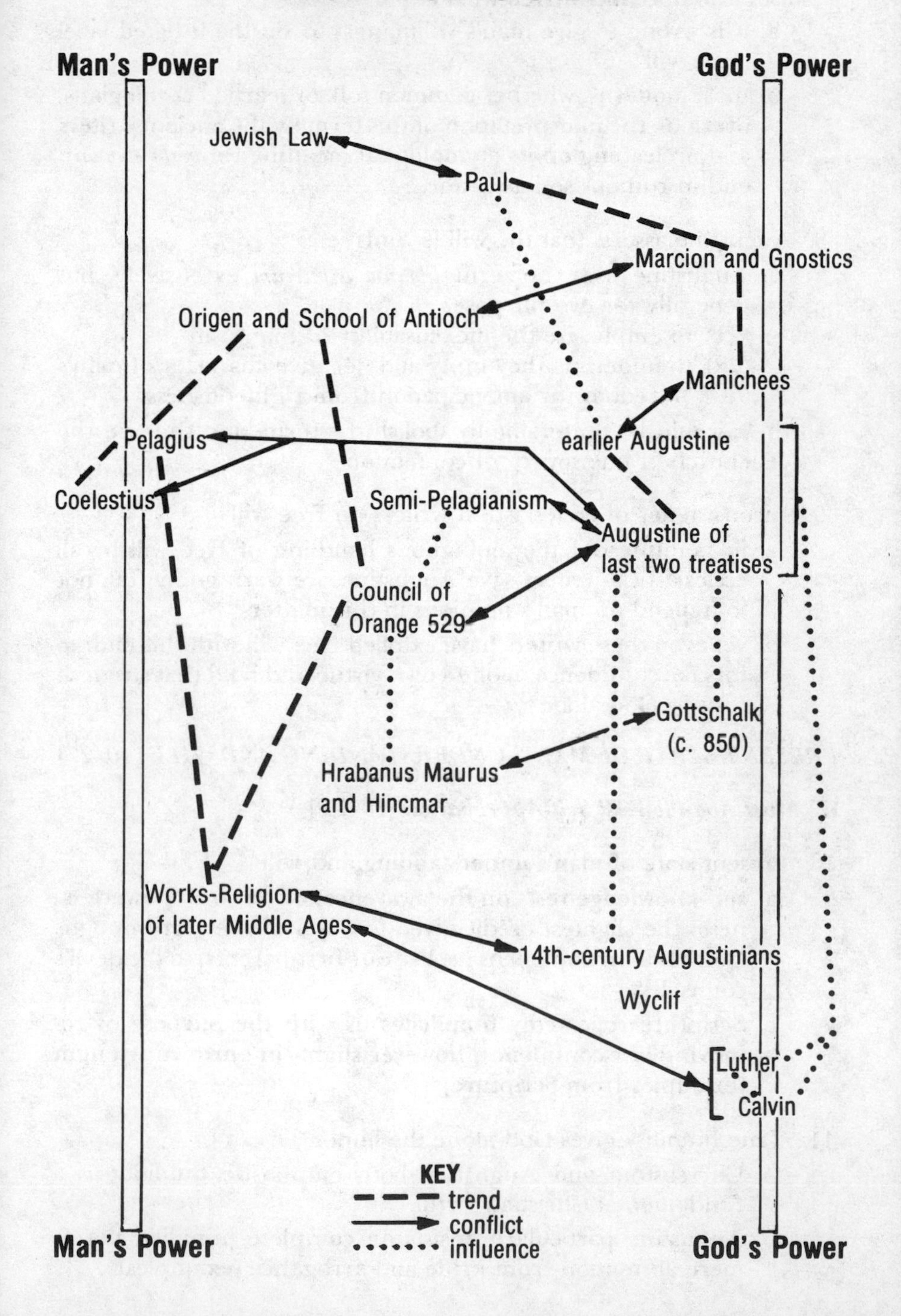
FREEDOM OF WILL
FROM PAUL TO CALVIN
Man's Power
God's Power
Jewish Law
Paul
Marcion and Gnostics
Origen and School of Antioch
Manichees
Pelagius
earlier Augustine
Coelestius
Semi-Pelagianism
Augustine of
last two treatises
Council of
Orange 529
Gottschalk
(c. 850)
Hrabanus Maurus
and Hincmar
Works-Religion
of later Middle Ages
14th-century Augustinians
Wyclif
Luther
Calvin
KEY
trend
conflict
influence
Man's Power
God's Power

7. That man necessarily, but without compulsion, is a sinner, establishes no doctrine of free will
   a. it is wrong to give man's willingness to sin the inflated label "free will"
   b. most moderns, whether common folk or learned theologians, overlook the interpretation of this term by the ancient writers and, in leaning on its etymological meaning [*in verbi etymon*], end in ruinous self-assurance

8. Augustine asserts that the will is "unfree"
   a. Augustine uses the term *liberum arbitrium* extensively, but generally for two purposes
      (1) to emphasize the inexcusability of man's sin
      (2) to underline the empty and negative character of man's "freedom" or emancipation from righteousness
   b. it would be preferable to abolish the term, and thus rid the church of one source of contention

9. Inconsistency of ecclesiastical writers on free will
   a. in pointing out the ambiguous handling of free will by all ecclesiastical writers save Augustine, we warn godly folk not to depend on man's opinions in this matter
   b. yet even these writers have extolled free will with this end: to forsake confidence in one's own virtue and hold that strength rests in God alone

PRESENT STATE OF MAN'S UNDERSTANDING AND WILL [*10–27*]

We Must Abandon All Self-Approbation [***10–11***]

10. Present state of man's understanding and will
    a. self-knowledge rests on the awareness of our own powerlessness; the slightest credit given to one's own effort impugns God's honor, and opens us, like our first parents, to the devil's counsel
    b. Scripture repeatedly humiliates us with the purpose of removing our confidence, however slight, in our own strength [examples from Scripture]

11. True humility gives God alone the honor
    a. Chrysostom and Augustine both emphasize humility as a fundamental Christian virtue
    b. Augustine particularly insists on complete humility, not as mere abstention from pride and arrogance [examples]

Corruption of the Understanding [***12–25***]

understanding of earthly things [*12–17*]

12. Though supernatural gifts are destroyed and natural gifts corrupted, enough of reason remains to distinguish man from brute beasts.
    a. supernatural gifts withdrawn by sin
        (1) includes faith, love of God, charity toward neighbor, zeal for holiness and righteousness
        (2) these are restored by Christ in us through grace of regeneration
    b. natural gifts (reason, will) not withdrawn, but corrupted by sin
        (1) if reason were completely removed, man would be indistinguishable from the beasts
            (a) hence some sparks of reason still gleam
            (b) but they are ineffective because they are cloaked with dense ignorance
        (2) the will, too, does not perish, but is bound to wicked devices so it cannot strive after the right
    c. introduction to discussion of the state of human understanding in sin [cf. 1.15.7; (a) understanding, (b) will]
        (1) it is wrong to condemn human understanding for its perpetual blindness: contrary to the Word of God and experience
        (2) human understanding is still capable of perception and longs for truth but shows its ineffectualness in investigating trifles—as the philosophers remark but cannot explain

13. The social order
    a. powers of the understanding vary with the object contemplated: distinction between earthly and heavenly "things"

earthly	*heavenly*
(1) not pertaining to God or His kingdom, true justice or blessed future life (2) but relating to present life	(1) pure knowledge of God, nature of true righteousness, and mysteries of the heavenly kingdom

-or-

(1) government	(1) knowledge of God and of His will
(2) household management	(2) the rule by which we conform our lives to God's will
(3) mechanical skills	
(4) the liberal arts	

b. innate and universal character of law as the basis of human organization: equity (*epiekeia*): some need of political order has been implanted in all men

c. the fact that some seed of political order has been implanted in all men is not disproved by criminal and other lawless types who reject law out of lust rather than understanding; their quarrels merely prove the weakness of the human mind

14. The arts—liberal and manual

a. while the arts are not shared in equal degree by all men, nearly all have some talent in some art: this is evidence of the continuing capacity (after the fall) of the human understanding

b. God's occasional creation of imbeciles demonstrates (by its absence) that capacity in the arts is a gift from God

c. man has, therefore, the beginning of the arts inborn in himself, and the capacity to improve on the arts as inherited (against Plato's doctrine of reminiscence)

15. The sciences

a. all human science comes from the Spirit of God, the sole fountain of truth

b. hence, we are not to depreciate any human truth, else we contemn the Spirit, its ultimate source, and thus are guilty of ingratitude to God

c. God, therefore, left some gifts to man even after his nature was despoiled of its true good

16. Human competence in art and science also derives from the Spirit of God

a. God's Spirit distributes natural gifts to mankind for the common good, to all, just and unjust; this is to be distinguished, however, from the spirit of sanctification

b. hence we can be tutored in the useful arts and the sciences even by the ungodly since they have received their gifts from God

c. Augustine teaches, and the Schoolmen agree, that the free gifts were withdrawn after the fall, while the natural ones remaining were corrupted: this does not mean that the gifts were defiled by themselves, but to defiled man were no longer pure

17. Summary
   a. by His general (common) grace, God limits the corruption of nature
   b. by a special grace, He endows each man according to his calling

understanding of heavenly things [*18–25*]

α Spiritual discernment is wholly lost until we are regenerated [18–21]

18. The limits of our understanding with regard to God's kingdom and spiritual insight
   a. spiritual insight consists in knowing
      (1) God [18]
      (2) His fatherly favor in our behalf (our salvation) [19–21]
      (3) how to frame our life according to the rule of His law [22–25]
   b. philosophers have enough insight into God to keep from hiding their impiety under ignorance, but apart from this slight flash, their books are full of confusion and lies

19. Man's spiritual blindness shown from John 1:4–5
   a. but our inflated opinion of this slight insight of ours makes us blind
   b. John, in the prologue to his Gospel, teaches us that we have absolutely no spiritual understanding unless illumined by the Spirit of God

20. Man's knowledge of God is God's own work, through the illumination of His Spirit; testimony of man's inability:
   a. John the Baptist and Moses
   b. Christ Himself
   c. Paul (clearest of all)

21. Without the light of the Spirit, all is darkness
    a. testimonies from Paul of enlightenment by the Spirit
    b. the light of the sun and the teaching of Jesus Himself are not available to men apart from the Spirit
    c. "he who attributes any more understanding to himself is all the more blind because he does not recognize his own blindness"

β Sin is distinct from ignorance (vs. Plato), but may be occasioned by delusion [22-25]

22. The evidence of God's will that man possesses makes him inexcusable but procures for him no right knowledge
    a. according to Paul, what the law of Moses does for the Jews, the natural law (conscience) does for the Gentiles
    b. definition of natural law: "Natural law is that apprehension of the conscience which distinguishes sufficiently between just and unjust, and which deprives men of the excuses of ignorance, while it proves them guilty by their own testimony."
    c. Plato's erroneous notion that sin is due to ignorance arises out of man's self-indulgence: when he commits evil he readily averts his mind, as much as he can, from the feeling of sin

23. Judgment of good and evil is unclear, so long as it takes place arbitrarily
    a. as Themistius shows, man is good at general definition but poor at applying it to specific cases: a man may consider murder or adultery evil, except when he is contemplating committing either of these crimes himself
    b. yet sometimes, against this general rule, man deliberately and knowingly rushes into wickedness
    c. this tendency is usefully explained by Aristotle's distinction between **ἀκράτεια** (incontinence) and **ἀκολασία** (intemperance)
        (1) in incontinence, passion (*παθή*) blinds the mind to the evil of its misdeed, but when passion subsides, repentance returns
        (2) in intemperance, there is stubborn persistence in sin

24. Human knowledge wholly fails as regards the first table of the law; as regards the second, fails in a critical situation
    a. our power to discriminate between just and unjust is only

sufficient to prevent us from evading the truth and using ignorance as our excuse

b. our blindness shown if we measure our reason by God's law, the pattern of perfect righteousness
   (1) first table: how could we have any inkling of the proper worship of God from our own natural perceptions?
   (2) second table: here we see a bit more clearly because of our concern with the preservation of civil society, but still imperfectly; the philosophers also do not penetrate beneath the outward vices to the inner evil desires

25. Every day we need the Holy Spirit that we may not mistake our way
   a. just as all sins cannot be imputed to ignorance, so not all sins are solely the result of malice and depravity
   b. testimony of Paul, David, and Augustine on man's inability, unaided, to understand the Lord's commandments rightly
      (1) Paul denies that even the right doing of anything can enter our mind
      (2) David repeatedly asks God for a new understanding of the law
      (3) Augustine likens the grace of illumination by the Spirit to the light of the sun—and just as needful

"Corruption of the Will"—Man's Inability to Will the Good [26-27]

26. The natural instinct that treats the "good" and the "acceptable" alike has nothing to do with freedom of will, and is no proof of the latter
   a. freedom of [moral] decision depends on the will rather than the understanding
   b. the natural instinct to pursue one's own well-being ("good") is an irrational impulse which man shares with animals
   c. we desire to follow the good, our eternal blessedness, but apart from the Holy Spirit's impulsion we do not and cannot

27. Our will cannot long for the good without the Holy Spirit
   a. the view that men do have innate feeble impulses to good, but needing energizing from the Holy Spirit, is based on a false reading by certain early fathers (on whom later Schoolmen have built) of Paul's description of the *bellum intestinum* [Rom. 7. 18ff.]

b. this verse has reference not to human nature, but to regenerated human nature, as Augustine came to realize
c. Augustine interprets Paul, Moses and David on this: "Nothing is ours but sin"

CHAPTER 3
Only Damnable Things Come Forth from Man's Corrupt Nature

Corruption of Man's Nature Is Such as to Require Total Renewal of His Mind and Will [*1–5*]

1. The whole man is flesh
   a. in John 3:6 and Rom. 8:6–7 there is an absolute contrast between Spirit and flesh
      (1) "flesh" means the whole natural, unregenerated man
      (2) "spirit" means the soul wholly renewed by the Holy Spirit
   b. this point is made even clearer in Eph. 4:17–23, where Paul contrasts the blindness and evils of unregeneration with the light of regeneration
   c. man's understanding, unrenewed by God, gives forth only stupid, frivolous, insane, and perverse thoughts

2. Romans, ch. 3, as witness for man's corruption
   a. this passage [using selections from the Psalms] describes not the depraved morals of one age or of particular individuals, but indicts the unvarying corruption of all of Adam's children, by nature, not merely by custom
   b. exegesis of passage
      (1) Paul strips man (in his apostate condition) of righteousness, then understanding
      (2) all have fallen away, become corrupt, and incapable of doing good
      (3) enumerates their shameful acts, not all manifested in each, but latent in all
      (4) the similitude of the diseased body, except that the diseased body still has some vigor of life, while the soul is utterly devoid of all good

3. God's grace sometimes restrains where it does not cleanse: the problem of the unregenerate virtuous

a. the virtuous of every age seem to warn us against adjudging man's nature wholly corrupted
b. but those merely illustrate a further working of God's grace—not to cleanse, but at least inwardly to restrain
c. the restraining grace of God is necessary, amid men's utter depravity, to make human life and society possible; modes:
   (1) restraint by shame
   (2) restraint by fear of the law
   (3) restraint because honesty is considered profitable
   (4) others rise above the common lot in order by their excellence to keep the rest obedient to them
d. summary: God by His providence bridles perversity of nature, that it may not break forth into action; but He does not purge it within

4. Uprightness is God's gift; but man's nature remains corrupted
   a. the problem of the righteous heathen: Camillus vs. Catiline
      (1) either Camillus = Catiline *or*
      (2) the natural man has some capacity to cultivate virtue
   b. solution: these "natural virtues" are the special gift of God, variously bestowed and in a certain measure, upon men otherwise wicked
   c. Summary: as for the virtues that deceive us with their vain show, they shall have their praise in the political assembly and in common remain among men; but before the heavenly judgment-seat they shall be of no value to acquire righteousness

5. Man sins of necessity, but without compulsion
   a. man is powerless to move toward good by himself: Scripture ascribes such movement entirely to God's grace
   b. in man's fallen state the will remains eager to sin
      (1) to will: (human)
      (2) to will ill: (of corrupt nature)
      (3) to will well: (of grace)
   c. distinction between necessity and compulsion
      (1) God is unable to do evil, not because of compulsion, but because of His boundless goodness: God's free will is not hindered or impaired by the fact that He must do good
      (2) the devil can do only evil, but sins with his will
      (3) man, though subject to the necessity of sinning, still sins willingly
      (4) man: freedom→sin→corruption (turning freedom into necessity)

d. point of this distinction: in the fall man sinned willingly and eagerly, not under compulsion from without; his now-depraved nature can now be moved or impelled only to evil, i.e., it is now subject to the necessity of sinning
e. Bernard's testimony concerning man's voluntary servitude

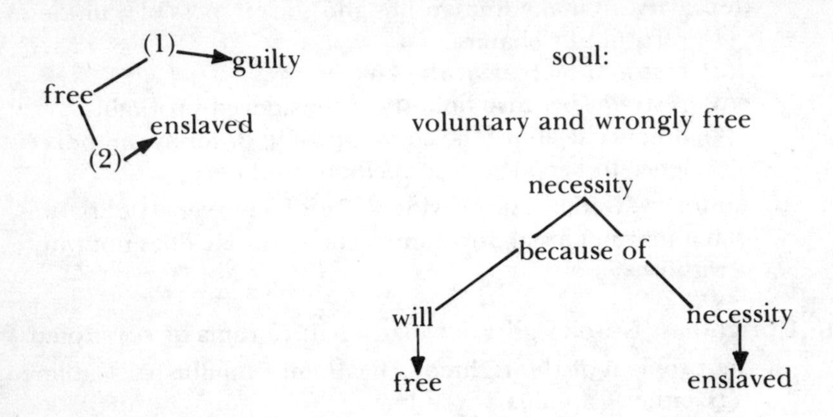

Conversion of the Will Is the Effect of Divine Grace Inwardly Bestowed [6–14]

6. Men's inability to do good manifests itself above all in the work of redemption, which God does quite alone
   a. God's method of supplying what we lack and of correcting and curing our corruption of nature
      (1) begins by arousing love and desire and zeal for righteousness in our hearts (or by bending, forming, and directing our hearts to righteousness)
      (2) completes by confirming us to perseverance
   b. exegesis of Ezek. 36:26–27: "I will remove the heart of stone from your flesh and give you a heart of flesh"
      (1) this comparison actually shows that nothing good can be wrung from our heart; what takes place is wholly from God
      (2) "created anew" does not mean that the will now begins to exist, but that it is changed from an evil to a good will
   c. supporting passages from Paul and Psalms teach that
      (1) God is the author of spiritual life from beginning to end
      (2) we are denied the least bit of credit as our salvation, God's free gift, comes from the second creation (antithesis: Adam vs. Christ)

   (3) all parts of good works, from their first impulse, belong to God
   (4) man has nothing to glory in, for the whole of salvation comes from God

7. It is not a case of the believer's "cooperation" with grace; the will is first actuated through grace
   a. erroneous teaching of cooperation: that the will, having been prepared by God's power, then has its own part in the action
      (1) Lombard here is twisting Augustine's use of *pedissequa,* the human will as the "attendant" of grace
      (2) Chrysostom erroneously states: "Neither grace without will, nor will without grace can do anything"
   b. Augustine contends that grace is prior to all merit

8. Scripture imputes to God all that is for our benefit
   a. method: to select without forcing some clear testimonies of Scripture to summarize the matter, but also with Augustine's attestation ("Whom the godly by common consent justly invest with the greatest authority")
   b. God (the sole source of Good)

grace

↓

faith

↓

willing
and } well
doing

   c. our conversion is the creation of a new spirit and a new heart; our reformed will, in so far as it is good, is from God, not from ourselves

9. The prayers in Scripture especially show how the beginning, continuation, and end of our blessedness come from God alone
   a. the prayer of Solomon, and those of David in the Psalms show
      (1) the antithesis between the heart's perverse motion and God's correction
      (2) the utter depravity of man, untouched by grace
      (3) cleanness of heart, once received, is wholly a gift, a "creation" of God

FAITH AND SALVATION: FROM PELAGIUS TO THE COUNCIL OF ORANGE (AD 529)

	BEGINNING	MIDDLE	END
PELAGIAN	unconditional freedom of will MAN'S EFFORT (plus assisting grace, but not necessary)		
SEMI-PELAGIAN	initial step taken by unaided free will	ALL ELSE THE GIFT OF GOD	
AUGUSTINIAN	initial step by prevenient grace ALL THE GIFT OF GOD absolute predestination	subsequent grace (gift of perseverance)	
COUNCIL OF ORANGE 529	God enables man to do the good he does *OR:* all, however, are able, after they have received grace through baptism, with the cooperation of God, to accomplish what is necessary for the salvation of their souls (synergism)		

b. John and Paul in the New Testament also assert that it is God alone who acts in us to do good
c. God's gift includes two parts
   (1) the will to do the good
   (2) the power to accomplish it (to surmount the burden of the flesh that weighs down the will)

10. God's activity does not produce a possibility that we can exhaust, but an actuality to which we cannot add
   a. Chrysostom falsely states: "Whom He draws he draws willing"; this wrong view has long been held by many in the church
   b. rather: the Lord by His Spirit directs, bends, and governs our heart and reigns in it as His own possession
   c. God does not indiscriminately deem everyone worthy of this grace (as some Scholastics hold)
      (1) this idea is that once grace is proffered by God, men are free to accept or reject it
      (2) rather, following Augustine, we must hold that the elect also are regenerated through the Holy Spirit and moved and governed by His leading

11. Perseverance is exclusively God's work; it is neither a reward nor a complement of our individual act
   a. the erroneous notion that perseverance is distributed according to men's merit, insofar as each man shows himself receptive to the first grace, contains two errors:
      (1) that our gratefulness for the first grace and our lawful use of it are rewarded by subsequent gifts
      (2) that grace does not work in us by itself, but is only a coworker with us [*cooperatrix*]
   b. point one suggests two warnings:
      (1) not to say that lawful use of the first grace is rewarded by later graces, as if man by his own effort rendered God's grace effective *or*
      (2) so to think of the reward as to cease to consider it of God's free grace
   c. point two uses the trite distinction between "operating" and "cooperating" grace
      (1) used by Augustine but not to divide the action between God and man; rather to emphasize the multiplying of graces
      (2) the good will of man is God's gift, freely given by God

12. Man cannot ascribe to himself even one single good work apart from God's grace
    a. false interpretation of I Cor. 15:10—Paul's insertion of the phrase "yet not I but the grace of God which was with me," they interpret as Paul correcting himself so as to teach that he was a fellow laborer with the Lord in grace: even otherwise good men trip on this straw!
    b. the ambiguity of the expression is heightened by the Latin translation which misses the force of the Greek article; the correct translation is that the grace present with him was the cause of everything
    c. this is Augustine's and Bernard's teaching

13. Augustine also recognizes no independent activity of the human will
    a. the Sorbonnists claim all ambiguity is against us, but they are only espousing Pelagius against Augustine
    b. Augustine:
        (1) Adam: *posse, sed non velle*
            we: *posse velle* (after grace)
        (2) three stages:
            (a) *posse non peccare* (before the fall)
            (b) *non posse non peccare* (after the fall)
            (c) *non posse peccare* (in grace)
    c. to summarize: in Augustine's own words: "Grace alone brings about every good work in us"

14. Augustine does not eliminate man's will, but makes it wholly dependent upon grace
    a. grace moves from within, changing the evil will to good; it does not act externally, uprooting the evil will and substituting a good one
    b. this grace is not given to all men, but when it is, it is given by free grace, not for man's merits
    c. subsequent grace, too, is freely given by God, not given because men worthily accept the first grace
    d. the human will does not obtain grace by freedom, but obtains freedom by grace
    e. "free will"—only by grace can it be converted to God, and whatever it can do it is able to do only through grace

CHAPTER 4
How God Works in Men's Hearts

Man under Satan's Control: but Scripture Shows God Making Use of Satan in Hardening the Heart of the Reprobate [*1–5*]

1. Man stands under the devil's power, and indeed willingly
   a. resumé of discussion
      (1) proved that man is so held captive by the yoke of sin that he can of his own nature neither aspire nor struggle toward good
      (2) by a distinction between compulsion and necessity, demonstrated that man sins both of necessity and voluntarily
   b. questions yet remaining
      (1) but what is the devil's and what is man's part in the action of sin?
      (2) does God have any role in the evil works in part ascribed to Him by Scripture?
   c. the [pseudo-]Augustianian simile of the horse (man) with two riders (God or the devil). Interpretation:
      (1) the will, captivated by Satan's wiles, of necessity obediently submits to all his leading
      (2) those whom the Lord does not make worthy, he abandons justly to Satan's action

2. God, Satan, and man active in the same event [the attack of the Chaldeans on Job (Job 1:17)]
   a. the whole thing stems from Satan
   b. but Job recognizes the Lord's work in it
   c. "division of labor"
      [(1) we are not dealing here with the universal activity of God which sustains all creatures and gives them the energy to do all they do]
      (2) special action which appears in every particular deed
         (a) Satan is God's instrument of wrath, of God's command to execute His just judgments [end]
         (b) Satan incites the Chaldeans (who have been handed over to him by God to execute this task) [manner]
         (c) the Chaldeans execute the evil deed

3. What does "hardness" mean?
   a. exegetical principle in reading the church fathers: the fathers

sometimes shrink from simple confession of truth in order not to let the impious speak irreverently of God's works

(1) this is acceptable if we adhere to Scripture

(2) Augustine sometimes shows this in attributing "hardening" and "binding" to mere foreknowledge and not to God's activity; but in *Contra Julianum,* Augustine clearly states that sins happen by God's might as a punishment for sins previously committed

b. two ways in which God "hardens"

(1) by taking away His light, only darkness and blindness remain

(2) by actively destining men's purposes and wills, God carries out His judgments through Satan as minister of His wrath

4. Scriptural examples of how God treats the godless

a. first way: Job 12:20; 12:24; Isa. 63:17

b. second way:

(1) the hardening of Pharaoh's heart

(2) the resistance of the indigenous tribes to the Israelites invading Canaan

Augustine's summary: "The fact that men sin is their own doing; that they by sinning do this or that comes from the power of God, who divides the darkness as He pleases"

5. Satan must also serve God

a. "evil spirit of the Lord" [I Sam. 16:14; 18:10; 19:9]: not the Holy Spirit, but a "spirit of God," because it responds to His will and power, and acts as God's instrument rather than by itself as author

b. how Satan reigns in a reprobate man, and how the Lord acts in both

(1) God makes these evil instruments, which He holds under His hand and can turn, wherever He pleases, to serve His justice

b. they, being evil, by their action give birth to a wickedness conceived in their depraved nature

***God's Providence Overrules Men's Will in External Matters** [6–8]*

6. In actions of themselves neither good nor bad, we are not thrown on our own

a. what about human actions in the physical as contrasted with the spiritual realm—does man have freedom to act here?
b. some [the Lutherans] allow free choice to man in the civil realm—this is not so important as to admit man is powerless to justify himself: this is the main point needful to know for salvation
c. but even here it is God's special grace that works to our advantage or steers us away from harm
d. numerous Scriptural examples demonstrate that men's minds were more subject to the Lord than ruled by themselves
   (1) Jacob's blessing on Joseph when he thought him a heathen Egyptian
   (2) Saul impelled to war by the Spirit of God
   (3) Absalom turned from Achitophel's counsel
   (4) Rehoboam persuaded by the young men's counsel
   (5) Rahab's confession that it was God who caused nations to tremble at Israel's coming, etc.

7. In each case God's dominion stands above our freedom
   a. but are these not special examples from which one cannot generalize?
   b. no, even our own daily experience shows that our minds are guided (even in external things) by God's prompting rather than our own freedom
   c. this the key to interpreting Prov. 20:12; 21:1
      (1) of all wills, the will of the king should be least of all under subjection
      (2) but even the king's will is in God's hand
      (3) therefore, our wills too are not exempt from that condition
   d. Augustine states that God's power (by his secret but righteous judgment) directs all human wills
      (1) to bestow benefits *or*
      (2) to inflict judgments

8. The question of "free will" does not depend on whether we can accomplish what we will, but whether we can will freely
   a. man's ability to choose freely is not dependent on the outcome of things or on outward success
   b. not the power to execute one's decisions, but freedom of judgment and of inclination of will are under discussion here
   c. Attilius Regulus the prisoner and Augustus the world ruler have no more or no less free will than one another

CHAPTER 5
Refutation of the Objections Commonly Put Forward in Defense of Free Will

***Answers to Arguments for Free Will Alleged on Grounds of Common Sense** [1-5]*

1. First argument: necessary sin is not sin; voluntary sin is avoidable
   a. Pelagius used this argument against Augustine; but we do not simply appeal to the weight of Augustine's name
   b. sin is no less sin because it is necessary sin
      (1) sin is not necessary by virtue of the creation, but by virtue of the fall man is enslaved to sin
      (2) the devil sins necessarily; but willfully
      (3) conversely, the will of the elect angels cannot turn from good but it does not therefore cease to be will
      (4) Bernard teaches that we are the more miserable because the necessity is voluntary
   c. sin is not avoidable because it is voluntary: to assert the opposite is to leap erroneously from "voluntary" to "free"

2. Second argument: reward and punishment lose their meaning unless both virtues and vices proceed from the free choice of the will
   a. this is Aristotle's argument
      (1) also used by Chrysostom and Jerome
      (2) Jerome also quotes the Pelagian opinion, "If it is the grace of God working in us, then grace, not we who do not labor, will be crowned."
   b. punishments are justly inflicted upon us since the guilt of sin takes its source from us (i.e. sins are our own; therefore, we are justly punished)
   c. it is absurd to say that the rewards of righteousness depend upon God's kindness rather than our own merits
      (1) Augustine says that the merits stem from God's gifts and thus God crowns His own gifts
      (2) the apostle Paul says that believers are crowned or glorified because they have been chosen, called, and justified by the Lord's mercy and not by their own efforts
      (3) God rewards the graces that He bestows upon us as if they were ours because He makes them ours

3. Third argument: all distinction between good and evil would be obliterated
   a. the argument stated by
      (1) Chrysostom: if to choose good or evil is not a faculty of our will, those who share in the same nature must be all bad or all good
      (2) Prosper of Aquitaine: no one would ever have departed from the faith if God's grace had not left us in a mutable condition
   b. they have somehow forgotten that
      (1) the election of God distinguishes between men
      (2) God's gift of perseverance imparted to some but not others

4. Fourth argument: all exhortation would be meaningless unless it be within the sinner's power to obey
   a. Augustine met this argument and answered it in
      (1) *On Rebuke and Grace:* "O man! Learn by precept what you ought to do; learn by rebuke that it is your own fault that you have it not; learn by prayer whence you may receive what you desire to have."
      (2) *On the Spirit and the Letter:* that God does not measure the precepts of His law according to human powers; rather He gives the elect capacity to fulfill it
   b. Christ and the apostle stand with us
      (1) Christ declares: "Without me you can do nothing"; but nonetheless reproves, chastises, and urges
      (2) Paul inveighs against the Corinthians for their neglect of love; yet prays that the Lord may give them love
   c. Paul indicates that teaching, exhortation, and reproof do change the mind
   d. Moses and the prophets exhort, yet confess that men become wise only through God's gift

5. The meaning of exhortation
   a. to the impious
      (1) today it presses them with the witness of conscience
      (2) in the Day of Judgment it renders them inexcusable
   b. to the pious
      (1) in connection with the inward work of the Holy Spirit it convicts of sin and
      (2) kindles the desire for good

Answers to Arguments for Free Will based on Interpretation of the Law, Promises and Rebukes of Scripture [6–11]

6. Are God's precepts "the measure of our strength"?
   a. our opponents cite numerous commandments of God from the Scripture and they say that either God is mocking us or He requires only what is within our power
   b. the law was put above us to show us clearly our own weakness
   c. Paul's witness concerning the sum of the law
      (1) the purpose and fulfillment of the law is love
      (2) Paul prays for the hearts of the Thessalonians to abound with love
      (3) yet he fully admits that the law sounds in our ears without effect unless God inspires in our hearts the whole sum of the law

7. The law itself points our way to grace
   a. Scripture clearly explains the manifold use of the law
   b. with the command are connected promises which proclaim that our support, and our whole virtue as well, rest in the help of divine grace
   c. as Augustine has said: "God bids us do what we cannot, that we may know what we ought to seek from him."

8. The several kinds of commandments clearly show that without grace we can do nothing [three classes; first mentioned in 6]
   a. first class: those which require man to be converted to God
      (1) but God testifies through Moses, Ezekiel, etc., that it is accomplished by Himself.
      (2) Augustine testifies: "What God promises, we ourselves do not do through choice or nature; but He Himself does through grace."
   b. second class: those which simply speak of observing the law; but many passages say that our righteousness, holiness, piety, and purity are gifts of God
   c. third class: those which bid man persevere in God's grace; but Paul prays and gives thanks that God fulfills every good resolve and work of faith in them

9. the work of conversion is not divided between God and man
   a. our opponents say:
      (1) that we may do our best and God will support our weak efforts and

(2) that Zech. 1:3 indicates an equal division of the work of conversion between God and ourselves

b. but God only enters into covenant with people when the Spirit enters and disposes their hearts to obedience

c. the conversion of God mentioned in Zech. 1:3 refers not to God's relationship to us but to the material testimony of His kind disposition toward us

10. The biblical promises suppose (according to our opponents' view) the freedom of the will
    a. as in the case of God's commandments, our opponents say that God mocks us when He invites us to merit His blessings, knowing us to be powerless
    b. I deny it and assert that the promises are intended
        (1) to prevent the impious from enjoying their sins and
        (2) to assist the commandments in kindling the desire for righteousness of the pious

11. The reproofs in Scripture, they further object, lose their meaning if the will be not free
    a. if the will is not free, God is cruel to reproach us for evils we could not escape
    b. but the pretext of necessity is a weak and futile defense. They are guilty and cannot shift the blame to an external cause
    c. sinners should harken to these reproaches and learn to hate their sins
    d. Dan. 9:4–19 is an example of how the reproaches serve the godly
    e. a collection of Scriptural exhortations and corresponding passages showing that the requisite power comes from God

Answers to Arguments Based on Special Passages and Incidents in Scripture. [*12–19*]

12. Deuteronomy 30:11ff.
    a. if these words apply to the basic precepts, they are important in the present case
    b. but the apostle declares that Moses spoke concerning the promise of the gospel
    c. but an obstinate person may contend that Paul twisted the passage

d. in Deut. 30:6 Moses taught that our hearts need to be circumscribed by God. Therefore the power is lodged in the Holy Spirit, not in man
e. the testimony of Paul agrees to this

13. God's "waiting" upon man's action is held to suppose freedom of the will
   a. in Hos. 5:15 the Lord says: "I shall go to my place, until they lay it upon their hearts to seek my face."
      (1) our opponents say this would be ridiculous if men were not free to incline their wills either way
      (2) they admit that God's grace is necessary for conversion
      (3) yet they concede grace to be necessary in such a way as to reserve to man his own ability
   b. what do such passages signify?
      (1) the withdrawing of God signifies the withdrawing of His Word in which He habitually reveals His presence
      (2) His considering what men might do means that He secretly tries them to humble them
      (3) this does not imply any power of free will

14. Are these works not then "our" works?
   a. our opponents argue that Scripture calls the good works "ours" and that
   b. we are not moved by God like stones and therefore, while God's grace plays the primary part, our effort plays a secondary part
   c. the bread for which we petition God is also called "ours"
   d. the second objection is disposed of by considering the way in which the Spirit acts upon the saints
      (1) God does not move us as we throw a stone
      (2) "To will is of nature, but to will aright is of grace."

15. The "works" are ours by God's gift, but God's by His prompting
   a. whatever is good in the will comes from the pure prompting of the Spirit
   b. but that is called "ours" which God does in us because
      (1) God does it *in* us; it is not of our own doing
      (2) it is our mind, will, and striving which He directs

16. Genesis 4:7 [Its appetite will be under you and you shall master it]
   a. our opponents say that the Lord here promised Cain that

sin's power would not have the upper hand in his mind if he willed to conquer it!

b. the passage has been misapplied

c. but supposing their application, the passage does not prove freedom of the will, for either

 (1) it is a command; in which case we have already demonstrated that no implication of freedom follows or

 (2) it is a promise; in which case there is no fulfillment

17. Romans 9:16; I Cor. 3:9

 a. our opponents say that since "It depends not upon him who wills or upon him who runs but upon God who shows mercy"

  (1) there is some will and some running

  (2) but Paul's meaning is simpler: only the mercy of the Lord is here; God accomplishes both willing and running in us

 b. similarly they twist the saying, "We are God's coworkers": this passage says that ministers are coworkers because God has furnished them the necessary gifts

18. Ecclesiasticus 15:14–17

 a. the author's authority is doubtful

 b. but if we do not reject him out of hand we find that

  (1) he says man was created with free will, which we grant

  (2) but we say he lost it

 c. I answer not only my opponents but this author by saying

  (1) if my opponents' interpretation is correct, we reject his authority

  (2) if this author only wishes to show that man is the cause of his own ruin, I agree

19. Luke 10:30

 a. our opponents make this an allegory of the fall of the human race

  (1) the human race is robbed by sin and the devil

  (2) but it is left "half alive"

  (3) this implies some portion of right reason and will remain

 b. suppose I reject the allegory which the fathers devised

  (1) the Word of God does not leave a "half-life" to men

  (2) the Scriptures clearly state that we were dead and were made alive

c. yet suppose we accept the allegory
   (1) what is left to man does not enable him to attain a true knowledge of God
   (2) Augustine's view, and the common consent of the schools, is that that on which salvation depends was taken from man after the fall

CHAPTER 6
Fallen Man Ought to Seek Redemption in Christ

Through the Mediator, God Is Seen as a Gracious Father [*1–2*]

1. Only the Mediator helps fallen man
   a. since the whole human race has fallen from life into death in the person of Adam, our knowledge of God the Creator, derived from the universe, is useless unless faith is added
   b. because we have profited so little from our contemplation of the created order, we are called to faith in Christ, which, because it appears foolish, the unbelievers despise
   c. faith is added to our estranged situation when we humbly embrace the preaching of the cross

2. Even the Old Covenant declared that there is no faith in the gracious God apart from the Mediator
   a. apart from the Mediator, God never showed favor toward the ancient people; but this is only to say that the blessed and happy state of the church always had its foundation in the person of Christ
   b. Old Testament personages cited to show that the church has always looked forward to its one Head, realized in Jesus Christ

Christ Essential to the Covenant and to True Faith [*3–4*]

3. The faith and hope of the Old Covenant fed upon the promise
   a. where solace is promised in affliction, the banner of trust and hope in Christ Himself is prefigured
   b. the promise and hope of the Redeemer is what gave stability to the covenant

4. Faith in God is faith in Christ
   a. from the beginning of the world, continuing through the promise made to David, Christ had been set aside before all the elect that they should look to him and place their trust in him
   b. even if many men once boasted that they worshiped the Supreme Majesty, the Maker of heaven and earth, yet because they had no Mediator it was not possible for them truly to taste God's mercy, and thus be persuaded that He was their Father

CHAPTER 7
The Law was Given, not to Restrain the Folk of the Old Covenant under Itself, but to Foster Hope of Salvation in Christ until His Coming

The Moral and Ceremonial Law Significant as Leading to Christ *[1–2]*

1. The Mediator helps only fallen men
   a. the Law was added about 400 years after Abraham, not to lead the people away from Christ but to strengthen them in their expectation of Him, thus renewing as it were the covenant of Abraham
   b. otherwise than as shadows of the coming Christ, the rites enjoined by the law would be utterly absurd
   c. the rites were intended to raise men's eyes to Christ

2. The law contains a promise
   a. in Moses' giving of the law and David's founding of the kingdom, Christ was set before ancient Israel as a mirror
   b. in their immaturity, they had to be led to Christ through the ceremonies: from their daily sacrifices, to the once-for-all sacrifice of Christ
   c. Paul's testimony that Christ is the end to which the law looks

We Cannot Fulfill the Moral Law *[3–5]*

3. The law renders us inexcusable and drives us into despair
   a. complete observance of the law is perfect righteousness before God, as Scripture promises

b. but do we fulfill that obedience? No!
c. thus we hang between the promise of life and the curse of death

4. Nevertheless the promises in the law are not without meaning
   a. the impasse: the law promises a blessedness which we, unable to keep it, cannot reach
   b. but this is not absurd or useless: for it leads us to realize that God freely bestows His gifts upon us, overlooking our imperfect obedience
   c. we will discuss this topic at greater length under "justification by faith"

5. The fulfillment of the law is impossible for us
   a. there has never been anyone—even a "saint"—who is without concupiscence
   b. Scriptural testimonies of this fact
   c. Augustine asserted this against the Pelagian attack

The First Use of the Law: the Law Shows Us the Righteousness of God, and as a Mirror Discloses Our Sinfulness, Leading Us to Implore Divine Help **[*6–9*]**

6. The severity of the law takes away from us all self-deception
   a. the law warns, informs, convicts, and condemns
   b. the law removes pride, and thus all false self-generated righteousness and covetousness which lurks secretly within man

7. The punitive function of the law does not diminish its worth
   a. in the law, as in a mirror, we see our weakness, our iniquity, and the resultant curse
   b. our corrupted will, which should be obedient to the law, persists in stubborn disobedience
   c. the law strikes our conscience increasingly with our iniquity and conversely heightens the sweetness of God's grace

8. The punitive function of the law in its work upon believers and unbelievers
   a. the law condemns all men
   b. but with two utterly different purposes
      (1) to terrify the wicked, but because of their obstinancy of heart

(2) to make the chosen ones realize they stand empty-handed before God, and must therefore seize upon God's mercy

9. The law, as Augustine says, by accusing moves us to seek grace
   a. a "cento" of quotations from Augustine which assert that the law drives us, through our inability to keep it, to call upon grace in Christ
   b. Augustine specifically deals with this first use of the law in *On the Spirit and the Letter;* the second use, for some reason or other, he does not discuss
   c. the first use of the law seen also in the reprobate, who by it are driven to terror and despair, but persist, despite this divine and equable foretaste of their end, in their desire to evade God's judgment

The Second Use of the Law: the Law Restrains Malefactors and Those Who Are Not Yet Believers [*10–11*]

10. The law as protection of the community from unjust men
   a. by fear of its punishment, the law restrains men otherwise untouched by what is just and right
   b. this restraint does not produce righteousness, for such men boil inwardly, curse God and the law, and yearn to break out in lawlessness
   c. but such restraining is needful for the community, whose welfare and tranquillity God certainly has in mind

11. The law a deterrent to those not yet regenerate
   a. two kinds of those not yet regenerate:
      (1) those confident of their own self-righteousness—to be brought down to humility
      (2) those uncontrolled in their lust—to be restrained
   b. those ignorant of God are led, gradually, by the fear engendered by the law, ultimately to love of Him

The Third Use of the Law: It Admonishes Believers and Urges Them on in Well-Doing [*12–13*]

12. Even the believers have need of the law
   a. this the principal use of the law

b. profits believers in two ways:
    (1) helps them to learn more each day the nature of the Lord's will
    (2) exhorts them to continuing obedience, thus aiding them in avoiding reversion to sin
c. these benefits described by David in a way not contradictory to Paul

13. Whoever wants to do away with the law entirely for the faithful, understands it falsely
    a. error of some who, ignorant of this distinction, reject the whole law of Moses as alien to Christians
    b. the statement that the life of a righteous man is a continual meditation on the law applies to all ages of history
    c. even if we cannot measure up to the law's requirements, it continually points us to our life's goal.

The So-Called "Abrogation" of the Law Has Reference to the Liberation of the Conscience, and the Discontinuance of the Ancient Ceremonies [14–17]

14. To what extent has the law been abrogated for believers?
    a. although for believers the law is now an exhortation, not a curse, one may not for this reason say it has been abrogated
    b. Paul and Jesus both emphasize that the law has not been set aside, but remains inviolable
    c. we must, therefore, distinguish what has been abrogated from what has not

15. The law is abrogated to the extent that it no longer condemns us
    a. Paul's reference to the "curse" applies solely to the force of the law to bind the conscience
    b. Christ, says Paul, was made a curse for us in order to release us from the law's harsh and unkeepable requirements
    c. yet we must continue to give the same veneration and obedience to the law

16. The ceremonial law
    a. by his coming Christ has abrogated in use, not in effect, the ceremonial law
    b. the ceremonial law, say Paul (Col. 2:17) and others, is only the

THE THREE USES OF THE LAW
Institutes 2.7.6ff.; cf. 4.20.14–21

III. The Pedagogical: admonishes believers and urges them on in well-doing (pars. 12–13)

II. The Restraining: restrains malefactors and those who are not yet believers (10f.)
- (a) protects community from unjust men[4]
- (b) deters those not yet regenerate
  - (i) brings those confident of their own self-righteousness to humility before God
  - (ii) restrains those uncontrolled in their own lust

I. The Punitive: mirrors our sin before God and leaves us inexcusable (pars. 6–9)
- (a) those to be redeemed thus realize their empty-handedness before God
- (b) the wicked are terrified, but because of their obstinacy of heart

THE THREE USES OF PUNISHMENT
Commentary Seneca De Clementia 1.22.1

I. To reform the man that is punished[1] (125.7–26)

II. By punishing him to make the rest better[2] (125.26–37)

III. (a) By removing bad men, to let the rest live in greater security (Seneca, *De Clementia* 1.22.1/ Calvin, *Comm. Seneca De Clementia* 125.37–126.1)

III. (b) To protect the dignity and authority of him against whom the sin has been committed[3] (Aulus Gellius, *Noctes Atticae* 7(6).14)

THE THREE USES OF CHURCH DISCIPLINE
Institutes 4.12.5ff

III. To overcome men with shame for their baseness, that they may begin to repent

II. To keep the good from being corrupted by the company of the wicked

I. To banish the wicked from the fellowship

NOTES

1. Greek: *nouthesia, kolasis parainesis;* Latin: *monitio, animadversio*
2. Greek: *paradeigma;* Latin: *exemplum*
3. Latin: *timoria*
4. Cf. *Institutes* 4.20.19

shadow of the reality in Christ, and drew its past validity from the promise of Christ's coming

17. The "written bond against us" is blotted out [Col. 2:13f.]
    a. two conflicting groups of expositors hold:
        (1) that the inexorable severity, but not the teaching, of the moral law is abolished; or
        (2) that the words refer solely to the ceremonial law, not to the moral law at all
    b. as opposed to both groups, the words of Paul here have a more inward reference (following Augustine)
        (1) the Jews' sacrifices served only to confess their own uncleanness, repeatedly, as the rites were repeated
        (2) yet, in Christ (not the law) the ancient Jews partook, as do we, in the same grace
        (3) so Paul is here warning the Christians not to revert to the law's ritual requirements, from which Christ has freed them

CHAPTER 8
Explanation of the Moral law (The Ten Commandments)

The Written Moral Law a Statement of the Natural Law [*1–2*]

1. What are the Ten Commandments to us?
    a. this is the place to introduce an explanation of the law, to confirm points already made
        (1) the public worship God prescribed is still in force
        (2) the law taught the Jews not only the true nature of godliness, but in demonstrating their incapacity to attain it, threw them (albeit unwillingly) on the Mediator
        (3) the contrast between God's majesty and our nothingness drives us inexorably to worship Him
    b. two purposes of the law
        (1) God calls us to reverence Him and specifies in what this reverence consists
        (2) thus pointing out our impotence, He reproves us for it
    c. relation in inward law to Decalogue
        (1) witness of conscience as accuser
        (2) failure of conscience because of our condition
        (3) thus the necessity of a written law

2. The inexorableness of the law
    a. law teaches us that we owe God glory, reverence, love, fear: to be expressed in a righteous, holy, pure life
    b. if we fail, as fail we do, we are inexcusable

We Learn from the Law that God Is Our Father, that He Is Merciful and All-Holy, and in Kindness Requires Obedience [*3–5*]

3. The severity of the law has a positive goal
    a. the law's teaching drives us to *descend into ourselves*
    b. steps in the awareness of our condition that follow:
        (1) compare our life with law: our failure
        (2) our powers are too weak to keep the law
        (3) in our impotence we are driven to fear eternal death
        (4) our despair leads us to seek help outside ourselves

4. Promises and threats
    a. beyond our mere reverence for God's righteousness thus obtained, God recognizes our blind inaction
    b. to overcome this, He adds
        (1) promises, to show His pleasure at man's keeping of the law
        (2) threats, to show how He detests unrighteousness, and to shock us out of our vices

5. The sufficiency of the law
    a. the law is the perfect rule of righeousness, obedience to which supremely pleases God
    b. but all men try, by contriving human precepts, to acquire righteousness apart from God's Word
        (1) seen in Moses' advice to Israel
        (2) seen in the debased practices that characterize our own age
    c. to overcome this tendency we must set before us the law and obedience to it as our goal

The Law Is Spiritually to Be Understood and Interpreted With Reference to the Purpose of the Law-Giver [*6–10*]

6. Since the law is God's law, it makes a total claim upon us
    a. God's law demands not only outward honesty but inward, spiritual righteousness, though few men take these twin demands to heart

b. contrast between human and divine law
   (1) human laws demand only outward conformity in action or at least no more than compliance in outward intention
   (2) divine law demands total obedience not only in outward *act* but also in inward intention: i.e., complete purity

7. Christ Himself has restored the right understanding of the law
   a. here we are adducing no new interpretation of the law, but only reasserting Christ's restoration of the law against the Pharisees' false interpretation
   b. any notion that Christ gave a new gospel law to supply the lack of Moses' law does a disservice both to God's law and the Old Testament Fathers, who were certainly no hypocrites

8. Ways to the right meaning
   a. exegetical principle: the commandments and prohibitions always contain more than is expressed in words: that is, *synecdoche*
   b. but there is a problem in applying this principle: to keep close enough to the words themselves so as not to gloss it with human accretions
   c. the best rule is to ask: Why was each commandment given to us? Examples:
      (1) fifth commandment: pay honor to those whom God has assigned it; dishonor toward them displeasing and prohibited
      (2) first commandment: worship God alone, impiety toward Him detested and forbidden
   d. two sides to every commandment:
      (1) something is enjoined, its opposite prohibited
      (2) something is prohibited, its opposite enjoined

9. Commandment and prohibition
   a. this last point means more than setting against a vice its corresponding virtue (commonly conceived as abstinence from that vice)
   b. its means positive right-doing: do not just refrain from harming a brother; do good for him!

10. By its strong language, the law shocks us into greater detestation of sin

a. why does God imply, by *synecdoche,* what He wills, rather than state it explicitly?
b. because we are always trying to make light of concealed sins, God calls them all to mind, shockingly, by labeling them by the worst sin in each category: for example, murder is more shocking than hatred or anger

The Two Tables of the Law, and the Commandments Rightly Assigned to Each [*11–12*]

11. The two tables: duties to God (1–4), duties to man (5–10)
   a. the whole law is divided into those duties which apply to the worship of God, and duties of love toward men
   b. worship of God is the foundation of righteousness
   c. only then are we in a position to act righteously in human society
   d. these two categories mentioned in Jesus' summing up of the law

12. The distribution of the commandments into two tables
   a. the two heads are detailed in the Ten Commandments to make clear precisely what God demands of us
   b. problem of grasping the precepts of the law
      (1) some divide it 3 and 7, suppress the commandment on images, and divide into two the final one
      (2) others divide it 4 and 6, but with 1 as preface, not command
      (3) I take 4 and 6, but with a preface (as Origen, Augustine sometimes, and in *Eruditi commentarii in Matthei Evangelium, opus imperfectum*)
      (4) Some, 5 and 5, as Josephus, but this mixes religion and charity

Detailed Exposition of the Individual Commandments [*13–50*]

first commandment [*13–16*]

13. The preface ("I am Jehovah your God . . .")
   a. in framing laws, care must be taken that they be not abrogated out of contempt
   b. three means ("proofs") provided to keep the law from contempt

(1) claiming authority over and demanding obedience of the people
(2) promises grace to draw them to holiness
(3) recounts His benefits to the Jews to prove their ingratitude if they do not respond

14. "I am Jehovah your God" [first and second "proofs"]
 a. claims authority and obedience
 b. attracts by sweetness of His promises not only for present life but for life to come; Scriptural examples

15. "Who brought you out of the land of Egypt, out of the house of bondage" [the third "proof"—recital of benefits, against ingratitude]
 a. freed from bondage by God, they are to serve and worship Him
 b. also uses titles to distinguish Himself from idols—to keep us in true worship of Himself; Scriptural examples
 c. beyond the intended effect on the Jews of their deliverance from Egypt, it is the type of our present spiritual bondage, from which He releases us
 d. thus the law is intended to draw all men to the Lawgiver

16. The first commandment
 a. purpose: the Lord wills alone to be preeminent among His people, and to exercise complete authority over them
 b. means: worship God truly and put all superstition and false gods away
 c. what we owe God; four classes:
  (1) *adoration:* the veneration and worship that each of us, in submitting to His greatness, renders to Him
  (2) *trust:* assurance coming from repose in and communion with Him
  (3) *invocation:* habit of calling upon Him whenever necessity presses us, as our only help
  (4) *thanksgiving:* gratitude with which we praise Him for all good things
 d. more than merely abstaining from a strange god, we are to cultivate true religion and beware of superstition
 e. meaning of "before my face": the offense thus made more heinous by reminding us that our every evil impulse is clear to the God who sees into the secret recesses of our hearts

second commandment [17-21]

17. Spiritual worship of the invisible God
    a. purpose: declares what sort of God He is, and with what kind of worship He should be honored
    b. sum: calls us away from paltry observances to His true and spiritual worship
    c. parts of the commandment:
        (1) restrains us from material representation of Himself
        (3) forbids us to worship any images; list of these

18. Threatening words of the second commandment
    a. to convince us to cleave to Him, He shows:
        (1) His power (EL = might)
        (2) His jealousy
        (3) His intention to vindicate His glory and majesty against idolatry
    b. God is as husband to us: He cannot bear to see His marriage bed defiled by our apostasy

19. "Who visits the iniquity of the fathers upon the children . . ."
    a. this apparently conflicts with Ezek. 18:20
    b. this difficulty variously "solved"
    c. since a wicked father is usually followed by a wicked son, the Lord's curse rests upon the whole house

20. Does not the visitation of the sins of the fathers upon the children run counter to God's justice?
    a. God's vengeance is upon men for their own iniquity
    b. Ezek. 18:20 is not in contradiction to this, but is in answer to the Jews who complained they were unjustly punished for their fathers' sins
    c. no, you are punished for your own sins—though it is true that children often follow the wicked ways of their parents

21. "And shows mercy to thousands . . ."
    a. God covenants His mercy to the children of the godly, and conversely His vengeance on the wicked offspring of the wicked—a fact that should strike greater terror into wrongdoers and comfort the righteous
    b. but this succession of mercy or judgment is not automatic—so as to detract from the freedom of God's judgment

c. a thousand generations = the largeness of God's mercy; four generations = limits of His vengeance

third commandment [22–27]

22. Interpretation of the commandment
    a. purpose: God wills that we hallow the majesty of His name
    b. corollary: do not treat His name with contempt
    c. three points to be observed:
        (1) all we think or say about God should savor of His excellence
        (2) we should not for any reason abuse His Word or mysteries
        (3) we should not defame His works
    d. the commandment particularly has to do with the perverse oath, discussed in both tables of the law
        (1) in reference to reverence and worship of God (first table)
        (2) in reference to human society (second table)

23. The oath as confession to God
    a. definition of oath: calling God to witness to confirm the truth of our word
    b. examples from Scripture showing that
        (1) a legitimate oath is a kind of divine worship
        (2) conversely, an oath by false gods arouses God's bitter anger

24. The false oath as a desecration of God's name
    a. because oath and worship of God's name coinhere, we must not profane His name by false swearing
    b. the normal mode of calling God to witness used, e.g., by Joshua (Old Testament) and by the Pharisees (New Testament): this implies that God will avenge our perjury if we deceive

25. The idle oath
    a. God's name is cheapened also by true but useless oaths
    b. oaths not used either for religion or love are offensive
    c. transferring oaths to God's servants as well as to strange gods demeans His Glory

26. Does not the Sermon on the Mount forbid this kind of oath?
    a. the Anabaptists literally interpret Matt. 5:34, 37
    b. but such interpretation sets Son against the Father, for the law is not set aside by Jesus
    c. exegesis of the difficulty
        (1) Christ's purpose is not to change the law but to restore it to its rightful purpose, from the Pharisees' and Scribes' corruption of it
        (2) hence "to swear" = "to swear in vain"
        (3) "at all" refers not to "to swear" but to the forms of oaths following thereafter
        (4) Christ is not correcting superstition here but rather forbidding idle, indirect oaths

27. The extrajudicial oath is therefore necessarily admissible
    a. only oaths forbidden by the law are referred to here: both Jesus and Paul used oaths where necessary
    b. some persons except only public (judicial) oaths from this prohibition
    c. but sober private oaths are also not condemned: Scripture examples
    d. to sum up, avoid all useless oaths: confine swearing to vindications of God's glory and to further brotherly edification

fourth commandment [*28–34*]

28. General interpretation
    a. purpose: dead to our own inclinations and works, we should meditate on God's kingdom in the ways He has established
    b. this commandment as a foreshadowing (according to early church fathers) requires special treatment: three conditions of keeping this commandment
        (1) repose of seventh day—spiritual rest
        (2) stated day of assembly to hear the laws and perform the rites
        (3) a day of rest for servants, etc.

29. The Sabbath commandment as promise [spiritual rest foreshadowed]
    a. Scripture repeatedly emphasizes the cruciality of this commandment; Scriptural examples

b. thus there is a close correspondence between outward sign and inward reality: only at rest are we receptive to God's working in us

30. The seventh day
    a. in keeping the seventh day the Jew was urged to imitate his Creator—a spur to zeal
    b. seven (the number of perfection in Scripture) = perpetuity
    c. through the seventh day, the Lord has sketched for His people the coming perfection of his Sabbath in the Last Day, to make them aspire to this perfection by unceasing meditation upon the Sabbath throughout life

31. In Christ the promise of the Sabbath commandment is fulfilled
    a. if such interpretation of the number seven is too subtle, at least it represents God's providing a model for us from His own example
    b. what interpretation we take makes little difference: the important thing is perpetual repose from our labors
    c. Christ's coming abolished the ceremonial part of this commandment

32. How far does the fourth commandment go beyond external regulation?
    a. what then is left of the Sabbath to us?
        (1) assembly on stated days for preaching, communion, and prayers
        (2) surcease from labor for servants and workingmen
    b. why not assemble daily then?
        (1) Scripture recognized that human weakness made daily meetings impossible
        (2) let us therefore keep what God has laid upon us

33. Why do we celebrate Sunday?
    a. some restless spirits are accusing Christian people of Judaizing
    b. on the contrary, we are not observing rigidly a ceremony, but using it to keep order in the church
    c. Paul's strictures against superstitious keeping of a new moon and sabbaths do not exclude lawful keeping of days that serves the peace of the Christian fellowship

d. the shift of the Lord's day was made to overthrow superstition and maintain order in the church

34. Spiritual observance of the sacred day
   a. the early Christians shifted to the day of the Lord's resurrection to symbolize the end of shadow-rites
   b. truth shadowed to the Jews is now set before the Christians unshadowed
   c. we reject the earlier Christian contention that only the "ceremonial part" of the law has been set aside, and that the day still remains
      (1) this is superstition, often worse than that of the Jews
      (2) we enjoin attendance at sacred meetings for the promotion of worship and piety

fifth commandment [*35–38*]

35. The wide scope of this commandment
   a. purpose: the God-established degrees of preeminence should be inviolable for us
   b. sum: look up to those placed over us by God and treat them with honor, obedience, gratefulness; not detracting from their dignity by contempt, stubbornness, or ungratefulness
   c. the wide meaning of *honor* in Scripture
   d. the divine pedagogy: by the easiest-to-tolerate subjection, the Lord leads us and accustoms us to all lawful subjection: God's titles of honor are shared by earthly leaders

36. The demand to
   a. universal rule: to him whom the Lord through His providence has placed over us we should render reverence, obedience, and gratefulness, whether he is worthy or unworthy of that honor
   b. the Lord explicitly enjoins us to reverence our parents, and even nature shows those who do not do so are monsters, not men
   c. confirmation in Scripture of the three parts of honor:
      (1) reverence: irreverence to parents punishable by death (Exod. 21:17; Lev. 20:9; Prov. 20:20)
      (2) obedience: disobedience to parents punishable by death (Deut. 21:18–21)
      (3) gratitude: by God's commandment we do good to our parents (Matt. 15:4–6)

37. The promise
    a. meaning: "Honor your father and your mother, that you may enjoy through a long period of life the possession of the land, which is to be yours as a testimony of His favor."
    b. length of present life is promised to us, as it was to the ancient Jews, not as containing blessedness itself, but as a symbol thereof

38. The threat
    a. the corollary: disobedient children are subject to sentence of death
    b. not mere longevity, but presence or absence of God's blessing during life is significant
    c. we are to obey our parents, as well as all other superiors, only so long as they do not incite us to transgress the law

sixth commandment [39–40]

39. The commandment
    a. purpose: the Lord having bound mankind together in a certain unity, each man ought to concern himself with the safety of all
    b. sum: harm to our neighbor's body forbidden
    c. this commandment applies not only to physical but also to spiritual righteousness: act and intention as well (i.e., murder—anger, hatred)

40. The reason for this commandment
    a. basis twofold: man is
        (1) image of God: therefore reverence His image in man
        (2) our flesh: embrace our own flesh in him
    b. guilt of murder includes not only the act but the plan, and even the wish to kill

seventh commandment [41–44]

41. General interpretation
    a. purpose: because God loves modesty and purity, all uncleanness must be far from us
    b. summary: do not become defiled with any filth or lustful intemperance of flesh

c. affirmative corollary: chastely and continently regulate all parts of life
d. man, created for life in society, is given marriage as the sole acceptable union to keep him from lust

42. Celibacy?
   a. God by special grace preserves some few in chaste virginity, temporarily or permanently
   b. the rest of us are subject to women's society both according to our created nature and because of our fallen state
   c. it is foolish to try to follow celibate continence when this gift is not given—in fact such struggle is a violation of God's ordinance

43. Marriage as related to this commandment
   a. each man is to recognize his own gift and determine from this whether to marry or remain celibate
   b. to avoid incontinence we must, if necessary, have recourse to marriage; unmarried incontinence or impure lust is sin against God's commandment

44. Modesty and chastity
   a. within marriage—sober control, not lust
   b. God who enjoins purity of heart, forbids not only fornication but seduction of others by wanton dress or conduct

eighth commandment

45. General interpretation
   a. purpose: since injustice is abominable to God, render to each man his due
   b. sum: do not pant after another man's possesions; rather, help him keep them, as all men's possessions are of God's distributing
   c. kinds of thefts:
      (1) by violence
      (2) by fraud
      (3) by legal craft
      (4) by flattering pretense of gift
   d. an anatomy of human greed in all its forms

46. This commandment obligates us to care for others' good
    a. honest and lawful gain excludes all forms of human exploitation
    b. our aim: help all men to keep what is theirs; but if they are deceitful, avoid contending with them—even to the point of giving up something of our own
    c. mutual duty in society
        (1) people/rulers
        (2) congregations/ministers
        (3) parents/offspring
        (4) age/youth
        (5) servants/masters
    d. sum: let each know his station in society and its duties

ninth commandment [*47–48*]

47. General interpretation
    a. purpose: God as truth abhors a lie; therefore we must practice truth toward one another
    b. sum: let us not harm anyone with slander or evil-speaking
    c. corollary: we should faithfully help everyone as much as we can in affirming the truth, in order to protect his name and possessions
    d. two aspects to falsehood
        (1) harming our neighbor's reputation
        (2) depriving him of goods
    e. principle of synecdoche again: the foulest vice represents the whole class
    f. while court perjury is dealt with under third commandment, here we are concerned with detraction that despoils our neighbor of his good name rather than his possessions

48. The good reputation of our neighbor
    a. human beings enjoy talking scandalously about others
    b. the evil-speaking that God here condemns is hateful accusation arising from evil intent and wanton desire to defame
    c. not only evil-speaking but listening to it and all encouragement of it forbidden

tenth commandment [*49–50*]

49. The meaning of this commandment
    a. purpose: God wills our soul to be disposed to love, therefore we must banish all desires contrary to love
    b. sum: no thought should steal upon us to move us to covet to our neighbor's loss
    c. corollary: whatever we conceive or attempt is to be for our neighbor's good and advantage
    d. why a second commandment so close to the one against adultery?
        (1) seventh commandment includes intent
        (2) but tenth commandment deals not with deliberate intent, but rather with covetousness, which can exist without deliberate intent
    e. thus not only inclination to evil, but even prompting thereto is forbidden

50. Innermost righteousness!
    a. why does God demand such uprightness?
        (1) the goal of the law is love; a covetous heart is diseased
        (2) are aimless fantasies evil? Here those that inspire self-centeredness are meant
        (3) God's pedagogy: evil desire denied to us by depriving us of the very things that prompt our reveling
    b. the duties enjoined in the second table must rest on the foundation of fear and reverence toward God
    c. it is wrong to divide this commandment into two, for it as a whole means: keep the possessions of others safe, both from injury and fraud, and from the slightest covetousness

Principles of the Law in the Light of Christ's Teaching [***51–59***]

51. The sum of the law
    a. purpose of whole law: to form human life to the archetype of divine purity
    b. Moses and Paul agree on the aim of the law
    c. the law is no rudimentary textbook but the perfect guide to all the duties of piety and love

52. Why does Scripture sometimes mention only the second table?
    a. no amount of exegesis can deny that Christ and the apostles often summarize the law by citing the second table alone

b. why? because the second table, through signs of Christian life, shows evidence of real fear of God (the aim of the first tablet)

53. Faith and love
    a. does the essence of righteousness lie more in living innocently with men than in honoring God with piety? No!
    b. love: the essence of the law
    c. the Lord means that the law only enjoins us to observe right and equity toward men, that thereby we may become practiced in witnessing to a pious fear of Him

54. Love of neighbor
    a. our life shall best conform to God's will and His law when it is most fruitful for our brethren
    b. self-love, being innate, needs no law to kindle it in us!
    c. holiness is measured in love of neighbor and of God
    d. God's pedagogy: take our strongest possession—self-love—and redirect it, with all of its dynamism, to other men and to God

55. Who is our neighbor?
    a. neighbor is not necessarily a term of physical proximity, but embraces the whole human race without exception
    b. we must turn first to God in order to realize the principle of love: whatever the character of a man, we must yet love him because we love God

56. "Evangelical counsels"?
    a. Schoolmen call these commandments of Christ, "evangelical counsels"
        (1) free to be obeyed or not
        (2) saddle on monks, not on simple Christians
    b. Scriptural examples showing the universal application of these precepts

57. The commandment to love our enemy is a genuine commandment
    a. not only monks, but all of us are to love our enemies as Augustine and Paul convincingly argue, and church fathers as late as Gregory I considered a commandment
    b. ask these Schoolmen if loving God (which they accept as bind-

ing upon all) is not harder than loving one's enemy (which they call an "evangelical counsel")

58. Distinction of mortal and venial sins invalid!
    a. Schoolmen's definition of venial sin: desire without deliberate assent, which does not long remain in the heart
    b. response: it is the failure of the soul to concentrate on the total demands of the law that leaves an empty space for such desires to enter
    c. sin is sin: we cannot make gradations of this sort

59. Every sin is a deadly sin!
    a. Matt. 5:19 surely applies to these extenuators of the law, who neglect content thereof and even Author
    b. they foolishly underestimate God's wrath
    c. our view: all sin, as rebellion against the will of God, is mortal

CHAPTER 9
Christ, Although He Was Known to the Jews Under the Law, Was at Length Clearly Revealed Only in the Gospel

The Grace of Christ Anticipated and Manifested [*1–2*]

1. The advantage of the community of the New Covenant
    a. God was known to the people of the Old Testament in the same image in which He with full splendor now appears to us
    b. the law served to hold the godly in expectation of Christ's coming
    c. the fact that Christ has now made God known does not exclude the pious who died before Christ from the fellowship of the understanding and light that shine in the person of Christ
    d. the mysteries which the ancient people only glimpsed in shadowed outline are now manifest to us; therefore, do not be blind at midday!

2. The gospel preaches the revealed Christ
    a. the word "gospel" may be taken in a two-fold sense

(1) as "forgiveness"—the gospel is that which promises free remission of sins which commonly occur in the law, whereby God reconciles men to Himself
(2) as "fulfillment"—the gospel is a new and unusual sort of embassy by which God has fulfilled what He had promised, the fulfillment realized in the person of Jesus Christ

b. the gospel as fulfillment is to be received as a higher definition, however, because in the person of Christ we have a living manifestation that our salvation has been accomplished

Refutation of Errors on the Relation of Law and Gospel: Intermediate Position of John the Baptist [*3–5*]

3. The promises are not abrogated for us
   a. yet we ought to beware of the devilish imagination of Servetus who pretends that by faith in the gospel we share in the fulfillment of all the promises
   b. believing in Christ we at once pass from death into life, but at the same time we must remember that saying of John's: although we know that "we are the children of God, it does not yet appear . . . until we shall become like him, when we shall see him as he is"
   c. we are bidden by the Holy Spirit to live in hope for the full enjoyment of Christ's spiritual benefits
   d. we must note a difference in the nature or quality of the promises: the gospel points out with the finger what the law foreshadowed under types

4. The opposition between law and gospel ought not to be exaggerated
   a. we refute those who always erroneously compare the law with the gospel by contrasting the merit of works with the free imputation of righteousness
   b. the gospel did not so supplant the entire law as to bring forward a different way of salvation

5. John the Baptist
   a. John stood between the law and the gospel, holding an intermediate office related to both
   b. he who is least in the kingdom of heaven is greater than John,

because as yet John had not witnessed the gospel in its greatest power, the resurrection and ascension

CHAPTER 10
The Similarity of the Old and New Testaments

The Covenant in the Old Testament Really the Same as That of the New [*1–6*]

1. The question
   a. all men adopted by God into the company of His people since the beginning of the world were covenanted to Him by the same law and by the bond of the same doctrine as obtains among us
   b. although the condition of the patriarchs in this fellowship differed from ours, we must guard against the assertions of Servetus and some Anabaptists, who babble that the Israelites were without any hope of heavenly immortality

2. Chief points of agreement
   a. the covenant made with the patriarchs is so much like ours in substance and reality that the two are actually one and the same
   b. three points are to be noted
      (1) carnal prosperity and happiness did not constitute the goal set before the Jews: rather, they were adopted into the hope of immortality
      (2) the covenant by which they were bound to the Lord was supported, not by their own merits, but solely by the mercy of the God who called them
      (3) they had and knew Christ as Mediator, through whom they were joined to God and were to share in His promises

3. The Old Testament looks to the future
   a. since Israel had the gospel promised in the law, and the gospel does not confine men's hearts to delight in the present life, it would be absurd to say that those to whom the gospel had been promised omitted and neglected the care of the soul, and sought after fleshly pleasures
   b. when Paul says that the promises of the gospel are contained

in the law, he proves with utter clarity that the Old Testament was particularly concerned with the future life

4. Even in the Old Covenant justification derives its validity from grace alone
   a. since the very heart of the gospel is the justification of sinners apart from the works of merit, and since the Jews are those to whom the doctrine of righteousness of faith was imparted, who dares separate the Jews from Christ?
   b. the salvation revealed in Christ is but the manifestation of the promises that the Lord had formerly made to Abraham and the patriarchs

5. Similar signs of the covenant
   a. the Israelites are equal to us not only in the grace of the covenant but also in the signification of the sacraments
   b. the similarities between our spiritual baptism and the Jews' crossing the sea
   c. the Jews ate the same spiritual food and drank the same spiritual drink, that is, Christ

6. Refutation of an objection based on John 6:49, 54
   a. some make the claim that the two statements of Christ, "Your fathers ate the manna in the wilderness, and they died," and "He who eats my flesh shall not die forever" demonstrate that the people of the old covenant are lost
   b. but these two statements agree, because Christ was accommodating His language to the capacity of His hearers
   c. the comparison was made by Christ to show how much greater benefit His hearers ought to expect of Him than what they said their fathers had received from Moses

Argument Concerning the Hope of Eternal Life, Showing that the Old Testament Patriarchs Looked for Fulfillment of the Promises in the Life to Come [*7–14*]

7. The fathers had the Word; with it they also had eternal life
   a. it is to be taken for granted that there is such life energy in God's Word that it quickens the souls of all to whom God grants participation in it
   b. since God of old bound the Jews to Himself by this sacred bond, there is no doubt that he set them apart to the hope of eternal life

c. by "Word" is meant that special mode of communication which both illumines the souls of the pious into the knowledge of God and, in a sense, joins them to Him

8. In the Old Covenant, God gave His people fellowship with Himself and thus eternal life
   a. Old Testament references to God's fellowship with His people
   b. if God's self-manifestation is a pledge of salvation, how can He manifest Himself to a man as his God without also opening to him the treasures of His salvation?

9. Even in the Old Covenant, God's goodness was stronger than death
   a. many passages in the Old Testament show that God was not only Israel's God in the present, but that He would never fail them in the future
   b. the statement, "I shall be the God of your seed after you," clearly shows that if God would declare His benevolence toward the dead by benefiting their offspring, much less would His favor fail the dead themselves
   c. the statement, "I am the God of Abraham, . . . Isaac, and . . . Jacob" made long after their death, certainly does not mean that God is the God of those who do not exist

10. The blessedness of the ancient people was not earthly
    a. because the manner of life divinely enjoined upon believers was a continual exercise by which they were reminded that they were the most miserable of all men if they were happy in this life only, they meditated on the heavenly
    b. examples of Adam, Abel, and Noah

11. The faith of Abraham
    a. we ought to esteem Abraham as one equal to a hundred thousand if we consider his faith, which is set before us as the best model of believing
    b. to be children of God, we must be reckoned as members of his tribe; yet what would be more absurd than for Abraham to be the father of all believers and yet not to possess even the remotest corner among them?
    c. experiences of his life

12. The faith of Isaac and Jacob
    a. Isaac as an example of one whose troubles do not permit him to be happy on earth
    b. Jacob as another example of extreme unhappiness
    c. conclusion: both men did not have their hope set upon earthly things

13. The patriarchs sought for everlasting life
    a. if these holy patriarchs looked for a blessed life, as they undoubtedly did, from God's hand, they both conceived and saw it as a blessedness other than that of earthly life
    b. they would have been more stupid than blocks of wood to keep on pursuing the promises when no hope of these appeared on earth, unless they expected them to be fulfilled elsewhere

14. Death for the saints the entrance to life
    a. in all their efforts in this life the saints set before themselves the blessedness of the future life
    b. examples of Jacob, Balaam, and David

This Argument Continued with References to Passages from David, Job, Ezekiel, and Others [*15–22*]

15. David as proclaimer of hope
    a. surely he who has confessed that there is nothing solid or stable on earth, yet holds fast to a firm faith in God, contemplates his happiness as reposing elsewhere
    b. examples from the Psalms illustrating David's hope

16. Additional passages applicable to the future life
    a. what David sings in many passages in the Psalms about the prosperity of believers may not otherwise be grasped unless it be applied to the manifestation of heavenly glory
    b. not even David disguises the fact that if believers keep their eyes fastened upon the present state of things, they will be smitten by very grievous temptation, as if there were for innocence neither favor nor reward with God

17. The hope of the godly rises above present calamities to the future life
    a. the example of David teaches us how rarely or never God fulfills in this world what He promises to His servants

b. David set before his eyes not what the changing course of the world brings, but what the Lord will do when He will sit in judgment

18. Their happy destiny contrasted with that of the wicked
   a. the saints suffer the cross at the Lord's hand only for a moment; the mercies they receive are everlasting
   b. on the other hand, they foresaw an eternal and never-ending ruin of the wicked who had for one day been happy as in a dream

19. Job as witness of immortality
   a. Job could not have made the statement: "I know that my Redeemer lives, and I shall be resurrected from the earth on the Last Day," if his aspiration had rested on earth
   b. we must therefore acknowledge that he lifted up his eyes to a future immortality, for he saw that his Redeemer would be with him even as he lay in the tomb
   c. these statements are not the private statements of only a few persons

20. The witness of the prophets to immortality
   a. the prophets represented God's goodness for the people under the lineaments, so to speak, of temporal benefits
   b. but the portrait they painted lifts up the minds of the people above the earth, which would of necessity arouse them to ponder the happiness of the spiritual life to come

21. The valley of dry bones in Ezekiel
   a. the Israelites first understood Ezekiel's prophecy as an announcement that decaying corpses were to be restored to life
   b. Ezekiel's vision served not only to correct a misinterpretation, but in the meantime it impressed upon the Jews how much the Lord's power extended beyond the restoration of the people from Babylon

22. Additional passages from other prophets
   a. example from Isaiah
   b. example from Daniel

23. Summary and conclusion: the agreement of the Testaments on eternal life

THE SUFFERINGS OF THE PATRIARCHS (Parallel between Hebrews 11 and Institutes 2:10)

INSTITUTES 2:10		EPISTLE TO THE HEBREWS 11	
Section		**Verse**	
10	Adam		
	Abel	4	Abel
		5	Enoch
	Noah	7	Noah
11	Abraham	8–10, 17–19	Abraham
12	Isaac	20	Isaac
	Jacob	21	Jacob
13	Hebrews 11:9–10, 13–16 quoted		
13	Joseph	22	Joseph
15	[Moses]	23–30	Moses
		31	Rahab
		32	Gideon
			Barak
			Samson
			Jephthah
15–18	David		David
18	[Samuel]		Samuel
19	Job		
21–22	The Prophets:		The Prophets
21	Ezekiel		
22	Isaiah		
	Daniel		

a. this then is our principle: the Old Testament or Covenant that the Lord had made with the Israelites had not been limited to earthly things, but contained a promise of spiritual and eternal life
b. Christ the Lord promises to His followers today no other "Kingdom of Heaven" than that in which they may sit at table with Abraham, Isaac, and Jacob
c. yet, it so pleased God in righteous judgment to strike blind the minds of those who by refusing the offered light of heaven voluntarily brought darkness upon themselves

CHAPTER 11
The Difference between the Two Testaments

THE OLD TESTAMENT DIFFERS FROM THE NEW IN FIVE RESPECTS

First Respect: Representation of Spiritual Blessings by Temporal [*1–3*]

1. Stress on earthly benefits which, however, were to lead to heavenly concerns
   a. the Lord of old willed that His people direct and elevate their minds to the heavenly heritage; yet, to nourish them better in this hope, He displayed it for them to see and, so to speak, taste, under earthly benefits
   b. but now that the gospel has more plainly and clearly revealed the grace of the future life, the Lord leads our minds to meditate upon it directly, laying aside the lower mode of training that He used with the Israelites
   c. the earthly possession the Israelites inherited was but a mirror in which they saw the future inheritance they believed prepared for them in heaven

2. The earthly promises corresponded to the childhood of the church in the Old Covenant; but were not to chain hope to earthly things
   a. keeping Israel under tutelage, the Lord gave, not spiritual promises unadorned and open, but ones foreshadowed, in a measure, by earthly promises
   b. examples of Abraham, David, and the prophets, based on Paul's argument in Galatians 4:1–3

3. Physical benefits and physical punishments as types
   a. the saints under the Old Testament esteemed mortal life more than we ought today because mortal life was the sphere in which types and symbols were given which testified to the coming spiritual happiness
   b. as God's benefits were more conspicuous in earthly things, so also were His punishments
   c. that God now punishes more gently and rarely is a consideration which points not to the action of different Gods but to the mode of God's dispensation

Second Respect: Truth in the Old Testament Conveyed by Images and Ceremonies, Typifying Christ [*4–6*]

4. The meaning of the difference
   a. the second difference between the Old and New Testaments consists in figures: that, in the absence of the reality, it showed but an image and shadow in place of the substance
   b. the New Testament reveals the very substance of truth as present
   c. argument from the Book of Hebrews, concluding that the function of the law was to be an introduction; the better hope manifested in the gospel, and, in like manner, the ceremonies of the Old Testament were observances waiting to find their confirmation in Christ

5. Childhood and manhood of the church
   a. it was the will of the Lord that the "childhood of the Jews be trained in the elements of this world and in little external observances, as rules for this children's instruction"
   b. the law and the prophets gave men of their own time a foretaste of that wisdom which was one day to be clearly disclosed

6. Even the great men of faith remained within the limits of the Old Covenant
   a. this view is not affected by the fact that almost no one can be found in the Christian church who in excellence of faith is to be compared with Abraham
   b. the object of our considerations here is not a comparison of grace given to a few, but the dispensation God has followed in teaching His people

Third Respect: The Old Testament Is Literal; the New, Spiritual [*7–8*]

7. Biblical origin and meaning of this difference
   a. comparison of law and gospel based on Jeremiah 31:31–34, and II Corinthians 3:6–11
   b.

the law	**the gospel**
literal doctrine	spiritual doctrine
carved on tablets of stone	written upon men's hearts
preaching of death	preaching of life
preaching of condemnation	preaching of righteousness
to be made void	to abide

8. The difference in detail, according to II Corinthians 3
   a. the Old Testament is the ministry of condemnation, for it accuses all the sons of Adam of unrighteousness, while the New Testament is the ministry of righteousness because it reveals God's mercy, through which we are justified
   b. this contrast is to be referred to the ceremonial law, for because the Old bore the image of things absent, it had to die and vanish with time, while the gospel, because it reveals the very substance, stands forever
   c. we are not to surmise from this difference between letter and spirit that the Lord had fruitlessly bestowed His law upon the Jews, and that none of them turned to Him

Fourth Respect: Bondage of the Old Testament and Freedom of the New [*9–10*]

9. Paul's teaching
   a. Scripture calls the Old Testament one of "bondage" because it produces fear in men's minds; but the New Testament, one of "freedom" because it lifts them to trust and assurance
   b. Hagar-Sarah analogy
   c. the holy patriarchs were no exception to the "bondage-freedom" comparison when we consider that common dispensation by which the Lord at that time dealt with the Israelites

10. Law and gospel
    a. while the word "law" refers to the Old Testament, it must be understood that "law" includes within itself also the promises published before the law

b. the children of the promise, reborn of God, who have obeyed the commandments by faith working through love, have belonged to the New Covenant since the world began
c. thus, all the saints whom Scripture mentions as being peculiarly chosen of God from the beginning of the world have shared with us the same blessing unto eternal salvation
d. the patriarchs so lived under the Old Covenant as not to remain there but ever to aspire to the New, and thus embraced a real share in it

Fifth Respect: the Old Testament Has Reference to One Nation, the New to All Nations [*11–12*]

11. The wall is torn down in Christ
    a. the fifth difference, which may be added, lies in the fact that until the advent of Christ, the Lord set apart one nation within which to confine the covenant of His grace
    b. Israel and the other nations compared

Israel	**other nations**
joined to God through His word	allowed to walk in vanity
the Lord's darling son	strangers
recognized and received into confidence and safekeeping	left to their own darkness
hallowed by God	profaned
honored with God's presence	excluded from all approach to God

    c. but in the fullness of time, God was revealed as the reconciler of Himself and all men

12. The calling of the Gentiles
    a. the calling of the Gentiles, therefore, is a notable mark of the excellence of the New Testament over the Old
    b. even Christ at the beginning of His preaching made no immediate progress toward the calling of the Gentiles

REPLY TO OBJECTIONS REGARDING GOD'S JUSTICE AND CONSISTENCY IN THESE DIFFERENCES OF ADMINISTRATION [*13–14*]

13. Why, in general, the differences?
    a. objection: some say it is not fitting that God, always self-

consistent, should permit such a great change, disapproving afterward what He had once commanded and commended

b. reply:
   (1) God ought not to be considered changeable merely because he accommodated diverse forms to different ages, as He knew would be expedient for each
   (2) that which is changeable is man's capacity

14. God's freedom to deal with all men as He wills
   a. second objection: but could not God just as well have revealed eternal life in clear words, without any figures, at the beginning as after Christ's advent?
   b. reply: this is as if they were to quarrel with God because He created the world so late, when He could have done it from the first

RELATION OF CHAPTERS 10 AND 11

CHAPTER 11		CHAPTER 10
Old Testament	**New Testament**	**Old Testament/New Testament**
temporal blessings represent spiritual blessings		not carnal prosperity and happiness
images and ceremonies	Christ the truth	but immortality the goal
literal	spiritual	Christ the Mediator and His promises shared by both
bondage	freedom	
one nation	all nations	in both OT and NT grace, not merit

CHAPTER 12
Christ Had to Become Man in Order to Fulfill the Office of Mediator

Reasons Why It Was Necessary that the Mediator Should Be God and Should Become Man [*1–3*]

1. Only He who was true God and true man could bridge the gulf between God and ourselves
   a. our Mediator had to be both true God and true man, not by simple necessity but by divine decree, our Father having decreed what was best for us
   b. no child of Adam, no angel, but rather the very majesty of God had to descend to us, since it was not in our power to ascend to Him
   c. the gulf between man's lowliness and God's majesty (even if man had not fallen) could be bridged only in this way
   d. Paul describes Him as "the man Jesus Christ" in order to accommodate to our weakness: Christ's human nature is our path to God

2. The Mediator must be true God and true man
   a. the enormous task of the Mediator: to restore men to God's grace—something only the Son of God Himself could do
   b. our adoption as sons of grace possible only by Christ's taking on completely our human nature and its consequences (except without sin)
   c. our Redeemer had to be both God and man: for to swallow up death man had to die, but Life had to bring alive
   d. therefore the only-begotten Son became our Redeemer

3. Only He who was true God and true man could be obedient in our stead
   a. only the perfect obedience of Christ to the Father's will could overcome our disobedience:
      (1) as man He felt death; as God He overcame it
      (2) those who break the union of God-man either way are dangerous to the faith of men
   b. Christ was not just any man, but the descendant of Abraham and David: thus we are even surer He is the Anointed one

Objections to this Doctrine Answered [4–7]

4. The sole purpose of Christ's incarnation was our redemption
   a. some speculate that Christ would still have become man even if no redemption of mankind had been needed
   b. but manifest testimonies of Scripture deny this and assert that Christ was incarnated for our redemption
      (1) Old Testament testimonies
      (2) New Testament testimonies

5. Would Christ have also become man if Adam had not sinned?
   a. (Osiander) claims Christ would have become incarnate to show His love for men, even if Adam had not sinned
   b. answer: man's condemned condition and Christ's coming are joined by eternal decree of God: it is not lawful, therefore, to speculate beyond this
   c. Osiander has stirred up the question anew: it is he, [rather than Calvin], who is presumptuous in speculating beyond the limits set by Scripture

6. Osiander's doctrine of the image of God
   a. Osiander's basis: man was created in God's image—the pattern of the Messiah to come
   b. thus infers: if Adam had never fallen, Christ would still have become man; Osiander thinks he was the first to see the nature of God's image in man: that God dwelt essentially in him
   c. yes [says Calvin], Adam bore God's image, as the highest of God's creatures, but no more so than the angels
   d. Christ the head over men and angels
      (1) angels have direct vision of God because they are like the Son
      (2) our future blessedness will be to take on the form of angels, and then enjoy the everlasting vision of God

7. Point-by-point refutation of Osiander
   a. Osiander objects that without an immutable decree concerning the incarnation of the Son, God is become a liar
   b. also, that if Christ had not been born as First Man (not as Redeemer) everything would have been tied to historical contingency—this is in opposition to Paul's teaching on the first and second Adam

c. Osiander thinks that only as man does Christ have primacy over the angels—this refuted by Paul
d. Osiander thinks that if Christ had not been man, men would not have had Him as King, as Head of His church—but [Calvin counters that] Christ, even not incarnate, could have headed His church, even as He heads the angels
e. Osiander now sets forth the "prophecy of Adam" ("bone of my bones and flesh of my flesh")
    (1) this is no "prophecy" but only concerns faithfulness in marriage
    (2) Paul's interpretation of this (Eph. 4:30-31) only uses the figure of marriage for our union with Christ

CHAPTER 13
Christ Assumed the True Substance of Human Flesh

***Referring to Ancient Heresies, Calvin Answers Menno Simons** [1-2]*

1. Proof of Christ's true manhood
    a. we have already proved Christ's divinity (1:13); our present task is to show how, incarnate, He was our Mediator
    b. Marcionites and Manichaeans long ago impugned the genuineness of Christ's incarnation
    c. Scripture otherwise copiously asserts the reality of Christ's incarnation

2. Against the opponents of Christ's true manhood
    a. detailed analysis of distorting of Scriptural passages to confirm error by
        (1) Marcion
        (2) Mani
    b. wrong interpretation of "Son of Man"
        (1) they say Christ is so called because He was promised to men
        (2) actually "Son of Man" is a Hebraic expression for "true man"; Scriptural texts confirming Christ's complete manhood
    c. wrong interpretation of "first born"
        (1) they say Christ, to be first born, should have been born of Adam at the very beginning

(2) but "first born" here refers not to age but to degree of honor and loftiness of power

d. wrong interpretation of statement that Christ received human, not angelic nature
   (1) they say this means He received humankind into grace
   (2) actually, Paul is here enhancing the honor Christ deigned to give us, by comparing us with the angels

e. the whole controversy is resolved by Gen. 3:15—that the seed of woman will crush the serpent's head:
   (1) this refers to the whole of mankind
   (2) we must acquire victory through Christ
   (3) hence Christ was begotten of mankind, because God addresses Eve to raise her hope against succumbing to despair

The Human Descent and True Humanity of Christ *[3–4]*

3. Christ's descent through the Virgin Mary: an absurdity exposed
   a. our opponents allegorize the term "seed" of Abraham: Paul, on the other hand, understands this in the sense of literal, biological descent
   b. they also bring up the fact that Matthew's genealogy of Christ is traced through Joseph; answer: Mary came from the same family
   c. they claim women are "without seed"; contra:
      (1) women share actively in the process of generation
      (2) but the political order gives a preferential position to the male sex
      (3) all genealogies name only males in Scripture—this is not to suggest that women are nothing!
      (4) testimony of law, forbidden degrees of marriage, etc., prove that the women contribute equally to the offspring
   d. when Matthew says that Christ was begotten of Mary he does not mean that the virgin was a mere channel through which Christ flowed

4. True man—and yet sinless! True man—and yet eternal God!
   a. they consider it shameful to Christ to derive His origin from men; then He would not be exempt from sin
   b. Christ had the same birth as we, but (as Paul says) preserved from sin

c. against their quibbles, Christ's freedom from sin is not to be explained by some mechanical process, but by the sanctification of the Spirit, which made His generation as pure and undefiled as that before Adam's fall
d. could the Word be confined within the narrowness of an earthly body? they ask; our answer [the "extra-Calvinisticum"]—"the Son of God descended from heaven in such a way that, without leaving heaven, he willed to be borne in the virgin's womb, to go about the earth, and to hang upon the cross; yet he continuously filled the world even as he had done from the beginning!"

CHAPTER 14
How the Two Natures of the Mediator Make One Person

Explanation of the Human and Divine Natures in Christ [*1–2*]

1. Duality and unity
   a. "the Word was made flesh" = the Son of God became the Son of man: not by confusion of substances, but by unity of person
   b. the best human analogue of this mysterious union is that of soul and body: some characteristics of the body and of the soul are distinct from one another; some are in common; others are capable of being transferred: but two diverse underlying natures make up the one human person
   c. so it is with Christ; the interchange of characteristics within the one person of the Mediator is called *communicatio idiomatum*

2. Divinity and humanity in their relation to each other [classification of Scriptural texts]
   a. of His divinity
   b. of His humanity
   c. of communication of properties

3. The unity of the person of the Mediator: texts comprehending both natures at once
   a. in John's Gospel
   b. in Paul

c. the two natures united in the person of the Mediator
   (1) these confused by some early writers
   (2) Mediator's office (which extends to the final judgment) comprehends both natures together
d. the same point is to be made about the title "Lord"

***Condemnation of the Errors of Nestorius, Eutyches, and Servetus** [4–8]*

4. The two natures may not be thought of as either fused or separated
   a. a devout examination of the mysteries of the office of Mediator would prevent the breaking of the union toward either extreme of man or of God
   b. we therefore hold that Christ, as He is God and man, consisting of two natures united but not mingled, is our Lord and the true Son of God even according to, but not by reason of, His humanity
   c. let us then avoid the twin errors of
      (1) Nestorius and his double Christ (the natures pulled apart)
      (2) Eutyches, who in trying to show the unity of person, destroys one nature or the other (the persons commingled)

5. The Christological error of Michael Servetus
   a. Servetus's erroneous views summarized:
      (1) supposes the Son of God to be a figment compounded from God's essence, spirit, flesh, and three uncreated elements
      (2) he denies the God-man, holding that before Christ came in the flesh there were only shadow-figures in God which were made plain only when the Word truly began to be the Son of God
   b. in answer, we assert the traditional view of the church: that the preexistent Logos, eternally God's Son, took human nature in a hypostatic union; further refutation and proofs

6. Christ as Son of God and Son of man
   a. Servetus claims that Christ could be accorded the name "Son of God" only because He took on flesh
   b. Scripture proves that Christ is Son according to both natures
      (1) Christ is by nature God's Son; we are sons by adoption and grace only

(2) while Christ is preeminently God's Son in His divine nature, sonship can be extended to the entire person of the Mediator

c. Scripture clearly teaches Christ's two natures, carefully distinguishing between them

(1) Son of man: of the posterity of Adam

(2) Son of God: by virtue of His deity and eternal essence

7. Servetus's flimsy counterevidence

a. Servetus quotes Rom. 8:32 and Luke 1:32 to support his claim that Christ was Son of God only by virtue of His incarnation

b. Servetus also claims that before He appeared in the flesh, Christ was nowhere called "Son of God," except figuratively

c. these views refuted from Scripture and Augustine, and support is also claimed (contrary to Servetus) for orthodoxy from Irenaeus and Tertullian

8. Comprehensive presentation and rebuttal of Servetus's doctrine

a. Servetus's claim that Christ was the Son of God only according to the flesh is redolent of the old Manichees' view that man has his soul by derivation from God

b. Servetus's views summarized: (based on false interpretation of "the Word was made flesh")

(1) the Son of God was from the beginning an idea, and even then was preordained to be the man who would become the essential image of God

(2) the Word of God is but outward splendor

(3) Christ's begetting: the will to beget the Son was begotten in God from the beginning, and extended itself by act to the creation itself

(4) Spirit and Word confused, for God distributed the invisible Word and the Spirit into flesh and soul

(5) Yet the Word has a seminal function, because the shadow Son was a length begotten through the Word

(6) to make Christ begotten of God's essence, Servetus compounds Christ out of three uncreated elements

(7) Christ's flesh was of the same substance with God; the Word was made man by the conversion of flesh into God

(8) Christ cannot be the Son of God unless his flesh came forth from God's essence; as a consequence Servetus reduces the eternal hypostasis of the Word to nothing,

snatching from us the Son of David, promised as our Redeemer

c. enough has been said here of Servetus's views; they are more fully refuted elsewhere; we conclude: if flesh were divinity itself, it would cease to be the temple of God

CHAPTER 15
To Know the Purpose for Which Christ Was Sent by the Father, and What He Conferred upon Us, We Must Look Above All at Three Things in Him: the Prophetic Office, Kingship, and Priesthood

Christ's Saving Activity Threefold: First the Prophetic Office [*1–2*]

1. The need of understanding this doctrine: Scriptural passages applicable to Christ's prophetic office
   a. the papists speak of the Son of God, using the traditional names, but emptily and ineffectually
   b. our task then is to understand the purpose and use of Christ's titles
   c. God provided an unbroken chain of prophets to teach salvation—but all these looked to a full understanding only with the coming of Christ

2. The meaning of the prophetic office for us
   a. the name Christ supposes three offices, all done by anointing with oil: prophet, priest, king
   b. Messiahship especially connected with the kingly office, but not to be overlooked in the other two
   c. Christ, as Scripture states, was anointed as prophet, but not only for Himself as teacher; His anointing as prophet applies also to His whole body, the church, in which the preaching of the gospel is to continue

The Kingly Office—Its Spiritual Character [*3–5*]

3. The eternity of Christ's dominion
   a. spiritual kingship

b. hence, efficacious and beneficial for us; and eternal in two ways:
   (1) in the church, which will weather all the storms, in perpetuity preserved
   (2) in the individual believer, inspired to hope for blessed immortality

4. The blessing of Christ's kingly office for us
   a. the happiness promised us by Christ does not rest in earthly prosperity, but in a heavenly life after death
   b. Christ enriches us with what we need to fight courageously and successfully against our spiritual enemies
   c. despite all our earthly tribulations, Christ our King will not leave us destitute: believers' hymn of assurance

5. The spiritual nature of His kingly office: the sovereignty of Christ and of the Father
   a. the "oil" not physical but the "spiritual oil of gladness" of the psalm [Ps. 45:7], received not for Himself, but for our benefit
   b. this sacred anointing visibly symbolized in baptism of Christ
   c. Paul's mention of Christ's turning over of His kingship to the Father, merely means that the perfect administration of the kingdom will not be as it is now
   d. "at the right hand of the Father" = the Father's deputy, as Paul explains in calling Christ the Head of the Church
   e. Christ is both King and pastor of the godly, and executor of judgment among the wicked

The Priestly Office: Reconciliation and Intercession [*6*]

6. The purpose and use of Christ's priestly office
   a. by his holiness, Christ our Mediator reconciles us to God
   b. but rightly accursed, we are barred from God; hence an expiation necessary for us to approach Him
   c. as the Epistle to the Hebrews shows, only the death of the priest Himself, Christ, can bring the benefit of His priesthood to us
   d. hence Christ is an everlasting intercessor and hence our trust in prayer, our peace of conscience, and our reliance on God's mercy
   e. Christ is our priest not only to make the Father propitious to us, but also to receive us as companions in His priestly office

f. the sacrifice of our high priest is once for all—no papist resacrificing!

CHAPTER 16
How Christ Has Fulfilled the Function of Redeemer to Acquire Salvation for Us. Here, also, His Death and Resurrection Are Discussed, as Well as His Ascent into Heaven

Alienated by Sin from God, Who yet Loved Us, We Are Reconciled by Christ [*1–4*]

1. The Redeemer
   a. our teaching on Christ so far has one objective:
      (1) Redeemer divinely sent to us
      (2) the minute we turn our gaze elsewhere, our salvation (grounded in Him) vanishes
   b. no one can descend into himself and seriously consider what he is without feeling God's wrath and hostility toward him: hence the sinner must seek no common assurance

2. The awareness of God's wrath makes us thankful for His loving act in Christ
   a. Paul's texts on God's enmity toward us until Christ's reconciling death are intended to accommodate to our understanding our ruin apart from Christ
   b. if Scripture had merely stated that God, by His own free favor, did not allow us to be estranged from Him, it would induce us to feel something of God's mercy
   c. but Scripture's more dramatic teaching of man's fearful plight until Christ's intercession, far more effectively portrays God's grace
   d. since, then, we have to be struck over the head with God's wrath by being taught God's hostility to us apart from Christ before we embrace God's love, Scripture so teaches

3. God's wrath against unrighteousness; His love precedes our reconciliation in Christ
   a. yet this manner of teaching is not mere accommodation to our weak capacity: God cannot abide our unrighteousness
   b. though sinners, we remain God's creatures, created for life

(though we have brought death on ourselves), and He loves us

c. by His love God goes before and anticipates our reconciliation in Christ

d. our assurance of God's favor rests in Christ alone

4. The work of atonement derives from God's love; therefore it has not established the latter
   a. the agreement of Scripture passages on God's love for us, and on His enmity toward us apart from Christ is obvious
   b. but if, beyond Scripture, you require the testimony of the ancient church, hear Augustine:
      (1) God's love is incomprehensible and unchangeable
      (2) God's reconciling love for us precedes His reconciling act in Christ
      (3) God hates what we have done with what He made, but loves what He made in us

The Effects of the Obedience and Death of Christ [*5–7*]

5. Christ has redeemed us through His obedience, which He practiced throughout his life
   a. Christ has obtained reconciliation for us through His lifelong obedience, as Paul has shown
   b. this is preeminently seen in Christ's death, however; the Apostles' Creed shows this by passing directly from Christ's birth to His death and resurrection
   c. yet other Scriptural texts refer to Christ's prior obedience as well

   the condemnation through Pilate

   d. the peculiar form of Christ's death, based on a trial and a judicial sentence, was necessary to transfer to Himself the condemnation determined for us—not just any death would serve
   e. all the circumstances of His death exemplify the condemnation of a sinless man for our own transgressions
   f. thus was our guilt transferred to Christ: a fact we must remember throughout life, to free us from fear and anxiety

6. "Crucified"
   a. the form of Christ's death also embodies a singular mystery
      (1) seen in the cross, the most accursed form of death
      (2) also foreshadowed in the Ashmoth, or sacrifices for purification of sin, of which Christ was the archetype
   b. Paul makes this explicit in many passages
      (1) making clear Isaiah's utterances about the suffering servant
      (2) emphasizing the need for a blood sacrifice both to satisfy God and to purify us

7. "Dead and buried"
   a. first fruit of Christ's death for us: liberation from the death to which we had been bound
   b. second fruit of Christ's death for us: mortification of our flesh

Explanation of the Doctrine of the Descent into Hell [*8–12*]

8. "Descended into hell"
   a. although this article of the creed was probably added later, it nevertheless mentions a commonly-held belief of the early church: Christ's descent into hell
   b. the creed itself, although not of apostolic authorship, is a trustworthy summary of our faith, drawn from Scripture
   c. the view of some that "descended into hell" is synonymous with burial is rejected on logical grounds

9. Christ in the nether world?
   a. another view: descent into hell was to release the souls of the patriarchs who had died under the law
   b. this is the source of "limbo," an underground prison of the souls of the dead
   c. I Peter 3:19, 20 interpreted by some; their interpretation corrected here

10. The "descent into hell" as an expression of the spiritual torment that Christ underwent for us
    a. a mere bodily death on Christ's part would have been ineffectual for us

b. therefore He underwent all the severity of God's vengeance to appease God's wrath toward us
c. some reject my interpretation on the ground that it thus puts what precedes His burial after it

11. Defense of this explanation from Scriptural passages
    a. Jesus Christ had to go through the sense of complete estrangement from God the Father, through a lively fear of death, in order completely to bear our nature
    b. Christ's cry of dereliction was no mere expression of others' opinion, but came out of the deep anguish of His own heart
    c. Christ had to fight and conquer the fear that torments all mortals, to enable us, too, not to be swallowed up by death

12. Defense of the doctrine against misunderstandings and errors
    a. but some persons here claim that Jesus could not have feared for the salvation of His own soul
    b. refutation of our opponents' views in detail:
        (1) Christ's grief and sorrow (denied by them) evidence that His soul as well as His body shared in the punishment in order that we may be totally redeemed
        (2) they deny anything evil to Christ: Christ voluntarily took our weakness, our fallen nature (but without sin)—not thereby detracting from His power
        (3) they then claim Christ feared death, but not God's curse and wrath, from which He knew Himself safe—Christ had a harsher and more difficult struggle than with common death
        (4) erroneous views, such as these, show that these persons do not really grasp how much our salvation cost the Son of God
    c. [Calvin here comes close to a kenotic view] the divine power of Christ's Spirit remained momentarily hidden, giving way to weakness of flesh, yet this pain and fear was not contrary to faith
    d. rejection of Apollinarian and Monothelite errors which make Christ only half a man
    e. the great paradox of John 12:27f.

Christ's Resurrection, Ascension, and Heavenly Session *[13–16]*

13. "On the third day He rose again from the dead" [three benefits of Christ's death for us]

a. it is in Christ's resurrection alone, not His death, that the victory of our faith over death lies
   (1) from Scripture, division of our salvation between death and resurrection of Christ is as follows:
      (a) through death—sin and death wiped out
      (b) through resurrection—righteousness restored and life raised up
      (c) thus, through resurrection power of His death manifested in us
   (2) in handling the relevant Scriptural passages, we are by synecdoche to understand "death" to include "resurrection," and vice versa
b. also, just as the mortification of our flesh rests in our participation in His cross, so we are benefited by His resurrection
c. His resurrection guarantees our own
d. conclusion: He suffered the same death that other men naturally die; and received immortality in the same flesh that, in the mortal state, He had taken upon Himself

14. "Ascended into heaven"
   a. Christ's ascent into heaven is to be present to us in a way more useful than His bodily presence
   b. as His body was raised up above all the heavens, so His power and energy were diffused and spread beyond all the bounds of heaven and earth
   c. Augustine harmonizes the words, "You will not always have me with you," and "Lo, I am with you always": we always have Christ according to the presence of majesty, but His physical presence with His church was only for a few days

15. "Seated at the right hand of the Father"
   a. "sitting" is taken from comparison with assessors at a king's court
   b. Christ's divine session means that He came into possession of the government committed to Him, until the Day of Judgment
   c. His heavenly session thus means more than the designation of His blessedness

16. Benefits imparted to our faith by Christ's ascension
   a. the Lord's ascent into heaven opened the way to the heavenly kingdom previously closed by Adam

b. Christ in heaven is our constant advocate and intercessor before the Father
c. our faith comprehends Christ's might, in which our strength against the powers of hell rests

Christ's Future Return in Judgment [*17*]

a. because Christ's kingdom lies hidden in the earth under the lowness of the flesh (despite His clear indication of His present power to those who believe), faith is called to ponder the visible, bodily presence of Christ which He will show in the Day of Judgment
b. no one—living or dead—can escape His judgment
c. while some writers explain differently the words "the living and the dead," it is clear that this is the correct meaning, in which Scripture and creed agree

Concluding Remarks on the Apostles' Creed and the Sufficiency of Christ [*18–19*]

18. The Judge is the—Redeemer!
    a. we have great assurance in our conviction that Christ as intercessor will not condemn those whom He has received into His charge and protection
    b. we follow the order of the Apostles' Creed because it conveniently sums up the main points of our redemption, even though we have no illusion of its apostolic authorship; it was obviously accepted by the early church as a public confession with the consent of all

19. Christ alone in all the clauses of the creed
    a. our whole salvation rests in Christ; no part of it comes from elsewhere:
        (1) our strength—in His dominion
        (2) our purity—in His conception
        (3) our gentleness—in His birth
        (4) our redemption—in His passion
        (5) our acquittal—in His condemnation
        (6) our remission from the curse—in His cross
        (7) our satisfaction—in His sacrifice
        (8) our purification—in His blood
        (9) our reconciliation—in His descent into hell

(10) our mortification of flesh—in His tomb
(11) our newness of life—in His resurrection
(12) our immortality—in the same
(13) our inheritance of the heavenly kingdom—in His entrance into heaven
(14) our protection, security, abundant supply of all blessings—in His kingdom
(15) our untroubled expectation of judgment—in the power given Him to judge

b. if we truly know Christ's blessings we will not, as some men, dash hither and yon after other sources of salvation

CHAPTER 17
Christ Rightly and Properly Said to Have Merited God's Grace and Salvation for Us

1. Christ's merit does not exclude God's free grace, but precedes it
   a. some men accept the view that we receive salvation through Christ, but in denying idea of "merit" they make Christ a mere instrument, not the author and prince of life
   b. quoting Augustine, we refute this and assert the following order:
      (1) God's good pleasure appoints Christ as Mediator to obtain salvation for us
      (2) thus we are freely justified by God's mercy alone, but at the same time, Christ's merit (subordinate to God's mercy) intervenes for us

2. Scripture couples God's grace and Christ's merit
   a. Scripture teaches God's love as the highest cause; faith in Christ the second or proximate cause
   b. in some ineffable way, God loved us and yet was angry toward us at the same time, until He became reconciled to us in Christ
   c. we sons of wrath estranged from God by sin have, by Christ's sacrifice, acquired free justification to appease God

3. The merit of Christ in the witness of Scripture
   a. as many passages of Scripture attest, Christ merited and acquired grace for us with His Father

b. meaning of key passages in Rom. 5
   (1) Rom. 5:10–11: God, to whom we were hateful because of sin, was appeased by the death of his Son to become favorable to us
   (2) Rom. 5:19: antithesis—as by the sin of Adam we were estranged from God and destined to perish, so by Christ's obedience we are received into favor as righteous

4. The substitution of Christ
   a. "grace was imparted to us by Christ's merit" means: by His blood we were cleansed, and His death was an expiation for our sins
   b. Christ is set over against all the sacrifices of the law, which prefigure Him (mainly from the Epistle to the Hebrews)
   c. we must accept the expiatory power of Christ's sacrifice: He became accursed to make satisfaction for sins

5. Christ's death the price of our redemption
   a. the apostles clearly testify that the penalty for our sins has been paid by Christ
   b. the character and efficacy of Christ's sacrifice for our sins clearly stated in the New Testament: the promise made by God for our works, unobtainable by our sinful selves, is fulfilled by Christ's death for us

6. Christ acquired no merit for Himself
   a. foolish question of Lombard and Schoolmen: Did Christ merit anything for Himself?
   b. by God's plan, as Scripture shows, Christ gave away Himself, forgot Himself, for our sake
   c. our opponents' use of Phil. 2:9 as proof of Christ's merits for Himself is wrong: Paul is here merely stating that Christ's humiliation is followed by His exaltation

BOOK THREE

The Way in Which We Receive the Grace of Christ: What Benefits Come to Us from It, and What Effects Follow

CHAPTER 1
The Things Spoken Concerning Christ Profit Us by the Secret Working of the Spirit

1. The Holy Spirit is the bond that unites us to Christ
   a. how do we receive those benefits which the Father bestowed on His Son, not for Christ's private use, but to enrich poor and needy men?
   b. outside of us, Christ would be separated from us, and we would not benefit salvifically from His work: therefore, He had to become one of us and dwell among us, and we have to grow into one body with Him; this we obtain by faith
   c. since not all enjoy this communion with Christ, we must climb higher and examine into the secret energy of the Spirit, by which we come to enjoy Christ and all His benefits
   d. Scriptural texts which describe how we experience Christ in the Spirit
   e. sum: the Holy Spirit is the bond by which Christ effectually unites us to Himself (cf. anointing: II.15.2)

2. How and why Christ was endowed with the Holy Spirit
   a. "Spirit of Sanctification": in general, for all living creatures; but especially the root and seed of heavenly life in us
   b. Spirit of the Father/Spirit of the Son: Son has the fullness of the Spirit to dispense to men

3. Titles of the Holy Spirit in Scripture
   a. Spirit of adoption [Rom. 8:15; Gal. 4:6]
   b. guarantee and seal of our inheritance [II Cor. 1:22; cf. Eph. 1:14]
   c. life [Rom. 8:10]
   d. water [Isa. 55:1; 44:3; John 7:37; Ezek. 36:25]
   e. oil and anointing [I John 2:20, 27]
   f. fire [Luke 3:16]
   g. spring [John 4:14]
   h. hand of God [Acts 11:21]

4. Faith the principal work of the Spirit
    a. hence terms used to express His power and activity are generally referred to faith
    b. the Spirit is the source of faith, the inner teacher of promised salvation, the energizer of Christ in us

CHAPTER 2
Faith: Its Definition Set Forth, and Its Properties Explained

The Object of Faith Is Christ [*1*]

a. resumé
    (1) by the law, God lays down our duty; when we fail, the sentence of eternal death is pronounced upon us
    (2) it is beyond our capacity to fulfill the law to the letter
    (3) there is only one means of liberation: Christ the Redeemer
b. current scholastic notions of faith are shallow and inadequate: e.g., common assent to the gospel history
c. faith has God as its object, but through Christ, by whom God has ordained to reveal His glory to us
    (1) Christ as God: the destination of our faith
    (2) Christ as man: the path of our faith

Faith Involves Knowledge; the True Doctrine Obscured by the Scholastic Notion of Implicit Faith [*2–5*]

2. Faith rests upon knowledge, not upon pious ignorance
    a. "implicit faith" destroys true faith
    b. believing does not mean
        (1) submitting to churchly prescription in blind obedience
        (2) but rather, knowing God as merciful Father through reconciliation effected in Christ

3. The Roman doctrine of "implicit" faith is basically false
    a. ignorance tempered by humility, unreasoning, gullible reverence for the church, is not true faith
    b. faith consists rather in the knowledge of God and Christ: Scripture teaches that understanding must be joined with faith

4. Even right faith is always surrounded by error and unbelief
   a. there is a place for "implicit" faith in us so long as we dwell in the ignorance and error of this life
   b. obscurities in Scripture humble us in our ignorance
   c. even the disciples displayed implicit faith before they attained full enlightenment

5. "Implicit" faith as prerequisite of faith
   a. evidences in the Gospels of a reverent attention on the part of some which disposed them to Christ's teaching: called "faith," it was actually only the beginning of faith
   b. this teachableness, however, is far different from the sluggish, dull ignorance which the papists dub "faith"

Relation of Faith to the Word and Brief Definition of Faith [*6–7*]

6. Faith rests upon God's Word
   a. the gospel leads us to faith
   b. the gospel, although anticipated in Moses and the prophets, is more fully set forth by Christ, the teacher of our Father's mercy
   c. faith and Word inextricably bound
      (1) hearing is believing
      (2) without the Word, faith lapses into mere credulity
      (3) the Word is a mirror in which we contemplate God
      (4) faith is obedience to the Word
   d. faith as knowledge
      (1) faith is more than knowing God exists—it is knowing God's will toward us
      (2) certainty can rest solely on believing the sacred and inviolable truth of His Word to us

7. Faith arises from God's promise of grace in Christ
   a. not words of vengeance in Scripture, but words of mercy and compassion, establish faith
   b. but knowledge of God's goodness, to be important for faith, must make us rely on that goodness
   c. definition of faith: "A firm and certain knowledge of God's benevolence toward us, founded upon the truth of the freely-given promise in Christ, both revealed to our minds and sealed upon our hearts through the Holy Spirit"

Various Unacceptable Significations of the Term "Faith" [*8-13*]

8-10. "formed" versus "unformed" faith

a. Schoolmen contend that a person devoid of the fear of God can still possess saving knowledge—a false notion [8]

b. I Cor. 13:2 is no proof of their distinction [9]

c. what is called "unformed" faith is only an illusion of faith [10]

11-12. "faith" among the reprobate?

a. the reprobate can, for a time, experience something of the same assurance as the elect [11]

b. there is a "lower" working of the Spirit among the reprobate, but always resulting in a confused, shadowy awareness of grace

c. but only the elect have faith as a permanent possession

d. this true and false faith contrasted out of Scripture [12]

13. Different meanings of the word "faith" in Scripture

a. sometimes means "sound doctrine of godliness"

b. sometimes confined to a particular object

c. sometimes means the gift of performing miracles (Paul)

d. sometimes means teaching by which we are established in faith

e. what sort of faith distinguishes the children of God from unbelievers?

Detailed Examination of What the Definition of Faith in Paragraph 7 Implies: the Element of Knowledge [*14-15*]

14. Faith as higher knowledge

a. this knowledge is not the comprehension commonly concerned with those things which fall under human sense-perception

b. this knowledge is more a persuasion of divine truth than instruction in rational proof

c. therefore the knowledge of faith consists in assurance rather than comprehension

15. Faith implies certainty

a. "sure and firm" means solid constancy of persuasion

b. full and fixed certainty of God's faithfulness is required

(1) to overcome the doubts that reveal our hidden weakness
(2) to overcome our anxiety which impairs our full reception of, and benefit from, God's mercy

c. hence we must have a quiet, bold, confident faith before God

16. Certainty of faith
    a. God's promises of mercy are true not only outside, but within us, if we have true faith
    b. portrait of the true believer

17. Faith in the struggle against temptation
    a. is certainty of faith incompatible with the terrible temptations that plague believers?
    b. we deny that such afflictions cut them off from the assurance of God's mercy and illustrate it from the vicissitudes of David as seen in the Psalms [note Calvin's self-identification with David]

18. The conflict in the heart of the believer
    a. the inner struggle is a reflection of the division of spirit and flesh in man
    b. despite the doubts inspired by the moral conflict, our assurance rests on no obscure and confused knowledge of the divine will toward us, for faith is never taken utterly from us, and ultimately triumphs over all perils

19. Even weak faith is real faith
    a. as faith grows in the believer, it is at all times sufficient to give us some assurance of God's promises
    b. its ignorance does not hinder the mind from gaining a clear knowledge of the divine will toward itself

20. The weakness and strength of faith [Paul]
    a. in this life we actually receive only a tiny portion of divine wisdom, though we keep learning
    b. yet tiny though it may be, and well-nigh overwhelmed by tumults, such faith brings us through the gospel to God's transforming presence

21. The Word of God as the shield of faith
    a. faith arms itself against all attacks with the Lord's Word
    b. to the doubts which trials raise about God's vengeance, faith

triumphantly asserts God's pardon and mercy: this is the common experience of the saints

c. so long as unfaith remains outside the heart, while faith remains secure within, the soldier-believer cannot be vanquished

22. Right fear
    a. believers, seeing God's vengeance upon the wicked, conceive a true fear of Him which strengthens rather than weakens their conscience
    b. this is exemplified in Paul's exhortation to the Gentiles to learn from the rejection of the Jews

23. "Fear and trembling" [Phil. 2:12]
    a. this means the reverent fear which despairs of self, but reposes full confidence in God's power
    b. but how can fear and faith dwell in the same mind?: "the very sweetness and delightfulness of grace so fills a man who is cast down in himself with fear and at the same time with admiration, that he depends upon God and humbly submits himself to His power"

24. The indestructible certainty of faith rests upon Christ's oneness with us
    a. some "half-papists" picture faith as an alternation between hope and fear; between contemplating Christ (which to do is salvation) and contemplating ourselves
    b. but Christ dwells within us: we do not contemplate Him from afar off, as they conceive hope
    c. despite the darkness of temptation, the believing soul ceases not its earnest quest for God

25. Bernard of Clairvaux on the two aspects of faith
    a. in our own hearts we are nothing
    b. in the heart of God we really are

26. Fear of God [as Lord] and honor of God [as Father]
    a. the fear of the Lord must be for us a reverence compounded of the son's honor of his father and the servant's fear of his lord
    b. if there were no hell, we ought still to dread offending him more than death

c. but due to the unrestrained wantonness of our flesh, we must ponder how the Lord hates all iniquity and how no evildoer will escape his vengeance

27. Childlike and servile fear [cf. I.4.4.]
    a. when John (1 John 4:18) says, "Perfect love casts out fear," he is talking about believers' fear, a free and voluntary kind
    b. unbelievers' fear is quite a different matter, as it arises not out of God's impending displeasure, but from His threatening vengeance which they would gladly circumvent if they could (cf. Eph. 5:6): a servile kind of fear
    c. some men interpolate a third intermediate variety which in the subduing of men's minds leads them willingly to yield a proper fear to God [Augustine, Peter Lombard, Thomas Aquinas]

28. Faith assures us not of earthly prosperity but of God's favor
    a. it is not length of life, honor, or riches that faith promises us
    b. rather faith gives us certainty that God will never fail
    c. the inward peace that God's grace brings, looking to the life to come, gives us blessing even amidst the miseries of the present life

Basis of Faith the Free Promise, Given in the Word, of Grace in Christ [29–32]

29. God's promise the support of faith
    a. the freely-given promise of God is the foundation of faith, wherein it begins, rests, and ends
    b. the promise of mercy is the proper goal of faith, but in the recognition that God is both avenger of wicked deeds and merciful to repentant sinners

30. Why faith depends solely on the promise of grace [in answer to Pighius]
    a. faith does not stand firm until a man attains to the freely-given promise
    b. faith does not reconcile us to God at all unless it joins us to Christ

31. The significance of the Word for faith
    a. faith needs the Word, as much as fruit needs the living root of a tree

b. unless the power of God, by which He can do all things, confronts our eyes, our ears will barely receive the Word, or not esteem at all its true value
c. memory of God's past benefits reminds us, in our despair, of God's saving power: Scriptural examples

32. The promise of faith fulfilled in Christ
a. there is no promise of God which is not a testimony of His love
b. God's benefits affect the reprobate and the elect differently
(1) the reprobate, showered with God's benefits, never became aware of God's mercy and only incur heavier judgment upon themselves
(2) the elect, despite passing unfaithfulness and ingratitude, never lose grasp of God's promises
c. no one is loved by God apart from Christ: apparent contradictory examples from Scripture dealt with

Faith Revealed in Our Hearts by the Spirit [*33–37*]

33. The Word becomes efficacious for our faith through the Holy Spirit
a. the dullness of our minds requires the illumination of the Holy Spirit before the Word can accomplish its work
b. faith is a double gift from God in that the Spirit
(1) illumines the mind
(2) strengthens and supports the heart
c. how Paul's notion of the "Spirit as the effect of faith," seemingly an inversion, is to be explained

34. Only the Holy Spirit leads us to Christ
a. human discernment, overwhelmed by things divine, is an untrustworthy guide and must be supplanted by the Holy Spirit
b. description of the illumination of the soul by the Holy Spirit and its effects
c. the Word cannot enter our blind minds unless they be illumined by the Spirit as inner teacher

35. Without the Spirit man is incapable of faith
a. man in his corrupted state is unfit to believe, so God's power, not man, initiates faith, and bestows it selectively (the more fully to show the glory of His gift)

b. Christ, when He illumines us into faith by the power of His Spirit, at the same time so engrafts us into His body that we become partakers of every good

36. Faith as a matter of the heart
    a. the Word of God is not received by faith if it merely enters the mind, but only if it is received in the heart itself
    b. the Spirit acts as a seal, to seal in our hearts the promises previously impressed upon our minds

37. Doubt cannot smother faith: reiteration of the believers' "song of triumph" over temptations and doubts

***Refutation of Scholastic Objections to This** [38–42]*

38. Scholastic error concerning the assurance of faith
    a. Scholastic notion: our confidence of faith is based on reasoning that God is favorable to us, provided our purity of life merits His favor
    b. our view rests upon no such "moral conjecture"
    c. God's alteration of favor and affliction in His dealings toward men proves man's innate folly

39. The Christian rejoices in the indwelling of the Spirit [refutation of the opponents' accusation that it is rash presumption to claim an undoubted knowledge of God's will]

40. The alleged uncertainty as to whether we will persevere to the end
    a. opponents capitalize on future uncertainty of the believer concerning salvation
    b. but they limit certainty of faith to some point of time, when faith actually looks to a future immortality in the life after death!
    c. we are not arrogant in boasting of such confidence

***Relation of Faith to Hope and Love** [41–43]*

41. Faith according to Heb. 11:1
    a. explanation of "substance of things to be hoped for" and "conviction of things not present"

- b. faith and love
  - (1) faith powerfully moves us to love God at the same time as we fear Him
  - (2) error of the Schoolmen's teaching that love is prior to faith and hope

42. Faith and hope belong together
  - a. hope logically follows from a living faith and without it faith is void
  - b. hope: an expectation of those things which faith has believed to have been truly promised by God
  - c. how hope supports faith (adduced from Scripture)

43. Faith and hope have the same foundation: God's mercy
  - a. Scripture often uses faith and hope interchangeably; sometimes they are yoked together
  - b. folly of Lombard's double foundation of hope
    - (1) grace of God
    - (2) merit of works
  - c. sole goal of faith: God's mercy
  - d. unlike Lombard's reliance on works, we rely on God's mercy alone, and hope in Him, not in self

CHAPTER 3
Our Regeneration by Faith: Repentance

Repentance the Fruit of Faith: Review of Some Errors Connected with this Point

1. Repentance as a consequence of faith
   - a. since the sum of the gospel consists in repentance and forgiveness of sins, any discussion of faith that left out these effects thereof would be incomplete
   - b. repentance is born of faith, all opponents to the contrary notwithstanding

2. Repentance has its foundations in the gospel, which faith embraces
   - a. the priority of faith to repentance means that the recognition

of God's grace precedes the sense of belonging to God (=faith), which in turn leads one to repentance
b. the hope of pardon goads man in his sluggishness
c. the folly of mechanically beginning from repentance and trying to reach faith by penitential exercises (cf. Anabaptists, Jesuits)

3. Mortification and vivification, called the two parts of repentance
   a. mortification: sorrow of soul and dread conceived from the recognition of sin and the awareness of divine judgment: contrition→ man laid low
   b. vivification
      (1) some understand it as "the consolation that arises out of faith"
      (2) clarification:
         (a) not the happiness received by the mind after its fear has been quieted
         (b) rather, the desire (arising from rebirth) to live holily and devotedly

4. Penance under law and under gospel [postulated by those who attempted to group the various meanings of the word in Scripture (examples given)]
   a. of the law: sinner stricken by God's wrath and his own sin, is caught inextricably in that disturbed state
   b. of the gospel: sore afflicted, yet the sinner rises above it and lays hold on Christ as his medicine and comfort

Repentance Defined: Explanation of Its Elements, Mortification of the Flesh and Vivification of the Spirit [*5–9*]

5. Definition
   a. faith and repentance permanently bound
   b. discussion of Hebrew and Greek terms
      (1) *shuv* = conversion or return
      (2) *metanoia* = change of mind or of intention
   c. the definition:
      (1) "true turning of our life to God" [sect. 6]
      (2) a turning that arises from a pure and earnest fear of Him [sect. 7]; and
      (3) it consists in the mortification of our flesh and of the old man, and in the vivification of the spirit" [sect. 8]

   d. this is the sense in which prophets and apostles exhorted men to repentance

6. Repentance as turning to God [part 1 of definition in par. 5]
   a. implies a transformation, not only in outward works, but in the soul itself
   b. this demonstrated from Ezek., Deut., Jer., James, Isa.

7. Fear of God the beginning of repentance [part 2 of definition in par. 5]
   a. to arouse the mind of the sinner to repentance it must think on divine judgment: hence the frequent yoking of judgment and repentance in Scripture
   b. sometimes lesser punishments are inflicted to alert the sinner out of his slothfulness of flesh and his obstinacy to an awareness of greater punishments to come: God has to be severe, as gentle dealings do not work
   c. all human virtue, shorn of worship due God, is sheer abomination

8. Mortification and vivification as component parts of repentance [part 3 of definition in par. 5]
   a. repentance requires first the destruction of the whole evil flesh, indeed a difficult thing: self-denial
   b. then only comes the second phase of repentance, wherein the Spirit steeps our souls with new thoughts and feelings

9. Rebirth in Christ!
   a. as our mortification is participation in Christ's death, so our vivification is participation in Christ's resurrection
   b. thus repentance is regeneration: the restoration of the disfigured image of God in us
   c. but the restoration of this image is a growing process throughout life

Believers Experience Sanctification, but not Sinless Perfection in this Life [***10–15***]

10. Believers are still sinners
    a. the freedom from bondage to the flesh which regeneration brings still does not end the life-long struggle, even for the saints

b. in disagreement with Augustine, we do not hesitate, on Paul's authority, to denominate post-regeneration tendencies toward evil as "sin"

11. In believers sin has lost its dominion, but it still dwells in them
    a. baptism purges the guilt, but not the substance of sin: the traces remain, as Scripture shows
    b. the precept to love God is not fulfilled unless our whole love is turned away from self to God: therefore any remaining transgression of the law is still sin

12. What does "natural corruption" mean?
    a. God, the author of nature, condemns only those inclinations in us which contravene His will (and which are the result of our fallen nature)
    b. this agrees with Augustine, although he is hesitant to call it flatfootedly "sin"

13. Augustine as witness to the sinfulness of believers [quotations adduced to buttress Calvin's interpretation of post-regeneration failings as sin (esp. *Against Julian*)]

14. Against the illusion of perfection
    a. the antinomianism of the Anabaptists rejected: that after spiritual regeneration man reenters the state of innocence, in which all moral controls can be removed, the Spirit leading the regenerate
    b. here is indeed a wrong view of Christ and of the Holy Spirit: inevitable when we seek Him outside the Scriptures
    c. rather, Scripture is the place to seek the Spirit of the Lord, where we are taught about Him:
        (1) the Holy Spirit is given to us for sanctification, to purge us and lead us into obedience to God's righteousness
        (2) we are purged by the Holy Spirit's sanctification, but still remain besieged by vices against which we must daily fight

15. Repentance according to II Corinthians 7:11 (exposition): Sorrow→
    a. earnestness or carefulness (to escape the devil's snares, and to keep under the Holy Spirit)→
    b. excuse (purification, asking pardon rather than denying one's offense or extenuating one's fault)→

c. indignation (the sinner inwardly finds fault with himself, recognizing his own perversity and ungratefulness toward God)→
d. fear (the trembling in the mind when we recognize what we deserve, and God's dreadful wrath toward sinners)→ humility, increased caution→
e. longing (recognition of our sins leads us to diligence in duty and readiness to obey)→
f. zeal (ardor aroused when these spurs are applied to us)→
g. avenging (the greater the severity we show to our own sins, the more hope we should have in God's favor and mercy): but with restraint, lest sorrow engulf us

The Fruits of Repentance: Holiness of Life, Confession and Remission of Sins; Repentance Is Lifelong [*16–20*]

16. Outward and inward repentance
    a. as the prophets frequently demonstrate, true repentance begins, not in external ceremonies, but in the inner disposition of heart
    b. the marks of sincere repentance will be systematically set forth in "The Life of the Christian Man" [chs. 6–10]
    c. there are certain useful outward exercises ("avenging") which promote repentance, but
        (1) (as the old writers sometimes tend to do) these are not to be relied on too much
        (2) nor to be made more rigid than the gentleness of the church calls for

17. The outward practice of penance must not become the chief thing
    a. repentance is the conversion of the entire heart to God, not the fasting and weeping that sometimes accompany this change of disposition
    b. however, there were in the Old Testament, and are today, times which call for such public manifestations of repentance: especially in times of impending disaster (cf. IV.12.17)

18. Confession of sin before God and before men
    a. yet repentance is improperly applied to this external profession

b. not only are daily offenses to be repented, but our graver offenses should compel us to recall to our minds sins long since buried: example of David harking back to his very birth
c. special versus ordinary repentance
   (1) God dramatically calls back some who have utterly fallen into spiritual death: special repentance
   (2) this should not, by contrast, lead us to slacken our day-to-day efforts of ordinary repentance for our corruption of nature

19-20. Repentance and forgiveness of sins
a. repentance and forgiveness of sins are interrelated: this is seen in the yoking of repentance and the kingdom of God/heaven in the Gospels [19]
b. repentance is the prior condition of forgiveness, but not the basis of our deserving pardon: rather, because the Lord has determined to have pity in the end that they may repent, He indicates in what directions one should proceed if one wishes to obtain grace [20]

Sins for Which There Is No Repentance or Pardon [*21-25*]

21. Repentance as God's free gift
a. repentance is a gift from God which He gives by the Spirit of regeneration to whom He wills, although He enjoins repentance upon all
b. faith, repentance, and God's mercy are inseparably bound: fear of God evidences the working of salvation in man
c. the teaching of Hebrews that post-baptismal sins are not to be forgiven is not to be interpreted broadly as some do: the only unforgivable sin is the sin against the Holy Spirit, which arises out of desperate madness

22. Unpardonable sin: knowingly to strive against the Holy Spirit
a. wrong definitions
   (1) Augustine: persistent stubbornness even to death, with distrust of pardon
   (2) envy of grace bestowed upon one's brother
b. the true definition: "They sin against the Holy Spirit who, with evil intention, resist God's truth, although by its brightness they are so touched they cannot claim ignorance": knowledge plus unbelief

23. How the impossibility of "second repentance" is to be understood [I John 2:19; Heb. 6 and 10]
    a. a return to the communion of Christ is not open to those who knowingly and willingly have rejected it
    b. not those of dissolute life who transgress God's Word, but those who deliberately reject its entire teaching; not any particular failing, but complete turning away from God—apostasy of the whole man

24. Those who cannot be forgiven are those who cannot repent
    a. because of their ungratefulness, such sinners are stricken by God's just judgment
    b. some Scriptural expressions which describe God's refusal to answer sinners' cries are shown to refer not to whole-hearted turning to God in repentance but rather to the blind torment that distracts the reprobate when he sees that he must seek God in order to find a remedy for his misfortunes, and yet flees at His approach

25. Sham repentance and honest repentance
    a. Scriptural instances of God's kindly answer to sham repentance explained as a temporary mitigation or suspension of punishments which will eventually come
    b. thus God, even by these acts of temporary kindness urges men to repentance, although He does not thereby bind himself by perpetual law to pardon obdurate sinners

CHAPTER 4
How Far from the Purity of the Gospel Is All that the Sophists in Their Schools Prate about Repentance; Discussion of Confession and Satisfaction

***The Scholastic Doctrine of Confession and Contrition, with its Alleged Scriptural Basis, Examined** [**1–6**]*

1. The Scholastic doctrine of penance
    a. we intend to cover as briefly as possible the Scholastic teaching on repentance
    b. ancient patristic clichés about repentance—uttered not to de-

fine it but to urge men not to fall again into sinfulness—misapplied by the Scholastics of our day

c. the doctrine of the later Scholastics is an outward practice calculated to tame the flesh and punish faults; but they do not touch at all the inward renewal of the mind

d. inadequacy of traditional division of repentance
   (1) contrition of heart
   (2) confession of mouth
   (3) satisfaction of works

e. the absurd questions they agonize over prove their ignorance of the whole matter

2. The Scholastic doctrine of penance torments the conscience
   a. they tie the three steps in repentance also to forgiveness of sins
   b. but in making the required contrition commensurate with the size of the sin confessed, and in requiring a full confession, they torture consciences, who cannot know for certain whether they are carrying out such requirements

3. Not the sinner's contrition, but the Lord's mercy awaits
   a. can the Scholastics show anyone who, believing their doctrine of contrition, has not
      (1) either been driven to desperation, or
      (2) met God's judgment with pretended rather than true sorrow?
   b. forgiveness of sins can never come to anyone without repentance, but it is not the cause of forgiveness of sins: let us fix our attention not on our own tears, but on the Lord's mercy
   c. those excluded from forgiveness:
      (1) Pharisees, sated with their own righteousness and unable thus to recognize their own poverty
      (2) despisers, who, oblivious of God's wrath, do not seek a remedy for their own evil
   d. the difference between the gospel and Scholastic teaching:
      (1) forgiveness of sins is deserved by a full contrition (not performable by the sinner) or
      (2) enjoin the sinner to hunger and thirst after God's mercy to show him—through the recognition of his own misery, vacillation, weariness, captivity—where to seek refreshment, rest, and freedom: in humility give glory to God

4. Confession not enjoined: refutation of Scholastic allegorical argument from the lepers that were cleansed
    a. conflict between canon lawyers and Scholastic theologians concerning confession:
        (1) canon lawyers: confession commanded only by ecclesiastical constitutions
        (2) scholastic theologians: confession enjoined by divine precept
    b. chief "proof text": (Matt. 8:4 and parallels)
        (1) priests to determine leprosy (Lev. 14:2–3)
        (2) sin is spiritual leprosy
        (3) therefore priests have duty to pronounce on this
    c. refutation:
        (1) all the priesthood and all its duties have been transferred to Christ
        (2) why then did Christ send the cured lepers to the priests?
            (a) to obey the civil (not ritual) law
            (b) thus the priests were compelled, even against their will, to acknowledge Christ's miracle
        (3) Chrysostom: Christ did this on account of the Jews, in order not to be considered a transgressor of the law

5. The unbinding of Lazarus misapplied (bad allegorization)
    a. John 11:44: the Lord, they say, bade the disciples unbind the risen Lazarus and let him go
    b. actually the Lord did not say this to His disciples, but rather to the Jews, to allay suspicion of fraud and display His greater power (Chrysostom)
    c. assuming that the disciples were the intended audience, though, it could be more aptly allegorized as meaning that those raised up by Him were to be reminded that their sins were forgotten and forgiven and were not to be more harshly treated by men than the Judge had treated them

6. Scriptural Confession
    a. what about the frequent Scriptural injunction that we are to "confess our sins to one another"?
    b. this has reference to fellow believers, not to priests exclusively:
        (1) we should lay our infirmities on one another's breasts, to receive among ourselves mutual compassion and mutual consolation

(2) we must confess our sins before our merciful God, before the angels, the church, before all men

Evidence for the Late Origin of Auricular Confession [*7–8*]

7. Compulsory confession unknown in the ancient church
   a. compulsory confession came with the fourth Lateran Council under Innocent III: previously all confession was free
   b. a learned witticism on "*omnis utriusque sexus*": everyone of both sexes—for hermaphrodites only?
   c. proof that compulsory confession was [a late ecclesiastical regulation]—nothing instituted by Christ, and not even by the early church
      (1) Sozomen's testimony concerning the *penitentiarius,* a special confession-hearing priest in the Eastern church
      (2) abandonment of this practice in Constantinople under Nectarius, because of scandal

8. Chrysostom does not enjoin confession to men
   a. Chrysostom repeatedly commends confession directly to God
   b. he was not setting men free from divinely enjoined commands, but (on good Scriptural grounds) keeping men's consciences free from encumbrances

Scriptural Confession of Sins, Public and Private [*9–13*]

9. Confession before God
   a. plan: first to relate the kind of confession taught in God's Word; then to examine our opponents' inventions
   b. mistranslation of Hebrew word אוֹדֶה in Ps. 7:17 and elsewhere as "to confess" (Septuagint and Vulgate)
   c. in Scripture: the Lord forgives; therefore let us pour out our hearts to Him: evidence from David (Psalms), Daniel, John

10. Confession of sins before men
   a. first, secret confession before God
   b. second, if there is need to proclaim God's mercy among men, public confession before men (but only if divine glory or our humiliation requires it)
   c. in Israel, after the priest recited the words, the people were to confess their iniquities publicly in the temple (Lev. 16:21); in like manner we are, by confessing our own wretchedness, to

show forth the goodness and mercy of our God, both among ourselves and before the whole world

11. General confession of sin
    a. two sorts of public confession
        (1) ordinary
            in a congregation, even if some be innocent, they partake in the guilt of the entire body, and should join in confession
        (2) extraordinary
            when all the people are guilty of some transgression in common, this calls for extraordinary public confession
    b. the order of service in a Christian congregation should begin with some public rite of confession, not only to pray for pardon, but also to shake off our great complacency and sluggishness
        (1) thus this ancient rite, part of the law's tutelage, pertains in a way to us as well
        (2) by framing a formula of confession in his own and the people's name, the minister opens the gate to prayer both to individuals in private and to all in public

12. Private confession in the cure of souls
    a. two forms of private confession
        (1) made for our own sake, for mutual counsel and consolation
        (2) made for our neighbor's sake, for reconciliation and making up to him for our injuries to him
    b. James (5:16) suggests we choose the most suitable person in the congregation (not necessarily the pastor) to confess to
    c. but to ministers especially is this task assigned, ordained to witness to and sponsor divine mercy
        (1) the believer, privately troubled and afflicted with a sense of sins, and unable to free himself from them without outside help, may freely use private confession to his own pastor
        (2) but this sort of confession is free and not bound by any man-made restrictions
        (3) pastors are to leave this freedom to the churches and are to defend it, in order to avoid tyranny in their ministry and superstition in the people

13. Private confession for the removal of an offense (second form)
    a. the classic pattern is seen in Matt. 5:23–24
    b. this may involve even excommunication from the fellowship for a time, until the sinner has obediently yielded to correction: Cyprian describes this practice of *exomologesis* in the early church
    c. frequent communion approved as a remarkable benefit for encumbered consciences, provided tyranny and superstition are excluded

The Power of the Keys, and Absolution [*14–15*]

14. Nature and value of the power of the keys
    a. power of keys has a place in three kinds of confession:
        (1) when the entire church with solemn recognition of its faults implores pardon
        (2) when an individual, who has by some notable transgression committed a common offense, declares his repentance
        (3) when one who needs a minister's help on account of a troubled conscience discloses his weakness to him
    b. absolution, public and private
        (1) when the whole church stands before God's judgment seat, confesses itself guilty and takes its sole refuge in God's mercy, it is a great benefit to have present there the ambassador of Christ, armed with the mandate of reconciliation
        (2) similar is the benefit when one estranged from the fellowship receives pardon and is restored to brotherly unity
        (3) equally beneficial is private absolution, when a man lays open his heart to his pastor, and receives from his pastor the gospel message that sets him free from tormenting anxiety
    c. but the "power of the keys" is never to be separated from the preaching of the gospel

15. Summary of the Roman doctrine of confession
    a. points on which the Romanists agree
        (1) all persons "of both sexes" as soon as they attain the age of discretion are to confess their sins at least once a year to their own priest

(2) their sins are not forgiven unless they have a firmly conceived intent to confess them
(3) further, if they do not carry out this intent when offered, paradise is no longer open to them
(4) the priest has this power to bind and loose from Matt. 18:18

b. points on which they disagree
(1) power consists in either one or two keys, or more
(a) some say one: the power to bind and loose, to which knowledge is joined as accessory
(b) some say two: discretion and power
(c) others add the authority to discern (in passing sentence), and power exercised in executing their sentence, and knowledge as counselor
(2) when it is objected that priests may have bound or loosed unworthy persons who will not be so bound or loosed in heaven, they assert
(a) keys are given to all priests by Christ and conferred by bishops on them at promotion
(b) sentence of priests approved by heaven if justly pronounced
(c) power of keys remains with priests so long as they perform their ecclesiastical functions; in a rusted and bound form with excommunicated and suspended clergy
(d) these are modest statements in comparison with those who teach the new doctrine of a treasury of merits (see III.5.2)

Criticism of Romanist Errors and Injurious Practices Related to Confession and Satisfaction [*16–25*]

16. The enumeration of all sins is impossible
a. are all sins to be recounted?
b. David in the Psalms cannot begin to number his own sins, when he confesses his innumerable sins before God
c. why, then, should we?

17. The requirement of complete (integral) confession is a measureless torment
a. the sinner, called upon to classify, weigh, and confess in detail every sin of which he is guilty can only end up in despair

b. then the Romanists offer this remedy: at least do everything within your power: but the sinner is then tormented—have I done everything I can?
c. then this remedy: at least repent of your negligence; if it is not utterly careless, it will be forgiven—but even this does not allay the terror struck by the voice resounding in the ears: "Confess all your sins"
d. reply: it is stupid to suppose that we can remember all the sins committed in a single day, let alone a whole year!

18. The pernicious effect of demanding complete confession
    a. such confession could only give a momentary surcease from a troubled conscience at best
    b. the true nature of this law of full confession
        (1) it is simply impossible and can only lead to despair
        (2) it turns men into hypocrites, for they are so busy cataloguing their outward sins that they overlook the mass of secret sins within
    c. is, then, not each single sin to be confessed? We are rather to pour out our whole heart to God, and having done so, ask that all our remaining secret errors be cleansed, as David said
    d. long ages of confessional practice in the church deny that sins are forgiven only when there is a firmly conceived will to confess, and that paradise is closed to anyone who has neglected an opportunity to confess; many men were absolved without confession to a priest, and without such conditions
    e. certainty of binding and loosing does not lie within the competence of earthly judgment, for the minister of the Word cannot know the faith and repentance of him who confesses (the ground of absolution) and when he duly performs his functions, can absolve only conditionally

19. Against auricular confession
    a. a plague upon the church, it should be abolished forthwith!
    b. sinning throughout the year, men vomit up their sins upon the priest as if they were transmitting God's judgment from themselves to the priest
    c. how reluctantly do men go to this yearly confession, except possibly priests, who enjoy exchanging anecdotes of their misdeeds as if they were amusing stories
    d. Nectarius knew what he was doing when he removed the

penitentiarius from his church to avoid scandal; these people are guilty of infinite scandals by their practice of auricular confession

20. Baseless appeal to the power of the keys
    a. the confessioners base this sort of confession on the power of the keys
    b. the true meaning of the power of the keys
        (1) given to the apostles: are their priestlings vicars or successors of the apostles?
        (2) the power of the Holy Spirit given prior to the power of the keys: have their confessioners received the power of the Holy Spirit?
        (3) if they claim that power, we ask: can the Holy Spirit err?
    c. conclusion: no priestlings have the power of the keys who without discrimination repeatedly loose what the Lord had willed to be bound, and bind what He had bidden to be loosed

21. The uncertainty of priestly binding and loosing
    a. the anomaly: the promise of binding and loosing given only to those who bind and loose rightly; but they entrust it sometimes to evil ministrants who usurp power without knowledge and misuse the power: are they then false in their claim, or has Christ made a lying promise?
    b. their evasion: Christ's statement is limited according to the merits of him who is being bound or loosed: we have the Word to measure this worthiness
    c. if, as they admit, a good many priests use the keys wrongly, how can I be sure I am being rightly absolved by a priest?
    d. this power which they claim, apart from God's Word, is nothing or is to be considered as nothing

22. The difference between perverted and right use of the power of the keys
    a. objection: if absolution depends on faith, it will always remain ambiguous and the minister, not qualified to judge of faith, is not sure about absolution
    b. answer:
        (1) their basis for absolution is a full confession, wisely weighed by the priest who hears; but if confession is not full (and how can it be?) the hope of pardon is impaired

   (2) the priest has to suspend judgment so long as he is unsure whether the sinner is recounting his confession in good faith
   (3) most priests are so ignorant that they cannot exercise this office anyway

c. so long as some sins remain unconfessed, whatever the priests may say by way of absolution is unfruitful; and the confessing one is left in anxiety because he is dependent upon the discretion of the priest, not the Word of God

d. Calvin's teaching:
   (1) absolution is conditional upon the sinner's trust that God is merciful to him, provided he sincerely seek expiation in Chirst's sacrifice and be satisfied with the grade offered him
   (2) the minister, functioning as a herald, cannot err when he publishes what has been dictated to him by the Word of God

23. Perverse claims exposed

a. we will deal with the power of the keys under the section on the government of the church (IV.12.1–13)

b. yet here it is necessary to separate Christ's utterances on excommunication and on the preaching of the gospel from their absurd application of them to auricular and secret confession
   (1) the power to absolve which they falsely claim by apostolic succession is really only the testimony of a pardon taken from the freely-given promise of the gospel
   (2) public confession, not secret confession, depends upon the discipline of the church and is, by way of example, to remove public offense from the church

c. Lombard and his tribe rake together all kinds of proofs that confession of sins always involves a priest as examiner; while God simply requires repentance and faith; they, by adding penalties and satisfactions of their own, sacrilegiously bind and limit God's grace

24. Summary

a. there is no function more proper to God than the forgiveness of sins, where our salvation rests; consciences are to be bound to the Word, not to men

b. these Romanists pass off man-made laws as divine, barbarously binding consciences to human regulations

c. main points of critique:
   (1) this tyranny was introduced at an ebb point in the history of the church
   (2) it is a pestilential law which drives God-fearers to despair and unconcerned unbelievers to a sluggish false sense of security
   (3) their mitigations of their teaching only serve to camouflage their impiety and to obscure and corrupt pure doctrine

25. General presentation and refutation of the Roman doctrine
   a. the third part of penance, according to their teaching, is satisfaction: they hold that men actually do obtain pardon for transgressions from God's kindness, but only through the intervening merit of works, by which the offense of our sins may be paid for, in order that due satisfaction may be made to God's justice.
   b. the answer of Scripture to this: freely-given remission of sins
      (1) it is not the receipt-giving Creditor who forgives, but He who, without any payment, willingly cancels the debt
      (2) "freely-given" means no satisfactions required
      (3) through Christ's name alone we receive forgiveness, and through nothing else

***The Grace of Christ alone Provides True Satisfaction for Sin and Peace to the Conscience** [26–27]*

26. Christ has provided full satisfaction
   a. Schoolmen's teaching summarized:
      (1) forgiveness of sins and reconciliation take place once for all when in baptism we are received through Christ into God's grace
      (2) after this, only through satisfactions can we overcome post-baptismal sins
      (3) these come to us through the keys of the church as the sole dispenser of Christ's blood
   b. answer: I John 2:lff. teaches Christ as our perpetual advocate, not as one possible satisfaction among others
   c. we share in the expiation made by Christ only if the whole honor therefore rests upon Him

27. The Roman doctrine deprives Christ of honor, and the conscience of every assurance

a. Christ's honor is to be kept whole
   (1) Christ by His own death slew the force and curse of sin, assuming the whole burden of our sins upon Himself
   (2) it is false to assert that after the initial purgation each one of us feels the efficacy of Christ's suffering solely in proportion to the measure of satisfying penance
b. consciences assured of pardon for sin are to have peace with God
   (1) it is absurd to assert that the grace of God operates in the first forgiveness of sins, but in subsequent sins our works cooperate in obtaining the second pardon
   (2) how can a conscience be quieted if told that sins are redeemed by satisfactions—and when have enough satisfactions been made?
   (3) Scripture teaches nothing but the repeated action of Christ's dying for us: again and again are our sins so redeemed

***Various Distinctions and Objections Critically Examined** [28–39]*

28. Venial and mortal sins
   a. our opponents take refuge in the distinction between venial and mortal sins, with their differing remedies
   b. but they cannot really distinguish the two categories except to call impiety and uncleanness of heart a venial sin
   c. with Scripture, we hold that all sins deserve death; but a sin is venial on a believer's part by God's mercy in Christ which wipes it away
   d. before God's law all sins equally deserve death
   e. it is impossible to make satisfaction for sin; for while men are doing this they are heaping up more sins

29. Forgiveness of sins involves remission of penalty
   a. their way out: distinction between penalty and guilt
      (1) guilt is remitted by God's mercy
      (2) but penalty remains thereafter to be paid to God's justice
   b. an anomaly: after admitting forgiveness of guilt is free, they teach that men must deserve it, work for it
   c. we have already shown that Scripture everywhere denies this distinction of guilt and penalty

d. however, here are other Scriptural testimonies to clinch the matter:
   (1) "God will remember our sins no more"
   (2) "will not reckon them to our account but keep them hidden"
   (3) sins: from scarlet to snow
   (4) conclusion: God remits all penalty of vengeance

30. Christ's unique sacrifice can alone remove both penalty and guilt
   a. "the chastisement (correction) of our peace" = the penalty Christ paid on our behalf
   b. *apolutrosis* in Paul means not mere redemption, but the price and satisfaction of redemption
   c. the law of Moses prescribes in detail the rites of expiation:
      (1) these are not works but sacrifices
      (2) the Israelite sacrifices look to Christ's unique sacrifice
   d. our opponents evasively distinguish between eternal and temporal penalities: in Scripture pardon of guilt includes remissions of penalties, and both are free

31. Misinterpretations of Scripture exposed: God's judgments, penal and corrective [Calvin answers his foes' use of proof texts by setting forth a twofold divine judgment]
   a. judgment of vengeance: the Judge toward the reprobate
   b. judgment of chastisement: the Father toward His chosen sons

32. God's judgment in vengeance has a wholly different purpose from that of His judgment in chastisement: the distinction
   a. first distinction:
      (1) punishment for vengeance: God's wrath
      (2) punishment for chastisement: God's love
   b. this basic distinction to be traced throughout Scripture; Scriptural passages adduced
   c. seeming contradiction: God's chastisement toward His elect: this is for their own good

33. Judgment of vengeance serves to punish; judgment of chastisement to improve
   a. second distinction: the scourges of the wicked are the beginning of the punishment they will suffer according to His judgment

b. but God punishes His church to bring it low and cause it to repent; Scriptural instances of this divine instruction
c. Augustine similarly distinguishes between God's dealing with the saints and the wicked

34. The believer undergoing God's chastisement is not to lose heart
a. the believer, unlike the unbeliever (who thinks God is a punishing judge) must recognize that God's severity is anger at vices, but love and mercy toward himself
b. sometimes, however, it seems that God is harsher toward His own people than toward the impious
c. the admonition of the law is a comfort here: the pious are being called back to the way of salvation, but unbelievers go down in error
d. there is no difference between everlasting and temporal penalties

35. The punishment of David
a. David was punished to teach him that God is displeased with murder and adultery; also the penalty for taking the forbidden census, a scourge of David's people, was for a public example of all ages and for David's humiliation (although God had freely forgiven David's guilt)
b. in like manner, though by grace we are forgiven by God, the penalties of original sin remain with us to teach us, thus humbled, to aspire more eagerly to true blessedness
c. God adjusts the severity of the penalties we suffer to our particular need
d. but why look only at the example of David? There are many other Scriptural examples of free absolution, without imposition of punishment

36. Good works as redemption of punishment
a. "recompense of punishment" in Dan. 4:27 refers not to God but to men: Daniel is asking the cruel Nebuchadnezzar to become kindly toward his people
b. "love covers a multitude of sins" in Prov. 10:12 applies to men, not to God
c. "by mercy and kindness sins are atoned for" (Prov. 16:6) does not refer to appeasing God by good works, but to God's pleasure toward those who have repented and turn toward Him (as proved in their actions)

37. The woman who was a sinner (Luke 7:36–50)
    a. the Pharisees' view:
        (1) Christ did not know the woman whom He pardoned
        (2) if He had known her He would not have pardoned her
        (3) consequently, thus deceived, Christ could not be a prophet
    b. but Christ told a parable to show she was not a sinner, because her sins were forgiven: her love was not the cause, but the proof of forgiveness of sins (argument *a posteriori*)

38. The Roman doctrine cannot claim the authority of the church fathers
    a. the fathers may have spoken sometimes in an untutored way about satisfactions—e.g., Chrysostom and "Augustine"—but never as our contemporary advocates of satisfactions
    b. "satisfaction" in its older meaning was not recompense for sins already committed, but caution lest future sins be committed

39. The Schoolmen corrupt the teaching of the fathers
    a. in the age of the fathers, satisfaction was not a payment paid to God but a testimony before the church of the sinner's repentance
    b. from this ancient rite the debased confessions and satisfactions of today took their origin
    c. the Schoolmen have indiscriminately put together from questionable sources their patchwork: e.g., from pseudo-Augustine's *On Repentance*

CHAPTER 5
The Supplements that They Add to Satisfactions, Namely, Indulgences and Purgatory

The Erroneous Doctrine of Indulgences and Its Evil Consequences [*1–5*]

1. Indulgences according to Romanist doctrine, and the mischief caused by them
    a. their definition: indulgences are the distribution of merits of Christ and the saints to supply for us the satisfactions we lack
    b. for centuries these pious frauds were tolerated by men, even though they were the cause of untold corruption and error

2. Indulgences contrary to Scripture
   a. many now see this as an evil traffic but do not know its true foundation: the so-called treasury of merits entrusted to the bishop of Rome and his underlings
   b. indulgences profane the blood of Christ, declaring against Scripture that it is insufficient
   c. antitheses:

(1) satisfaction in the blood of martyrs	(1) Christ was made sin, to make us righteous (II Cor. 5:21)
(2) Paul and others died for us	(2) Christ alone was crucified and died for them (I Cor. 1:13)
(3) another purchase price established: the blood of martyrs	(3) Christ acquired the church with His own blood (Acts 20:28)
(4) sanctification, otherwise insufficient, is perfected by the martyrs	(4) by a single offering Christ has perfected for all time those who are sanctified (Heb. 10:4)
(5) they wash their robes in the blood of the saints	(5) all the saints have washed their robes in the blood of the Lamb (Rev. 7:14)

3. Authorities against indulgences and merits of martyrs
   a. two authorities
      (1) Leo the Great: "the righteous have received, not given, crowns"
      (2) Augustine: "though as brethren we die for our brethren, no martyr's blood is shed for the forgiveness of sins"
   b. effect of this pernicious doctrine on the place of Christ
      (1) mingles the blood of martyrs with the blood of Christ: they having reputedly given to God more than they needed for themselves
      (2) they claim the martyrs' blood is fruitful only if shared for the good of the church, to be drawn upon in satisfactions
      (3) we assert that the saints' example kindled the church's zeal

4. Refutation of opposing Scriptural proofs
   a. their proof text: Col. 1:24: Paul in his own body supplies what was lacking in Christ's sufferings
   b. these sufferings actually refer not to the work of redemption, which is Christ's alone, but to the daily sufferings of the church, in which Christ shares, and which are for the church's upbuilding
   c. Augustine: expresses essentially the same interpretation of this verse

5. Indulgences oppose the unity and the comprehensive activity of the grace of Christ
   a. who taught the Pope to inclose in lead and parchment the grace of Jesus Christ?
   b. either the gospel of Christ or indulgences must be false
   c. probable origin: penitents upon whom severer exactions than they could bear were enjoined, sought relief from the church

Refutation of the Doctrine of Purgatory by an Exposition of the Scriptural Passages Adduced to Support It [*6–10*]

6. Refutation of the doctrine of purgatory is necessary
   a. some persons (e.g., Melanchthon) leave purgatory unmentioned in order to avoid excessive controversy: this is wrong, for this doctrine is grossly unscriptural and cannot be winked at
   b. purgatory is a deadly fiction of Satan, nullifies the cross of Christ, inflicts unbearable contempt upon God's mercy, and overturns and destroys our faith
   c. now that we have disposed of the Romanist doctrine of satisfactions, the very root of purgatory has been removed: all we really need to say now is that it is a dreadful blasphemy against Christ

7. Alleged proofs of purgatory from the Gospels
   a. Matt. 12:32; Mark 3:28f; Luke 12:10: "Sin against the Holy Spirit is not to be forgiven either in this age or in the age to come"
      (1) this hints that some sins are to be forgiven "in the age to come"
      (2) answer: the Lord is there speaking of the guilt of sin

b. Matt. 5:25-26: "Make friends with your adversary . . . lest sometime he hand you over to the judge, and the judge to the constable, and the constable to the prison . . . whence you cannot get out until you have paid the last penny"
   (1) if the judge signifies God; the accuser, Satan; the guard, the angel; then the prison does signify purgatory
   (2) but actually, Christ is here suggesting that men must act toward one another not according to the letter of the law (*summum jus*), but according to equity (*aequitas, epiekeia*); thus it does not refer to purgatory

8. Proofs alleged from Philippians, Revelation, II Maccabees
   a. Phil. 2:10: the knees of those in heaven, in earth, and in the nether regions bow to Christ
      (1) they claim that "nether regions" cannot refer to those eternally damned; it must apply to souls agonizing in purgatory
      (2) it actually means that dominion over all has been given to Christ, and "nether regions" simply means the devils who will at the end be brought before God's judgment seat
   b. Rev. 5:13: "I heard every creature in heaven and on earth and under the earth and in the sea . . .": merely means that all parts of the world, from the very peak of heaven even to the center of the earth, in their own way declare the glory of their Creator
   c. II Macc. 12:43: Judas Maccabeus sent an offering for the dead to Jerusalem
      (1) Maccabees is uncanonical [Calvin turns Augustine's support of this book against his opponents, also quoting Jerome against it]
      (2) Judas's act was not without superstition and wrong-headed zeal, but he did it in order that they might share in eternal life with the remaining believers who had died for country and religion—this has nothing to do with purgatory!

9. The crucial passage: I Cor. 3
   a. the Romanists interpret this as the fire of purgatory, by which the filth of sins is cleansed away that we may enter into the kingdom of God as pure men
   b. many early authorities, however, interpret the fire as refer-

ring to tribulation on the cross, through which the Lord tests His own that they may not linger in the filth of the flesh

c. but there is a clearer and truer interpretation even than this:
   (1) preliminary question: Do all the apostles and saints have to go through this so-called purgatorial fire? They answer, no. But Paul is talking about *all* men
   (2) "wood, hay, and stubble" are a metaphor for the doctrines devised by men's brains, which are tested by the fire of the Holy Spirit, and the works done on such a human foundation are lost

10. The appeal to the early church cannot help the Romanists
   a. but they say: it was a most ancient observance of the church; Paul answers that all must lose their work who build the church on an unsuitable foundation
   b. they say: it was a custom for 1,300 years; answer: by what authority, by what revelation of the Word of God?
      (1) mourning and burial are there; but not prayers for the dead
      (2) ancient writers who did use prayers for the dead realized they lacked both the command of God and lawful example: they did it by way of concession to human nature—therefore they are no example to imitate
   c. rites for the dead and annual rites for the cleansing of their souls were practiced among all Gentiles
      (1) these were imposed by Satan to delude mortals
      (2) but they did serve, nevertheless, to remind men that death is not destruction but a crossing over from this life to another
      (3) Scripture is superior here: blessed are the dead who die in the Lord, for henceforth they have rest from their labors (Rev. 14:13)
   d. the practice of the ancient church reviewed (prayers for the dead)
      (1) ancient writers allowed this because of public custom and common ignorance
      (2) some of the church fathers, including Augustine, were carried off into error
         (a) Augustine was dutifully carrying out his aged mother's request, not testing it by Scripture first
         (b) his book, *The Care to be Taken for the Dead,* is full of doubts and ought to cool off any foolish zeal on the

part of anyone who wants to play intercessor for the dead

e. the true rule to be followed: we are not to inject anything in our prayers not commensurate with the Word of God

f. even though the ancient church did use prayers for the dead, they did this far differently from the modern users of purgatory: the ancients were concerned with memory of the dead, and were quite clearly in doubt regarding the state of the dead—a far cry from the pipe dreams of purgatory of the Romanists, who preach care of the dead and preach it over all works of love

g. even the church fathers can be quoted against the prayers for the dead, including Augustine

h. enough has now been presented to disprove purgatory; why trouble readers with an endless recital of grosser superstitions?

THE LIFE OF THE CHRISTIAN MAN (6–10)

CHAPTER 6
The Life of the Christian Man; and First, by What Arguments Scripture Urges Us to It

1. Plan of the treatise
   a. object of regeneration: to manifest in the life of believers a harmony and agreement between God's righteousness and their obedience, and thus to confirm the adoption they have received as sons
   b. while God's law is capable of renewing our lost image, our slowness is such that we need help: hence here is culled from Scripture a pattern of living
   c. this collection of Scripture passages will be concise (I love brevity): for fuller disquisitions on individual virtues, see the church fathers
   d. both the philosophers and Scripture deal with the virtues, each with their own order, but the philosophers with pretentious affectation and explicit order; Scripture (Holy Spirit) without affectation and with order implicit

2. Motives for the Christian life
   a. two chief aspects of Scripture's moral teaching:
      (1) to instill the love of righteousness in our hearts
      (2) to provide us with a rule to keep our zeal for righteousness in the proper path
   b. Scripture calls us to holiness; not our own holiness, but a holiness infused in us when we cleave to God

3. The Christian life receives its strongest motive to God's work through the person and redemptive act of Christ
   a. while the philosophers merely exhort us to live according to "nature," God has given us a living pattern to follow in Jesus Christ, who is also our Savior
   b. failure to pursue righteousness is revolt both from God our Father, and Christ our Savior
   c. Scripture continually exhorts us to gratefulness to God for His gift of Christ to us
   d. the Scriptural foundation of life is far richer than the philosophers' commendation of the mere natural dignity of man

4. The Christian life is not a matter of tongue but of the inmost heart
   a. some emptily boast of the name "Christian" but are not touched by the gospel
   b. doctrine dealt with first, but it must enter our lives
   c. even the philosophers reject those who merely chatter about purity of life: why shouldn't we all the more be moved by the gospel than by cold exhortations of philosophers?

5. Imperfection and endeavor of the Christian life
   a. perfection is our goal, but imperfection is our earthly lot; so exclude no one from the church because he has not yet attained it
   b. integrity is our goal: sincere simplicity of mind, free from guile and feigning: the opposite of a "double heart"
   c. we are all encumbered, in varying degrees, so we must progress in the Christian life at varying rates

CHAPTER 7
The Sum of the Christian Life: The Denial of Ourselves

***The Christian Philosophy of Unworldliness and Self-Denial; We Are Not Our Own, We Are God's** [1–3]*

1. We are not our own masters, but belong to God
   a. man enabled to follow the Christ (the best plan of living) by a more explicit plan than that given in the law
      (1) beginning: "to present their bodies to God as a living sacrifice, holy and acceptable to Him"
      (2) basic exhortation: "be not conformed to the fashion of this world, but be transformed by the renewal of your minds"
   b. we are not our own, but the Lord's:
      (1) forget ourselves
      (2) live and die for God
   c. the first step in the Christian life: departure from self to total obedience to God—the sum of the Christian philosophy

2. Self-denial through devotion to God
   a. the second step: seek the Lord's will, not our own
      (1) Scripture, in enjoining self-denial, erases desire for power, glory, etc.
      (2) throughout life, the Christian's business is with God
   b. crucial place of self-denial
      (1) when we deny ourselves we leave no place to human vices spawned by self-love
      (2) when we fail to deny ourselves, these vices rage in us
      (3) prideful commendation of virtue by the philosophers contrasted to Christ's preference for harlots and publicans over the spiritually proud

3. Self-renunciation according to Titus, ch. 2
   a. grace of God offered
   b. two obstacles to it removed:
      (1) ungodliness
      (2) worldly desires
   c. all actions of life limited to three parts, which, when joined, mean perfection:
      (1) soberness
      (2) righteousness
      (3) godliness

d. but despite our efforts to devote ourselves to God and brethren, we find it difficult: hence Paul reminds us of our immortal hope

The Principle of Self-Denial in Our Fellow Men [*4–7*]

4. Self-denial gives us the right attitude toward our fellow men
   a. self-love is the chief impediment to righteousness
   b. the genesis of pride in self and envy and spite toward others
   c. the only remedy: to pluck out love of strife and of self, as Scriptural teaching bids; to remember all our gifts are from God and to acknowledge this in humble gratefulness
   d. a call to humility toward self and reverence toward others

5. Self-renunciation leads to proper helpfulness toward our neighbors
   a. the "works of love" can only be accomplished if we "get out of ourselves" and share our benefits with others
   b. the church as body with many members: stewardship of our God-given gifts to be tested by the rule of love

6. Love of neighbor is not dependent upon manner of men but looks to God
   a. we are to love our fellows not for their own merits but because they bear in themselves the image of God
   b. in this loving of those who hate us, we have to go against human nature

7. The outward work of love is not sufficient, but it is intention that counts!
   a. not the complete outward discharge of duties, but the inward sincerity in fulfilling them is what counts
   b. today alms are often given contemptuously—an attitude even the pagans did not tolerate
   c. true philanthropy has no other limit than that of the giver's resources

The Principle of Self-Denial in Our Relation to God [*8–10*]

8. Self-denial toward God: devotion to his will!
   a. an anatomy of human ambition: we madly seek after wealth or power, and fear and hate poverty and lowly station

b. against this "natural" tendency must be set the desire and hope of the Lord's blessing

9. Trust in God's blessing only
   a. if we believe that all our good rests upon God's blessing, we will stop pursuing worldly wealth and power
   b. bear in mind that God's blessing will not come upon those who use fraud, robbery, wickedness
   c. so minded, we will like David give God the credit for any good that comes to us

10. Self-denial helps us bear adversity
   a. self-denial: total resignation of every part of one's life to God's will
   b. this attitude must prevail over every affliction our lives are heir to
   c. keep our confidence that God will in all adversity give us the needed strength and support
   d. do not, like the pagans, charge all this up to fortune: God is the sole judge and governor of all that happens

CHAPTER 8
Bearing the Cross, a Part of Self-Denial

We Are to Take Up Our Cross, as Followers of Christ *[1–2]*

1. Christ's cross and ours
   a. God's will is that His adopted children lead a hard and unquiet life, just like Christ's own
   b. in our sufferings we share Christ's, and follow Him from earth to heaven
   c. thus our very sufferings are blessed and salvation-bearing

2. The cross leads us to perfect trust in God's power
   a. while Christ suffered affliction only to show His obedience to the Father, there are many reasons why we are afflicted
   b. God's method in affliction:
      (1) He afflicts
      (2) we succumb
      (3) we learn to call upon His power

(4) but even after becoming aware of God's grace, we tend to fall back in self-complacency (as David did), so new afflictions must come

c. in prosperity, confidence; shattered by adversity; we then betake ourselves to God's grace

This Is Needful to Teach Us Patience and Obedience [*3–6*]

3. The cross permits us to experience God's faithfulness and gives us hope for the future
   a. the cross is the source of all our blessings, as Paul teaches
   b. how the cross strengthens hope
      (1) our blind love cleansed
      (2) we feel our incapacity
      (3) distrust self
      (4) trust in God
      (5) persevere to the end
      (6) stand in His grace and understand His promise
      (7) our hope strengthened

4. The cross trains us to patience and obedience
   a. God has already, of course, conferred His blessing on the saints; but in their lives He tests and trains their obedience so it may come forth and become active, visible to them
   b. the cross also teaches them to live not according to their own whim, but according to God's will

5. The cross as medicine
   a. like horses fattened and idle for several days, we self-indulgently try to throw off God's yoke
   b. against this tendency to fall back into self-indulgence, the cross is our restraint and remedy
   c. God, as physician, treats each man as he requires

6. The cross as fatherly chastisement
   a. present affliction is also to remind us of, and to correct, past transgressions
   b. but chiefly to promote our salvation, for which we should be grateful
   c. differing purpose of affliction for believers and unbelievers: every cross attests to us God's steadfast love: Follow God! (cf. Cicero and Seneca)

Bearing the Cross in Persecution and Other Calamities [*7–8*]

7. Suffering for righteousness' sake
   a. to suffer persecution for righteousness is a comfort whether we experience it in proclaiming God's truth or in protecting the innocent
   b. all evils, even death itself, become happiness for us when God breathes upon us

8. Suffering under the cross, the Christian finds consolation in God
   a. we should cheerfully undergo afflictions at the Lord's hand
   b. but our joy will always be tempered by pain—how could one in indifference really benefit from such tribulation?

The Christian Meets Suffering as Sent by God, but with No Stoic Insensibility [*9–11*]

9. The Christian, unlike the Stoic, gives expression to his pain and sorrow
   a. Christian forebearance is no Stoic *apatheia*
   b. Christ's own experience of pain and suffering gives the lie to the Christian "new Stoics" who teach a like doctrine of emotionlessness

10. Real sorrow and real patience in conflict with each other
    a. the reality of the "double will" in the saints: torn one way by natural sense, another by disposition to godliness
    b. we feel the emotions of our nature—but we do not let them ultimately swamp us
    c. beyond all sorrow, be of good cheer in the conviction that God has willed all for us to follow

11. Patience according to philosophic and Christian understanding
    a. philosophers say: obey God because you have to
    b. Scripture has us see in God's will:
       (1) righteousness and equity
       (2) concern for our salvation
    c. our consolation is in the assurance that our cross is for our salvation
    d. our bitterness in bearing our cross is to be tempered with spiritual joy, and hence, thanksgiving and praise to the Lord

CHAPTER 9
Meditation on the Future Life

By Our Tribulations God Weans Us from Excessive Love of this Present Life [*1–2*]

1. The vanity of this life
   a. God, knowing our propensities, uses the best ways to draw us from love of the present world to contempt of it
   b. our aspiration for heavenly immortality is what sets us off from beasts
   c. but our nature constantly pulls us back to wallow in the present life
   d. to counter this tendency in us, God metes out appropriate afflictions for each man's particular failing
   e. the discipline of the cross teaches us that
      (1) this life, by itself, is vain and vitiated by many evils
      (2) but we are, conversely, to raise our eyes to heaven

2. Our tendency to leave unnoticed the vanity of this life
   a. there is no compromise between rejection and acceptance of the world
   b. we act as if the present life were going to go on forever for us
   c. hence we need constant and strong reminding of what life is truly like

A Right Estimate of the Present Life, which Is Transient and Unsatisfying, Leads Us to Meditate on the Life to Come [*3–6*]

3. Gratitude for earthly life!
   a. contempt of the present life does not mean ingratitude toward God
   b. daily earthly benefits are a preface to eternal glory
   c. both testimonies of Scripture and nature itself exhort us to thank the Lord for these benefits
   d. these benefits are a preparation for, a foretaste of the life to come

4. The right longing for eternal life
   a. men without the light of true religion were wise in wishing not to have been born or in rejoicing at funerals and lamenting at birthdays

b. in comparison with the heavenly life the present is to be despised; yet we are not to despise life itself, but treat it as a sentry's standing guard, for it is for God to determine the time of our departure from this life

5. Against the fear of death!
   a. nature prompts us to fear death, but Christian piety reminds us that the incorruptibility to come overrules that fear and comforts us
   b. all living things by nature crave to go on existing here, but also long for the final resurrection; men, endowed with understanding and illumined by the Spirit, should especially do so
   c. no further talk about this here: let those who wish more discussion ask the philosophers about contempt of death
   d. the more joyfully we await the day of death, the greater progress we have made in the school of Christ

6. The comfort prepared for believers by aspiration for the life to come
   a. our present happiness is to consist in our intent gaze (beyond present anguish) toward heaven
   b. then we can without difficulty bear the earthly prosperity of the wicked, knowing their ultimate destiny
   c. *in fine,* gazing upon the power of the resurrection, we will experience in our hearts the final triumph of Christ's cross over all wickedness

CHAPTER 10
How We Must Use the Present Life and Its Helps

The Good Things of This Life Are to Be Enjoyed as Gifts of God [1–2]

1. Double danger: mistaken strictness and mistaken laxity
   a. in the pilgrimage through this life, we are to use our God-given earthly benefits—whether for necessity or for delight—to help us on our way
   b. two extreme errors to be avoided
      (1) to govern one's life by a severe necessity, abstaining from all things one can do without
      (2) to use the things of this life without any restraint upon one's conscience whatsoever

c. both extremes are to be countered by the moderation of Scripture's teaching

2. The main principle
   a. God created earthly gifts for our good, not our ruin: let us therefore so use them
   b. a dual purpose—delight, as well as need—seen in:
      (1) teaching of Scripture
      (2) natural qualities of things themselves: beauty, savor, taste, etc.

We Are Not to Use these Blessings Indulgently, or to Seek Wealth Greedily, but to Serve Dutifully in Our Calling [*3–6*]

3. A look at the Giver of the gift prevents narrow-mindedness and immoderation
   a. against Stoicism with its emphasis on necessary use to the exclusion of lawful delight
   b. but also against freedom to lust, which equally leaves us incapable of thankfulness to God
   c. excessive food, elegant clothing, and all ostentation in living turn our minds from God

4. Aspiration to eternal life also determines aright our outward conduct of life
   a. contempt of the present life and meditation on the life to come is the basic principle
   b. this leads us to two rules for the conduct of life:
      (1) use this world as if not using it
      (2) bear poverty patiently; bear abundance moderately
   c. the first rule means: avoid excessive indulgence, cutting off superfluous wealth and licentiousness

5. Frugality, earthly possessions held in trust
   a. the second rule: moderation in both poverty and prosperity
   b. a third rule: all gifts are ours by God's kindness, entrusted to us for our benefit; an account of them is to be rendered at the end

6. The Lord's calling a basis of our way of life
   a. like a sentry set at his post by his commander, each man has a calling set out for him by the Lord

(1) this is to restrain man's fickleness and overweening ambition, and to give direction and purpose to his life

(2) for example, a private citizen cannot take political action to remove a tyrant; only a public man, called to political life, can do this

b. how the practice of one's calling is the very foundation of well-doing in our daily life

(1) God rejects even those seemingly good efforts we make outside our appointed calling

(2) we are to stay where God has placed us, following the divine guidance, in our misery and difficulty taking our consolation in the fact that God Himself has laid these burdens upon us, and that no task, however menial, is not precious in God's sight

CHAPTER 11
Justification by Faith: First the Definition of the Word and of the Matter

Justification and Regeneration, the Terms Defined [*1–4*]

1. Place and meaning of the doctrine of "justification"

a. summary of material already presented on faith and its benefits

(1) faith is that which enables us to grasp and possess Christ

(2) benefits of this faith are twofold

(a) being reconciled to God through Christ's blamelessness, we may have in heaven instead of a Judge a gracious Father

(b) sanctified by Christ's spirit we may cultivate blamelessness and purity of life

b. the importance of justification

2. The concept of justification

a. he is said to be justified in God's sight who is both reckoned righteous in God's judgment and has been accepted on account of his righteousness

b. justification by works and by faith compared

(1) he in whose life that purity and holiness will be found which deserves a testimony of righteousness before God's throne will be said to be justified by works

(2) he who, excluded from the righteousness of works, grasps the righteousness of Christ through faith, and clothed in it, appears in God's sight not as a sinner but as a righteous man, is said to be justified by faith

3. Scriptural usage
   a. difference in applying the term to God and to man
      (1) applied to God, "to justify" simply means to render to God and His teaching the praise they deserve
      (2) applied to man, "to justify" means nothing else than to acquit of guilt him who was accused, as if his innocence were confirmed
   b. since God justifies us by the intercession of Christ, He absolves us not by the confirmation of our own innocence but by the imputation of righteousness, so that we who are not righteous in ourselves may be reckoned as such in Christ
   c. justification is really an interpretation of forgiveness

4. Justification as gracious acceptance by God and as forgiveness of sins
   a. justification as "acceptance"
   b. justification as "imputation of righteousness," where righteousness means opposition to guilt
   c. justification as reconciliation

Refutation of Osiander's Doctrine of "Essential Righteousness" [*5–12*]

5. Osiander's doctrine of essential righteousness
   a. the whole problem is raised because Osiander does not understand that the bond of our union with Christ is the secret power of His Spirit
   b. Osiander is not content with the righteousness which has been acquired for us by Christ's obedience and sacrificial death, but pretends that we are substantially righteous in God by the infusion both of His essence and of His quality

6. Osiander erroneously mixes forgiveness of sins with rebirth
   a. Osiander's claim: that God justifies not only by pardoning but by regeneration; that is, God does not leave as they were by nature those whom He justifies, but rather changes their vices
   b. answer: indeed, righteousness and sanctification are inseparable, but reason itself forbids us to transfer the peculiar qual-

ities of the one to the other, as in the analogy of light and heat from the sun

7. The significance of faith for justification
   a. Osiander's objection: something else other than faith is necessary in order to produce justification, namely, the conveying of essential righteousness by God rather than Christ alone
   b. reply: indeed, faith alone cannot justify, for faith is always weak and imperfect
   c. properly speaking, God alone justifies; then we transfer this same function to Christ because He was given to us for righteousness

8. Osiander's doctrine that Christ is, according to His divine nature, our righteousness
   a. Osiander's opinion is that, since Christ is God and man, He is made righteousness for us with respect to His divine nature, not His human nature
   b. reply: but if our righteousness lies in Christ's divinity, we receive this gift not peculiarly from Christ; then in what sense would it be consistent to say that He was "made for us"
   c. refutation based on Jer. 51:10

9. Justification as the work of the Mediator
   a. Osiander's objection: the work of justification can be ascribed only to divine nature
   b. reply: Christ fulfilled the office of priest according to His human nature; in His flesh, Christ's righteousness has been manifested to us
   c. we are justified in Christ, insofar as He was made an atoning sacrifice for us: something that does not comport with His divine nature

10. What is the nature of our union with Christ?
    a. we are deprived of this utterly incomparable good until Christ is made ours
    b. the joining of Head and members is a mystical union; a spiritual bond
    c. Osiander's doctrine of essential righteousness and essential indwelling has a twofold result:
       (1) Osiander holds that God pours Himself into us as a

gross mixture, just as he fancies a physical eating in the Lord's Supper

(2) God breathes His righteousness upon us, by which we may be really righteous with Him, since according to Osiander this righteousness is both God Himself and the goodness or holiness or integrity of God

11. Osiander's doctrine of the essential righteousness nullifies the certainty of salvation
    a. Osiander's teaching that we are righteous together with God tries to waft us above the clouds, thus preventing our calling upon God with quiet hearts
    b. Osiander's objections
        (1) "to be justified" is not a legal term
        (2) we are not justified by free imputation
    c. reply:
        (1) the antithesis between pardoning and accusation clearly shows that the expression was taken from legal usage
        (2) the pardoning of sins is not a partial gift; it is complete, and includes the whole of righteousness in free remission
    d. Osiander's objection: it would be insulting to God and contrary to His nature that He should justify those who actually remain wicked
    e. reply: justification and regeneration must be kept distinct because traces of sin always remain in the righteous; therefore justification must be granted not in part but liberally, while regeneration is a gradual process of reformation into newness of life

12. Refutation of Osiander
    a. Osiander's objection: Christ has become wisdom for us, but this applies only to the eternal Word; therefore Christ the man is not righteousness
    b. reply: the only-begotten Son of God was indeed His eternal wisdom, but what Paul here says applies not to the essence of the Son of God but to our use, and rightly fits Christ's human nature
    c. further argument from Osiander that our righteousness is derived from the divine nature of Christ
    d. reply: it is not to be denied that the righteousness Christ bestows upon us is the righteousness of God, which proceeds

from Him; yet, in Christ's death and resurrection there is righteousness and life for us

e. while righteousness is defined by Osiander as that by which we are moved to act rightly, and that this is the action of God alone, it must be seen whether He does this of Himself and directly or through the hand of His Son

f. in short, whoever wraps up two kinds of righteousness in order that miserable souls may not repose wholly in God's mere mercy, crowns Christ in mockery with a wreath of thorns

Refutation of Scholastic Doctrines of Good Works as Effective for Justification [*13–20*]

13. Righteousness by faith and righteousness by works
    a. faith-righteousness so differs from works-righteousness that when one is established the other has to be overthrown
    b. a man who wishes to obtain Christ's righteousness must abandon his own righteousness
    c. it is necessary that there be no occasion for our own boasting, which would result in our pointing to works-righteousness

14. Likewise, the works of the regenerated can procure no justification
    a. the Sophists evade the issue when they explain "works" as meaning those which men not yet reborn do only according to the letter by the effort of their own free will, apart from Christ's grace
    b. reply: they do not observe that in the contrast between the righteousness of the law and of the gospel, all works are excluded, whatever title may grace them

15. The Roman doctrine of grace and good works
    a. we confess with Paul that the doers of the law are justified before God; but, because we are all far from observing the law, we infer from this that those works which ought especially to avail for righteousness give us no help because we are destitute of them
    b. the Schoolmen's definition of faith and grace
        (1) faith—an assurance of conscience in awaiting from God their reward for merits

(2) grace—the Spirit helping in the pursuit of holiness

c. Lombard's explanation of the twofold manner in which justification is given to us

(1) Christ's death justifies us, while love is aroused through it in our hearts and makes us righteous

(2) through the same love, sin is extinguished by which the devil held us captive, so that he no longer has the wherewithal to condemn us

d. grace must never, as in Augustine, be subsumed under sanctification

16. Our justification according to the judgment of Scripture

a. the Scriptural understanding of faith-righteousness means turning aside from our own works and looking solely upon God's mercy

b. the order of justification

(1) God embraces the sinner in his miserable condition

(2) with a sense of God's goodness the sinner is touched; thus despairing of his own works, he grounds his salvation in God's mercy

c. the order may differ, but the content remains the same

17. Faith-righteousness and law-righteousness according to Paul

a. faith justifies because it receives and embraces the righteousness offered in the gospel

b. while the law attributes righteousness to works, the gospel bestows free righteousness apart from the help of works

c. this teaching illustrated from Rom. 10 and Gal. 3:18

18. Justification not the wages of works, but a free gift

a. the argument from Gal. 3 extended

b. one does not have to work for righteousness under the law if through faith that righteousness is received which the gospel freely bestows

c. Paul's example of Abraham

19. Through "faith alone"

a. the Sophists will not allow the word "alone" by demanding that ceremonial works of the law are excluded, not the moral works

b. reply: when the ability to justify is denied to the law, these words refer to the whole law

20. "Works of the law"
    a. though works are highly esteemed, they have their value from God's approval rather than from their own worth
    b. works have value because through them man intends to show obedience to God
    c. the fact that faith issues in works of love does not mean that we are justified from that working of love

Sins Are Remitted Only Through the Righteousness of Christ [21–23]

21. Justification, reconciliation, forgiveness of sins
    a. definition: the righteousness of faith is reconciliation with God, which consists solely in the forgiveness of sins
    b. reconciliation: sin is division between man and God, whereby man is God's enemy until he is restored to grace through Christ
    c. justification: thus, him whom He receives into union with Himself the Lord is said to justify, because He cannot receive him into grace unless He turns him from a sinner into a righteous man
    d. forgiveness of sins: if those whom the Lord has reconciled to Himself be judged by works, they will indeed still be found sinners; therefore reconciliation takes place by the forgiveness of sins

22. Scriptural proof for the close relation between justification and forgiveness of sins
    a. in II Cor. 5:19, 21, Paul mentions righteousness and reconciliation indiscriminately to have us understand that each one is reciprocally contained in the other
    b. Paul's example of David
    c. statements of Augustine and Bernard

23. Righteous—not in ourselves but in Christ
    a. man is not righteous in himself but because the righteousness of Christ is communicated to him by imputation
    b. Christ shares His righteousness with us that, in some wonderful manner, He pours into us enough of His power to meet the judgment of God
    c. the example of Jacob stated by Ambrose

CHAPTER 12
We Must Lift Up Our Minds to God's Judgment Seat that We May Be Firmly Convinced of His Free Justification

Justification in the Light of the Majesty and Perfection of God [*1–3*]

1. No one is righteous before God's judgment seat
   a. we are concerned with the justice not of a human court but of a heavenly tribunal; therefore we cannot measure by our own standards the integrity of works needed to satisfy the divine judgment
   b. the supreme Judge as He is depicted in Scripture
   c. examined by the standard of the written law, we ought to be tormented by a horrid fear

2. Righteousness before men and righteousness before God
   a. it is easy to think of ourselves as having something, as long as the comparison stops with men
   b. but this assurance vanishes in a flash and dies when we rise up toward God
   c. this is true for our souls as well as for our bodies

3. Augustine and Bernard of Clairvaux as witnesses of true righteousness
   a. Augustine: "All the pious who groan under this burden of corruptible flesh and in this weakness of life have one hope: that we have one Mediator, Jesus Christ the righteous one, and He is the appeasement for our sins"
   b. Bernard: "Where, in fact, are safe and firm rest and security for the weak but in the Saviour's wounds . . . ?"

Conscience and Self-Criticism Before God Deprive Us of All Claims to Good Works and Lead Us to Embrace God's Mercy [*4–8*]

4. The gravity of God's judgment puts an end to all self-deception
   a. for if the stars, which seem so very bright at night, lose their brilliance in the sight of the sun, what do we think will happen even to the rarest innocence of man when it is compared with God's purity?
   b. as for us, purity of will alone will be demanded

5. Away with all self-admiration
   a. let us not be ashamed to descend from this contemplation of divine perfection to look upon ourselves without flattery and without being affected by blind self-love
   b. while man flatters himself on account of the outward mask of righteousness that he wears, the Lord meanwhile weighs in His scales the secret impurity of the heart

6. What humility before God is
   a. humility consists in acknowledging ourselves poor and destitute, and therefore yielding to God's mercy
   b. if we think we have anything left to ourselves, we do not have humility
   c. the difference between true and false humility

7. Christ calls sinners, not the righteous
   a. the parable of the publican and Pharisee
   b. Christ invites to share His beneficence only those who labor and are heavy-laden

8. Arrogance and complacency before God block our way to Christ
   a. arrogance arises from a foolish persuasion of our own righteousness, when man thinks that he has something meritorious to commend him before God
   b. complacency can exist even without any belief in works, in those persons who think they need not aspire to the mercy offered to them
   c. supporting quotations from Augustine and Bernard

CHAPTER 13
Two Things to Be Noted in Free Justification

Glory to God and Peace to Our Consciences [*1*]

1. Justification serves God's honor; and revelation, His justice
   a. the two items to be noted:
      (1) the Lord's glory should stand undiminished and, so to speak, in good repair
      (2) our consciences in the presence of His judgment should have peaceful rest and serene tranquillity

b. the righteousness of God is not sufficiently set forth unless He alone be esteemed righteous, and communicate the free gift of righteousness to the undeserving
c. so long as man has anything to say in his own defense, he detracts somewhat from God's glory

Effect on Our Own Righteousness [2-4]

2. He who glories in his own righteousness robs God of His honor
   a. we never truly glory in Him unless we have utterly put off our own glory
   b. whoever glories in himself, glories against God
   c. the praise of righteousness remains perfect and whole in the Lord's possession, since it was to manifest His own righteousness that He poured out His grace upon us

3. A glance at one's own righteousness provides no peace for the conscience
   a. the conscience can be made quiet before God if unmerited righteousness be conferred upon us as a gift of God
   b. when our souls possess that by which they may present themselves fearless before God's face and receive His judgment undismayed, then only may we know that we have found no counterfeit righteousness
   c. to have faith is to strengthen the mind with constant assurance

4. Attention to one's own righteousness also nullifies the promises
   a. the fulfillment of the promise depends not upon merit but upon faith
   b. the inheritance arises from faith in order to establish the promise according to grace
   c. the promise is confirmed when it rests with God rather than with man
   d. support from Augustine and Bernard
   e. Scriptural support

Faith in God's Free Grace [5]

5. Faith in God's free grace alone gives us peace of conscience and gladness in prayer
   a. further refutation of Osiander's "essential righteousness"

b. our confidence lies not in our becoming regenerated, which is always imperfect in the flesh, but rather in our being engrafted in the body of Christ, thereby freely accounted righteous

CHAPTER 14
The Beginning of Justification and its Continual Progress

Man in His Natural State Dead in Sins and in Need of Redemption [1-6]

1. Four classes of men with regard to justification
   a. fourfold classification of men, who are either
      (1) those endowed with no knowledge of God and immersed in idolatry
      (2) those initiated into the sacraments, yet by impurity of life denying God in their actions while they confess him with their lips; they belong to Christ only in name
      (3) hypocrites who conceal with empty pretenses their wickedness of heart
      (4) those regenerated by God's spirit, who make true holiness their concern
   b. in the first instance, not one spark of good will be found in them
   c. even though this first class of men excel in morals, we must examine from what disposition of the heart these works come forth

2. The virtues of unbelievers are God-given
   a. comparison of virtues and vices in notable figures
   b. the Lord has placed the discernment between honorable and wicked deeds in the minds of men
   c. all virtues—or images of virtues—are gifts of God, since nothing is in any way praiseworthy that does not come from Him

3. No true virtue without true faith
   a. if the goal of that which is right is to serve God, then whatever strives to another end already deservedly loses the name "right"
   b. duties are weighed not by deeds but by ends

4. Without Christ there is no true holiness
   a. those who have no part in Christ, no matter what they do, hasten all their lives to destruction and to the judgment of eternal death
   b. Augustine: "our religion distinguishes the just from the unjust not by the law of works but by that of faith"

5. Righteousness before God comes not from works, though ever so good, but from grace
   a. Scriptural passages showing that God finds nothing in man to arouse Him to do good to him; to man God first comes in His free generosity
   b. who of us can boast that he has appealed to God by his own righteousness when our first capacity for well-doing flows from regeneration?

6. Man can contribute nothing to his own righteousness
   a. further Scriptural testimonies against works-righteousness
   b. if justification is the beginning of love, what righteousness of works will precede it?

Hypocrites and Nominal Christians, Under Condemnation [*7–8*]

7. Righteousness is a thing of the heart
   a. under this condition are included those who are listed as the second and third classes above
   b. the absence of regeneration in them shows their lack of faith
   c. therefore they have not been reconciled to God, nor justified in His sight, since men attain these benefits only through faith
   d. such men can bring forth only what is hateful to God's judgment
   e. no sanctification can be acquired unless the heart has first been well cleansed

8. Person and work
   a. in men not yet truly sanctified, works manifesting even the highest splendor are so far away from righteousness before the Lord that they are reckoned sins
   b. favor with God is not obtained by anyone through works; works please Him only when the person has previously found favor in His sight

Those Who Are Regenerated Are Justified by Faith Alone [*9–11*]

9. Also, true believers do no good works of themselves
   a. the righteousness possessed by those of the fourth class
   b. such men are consecrated to the Lord in true purity of life, with hearts formed to obedience to the law
   c. nevertheless, traces of our imperfection remain to give us occasion for humility
   d. even our best works are still spotted and corrupted with some impurity of the flesh

10. He who thinks he has his own righteousness misunderstands the severity of the law
    a. one sin is enough to wipe out every memory of previous righteousness
    b. God does not, as many stupidly believe, once for all reckon to us as righteousness that forgiveness of sins concerning which we have spoken in order that, having obtained pardon for our past life, we may afterward seek righteousness in the law

11. Believers' righteousness is always faith-righteousness
    a. the difference between our teaching and that of the Schoolmen lies in the fact that we claim man's works to be without efficacy toward justification, while the Schoolmen claim that a man once for all reconciled to God through faith in Christ may be reckoned righteous before God by good works and be accepted by the merit of them
    b. for Abraham, however, the Lord reckoned faith as righteousness
    c. the embassy of free reconciliation with God is published not for one day or another but is attested as perpetual in the church

Scholastic Objections to Justification by Faith, and Doctrine of the Supererogatory Merits of the Saints Examined and Refuted [*12–21*]

12. Evasions of opponents
    a. the Schoolmen maintain that good works are not as important in their intrinsic worth as to be sufficient to obtain righteousness, but their great value lies in "accepting grace"
    b. they admit we need forgiveness of sins to supply the defect of

works, but that the transgressions committed are compensated by works of supererogation

c. reply: "accepting grace" is nothing else than His free goodness

13. One who speaks of "supererogatory" works misunderstands the sharpness of God's demand and the gravity of sin
    a. there is no such thing as partial righteousness
    b. their error is this: he who partly keeps the law is to that extent righteous by works
    c. there is no righteousness of works except in the perfect observance of God's law
    d. what perversity is it for us, lacking such righteousness, to boast of some little bits of a few works and try through other satisfactions to pay for what is lacking!
    e. those who talk such nonsense do not realize what an execrable thing sin is in God's sight

14. Even the perfect fulfillment of our obligation would bring us no glory; but this also is not at all possible
    a. how can works of supererogation square with Luke 17:10?
    b. let us not boast of voluntary liberality when we are constrained by necessity

15. God is entitled to all that we are and have; hence there can be no supererogatory works
    a. argument continued from I Cor. 9 and Luke 17
    b. works of supererogation God neither commanded nor approves

16. No trust in works and no glory in works
    a. avoid these two plagues:
        (1) placing confidence in the righteousness of works
        (2) ascribing to works any glory
    b. what is important is not works, but God's pardon

17. In no respect can works serve as the cause of our holiness
    a. none of the four kinds of causes postulated by the philosophers has anything to do with works
    b. the four causes and their Scriptural counterpart [see table p. 226]

(1) efficient cause—the mercy of the Heavenly Father and His freely given love toward us
(2) material cause—Christ, with His obedience, through which He acquired righteousness for us
(3) formal or instrumental cause—faith
(4) final cause—proof of divine justice and in the praise of God's goodness

c. these four causes applied to Rom. 3:23-26

18. The sight of good works, however, can strengthen faith
    a. in two ways, the saints recall their own uprightness
        (1) comparing their good cause with the evil cause of the wicked, they thence derive confidence of victory, not so much by the commendation of their own righteousness as by the just and deserved condemnation of their adversaries
        (2) without comparison with others, while they examine themselves before God, the purity of their own conscience brings them some comfort and confidence
    b. regarding the second, the saints certainly may undergird and strengthen themselves in the faith by these signs of the divine benevolence toward them; yet, as far as salvation is concerned, they at the same time rely wholly on the free promise of righteousness

19. Works as fruits of the call
    a. recollection of works: signs of the indwelling of the Holy Spirit rather than matters that have any place in laying a foundation to strengthen the conscience
    b. prior to the occasion for exulting must come the apprehension of God's goodness, sealed by nothing else than the certainty of the promise

20. Works are God's gift and cannot become the foundation of self-confidence for believers
    a. the saints regard works solely as gifts of God from which they may recognize His goodness and as signs of the calling by which they realize their election
    b. works do not in any degree diminish the free righteousness we attain in Christ
    c. supporting statement from Augustine

THE CAUSALITY OF SALVATION

	CALVIN	COUNCIL OF TRENT
Efficient Cause:	God the Father	God's mercy
Material Cause:	Christ	sacrament of baptism
Formal or Instrumental Cause:	faith	God's justice
Final Cause:	(1) proof of divine justice (2) praise of God's goodness	glory of God and Christ
Meritorious Cause:	— — — — — — —	Our Lord Jesus Christ, God's only begotten Son
Head and Primal Source	that God embraced us with His free mercy	
Eternal Life	[exegesis of Rom. 3:23–26]	

Calvin claims that the Roman Catholics "falsely represent the material and the final cause, as if our works held half the place along with faith and Christ's righteousness."

Cf. *Acta Synodi Tridentinae,* Sess. VI, c. 8 (Corpus Reformatorum 7.432f), and Calvin, *Antidote* (Corpus Reformatorum 7.449)

Also see Louis Goumaz, *La Doctrine du salut d'après les commentaires de Jean Calvin sur le Nouveau Testament* (1917), Theses and Conclusions, XI

21. Sense in which good works are sometimes spoken of as a reason for divine benefits
    a. why does Scripture show that the good works of believers are reasons why the Lord benefits them?
    b. although the efficient cause of our salvation consists in God's love, the Lord also embraces works as inferior causes
    c. in this sense, what goes before in the order of dispensation He calls the cause of what comes after
    d. the order may look like this:
        (1) God choosing
        (2) God justifying
        (3) man producing good works
        (4) God glorifying in the good works (man's eternal life), in which case eternal life is derived from good works, but not ascribed to good works
    e. the true cause is the choosing and justifying action of God

CHAPTER 15
Boasting About the Merits of Works Destroys Our Praise of God for Having Bestowed Righteousness, as Well as Our Assurance of Salvation

Doctrine of Human Merit in Justification Opposed by Augustine and Bernard as Well as by Scripture [*1–4*]

1. False and true questioning
    a. no man is justified by works unless he is free of the least transgression
    b. therefore this question arises: though works may by no means suffice for justification, should they not yet deserve favor with God?

2. "Merit" an unscriptural and dangerous word
    a. whoever first applied the term "merit" to men's works over against God's judgment provided very badly for sincere faith
    b. the terms "merit" and "grace" in Augustine, Chrysostom, and Bernard

3. The whole value of good works comes from God's grace
    a. our good works in and of themselves are full of uncleanness

b. good works are "good" because God's kindness has of itself set this value on them

4. Defense against counterevidence: how God really takes good works into account
   a. sophists have mistranslated Ecclesiasticus 16:15, and misrepresented the spirit of Heb. 13:16
   b. the distinction that good works deserve the graces that are conferred upon us in this life, while everlasting salvation is the reward of faith alone, is to be rejected
   c. everything given to the godly, even blessedness itself, is of God's beneficence and is intended to make both us and the gift given to us worthy of Him

Rejection of the Substitution of Man's Merit for Christ's; the Scholastic and Semi-Pelagian Doctrine [*5–8*]

5. Christ as the sole foundation, as beginner and perfecter
   a. Christ did not become the foundation of our salvation only to see its fulfillment follow from ourselves
   b. because all benefits of Christ are ours and we have all things in Him, in us there is nothing

6. Roman theology curtails Christ's might and honor
   a. Rome has misrepresented the truth in discovering "moral" good works whereby men are rendered pleasing to God before they are engrafted into Christ
   b. it is only such engrafting into Christ through faith by which we gain merit, and merit here is not ours but Christ's

7. Roman theology understands neither Augustine nor Scripture
   a. Roman theology mistakenly derives good works from free will, through which, they say, all merit exists
   b. Peter Lombard did not understand Augustine, though Lombard may be called sane and sober when compared with the Schools of the Sorbonne
   c. Roman theology actually discourages confidence in God's favorable disposition to the works of people

8. Admonition and comfort on the basis of right doctrine
   a. the example of Christ as the fulfillment of piety and holiness
   b. passages of consolation for disciples of Christ

CHAPTER 16
Refutation of the False Accusations by Which the Papists Try to Cast Odium upon this Doctrine

Objection I

1. Does the doctrine of justification do away with good works?
   a. charges brought against the doctrine
      (1) it abolishes good works
      (2) it seduces men from the pursuit of good works
      (3) it makes the path to righteousness too easy
      (4) it lures into sin men who are already too much inclined to sin
   b. good works are, however, not destroyed by the doctrine of justification of faith, because you cannot grasp this without at the same time grasping sanctification also
   c. Christ justifies no one whom He does not at the same time sanctify

Objection II

2. Does the doctrine of justification stifle zeal for good works?
   a. there are two reasons why the second charge, that our doctrine seduces men from the pursuit of good works, is false:
      (1) if the only reason good works are performed is the hope of ultimate reward, the whole foundation of such good works is completely in error
      (2) the right foundation of good works is gratitude by which we reciprocate the love of Him "who first loved us"
   b. Scriptural texts supporting the correct foundation for the right regulation of life

3. God's honor and God's mercy as motives for action: subordination of works
   a. the apostles of Scripture derive their most powerful exhortations from the thought that our salvation stands upon no merit of ours but solely upon God's mercy
   b. it is the remembrance of God's benefits which will amply suffice to arouse men to well-doing
   c. while Scripture says that "God will render to every man according to his works" (Rom. 2:6–7; Matt. 16:27; I Cor. 3:8,

14–15; etc.), it is to be denied that this is the only thing, or the principal thing, or that we should take our beginning from that point

Objection III

4. Does the doctrine of justification incite man to sin?
   a. it is the most worthless of slanders to say men are invited to sin, when we affirm the free forgiveness of sins in which we assert righteousness consists
   b. while righteousness for us is free, it was not so for Christ, who bought it at the cost of His own blood
   c. when men are so taught, they are made aware that they cannot do anything to prevent the shedding of His most sacred blood as often as they sin
   d. righteousness is too precious to be matched by any compensation of works

CHAPTER 17
The Agreement of the Promises of the Law and of the Gospel

Works as Related to the Law: the Instance of Cornelius, Acts 10:13 [*1–5*]

1. Scholastic arguments stated and confuted
   a. the charge: justification is not by faith alone if we are to be keepers of the law
   b. reply: the freedom from the power of the law of which we speak is not carnal freedom which incites license
   c. the freedom of which we speak is spiritual freedom, which comforts the stricken conscience, showing it to be free from the curse and condemnation with which the law pressed it down

2. We cannot bring the promises of the law to fulfillment through our works
   a. the promises of God are based on the complete fulfillment of the conditions of the law, conditions which will never be fulfilled
   b. thus the righteousness we tried to attain through fulfillment of the law is accomplished not by our efforts but by Christ

3. The promises of the law are put into effect through the gospel
   a. the promises of God have no beneficent effect upon us so long as they have reference to the merits of works
   b. but when the promises of the gospel are substituted, which proclaim the free forgiveness of sins, these not only make us acceptable to God but also render our works pleasing to Him
   c. three reasons why works win God's favor:
      (1) they are the works of believers who base their reconciliation with God on faith rather than on works alone
      (2) they are works raised to the place of honor by God Himself, without considering their worth
      (3) they are works received with pardon rather than the imputation of their intrinsic imperfection

4. The twofold acceptance of man before God
   a. the double acceptance of man before God consists in
      (1) man, by virtue of his miserable condition, being totally unworthy of God's acceptance
      (2) man, by virtue of God's grace, being totally worthy of his heavenly calling
   b. summary statement of the doctrine: God's sole reason to receive man unto Himself is that He sees him utterly lost if left to himself, but because He does not will him to be lost, He exercises His mercy in freeing him

5. In what sense the Lord is pleased with the good works of the regenerate
   a. good works acceptable because God is their source
   b. but even the godly are still sinners, and their good works need to be embraced in Christ

Passages that Relate Justification to Works Examined [*6–15*]

6. The promises of grace of the Old Covenant as distinct from the promises of the law
   a. "promises of the law" means promises which declare that there is recompense ready for you if you do what they enjoin
   b. God's reward to the children of God is given not on the basis of law which has been kept, which ought to be perpetual anyway, but on the basis of adoption
   c. Old Testament passages supporting this doctrine

7. Does not Scripture speak of the "righteousness" of the works of the law?
    a. while we willingly confess that perfect obedience to the law is righteousness, we deny that such a form of righteousness exists
    b. we do not attain righteousness save by observing the whole law; but such righteousness is broken by every transgression

8. Twofold value of work before God
    a. charge of opponents: were not both the "faith of Abraham" (Rom. 4:3) and the "deed of Phinehas" (Ps. 106:31) reckoned as righteousness? Therefore, while we are not justified without faith, we are also not justified by faith alone
    b. reply: the difference between the value of works themselves and the value of works after faith-righteousness has been established
    c. after forgiveness of sins is set forth, the good works that now follow are appraised otherwise than on their own merit

9. Justification by faith is the basis of works-righteousness
    a. why do opponents try to destroy justification of faith when, following such justification, works which otherwise would be impure and half done are accounted righteousness?
    b. if works-righteousness depends on justification of faith, the latter is strengthened and its power shines forth even stronger

10. Works acceptable only when sins have been pardoned
    a. a work begins to be acceptable only when it is undertaken with pardon
    b. as we, engrafted into Christ, are righteous in God's sight, so are our works, despite their faults, which are covered by Christ's sinlessness

11. James against Paul?
    a. the intention of James was not to contradict Paul, but to correct those who overlooked all the proper works of believers
    b. James was making a careful distinction between a dead faith and true faith

12. The word "justify" used by James in a sense different from Paul's
    a. Paul and James use the word "justify" in two senses

   b. for Paul, we are justified when the memory of our unrighteousness has been wiped out, but James is speaking of the declaration, not the imputation of righteousness
   c. James is fighting an empty show of faith which cannot justify, and says that a justified person declares his righteousness by good works

13. Romans 2:13
   a. when Paul says "the doers of the law, not the hearers, are justified," the apostle is casting down the foolish confidence of the Jews who claimed sole knowledge of the law while they were its greatest despisers
   b. it is obvious that the righteousness of the law consists in works, but that does not mean we are justified by such works
   c. since no one can boast that he has fulfilled the law through works, Paul affirms there is no righteousness arising from the law

14. What does it mean when before God believers appeal to their works?
   a. even the saints, appealing for God's approval of their innocence, do not present themselves as free from all guilt
   b. the basis of their appeal is still their assurance of salvation resting in God's goodness alone
   c. also, the saints are not afraid to call upon God as judge of their own sincerity and righteousness in comparison with their adversaries' dishonesty and wickedness

15. Perfection of believers?
   a. passages alluding to those who keep uprightness, yet none of Adam's children has lived up to this standard
   b. works of "accepting grace" (scholastic teaching) have value only through God's pardon
   c. passages which require perfection of believers still to be heeded, yet acknowledging imperfection in perfection (Augustine)

CHAPTER 18
Works-Righteousness Is Wrongly Inferred from Reward

***Passages Referring to Reward do Not Make Works the Cause of Salvation** [1–4]*

1. What does "recompense according to works" mean?
   a. the several passages which refer to God rendering to every man according to his works indicate an order of sequence rather than the cause
   b. the word "to work" is not opposed to grace, but rather refers to the good work of God accomplished through believers

2. Reward as "inheritance"
   a. the kingdom of Heaven is not servants' wages but sons' inheritance
   b. the example of Abraham shows that reward follows adoption and is received as promise prior to works

3. Reward as grace
   a. still, the Lord does not mock us in saying He will reward works with what He had given free before works
   b. good works are a "training" which point a finger forward to the fruition of the promise
   c. the parable of the laborers and the vineyard as interpreted by "Ambrose"

4. The purpose of the promise of reward
   a. reward is given not for works, but signifies compensation for miseries, tribulations, slanders, etc.
   b. recompense therefore refers to the contrast between repose and toil, joy and sorrow, affluence and poverty, glory and disgrace, marking the inheritance into eternal life from life in the world

***Answers to Objections Against this View** [5–10]*

5. Reward rests upon forgiveness
   a. righteousness exists because grace justifies the ungodly (Augustine)

   b. similarly, righteousness is imputed to our works, covering over that which is unrighteousness in them
   c. thus, more crucial than good works is God's pardon

6. On "treasures in heaven"
   a. good works likened to the riches we shall enjoy in the blessedness of eternal life
   b. none of our good works will ever be lost, even though they are unworthy of God's glance

7. Reward for tribulation endured?
   a. tribulations are sent in order that we may be worthy of God's kingdom
   b. to stir up our sluggishness God has assured us the trouble we have borne to the glory of His name will not be in vain
   c. yet our whole promised assurance rests upon the free covenant of God's mercy, going before

8. Justification through love: Scholastic arguments drawn from Paul refuted exegetically
   a. contention from I Cor. 13:2 and I Cor. 13:13 that we are justified by love rather than by faith. Answer:
      (1) love is greater than faith, not as being more meritorious, but because it is more fruitful
      (2) but this does not mean that love justifies more, for justification does not lie in any worth of works, but in God's mercy
   b. contention from Col. 3:14: love as the "bond of perfection" is therefore aiso the bond of righteousness. Answer: What man can even suggest that he has attained the perfection of love?

9. Matt. 19:17: Scholastic claim that "keep the commandments" is the "royal road" to salvation
   a. to a lawyer accustomed to the persuasion of law-righteousness, Christ accommodates His teaching, sending him back to the law, the perfect mirror of righteousness, that he may be disabused of his empty confidence in works
   b. if we seek righteousness in works, we should keep the law perfectly; unable to do so, we must turn, humbled, to faith in Christ
   c. for those already humbled, Christ does not need to refer to the law

10. Righteousness and unrighteousness are not comparable with each other by the same rule
    a. charge: since faith is sometimes called a "work," it is wrong to oppose faith to works
    b. reply: as if faith, insofar as it is obedience to the divine will, obtains righteousness for us on its own merits!
    c. faith embraces God's mercy, and seals upon our hearts Christ's righteousness, not our own
    d. it is foolish reasoning to conclude from the statement that death is the just payment for each sin, that man can be reconciled by a single good work

CHAPTER 19
Christian Freedom

Necessity of a Doctrine of Christian Freedom, which Has Three Parts, the First, Freedom from the Law, Seen in Galatians [*1–3*]

1. Need for a right understanding of the Christian doctrine of freedom
    a. Christian freedom is a necessary part of the gospel and an appendage of justification
    b. the very thought of Christian freedom stirs up wild tumults
    c. now is the right time to introduce this doctrine, so necessary, yet to be presented with refutation of the usual objections

2. Freedom from the law
    a. the first of three parts of Christian freedom; freedom from the law and all works-righteousness
    b. not how we may become righteous, but how we may be reckoned righteous—this is the question
    c. yet the law never stops teaching even believers: the whole life of Christians should be a practice of godliness—sanctification

3. The argument of Galatians
    a. the letter to the Galatians deals with more than mere freedom of ceremonies
    b. the drift of Paul's argument:
        (1) in Christ is a perfect disclosure of what was foreshadowed in the Mosaic ceremonies

(2) believers cannot obtain righteousness before God by any works of the law
(3) through the cross of Christ, believers are free from the universal condemnation by the law
(4) claims for consciences of believers their freedom from things unnecessary

The Second, Freedom of Conscience Willingly Obeying Without Compulsion of the Law [*4–6*]

4. Freedom from the constraint of the law establishes the true obedience of believers
   a. consciences, once freed from the constraining necessity of the law, willingly observe it
   b. the law requires that we love our God with all our heart, etc.; this perfection is not attainable by any of us in this life
   c. let us then ponder our imperfect works (hence, transgressions of the law)—there is no wonder they cannot be judged good!

5. Freedom from constraint makes us capable of joyous obedience
   a. our works, measured by the standard of the law, are under its curse: the law is then a source for our unhappiness; we are like servants under a harsh taskmaster
   b. once freed from the severe requirement of the law, we eagerly and cheerfully follow God's leading—now we are like sons of a generous father

6. Emancipated by grace, believers need not fear the remnants of sin
   a. the Epistle to the Hebrews refers to all the good works done by the holy fathers to faith, and judges them by faith alone (ch. 11)
   b. Paul in Rom. 6 describes our freedom from the law, not in terms of leave to sin, but of encouragement to do good

The Third, Freedom in "Things Indifferent" with Proofs from Romans [*7–9*]

7. There are some things which we are not religiously bound to use, but can use or not use them as we please
   a. some persons resent our stirring up discussion about ritual

regulations (fasting, holidays, vestments, etc.) as if these were vain frivolities

b. but these matters must be brought into the open, else persons will torture themselves over minute questions of food, dress, etc., and be inextricably entangled in doubts

8. Freedom in the use of God's gifts for His purposes
   a. in perplexities of conscience two opposite stances are possible:
      (1) daring confidence that turns away from God
      (2) overpowering fear of God
   b. both lack thankfulness for God's gifts
   c. the goal of this freedom: we should use God's gifts for the purpose for which He gave them to us, with no scruple of conscience, no trouble of mind

9. Against the abuse of Christian freedom for gluttony and luxury!
   a. Christian freedom a spiritual thing—to bring peace of mind before God
   b. two errors in its use:
      (1) those who use Christian freedom as an excuse for their own lust (first error: description of offensive opulence; cf. *De Luxu*)
      (2) those who consider Christian freedom consists in using it before men even to the harm of weaker brethren (second error)
   c. the Christian answer to such opulence: soberness and moderation in using the goods of this world

***Relation of Christian Freedom to the Weak and to the Question of Offenses** [10–13]*

10. Against the abuse of Christian freedom to the injury of the weak (second error)
    a. the indiscriminate use of freedom, as if to safeguard it, may offend weak brothers
    b. Christian freedom is in God's sight, not in man's, and may consist as much in abstaining as in using
    c. sometimes we must declare our freedom before men, but always with concern for weaker brethren

11. On offenses
    a. useful Scriptural distinction between offense given and offense received
    b. offense given (of the weak); includes: doing anything with unseemly levity, wantonness or rashness, out of proper order or place, so as to cause the ignorant and simple to stumble
    c. offense received (of the Pharisees); includes: something, otherwise not wickedly or unseasonably committed, which is by ill-will or malicious intent wrenched into occasion for offense
    d. the teaching of Paul and of Jesus is that we avoid offense to the weak, but not worry about offending the Pharisees' rigor

12. On the right use of Christian freedom and the right renunciation of it
    a. whether we keep or renounce Christian freedom to avoid offense depends on whether we are dealing with weak persons or Pharisees
    b. this varied strategy seen in Paul's circumcision of Timothy and refusal to circumcise Titus
    c. the rule: we should use our freedom if it results in the edification of our neighbor, but if it does not help our neighbor, then we should forego it

13. We must not on pretext of love of neighbor offend against God
    a. avoiding offenses applies only to things indifferent
    b. priorities:
        (1) purity of faith, then
        (2) love, then
        (3) our freedom
    c. wrong Romanist practices must not be passed off as "milk," for milk is not poison
    d. no further refutation here because:
        (1) their banalities are scarcely worth refuting
        (2) special treatises are already written on this

***Freedom and Conscience in Relation to Traditions, and to Civil Government** [14–16]*

14. Freedom of conscience from all human law
    a. believers in Christ are freed from humanly devised observances

b. Paul in Galatians is trying to show how Christ is wiped away unless our consciences stand fast in their freedom
c. a fuller treatment of these human constitutions will be given later

15. The two kingdoms; the nature of conscience [Note: III.19.15f.-IV.10.3f.]
    a. the distinction: a twofold government in man
        (1) spiritual: whereby the conscience is instructed
        (2) political: whereby man is educated for the duties of humanity and citizenship that must be maintained among men
    b. value of the distinction
        (1) not to misapply to the political order the gospel teaching on spiritual freedom: Christians are still subject to the laws, even though their consciences are free in God's sight
        (2) constitutions related to the spiritual kingdom may be adjudged lawful if consonant with God's Word
    c. the difficulty: men fail to distinguish sharply enough the external forum from the forum of conscience
    d. resolution of difficulty: in understanding the nature of conscience
        (1) when men grasp the conception of things with the mind and the understanding, they are said "to know"
        (2) in like manner, when men have an awareness of divine judgment adjoined to them as a witness which does not let them hide their sins but arraigns them as guilty before God's judgment-seat—this awareness is called "conscience"

16. Bondage and freedom of conscience
    a. works refer to men; conscience to God, i.e., inward uprightness of heart
    b. but sometimes conscience is extended to men (e.g., Acts 24:16): the fruit of a good conscience flows forth and comes even to men
    c. *adiaphora:* we should abstain from anything that might cause offense, but with a free conscience (e.g., meat offered to idols—I Cor. 10:28f.)

Chapter 20
On Prayer

FIRST DIVISION: THE NECESSITY OF PRAYER [1-3]

1. Place of prayer in Christian doctrine
   a. man's helplessness is the basis of prayer
   b. faith instructs us to recognize whatever we need and lack is in God and in Jesus Christ
   c. then we must ask of Him in prayers what we have learned to be in Him
   d. gospel→faith→invocation of God

2. Definition, necessity, and usefulness of prayer
   a. prayer: communion of men with God in which they seek from Him in fact that which He has already promised in words
   b. through prayer we invoke God's overarching providence, sustaining power, and merciful goodness

3. Objection to prayer, and refutation of objection
   a. contention that, because God is omniscient, prayer is superfluous (Seneca, *Ep.*, 31:5)
   b. six principal reasons to pray:
      (1) that our hearts may be fired with a zealous and burning desire ever to seek, love, and serve Him and to take refuge in Him in time of need
      (2) that no desire and wish may enter our minds of which we may be ashamed to let Him witness, while we learn to set all our wishes before His eyes and even to pour out our whole hearts
      (3) that we be prepared to receive His benefits with true gratitude of heart and thanksgiving, benefits of which we are reminded by our prayer as having come from His hand
      (4) that, having obtained what we were seeking and being convinced that He has answered our prayer, we should be led to meditate upon His kingdom more ardently
      (5) to embrace with greater delight those things we acknowledge to have been obtained by prayers
      (6) to confirm His providence in our minds—that He is a never-failing help in our every need

SECOND DIVISION: HOW SHALL WE PRAY?: THE RULES OF PRAYER [4-16]

First Rule: We should be composed in mind and heart as befits those who enter conversation with God [4-5]

a. the thoughts which are required for conversation with God [4]
   (1) concentration of mind [5]; in prayer avoid distraction by wandering thoughts
   (2) moderation in request: do not ask more than God allows
b. the Holy Spirit as our guide and teacher in prayer
   (1) but we are too weak in mind and effort, unaided, to achieve this
   (2) the Holy Spirit then supplies the lack in our natural powers
   (3) but Paul's exhortation to pray in the Spirit does not mean that we are to cease watchfulness

Second Rule: In our petitions we should always sense our own insufficiency; and earnestly pondering how we need all that we seek, we should join with this prayer an earnest, nay burning, desire to attain it [6-7]

a. wrongly-conceived prayers [6]
   (1) prayers perfunctorily performed out of a sense of duty
   (2) prayers mumbled without meditation, for the sake of appeasing God
b. all times are opportune for prayer [7]
c. true prayer requires repentance

Third Rule: Stand humbly before God, abandoning all self-glory, giving glory completely to Him, and putting away all self-assurance [8-9]

a. Scriptural instances of self-abasement before God [8]; Daniel, David, Isaiah, Jeremiah, Baruch (?)
b. plea for forgiveness the most important part of prayer [9]; the beginning and preparation of proper prayer—the plea for pardon with a humble and sincere confession of guilt
c. general and special confession
   (1) general confession involves a prayer for God's freely-given mercy, for without this no prayer will reach God
   (2) special confession of present guilt, together with a plea for remission of every sin and penalty

d. in what sense do the saints claim self-righteousness in prayer to God? [10]
The godly may enjoy the awareness of his own purity before God in order to confirm himself in the promises with which the Lord comforts and supports His true worshipers—but the assurance of being answered rests solely upon God's clemency, apart from all consideration of personal merit

Fourth Rule: In true humility, we nevertheless are impelled to pray with a sure hope that our prayer will be answered [11-16]

a. fear and hope is the basis for all godly prayer [11]
b. relation of prayer to faith
c. certainty that prayer is granted is based upon Scripture [12]
d. this assurance is founded upon God's goodness, which joins promise and command to pray [13]
e. we enter into the fellowship of answered prayer with patriarchs, prophets, and apostles, not because of our holiness, but because of our common command to pray and common faith in God's Word [14]
f. why does God sometimes answer prayers that do not conform to His Word? [15]
    (1) these exceptions do not invalidate the universal rule
    (2) that God sometimes answers even the prayers of unbelievers serves to illumine His mercy to sinners
    (3) this should not drive believers to unbelief or to envy of unbelievers whose prayers have been answered
g. How could Abraham, Samuel, and Jeremiah pray against God's will?
    (1) the prayers of the saints are a mixture of faith and error
    (2) but God so tempers the outcome of events according to His incomprehensible plan that these prayers are not nullified
    (3) thus despite their being deceived in their opinion, they are not utterly lacking in faith

Discussion of the Four Rules [16]

Our prayers are answered only through God's forgiveness, not because they conform to the four above-mentioned rules

a. God even overlooks our rash ejaculations arising out of sorrow, ignorance, or strong emotions—though they run counter to the first rule of prayer

b. God also overlooks violations of the second rule, when men's intention falters out of apathy

c. also despite the inadequacy of our beseechings for forgiveness, God overlooks our failure to measure up to the third rule

d. the weakness or imperfection of our faith is offset by God's mercy and pardon

THIRD DIVISION: CHRIST THE ONLY INTERCESSOR [17–20]

17. Prayer in the name of Jesus
    a. we are unworthy to present ourselves before God
    b. hence God has given us His Son as our advocate to free us from the shame and fear we feel before God's dread majesty
    c. the use of any other name than Christ in calling upon God is obstinately to flout His commands and nullify His will and promises to us

18. The risen Christ as our intercessor
    a. the priest entering the sanctuary on behalf of the twelve tribes of Israel foreshadows our need for a Mediator in approaching God
    b. Christ bade His disciples regard Him as their intercessor after His ascension into heaven to compensate for His physical removal from their midst

19. Christ is the only Mediator, even for the mutual intercession of believers
    a. if we forsake Christ, we have no access to God
    b. the saints commend one another to God in prayer, yet solely depending upon Christ's intercession
    c. . . . we should direct all intercession of the whole church to Christ as sole intercessor

20. Christ is the eternal and abiding Mediator
    a. Christ is both our redemption and our intercession
    b. our mutual prayers for one another and for all members laboring on earth rise to Christ our Head who has gone before us
    c. Christ does not perpetually kneel in supplication on our be-

half before God, but the power of His death avails as an everlasting intercession in our behalf

FOURTH DIVISION: ON THE INTERCESSION OF THE SAINTS [21-27]

1. Harmful effects of the intercession of the saints [21-22]
   a. whoever takes refuge in the intercession of the saints robs Christ of the honor of Mediator [21]
      (1) Scripture recalls us to Christ alone
      (2) but in various periods of the church, and especially under the papacy, the merits of the saints are commended
         (a) there are no grounds for this in Scripture
         (b) but it arises out of anxiety that Christ is insufficient or too severe to approach directly
   b. belief in the intercession of the saints leads to their veneration and many attendant errors and superstitions [22]
      (1) "division of labor" among the saints creeps in with special needs and for particular individuals
      (2) the saints really pray for the coming of God's kingdom, not with partiality for their "pets"
      (3) some even look upon saints as determiners of their salvation, and pastors out of greed fail to curb this cult

2. Refutation of Roman proof-texts for intercession of the saints
   a. departed saints are not angels [23]
   b. Jer. 15:1 does not prove the intercession of the dead
   c. departed saints are not engaged in earthly cares, and thus have no contact with us [24]
   d. prayers of man on earth for one another is no analogue of departed saints' intercession for men yet living
   e. how can the saints in heaven observe our needs even though they may be bound with us in love based on a common faith?
   f. invocation of names of the patriarchs is not relevant [25], but merely to remind us of God's covenant which we have inherited from them
   g. "for David's sake" is no support for intercession of the saints
   h. Scriptural evidence that saints' prayers have been heard by God no proof of intercession of the saints, but an example to us, that we might through Christ appropriate divine power to us [26]

3. Summary of refutation of intercession of the saints [27]
   a. since Scripture enjoins prayer to God alone as the prime duty of piety, direct prayer to others is manifest sacrilege
   b. faith and prayer
      (1) prayers are to be conformed to the measure of His Word
      (2) faith grounded upon the Word is the mother of right prayer; deflected from the Word, it is corrupted
      (3) prayer rightly begun springs from faith, and faith from hearing God's Word
   c. the true intercession
      (1) Christ alone mediates for us
      (2) the papacy exemplifies lack of faith in urging other mediators
      (3) reliance upon human mediators leaves Christ with nothing to do

FIFTH DIVISION: PRIVATE PRAYER [28]

1. Interconnection of petition and thanksgiving
   a. in asking and beseeching we seek: { (1) that makes for His glory and name; (2) benefits for our own advantage }
   b. in giving thanks we: { (1) praise His benefits to us; (2) credit to His generosity every good }

2. God is the Author of all blessings, and to be praised and thanked without ceasing
   a. all that we are, have, and do is to be committed to Him, the sole source of our good and our only help
   b. we are accursed of God when we have confidence in ourselves
   c. Paul's "sanctified by the word and prayer" and David's "new song," as well as other passages of Scripture attest to this
   d. God's benefits also, beyond the extolling of the tongue, engender love for themselves

SIXTH DIVISION: ON THE COMMON PRAYERS OF THE CHURCH [29–33]

1. Necessity and danger of public prayer [29]
   a. constancy applies not only to private prayers but also to public ones

(1) by common consent, certain hours (indifferent to God but necessary for men) are agreed upon
(2) but prayer may be intensified in a particular church if the need arises

b. dangers
(1) vain repetitions
(a) not to be confused with persistence in real prayer
(b) repetitious prayers of the present-day papacy redolent of the Pharisees' prayers
(2) hypocritical praying in public—reminiscent of the "chief seats"

c. true prayer
(1) the true goal of prayer—to arouse and bear hearts to God; either to praise Him or ask His help
(2) prayer is an emotion of the heart within, poured out and laid before God, the searcher of hearts
(3) Christ taught us to pray in secret that we might enter with our whole heart into what is something inward and requiring tranquillity
(4) Christ exemplifies this in His own periodical withdrawal to pray; though at times He prayed even in the midst of a crowd
(5) public and private prayer feed one another
(6) the biblical term "house of prayer" commends public prayers to us, to foster unity of faith among us

2. The significance of church buildings [30]
a. public temples are analogous to divinely ordained public prayers
b. lawful use of church buildings excludes
(1) belief that God is preeminently present there
(2) belief in a special holiness inherent there which makes prayers offered there more efficacious
c. but the New Testament has interiorized the Old Testament teaching on the temple: we are all living spiritual temples of God

3. Speaking and singing in prayer [31–32]
a. the tongue was created to praise God in word and song [31]
(1) voice and song in prayer must come from deep feeling of heart
(2) yet, associated with the heart, they are commended
(3) the glory of God ought to shine in the various parts of

our bodies, especially in the tongue, the instrument for common prayer of men to God

b. church singing [32]
  (1) dates from apostolic times, but fell into disuse in the West and was reintroduced in Ambrose's and Augustine's time
  (2) properly conceived, it lends dignity to sacred actions and is invaluable in kindling zeal and eagerness to pray in our hearts
  (3) but the words must always stand over the melody

4. Prayer should be in the language of the people [33]
  a. prayer, done for the edification of the whole church, must be in a language the worshipers can understand
  b. the papists, in their practice, run counter to Paul's advice on this

5. Feeling and thought and gesture in relation to prayer
  a. normally, tongue and mind should join in prayer
  b. in private, unspoken prayers are sometimes the best, but when feelings are aroused the tongue breaks forth into speech and bodily members into unostentatious gesture
  c. the customary bodily gestures (such as uncovering the head, kneeling) are attempts to heighten our reverence toward God

SEVENTH DIVISION: THE LORD'S PRAYER [34–49]

Introduction [*34–35*]

1. The uses of the Lord's Prayer [34]
  a. helps us to acknowledge His boundless goodness and clemency
  b. sends us to Him in our every need
  c. provides, to meet our ignorance and insufficiency, a form setting forth
    (1) all that He allows us to seek of Him
    (2) all that is of benefit to us
    (3) all that we need ask

2. Division of the Lord's Prayer into six petitions grouped in two parts [35]
  a. six, not seven, petitions

b. while the whole prayer ascribes to God's glory the chief place, the first three petitions particularly apply to it, the second three are concerned with the care of ourselves

Interpretation [*36-47*]

Invocation

1. Our Father . . . [36-39]
   a. the invocation "Our Father" bespeaks God's loving fatherhood of us, transcending all human fatherhood, and our sonship toward Him through our adoption as children of grace in Christ [36]
   b. "Our Father"—a form of address that should encourage us in our fear and hesitation [37]
      (1) the Father of mercies is moved by our prayers of sincere confession of sin
      (2) our narrowness of heart keeps us from comprehending God's favor, but Christ is pledge and guarantee of our adoption and also gives the Spirit in witness of it
      (3) thus we are to pray boldly in the Spirit
   c. "Our Father"—a form of address that sets us in fellowship with the brethren [38]
      (1) He is Father of us collectively, not individually: this is the basis of our brotherly love
      (2) prayers of the Christian man should be general and embrace all who are brothers in Christ, not only those whom He at present sees and recognizes as such, but all men who dwell on earth
      (3) all prayers ought to be such that they look to the fellowship which our Lord has established in His kingdom and His household
   d. comparison of prayer and almsgiving [39]
      (1) we can, nevertheless, pray especially for ourselves and certain others, provided the sense of community is constantly kept in mind and all things referred to it
      (2) this parallel to almsgiving, which though enjoined for all poor, we can carry out only for some because we cannot know all who need and are unable to help all
      (3) still, in prayer, distances can be leaped that are impossible in almsgiving, and we can pray for foreign and unknown persons through the general form of prayer that includes all children of God

2. "Who art in heaven . . ." [40]
   a. while this does not mean that God is confined to a particular place (for He is everywhere diffused), the expression is intended for our incapacity which cannot otherwise comprehend His unspeakable glory: incomprehensible essence
   b. threefold meaning of "in heaven"
      (1) God transcends all place; we must rise above all perception of body and soul to seek Him: greatness
      (2) He is lifted above all chance or change: everlasting immortality
      (3) He embraces and holds together the entire universe and controls it by His power: infinite power

3. Meaning of "Father"; summary:
   a. engenders trust in God-in-Christ and protects us from false gods, thus leading us from the Son to the Father
   b. His throne in heaven reminds us of His governing of the universe, thus of His care for us

First Part [41–43]

1. First petition: "Hallowed be thy name . . ." [41]
   a. calls upon men to give honor to God: not to speak or think of Him without the highest reverence
   b. thus all impiety, detraction and mockeries of God's name are to be banished, and hence God's majesty may more and more shine forth

2. Second petition: "Thy Kingdom come" [42]
   a. though not separate in content from the first petition, it is separated from it to overcome our sluggishness
   b. meaning of "kingdom": God reigns where men pledge themselves to His righteousness to aspire to a heavenly life
      (1) by denial of self: God corrects all desires of the flesh that war against Him
      (2) by contempt of the world: God shapes all our thoughts in obedience to His rule
   c. God's setting up of His kingdom through the two ways of humbling the world
      (1) through the secret inspiration of His Spirit: we must daily desire that God gather churches unto Himself from all parts of the world, etc.

(2) the impious who resist His authority He casts down

d. the function of this petition
   (1) to draw us back from worldly corruption that separates us from God and keeps His kingdom from thriving within us
   (2) to kindle zeal for mortification of the flesh
   (3) to instruct us in bearing the cross

3. Third petition: "Thy will be done" [43]
   a. though not to be separated from His kingdom, His will is separately mentioned here on account of our ignorance
   b. meaning: God will be King in the world when all submit to His will
   c. God's two "wills"
      (1) here is meant not God's secret will by which He controls all things and directs them to their end by His incomprehensible plan [III.21-24 and I.16-18]
      (2) rather here is meant God's other will to which voluntary obedience corresponds—described in terms of conforming earth to the obedient, peaceable, and upright ways of heaven
   d. the function of this petition
      (1) to renounce the desires of our flesh (which are contrary to God's will)
      (2) to be formed to self-denial
         (a) that God may rule in us according to His decisions, and
         (b) create new minds and hearts in us
      (3) in sum: that His Spirit may govern our hearts and teach us inwardly that we may learn to love what pleases Him and hate what displeases Him

4. Conclusion of the first part
   a. all these things will come to pass even without any thought or desire or petition of ours
   b. yet it is good and valuable for us to desire and request them, for thus we testify ourselves servants and children of God
   c. those who do not hallow God's name, or pray for the coming of His kingdom and that His will be done, are not to be received among God's children and servants, and will inexorably go to their confusion and destruction

Second Part: in which we descend to our own affairs, but without losing sight of God's glory [44–47]

1. Fourth petition: "Give us this day our daily bread [44]
   a. the general intent of this petition
      (1) by it we ask of God all things our bodies need in this world, thus giving ourselves over to His providential care
      (2) thus those of us who would give our souls to God but are troubled and worried in body are set at rest in order that our expectation of eternal life may not be impaired—a great exercise of faith!
   b. the exposition of the several parts
      (1) "daily" bread
         (a) "supersubstantial" bread is an erroneous interpretation because God is concerned with the whole man—here and hereafter—not just with his spiritual side
         (b) Christ accommodates His teaching to our slowness of mind by working gradually from the physical (petition 4) to the spiritual (petition 5, 6)
         (c) the adjective "daily"
            (1) emphasizes God's care for us day by day and hour by hour, by physical as well as spiritual means
            (2) restrains our greedy amassing of physical goods
            (3) reminds us that God gives us not only the bread but the capacity to ingest it and benefit from it
         (d) "our"
            (1) by divine gift and not by our own right
            (2) yet earned by our own honest toil and not through others' harm
         (e) "given"
            (1) a simple and free gift of God whatever its source
            (2) by His blessing alone do our labors prosper

2. Fifth petition: "Forgive us our debts . . . " [45]
   a. the final two petitions sum up God's spiritual convenant for the salvation of the church: forgiveness of sins and protection against temptations
   b. exposition of the separate points
      (1) "debts": so-called because we owe penalty for them
         (a) God pardons us through His free mercy given in Christ our ransom

(b) the "Spirituals" who believe in earthly perfectibility run counter to this true doctrine and thus call judgment, not mercy, upon themselves; they lure their disciples away from Christ

(2) "as we forgive . . ."

(a) forgiveness belongs to God alone

(b) but we can willingly cast from the mind wrath, hatred, desire for revenge, and remembrance of injustice, thus opening ourselves up to God's forgiveness

(c) but by forgiving others we do not "deserve" God's forgiveness—this phrase is added here to comfort the weakness of our faith, and to mark us as children of God

3. Sixth petition: ["Lead us not into temptation . . ."] [46]

a. corresponds to the promise that the law is to be engraved upon our hearts, but because of our continual warfare, this petition asks for God's help and protection so we may be victorious

b. our double need of the Spirit

(1) to soften our hearts and lead them to obey God

(2) to render us invincible against temptation

c. exegesis of separate points

(1) "temptations": many and varied

(a) from our own inordinate desire or the devil's devices

(b) temptations of the "right" (prosperity) or of the "left" (adversity)

(c) it is against all these that we pray God's help to withstand

(d) yet temptations are necessary to "keep us on our toes"; so we do not ask to be relieved of all temptations, but only not to succumb to them

(e) God and the devil use temptations in antithetical ways:

(1) God—to test the sincerity of His children and by exercising it to strengthen them; always providing a means of escape

(2) Satan—to crush men

(2) "evil" or "evil one"

(a) either interpretation correct

(b) our plea: not to be vanquished or overwhelmed by any temptations but may stand fast by the Lord's power against all attacking powers

d. it is not in our power, but only by God's spirit that we engage the devil in conflict
   (1) it would be pointless to pray thus if we felt sufficient in ourselves
   (2) in this petition we anticipate not only the initial help to be freed of Satan and sin, but also continual increases of God's grace, leading to final victory
e. the objection raised for James 1:13 solved
   (1) James says it is against God's nature to lead us into sin
   (2) but James means we must not transfer to God the vices we ourselves are guilty of
   (3) but God can sometimes, when it seems good to Him, turn us over to Satan, by a just and often secret judgment: the cause, hidden from men, is certain with God

   [N.B.: God's freedom chs. 21–24 anticipated]

Conclusion [47]

1. Resumé of second part
   a. here we commend to God ourselves and all our possessions
   b. these prayers ought to be public, looking to the public edification of the church and the advancement of the believers' fellowship
   c. all our prayers must be social, not individual

2. First doxology
   a. while omitted from the Latin versions, this clause ought to be here, for it tells why we should be bold to ask and confident to receive
   b. God's kingdom, power, and glory are eternal basis for our assurance and prayer

3. "Amen"
   a. expresses the warmth of our desire to obtain what we have asked of God
   b. strengthens our hope that these things have already been brought to pass by God's undeceiving promise

Perfection and Fullness of the Lord's Prayer [*48–49*]

1. The Lord's Prayer as a binding rule [48]
   a. in the Lord's Prayer we have the perfect sum of all prayers we can lawfully utter

b. nothing can be taken away or added to it: those who do
    (1) wish to add to God's wisdom for their own blasphemy
    (2) are contemptuous of God's will, and wander beyond it in their uncontrolled desire
    (3) will never obtain anything thus, because their prayers are apart from faith

c. thus Tertullian rightly calls it the "lawful" prayer: all other prayers lie outside the law and are forbidden

2. The Lord's Prayer does not bind us to its form of words but to its content [49]
    a. there are many other prayers in Scripture, utterly different in phraseology, yet composed by the same Spirit and profitable for us
    b. but in this perfect prayer, in sum but not in exact language, are contained all other prayers; by it the content of every prayer must be guided
    c. the Lord's Prayer: the teaching of divine wisdom, teaching what it willed, and willing what was needful

EIGHTH DIVISION: PERSEVERANCE IN PRAYER [50–52]

1. Times and occasions of prayer [50]
    a. prayer at regular times
        (1) we should especially exercise ourselves in prayer on arising, at meals, and upon retiring
        (2) this practice is to help us in our sluggishness, not superstitiously "to pray God" for the remaining hours
        (3) in our or other's adversity or prosperity, we must turn to God in prayer
    b. our prayers must impose no law upon God
        (1) we must leave God free to decide what He is to do and when and how He is to do it
        (2) by praying first of all that His will be done, we retain our own will, and keep ourselves within our creaturely limits

2. Patient perseverance in prayer [51]
    a. God does not always respond to our first request, but in His own time will show He has not been deaf to our entreaty
    b. like David, we should persist in prayer with even-tempered minds
    c. superstitious "bargains" with God are ruled out: God some-

times grants to such in wrath what He withholds from others in mercy

3. Unheard prayers? [52]
   a. our faith in God is stronger than our sense perception which fails to see how God answers our prayers:
      God will never forsake His people; the good destined for them will be revealed at the Judgment Day
   b. even when God grants our prayers, it is not always in the exact form of our request, but never are our prayers in vain
   c. prayer without perseverance is prayer in vain

CHAPTER 21
Eternal Election, by Which God Has Predestined Some to Salvation, Others to Destruction

Importance of the Doctrine of Predestination Excludes both Presumption and Reticence in Speaking of It [*1–4*]

1. Necessity and beneficial effect of the doctrine of election; danger of curiosity
   a. covenant of life not preached equally among all men; and unequally heeded among those to whom preached
   b. this unequal treatment of men by God raises agonizing questions for many
   c. our answer: until we come to know God's eternal election, we shall never really be persuaded that our salvation flows from God's free mercy
      (1) Paul's description of the remnant of the people saved shows God as willing out of His good pleasure, and paying no reward
      (2) how can we be properly humbled before God unless the doctrine of predestination be made clear?
   d. two kinds of men in their attitude toward predestination: the curious who madly rush into an investigation of it; the cautious who want to avoid controversy by side-stepping the topic
      (1) restraint enjoined on the first kind of men
      (2) for it is not lawful for man to try to penetrate more deeply than the Lord intended

2. Doctrine of predestination to be sought in Scripture only
   a. let us seek about predestination only what the Word of God discloses, maintaining a "learned ignorance"
   b. to go beyond this limit is to plunge ourselves into ruin

3. The second danger: anxious silence about the doctrine of election
   a. some men practically tell us to bury any mention of predestination
      (1) their moderation is laudable
      (2) but they make little progress with the human understanding
   b. we prefer to let Scripture as the school of the Holy Spirit speak to our open minds, but never to try to go beyond this limit

4. The alleged peril in the doctrine dismissed
   a. we must not let the blasphemies of wicked men deter us from speaking of predestination, any more than they should deter us from discussing the doctrines of the Trinity or of creation
   b. this is the line taken by Augustine in his *The Gift of Perseverance*

Predestination Defined and Explained in Relation to the Israelitish Nation, and to Individuals [5–7]

5. Predestination and foreknowledge of God; the election of Israel
   a. while predestination is generally accepted by religious men, many confuse predestination for foreknowledge: actually both doctrines are in God but one is not to be subjected to the other
   b. definitions
      (1) foreknowledge: all things always were, and perpetually remain, under God's eyes, so that to His knowledge there is nothing future or past, but all things are present
      (2) predestination: God's eternal decree, by which He determined with Himself what He willed to become of each man
   c. Scriptural evidence of Israel: in God's choice rests the future condition not only of individuals but of nations

d. Scripture gives the lie to those who bind God's election either to men's worth or merit of works: supporting texts

6. The second stage: election and reprobation of individual Israelites
   a. but not all of Israel was chosen: the second, more limited, degree of election: e.g., that of Isaac over Ishmael; Jacob over Esau
   b. God's freedom seen in the very inequality of His grace

7. The election of individuals as actual election
   a. God's election preeminently seen in His election of individual persons: out of Abraham's race only certain ones were chosen to ascend to the Head, Christ
      (1) Paul teaches this from Mal. 1:2 (Rom. 9:13)
      (2) experience also shows that out of a great multitude many fall away
   b. intermediate between rejection of all mankind and election of a meager number of the godly is the fact that God makes covenant with some who are outwardly changed but in whom inner grace does not work to regenerate them and keep them in the covenant to the end
      (1) this the doctrine of the remnant
      (2) seen in Paul's distinction between children of Abraham according to the flesh and according to the spirit
   c. summary survey of the doctrine of election
      (1) God once established by His eternal and unchangeable plan those whom He long before determined once for all to receive into salvation, and those whom, on the other hand, He would devote to destruction
      (2) election is founded upon God's mercy; reprobation upon His just but incomprehensible judgment
      (3) signs of both states
         (a) call and justification—of election
         (b) shutting off from knowledge of His name and from sanctification—of reprobation
      (4) remaining chapters on this topic to deal with quibble of the learned on this and arguments of the impious dangerous to the simple-minded

Outline of Presentation

1. Related doctrines (a partial list)
   (a) providence (God's working from God's side; predestination is

God's working from man's side: predestination and providence are together in *Inst.* 1539–1550)

(b) faith

(c) justification

(d) the Church

(e) Christ

2. Growth of this doctrine in Calvin
   (a) work on Stoic doctrine of *pronoia* in Seneca (1532)
   (b) 1536 *Institution* [II.138–147]
   (c) 1537/38 Catechism, par. 13. [Fuhrmann, *Instruction in Faith, 1537,* pp. 36f.; Battles, *John Calvin: Catechism, 1538,* pp. 16f.
   (d) 1539 *Institutes* (effect of reading Augustine, and of Bucer) ch. 8
   (e) 1551–52 Jerome Bolsec incident
   (f) *De Aeterna Praedestinatione* (1552)
   (g) 1559 *Institutes* (III.21–24)

3. Scriptural basis: history of Israel as seen through Paul's eyes, and as interpreted by the later Augustine.
   Predestination in Christian history
   (a) predestination is historically a counter-principle of authority to ecclesiastical absolutism (e.g. Wyclif).
   (b) freedom of will: New Testament to Reformation (diagram 2:2, p. 91)

4. Some presuppositions of Calvin's doctrine of predestination
   (a) Calvin starts with two poles (based on own religious experience and upon Paul and Augustine)

*God's Freedom**	*Man's Bondage*
(free because grace is given to whom He will)	(cannot accept God's grace, and hence, freedom, unless by God's act wholly)

---

*Corpus Reformatorum 52:266, sermon 2 on the Epistle to the Ephesians: "Car si nous voulions assubietir Dieu à estre égal envers tout le monde, il auroit moins de liberté que les creatures mortelles" ("For if we would subject God to being equal toward all the world, He would have less freedom than mortal creatures").

(b) Passages from which the notion of God's freedom may be inferred:

III.21.6	*III.22.1*
God's mere generosity is free, bound by no laws—cf. Israel vs. other nations inequality of God's grace—proves it free	God has always been free to bestow His grace on whom He would: example of Christ.

Thus behind the *decretum arcanum,* the *decretum horribile,* lies God's freedom. Calvin, thus, posits for God a freedom which negates for man freedom in the religious sphere; yet Calvin insists upon man's moral responsibility and guilt, despite his bondage.

(c) three basic presuppositions:
  (1) God is free: III.21.5f; cf. III.2.35 (inequality of God's grace proves it and its Giver are free)
  (2) God is active, not passive
    a) in election: III.22
    b) in reprobation: III.23
  (3) But man is still responsible: III.24

Cf. Beza, *Life of Calvin,* Eng. Tr. Calvin's Tracts, I, lviii (on the Jerome Bolsec incident: 16 Oct.–23 Dec. 1551): "Meanwhile the Consistory of Geneva, at a public meeting, declared the true doctrine of predestination, and afterwards approved of it, as comprehended in a public document drawn up by Calvin. All that Satan gained by these dissensions was, that this article of the Christian religion, which was formerly most obscure, became clear and transparent to all not disposed to be contentious."

5. Plan of treatment of the doctrine
  (a) [chapter 21]: basic exposition of double predestination [note summary at end]
  (b) [chapters 22–24]: answers to objections of learned and impious critics of predestination
    (1) [chapter 22]: Scriptural foundations of the doctrine/its literary history in Christian history
    (2) [chapter 23]: specific refutation of the five chief objections to predestination

(3) [chapter 24]: the call of the elect/the judgment of the reprobate

Chapter 22
Confirmation of This Doctrine from Scriptural Testimonies

***Election Is Not From Foreknowledge of Merit but Is of God's Sovereign Purpose* [*1–6*]**

1. Election vs. foreknowledge of merits
   a. many authorities have held and now hold the wrong notion that God distinguishes among men according as He foresees the merits or evil inclinations men are going to have
   b. Calvin's contrary view borne out by clear Scripture and by experience as well
   c. this unequal treatment by God they find more objectionable in individual cases than in nations: what, then, about the case of Christ, of the seed of David?—for Augustine, Christ is the clearest mirror of election
   d. Paul: we were chosen in Christ "before the creation of the world"—therefore the choice of us is apart from our worth: (Eph. 1:4–5) plus other proofs from Paul's letters

2. Election before creation and not associated with foreknowledge of merit [exegesis of Eph. 1:4–5 in detail]
   a. all regard for human worth removed by words "before the creation of the world"
   b. "elected to be holy": all human virtue is the result of election
   c. thus God has chosen whom He has willed, and before their birth

3. Elected to be holy, not because already holy
   a. combine II Tim. 1:9 and Eph. 1:4: you then have a clear repudiation on Paul's part of election through human merit
   b. merits, whether past or future, are ruled out clearly in Scripture, e.g., "You did not choose me, but I chose you" (John 15.16): God's will solely determinative in election

4. Romans, chs. 9 to 11, and similar passages
   a. Paul: Israel chosen, but not all descendants of Israel are true Israelites

b. just as the ancient Jews claimed the name "church" for themselves, holding the gospel to depend on their decision, so today do the papists act
c. over against their claims we set God's special election as the sole cause of His adoption of men as sons
d. the choice of Jacob over Esau, as Paul shows, rests not on God's foreseeing of future merits of the one over the other, but on God's call only

5. The case of Jacob and Esau refutes the argument from works
   a. Paul contends that the distinction between the brothers depends not upon any basis of works but upon the mere calling of God, because it was established between them before they were born
   b. Paul: the salvation of believers has been founded upon the decision of divine election alone, and rests not at all upon works
   c. God's free choice of Jacob over Esau is even accentuated by His overlooking Esau's right of primogeniture
   d. other cases of God's free choice:
      (1) Isaac/Ishmael
      (2) Ephraim/Manasseh

6. Jacob's election not to earthly blessings
   a. can one, from Jacob's earthly elevation to first-born, infer his adoption into the inheritance of heaven? (even Paul twisted Scripture, they say)
   b. answer: God willed by an earthly symbol to declare Jacob's spiritual election (otherwise hidden in God's inaccessible judgment)
   c. Jacob's claim then a proof of God's freely given mercy (Rom. 9:15, quoting Exod. 33:19)
   d. Paul's "foreknown of God" (Rom. 11:2) are people actively chosen by God, not passively "watched"
      (1) God's secret predestination also taught by Peter (I Peter 1:2, 19f.)
      (2) Paul's "people foreknown" = only a fraction mixed with the multitude that falsely claims God's name
      (3) Exod. 33:19 (Rom. 9:15): God will have mercy on those toward whom He is merciful: proof of God's special grace

***Answers to Opponents of this Basis of Election, Which also is Reprobation** [7–11]*

7. Christ's witness concerning election
   a. Christ in John's gospel asserts that our reception into His keeping is the Father's gift
   b. therefore none excel by their own effort or diligence
   c. but by free adoption God makes those whom He wills to be His sons: the intrinsic cause of this is in Himself, for He is content with His own secret good pleasure

8. The church fathers, especially Augustine, on God's "foreknowledge"
   a. Ambrose, Origen, Jerome, taught predestination by foreknown merits
   b. Augustine, after initially holding this view, in his controversy with Pelagius saw the light—a whole volume could be woven from his words on this
   c. Paul could easily have vindicated God's righteous (but selective) dealing with men, by an appeal to works, but the Holy Spirit prevented him from asserting this false view

9. Is not election joined to God's "foreknowledge" of man's merits in so far as free grace makes just such merits possible?
   a. Thomas Aquinas: foreknowledge of merits is not the cause of predestination on the side of the predestinator's act but on our side it may in a way be so called: namely, according to the particular estimate of predestination, as when God is said to predestine glory for man on account of merits, because He has decreed to bestow upon him grace by which to merit glory
   b. this would subordinate predestination to grace, to predestination to glory: absurd!
   c. a wise retort: "Those who assign God's election to merits are wiser than they ought to be"

10. The universality of God's invitation and the particularity of election
    a. a paradox: God calls all but elects only a few. Why?
       (1) some moderates (e.g., Melanchthon) emphasize the universality of the promises over special grace in order to avoid thorny questions
       (2) Calvin however will not tolerate any evasion

b. Scripture's harmonization of the call of all to repentance and faith by outward preaching, but the giving of the spirit of repentance and faith only to some—has been treated before but will be treated again; for now:
   (1) gospel addresses all, but gift of faith is rare
   (2) is there not mutual agreement between faith and the Word? Augustine asserts the sublime mystery of God's call to all but the response of some, as Paul everywhere declares
   (3) cf. also Bernard of Clairvaux
   (4) further texts, from John's Gospel

11. Rejection also takes place not on the basis of works but solely according to God's will
   a. Paul makes Esau's rejection, as Jacob's acceptance by God, lie outside any merits
   b. this shows that reprobation (as well as predestination) rests on God's decision alone

CHAPTER 23
Refutation of the False Accusations with Which This Doctrine Has Always Been Unjustly Burdened

Reprobation the Concomitant of Election and an Act of God's Will [*1 –3*]

1. Election—but no reprobation?
   a. human understanding boggles at this teaching of Scripture; as a consequence many try to avoid reproaching God by divorcing election from condemnation
   b. Calvin answers this "childish argument": God condemns those He passes over—and on the basis of His own will solely
   c. Paul's mention of God's "patience" is not to be read as God's patient waiting upon men on the chance they may of themselves repent; Augustine: where might is joined to longsuffering, God does not permit but governs by His power
   d. this inference from Paul's statement that "God has prepared vessels of mercy" but that vessels of wrath are for good reason "fashioned for destruction," answered: God in both cases is pursuing His secret plan although all men are, Paul reminds us, blameworthy

α First Objection: the Doctrine of Election Makes God a Tyrant (2–3)

2. God's will is the rule of righteousness
   a. this should be enough refutation, but we must needs continue our individual refutations
   b. is God, they ask, such a tyrant as to destroy capriciously those who have not previously offended Him?
   c. for the pious, who revere God's will as ultimate cause of all that is, this is an impious question which tries to find a cause beyond the ultimate cause
   d. Calvin here repudiates the "absolute might" of the theologians: God, as highest perfection, is the law of all laws

3. God is just toward the reprobate
   a. they ask: why did God from the beginning predestine some to death, even before they could, by existing, deserve that judgment?
   b. answer: mankind as fallen is odious to God, and can deserve no other judgment

God's Justice Not Subject to Our Questioning [4–7]

4. God's decree is also hidden in His justice
   a. they ask: did God not predestine them to the very corruption now viewed as the cause of condemnation?
   b. to this charge that God would then be made unjust, Calvin answers with Paul's question: "Who are you, O man, to argue with God?"
   c. they respond that Calvin is not truly defending God's righteousness but only reaching for a subterfuge
   d. Calvin answers: God's judgments, while wholly righteous, are inscrutable to men, as Paul and Prov. 26:10 clearly assert: our meager understanding is no basis for condemning God's apparent injustice

5. God's hidden decree is not to be searched out but obediently marveled at
   a. why God so willed is not for our reason to inquire, for it cannot comprehend God's will
   b. meditation on the contrast between man's puny understand-

ing and the deeps of God's will: "Ignorance that believes is better than rash knowledge" (Augustine)

c. God Himself by His Holy Spirit spoke the final word through Paul's mouth

β Second Objection: the Doctrine of Election Takes Guilt and Responsibility away from Man

6. a. They now ask, not directly accusing the Judge, but excusing the sinner: Why should God impute those things to men as sin, the necessity of which He has imposed by His predestination?
   b. the older church fathers answered this one by their doctrine of God's foreknowing man's merits (or demerits)
   c. Calvin's answer: "God has made everything for Himself, even the wicked for the evil day" (Prov. 16:4)
   d. some of the church fathers solve the difficulty by asserting that God has imposed no necessity on men but has merely foreseen their wickedness to come
      (1) this dodge is eagerly picked up by the Schoolmen
      (2) but even Valla disproves it by saying that both life and death are acts of God's will more than of His foreknowledge

7. God has predestined the fall into sin
   a. they assert that it is not stated explicitly that God decreed Adam should perish for his rebellion, and hold that Adam had free choice to shape his own fortune, and was to be treated only as he deserved
   b. answer: God's omnipotence demands a creation to no uncertain end; predestination seen in Adam's posterity—then it must also apply to Adam himself
   c. the dreadful decree: it must have been God's will to decree in Adam's fall the fall of countless others
   d. God's wisdom foreknows everything; God's might controls and rules everything; Augustine concurs in this statement

God Willed, Not only Permitted, Adam's Fall and the Rejection of the Reprobate, but with Justice [*8–11*]

8. No distinction between God's will and God's permission
   a. they assert that God wills salvation; but only "permits" reprobation

b. Augustine answers: "the will of God is the necessity of things"
c. God acts justly, and for His own glory: our task is not to seek the ultimate reason why God has so acted, but to recognize the immediate cause of man's reprobation in man's own inherited fault: before God's secrets a "learned ignorance" is best

9. Summary refutation of the second objection
   a. the reprobate seek an excuse for their sinning in the necessity laid upon them by God's ordination
   b. we reply that God's ordinance, which destines them to destruction, has its own equity (though unknown to us) and consequently they are rightly judged by God

γ Third Objection: the Doctrine of Election Leads to the View that God Shows Partiality toward Persons

10. a. they state: if you put the release of some from eternal destruction solely on the divine will, then you make God a "respecter of persons"
    b. answer:
       (1) Scripture here means by "person" not a man but conspicuous human qualities, either attractive or repulsive
       (2) God is not partial toward persons—Jew or Greek, poor or wealthy, slave or free
    c. further answer: how is it that of two men indistinguishable in merit, God passes over one but takes the other?—free mercy is the only consideration

11. God's mercy and righteousness in predestination
    a. they say: if God is to be fair, then He should either condemn all or show mercy to all
    b. with Augustine, Calvin holds that God, in freedom, shows His mercy to some, His justice in judging others

Preaching of Predestination Not Injurious but Useful [*12–14*]

δ Fourth Objection: the Doctrine of Election Destroys All Zeal for an Upright Life

12. a. they assert: predestination will extinguish any desire for well-doing: if God alone decides, what difference does it make how one acts?

b. answer:
  (1) some indeed criminally so act in this manner
  (2) but Scripture instructs us far otherwise, to be humbled to tremble before God's justice and esteem His mercy
  (3) with Paul, Calvin asserts the great difference between ceasing well-doing because election is sufficient for salvation, and devoting ourselves to the pursuit of good as the appointed goal of election

c. they reply: then if a man condemned by God tries to make himself approved by God by innocent life, he is wasting his time

d. answer: this effort, too, comes from God's election

ϵ Fifth Objection: the Doctrine of Election Makes All Admonitions Meaningless

13. a. they claim predestination overthrows all exhortation to godly living
  b. on this, see Augustine, *Rebuke and Grace*
    (1) Paul preaches both election and moral exhortation, and harmonizes them
    (2) let preaching, then, take its course, that it may lead men to faith, and hold them fast in perseverance with continuing profit
    (3) as Augustine asserts, we are to proclaim God's truth without holding back anything—for God's will shall prevail over all

14. Augustine as the pattern for the right manner of preaching divine predestination
  a. Augustine nevertheless tempers his preaching of truth in such a way as to promote edification, yet avoid offense
  b. God acts within man; we cannot know who belongs to the number of the predestined, who does not
    (1) we are not to teach by cursing men as already condemned or to be condemned in the future because they are now unbelieving
    (2) rather, we are to wish that all men be saved

CHAPTER 24
Election Is Confirmed by God's Call; Moreover, the Wicked Bring upon Themselves the Just Destruction to Which They Are Destined

***The Elect Are Effectually Called, and Incorporated into the Communion of Christ** [1–5]*

1. The call is dependent upon election and accordingly is solely a work of grace
   a. we will discuss more explicitly the calling of the elect and the blinding of the wicked
   b. Paul's order: God
      (1) appoints
      (2) calls
      (3) justifies
   c. gospel preaching, though originating in election, is shared with the wicked; hence it cannot be a full proof of election
   d. John 6:45: "Every man who has heard and learned of the Father, comes to me"—but the "hearing and learning" are of God's deciding
   e. God's appointment of Himself as Father and His call of His children into the one family of faith are coupled in Scripture as evidence of God's free mercy, not of a synergistic mixing of God's call with man's response (as allowing some human merit)

2. The manner of the call itself clearly indicates that it depends on grace alone
   a. the call consists in
      (1) the preaching of the Word
      (2) the illumination of the Spirit
   b. God, in offering His Word even to those who do not seek Him, shows His free goodness
      (1) those who then reject His Word thereby bring an even heavier judgment upon themselves
      (2) God, in withdrawing the effective working of His Spirit from them, shows forth His own glory
      (3) the inner call that remains with the elect, however, is a sure pledge of salvation

3. Faith is the work of election, but election does not depend upon faith
    a. two errors to be avoided
        (1) man, as God's coworker, ratifies election by his own consent
        (2) election doubtful unless confirmed by faith
    b. the right view:
        (1) our assurance of salvation must never so bedazzle us as to obscure the ultimate cause: God's election
        (2) we must never let the pipe detract from the honor due the fountain alone

4. The right and wrong way to attain certainty of election
    a. Satan, to unsettle the certainty of our election, tempts us to seek our certainty "outside the way": i.e., to try to penetrate into the inner recesses of divine wisdom
    b. to inquire outside of God's Word about our election is a deadly abyss; our "inquiry" should begin with God's call and end with it
    c. the peace and joy brought by the feeling of God's election, according to Bernard of Clairvaux

5. Election is to be understood and recognized in Christ alone
    a. if we are truly in communion with Christ, we have a sufficiently firm testimony that we have been chosen as God's adopted sons
    b. that this communion in Christ is given to us is testified through the preaching of the gospel
    c. since Christ is our ultimate goal, to seek outside and beyond Him anything at all is insane
    d. in our prayers we must not bargain with God, but rest secure in His promises

***Under Christ's Protection the Perseverance of the Elect Is Secure: Scriptural Passages Cited in Objection Interpreted** [**6–11**]*

6. Christ bestows upon His own the certainty that their election is irrevocable and lasting
    a. does God care for our salvation? Yes, if He has led us to Christ, the sole Savior of His people
    b. let us therefore embrace Christ as our shepherd; He will enfold us

c. still there is anxiety about our future state: "Many are called but few are chosen": for this, the gift of perseverance as John and Paul both assert

7. He who truly believes cannot fall away
   a. those who seem for a time to be Christ's, but fall away, have never really cleaved to Christ with the heartfelt trust of certain election (John)
   b. let us not then be discouraged by their failure
   c. Paul, however, cautions against haughty pride and self-centered confidence, inimical to reverence toward God; and he also commends fear to prepare us humbly to receive God's grace
   d. our hope, which extends beyond death, stands against all doubt

8. General and special calling: exegesis of "Many are called but few are chosen" (Matt. 22:2ff.)
   a. this text, badly understood, is unambiguous when we realize that there are two kinds of calls
      (1) general call: by which God invites all equally to Himself by the outward preaching of the Word
      (2) special call: plus the inward illumination of Spirit, by which He causes the preached Word to dwell in their hearts
         (a) given usually to believers alone
         (b) but occasionally to others for a time—their ungratefulness, then, is even more culpable

9. The example of Judas is no counterevidence
   a. distinction between God's choice of His elect, and His choice of Judas for the apostolic office, from which he was to fall away in unfaith
   b. Gregory the Great is in error when he states we are aware of our call but unsure of our election—due to his making election depend on the merit of works
   c. predestination, rightly understood, is the best confirmation of faith

10. The elect before their call; there is no "seed of election"
   a. the call to election can come at any time of a man's life; throughout life the elect differ not at all from all sinful men, except that they are protected from ruin by God's special mercy

b. they are in error who think the seed of election was planted in them at birth; refutation of their examples

11. Not growth from seed but divine deliverance
   a. no Scriptural warrant for a "seed of election" in man
   b. election is God's deliverance of man: those whom the Lord has once determined to snatch from this gulf of destruction He defers until His own time; He only preserves them from falling into unpardonable blasphemy

How God Deals with the Reprobate [*12–17*]

12. God's administration of justice toward the reprobate
   a. God's call to the elect has its analogue in His judgments against the reprobate
   b. varied divine strategy toward the reprobate:
      (1) deprivation of capacity to hear the Word: e.g., 4,000 years of ignorance for the Gentiles, before Christ
      (2) blinding or stunning of reprobate after they hear the Word: of a hundred people who hear the Word, twenty receive it in faith, the rest reject it—all the result of God's choice

13. The preaching of the Word itself can conduce to hardness of heart
   a. God's bestowal of grace on some but not on others rests with His own almighty but secret will
   b. Chrysostom erroneously makes God's drawing of men to Himself rest not in God's judgment but solely in man's decision
   c. Scriptural examples show that God sometimes sends His Word to those whose blindness He intends to increase: e.g., Pharoah; people to whom Ezekiel was sent, etc.
   d. to those whom God decides not to illumine, God transmits His doctrine in an obscure form, so they will not profit by it but become even more stupid—yet the Word of God always has enough light to convict the wicked conscience

14. The cause of hardness of heart
   a. why does the Lord do as He does?
   b. two reasons:
      (1) because the reprobate do not obey God's Word when it is made known to them

(2) because the reprobate have been raised up by God's righteous but inscrutable judgment to show forth His glory in their condemnation

c. the impious complain that God abuses His creatures for His cruel amusement

d. our response: the wicked suffer nothing out of accord with God's most righteous judgment

15–16. Scriptural Passages that seem to prove the opposite of the stated doctrine

(i) Ezekiel 33:11 (15)

a. some Scriptural passages are brought forward to prove that the wicked bring death upon themselves; and do not die by God's ordination

b. Ezek. 33:11: "God does not will the death of the wicked but wills that the wicked turn back and live"—interpretation: the prophet's instruction that the death of the sinner is not pleasing to God is designed to assure believers that God is ready to pardon them as soon as they are touched by repentance but to make the wicked feel that their transgression is doubled because they do not respond to God's great kindness and goodness

(ii) I Tim. 2:3–4, and similar passages (16)

a. I Tim. 2:3–4: God "wills all men to be saved": by this Paul surely means only that God has not closed the way unto salvation to any order of men (e.g., kings and rulers); rather, He has so poured out His mercy that He would have none without it

(iii) the other passages do not declare what God has determined in His secret judgment regarding all men, but proclaim that there is ready pardon for sinners provided they turn back to seek it: e.g., Rom. 11:32; II Peter 3:9: answer—but the turning back itself is God's own doing!

17. Answers to further objections

a. first objection: has God a "double will"? Answer:

(1) do not take literally the Scriptural passages attributing human emotions to God

(2) by these God teaches us emphatically that what seems momentarily against His will is really consonant with it

b. second objection: will the Father of all be so unjust as to forsake any but those who by their own guilt previously have deserved this punishment? Answer: why did God pick one people for His very own, as a flower?

c. third objection: how can God hate anything He has made? Answer: true, but the reprobate are for good reason hateful to God: deprived of His Spirit they can bring forth nothing but cursing

d. final answer:
   (1) with Paul: "Who are you, O man, to argue with God?"
   (2) with Augustine: they who measure divine justice by the standard of human justice are acting perversely

CHAPTER 25
The Final Resurrection

Assertion of the Doctrine of the Final Resurrection [*1–4*]

1. Importance of and hindrances to the resurrection hope
   a. hope and faith as related to the resurrection texts of Scripture
   b. temptations of doubt overcome when we are bound to the heavenly life

2. Longing for union with God as motive for the hope of resurrection
   a. man's highest good as union with God faintly glimpsed only by Plato among the ancient philosophers
   b. those alone receive the fruit of Christ's benefits who raise their minds to the resurrection, a happiness kindled more and more each day
   c. all the parts of our resurrection have already been completed in Christ, but for us He will appear a second time unto salvation

3. The resurrection hoped for is that of the body: Christ's resurrection the prototype and basis for ours
   a. two foundations for our hope
      (1) the parallel of Christ's resurrection
      (2) the omnipotence of God
   b. it was not for Himself alone that Christ both died and rose; what was begun in the Head must be completed in the body
   c. Scriptural evidences of Christ's resurrection

4. God's omnipotence as foundation of the resurrection of the body
   a. no one is truly persuaded of the coming resurrection unless he is seized with wonder, and ascribes to the power of God its due glory
   b. the resurrection enables us to triumph over present battles

Objections of Various Classes of Opponents to the Doctrine Refuted [*5–9*]

5. Pagan denial of resurrection countered by burial rites
   a. by an unbelievable prompting of nature men always had before their eyes an image of the resurrection
   b. the custom of burial as earnest of new life

   The error of the chiliasts
   a. the chiliasts do not understand that the number one thousand in Revelation (20:4) refers only to disturbances that awaited the church
   b. if the "thousand-year reign" is terminal, then so is Christ's kingdom
   c. God's justice, as well as His majesty, are eternal

6. Resurrection of the flesh but immortality of the soul: (cf. *Psychopannychia*)
   a. two errors:
      (1) the whole man dies and souls are resurrected with bodies
      (2) immortal spirits are clothed with new bodies
   b. but, to refute the first error, the spirit, which is formed after the image of God, is more than a fleeting breath
   c. Scriptural testimonies that our souls may be entrusted to God
   d. do not be over-curious about the soul's immediate state

7. Resurrection of that body in which we have been clothed in this life
   a. to refute the second error, we must affirm that whatever now exists in us that is unworthy of heaven does not hinder the resurrection
   b. if our bodies are members of Christ and sanctified to Him, how could that which is sacred to God be condemned to eternal corruption?
   c. Scriptural testimonies to the resurrection of the body

8. Significance of rites honoring the body
   a. charge: in the resurrection there will be a creation of new bodies
   b. but Scripture urges us to hope for the resurrection of our flesh
   c. burial rites let men know that a new life is prepared for the bodies laid away, and raise our eyes from a grave to the vision of renewal

   The manner of resurrection

   d. as to substance we shall be raised in the same flesh, but different in quality
   e. remarks based on I Cor. 15

9. The resurrection of the ungodly
   a. there will be a resurrection of judgment and a resurrection of life
   b. in the present life, Christ's liberality flows to both the godly and the wicked, but the final judgment will separate the lambs from the goats

Man's Life in the Hereafter: Eternal Enjoyment of God's Presence, or Eternal Misery in Alienation from God [*10–12*]

10. Everlasting blessedness
    a. the difficulty of words to express the coming spiritual blessedness
    b. nothing beyond the presence of God is to be sought, since God contains the fullness of all good things
    c. it is harmful to indulge in dangerous speculations

11. Disposing of superfluous questions
    a. to discuss the future difference between prophets and apostles, virgins and married women is useless investigation
    b. we ought to be satisfied with the "mirror" and its "dimness" until we see him face to face

12. The lot of the reprobate
    a. despite the figurative representations of physical torments, the worst wretchedness is to be cut off from all fellowship with God

b. those who are the object of God's wrath will experience all that exists aflame with dire anger against him
c. thus with one glance God scatters mortal men, but urges His worshipers on until He Himself is "all in all"

BOOK FOUR

The External Means or Aids by Which God Invites Us into the Society of Christ and Holds Us Therein

CHAPTER 1
The True Church with Which as Mother of All the Godly We Must Keep Unity

The Holy Catholic Church, our mother *[1–4]*

1. The necessity of the church
   a. Christ becomes ours through faith in the gospel, but in our sluggishness we need outward helps
   b. God has provided such for us, through
      (1) pastors and teachers
      (2) sacraments
   c. our plan of instruction:
      (1) church: its government, orders, and power
      (2) sacraments
      (3) civil order
   d. the church is the starting point of our discussion

2. What is the relationship of church and creed?
   a. "believe the church":
      (1) visible church
      (2) all the elect, including the dead
   b. "believe" vs. "believe in"
      (1) "believe in God": our mind reposes in Him as truthful and our trust rests in Him
      (2) "believe the church," without the preposition, is correct, to distinguish from belief in God
   c. underneath a huge pile dwells a small number of God's elect, undaunted by Satan's savage attack
   d. the unity of believers under Christ the Head is the sole basis of hope for future inheritance
   e. the unity of the true catholic church, though at times it may be a tiny secret remnant

3. "The communion of saints"
   a. "communion of saints": benefits shared by Christ with them should be shared with one another

b. yet this sharing does not rule out
   (1) diversity of gifts
   (2) civil order, with private property
c. our faith rests upon a church that cannot fail
   (1) it stands by God's election, and cannot waver or fail any more than His eternal providence can
   (2) it has been joined to Christ's steadfastness; He will no more allow His believers to be estranged from Him than that His members be rent and torn asunder
   (3) while we remain within the bosom of the church, the truth will always abide with us
   (4) such promises as, "There will be salvation in Zion," etc., apply to us
d. so to embrace the unity of the church does not require a visible, tangible church, for it belongs to the realm of faith
   (1) it is not for us to distinguish between reprobate and elect (God's prerogative)
   (2) rather to establish with certainty in our hearts that all those who, by the kindness of God the Father through the Holy Spirit, have entered into fellowship with Christ are set apart as God's property and personal possession, to share His grace

4. The visible church as mother of believers
   a. but since our task here is to discuss the visible church, we should reflect on the title, "mother"
   b. church as mother
      (1) we cannot enter the spiritual life except through her
      (2) we must be pupils at her school all our lives
      (3) away from her we cannot hope for forgiveness of sins or salvation
   c. thus it is always disastrous to leave the church

Her Ministers, Speaking for God, Not to Be Despised [5–6]

5. Education through the church, its value and its obligation
   a. God's plan in human ministry
      (1) although God could do as He pleased, He chose human means
      (2) God ordained holy assemblies at the sanctuary with preaching
      (3) just as God did in biblical times, so today God wills to teach us through human means; double use:

(a) to test our obedience through His ministers
(b) to accommodate to our weakness

b. objections
   (1) authority of the Word dragged down by baseness of incumbents—ungratefulness
   (2) apostates try to split churches

c. our response
   (1) with Paul we must assert that the church is built up solely by outward preaching, and that the saints are held together by one bond only: that with common accord, through learning and advancement, they keep the church order established by God
   (2) believers have no greater help than public worship, for by it God raises His own folk upward step by step (this is why David longs for the temple)
   (3) by His Word, God alone sanctifies temples to Himself for lawful use
   (4) if we attempt anything without His express command, strange inventions forthwith cling to the bad beginning and spread evil without measure

6. Meaning and limits of the ministry
   a. two sides of a controversy:
      (1) some exaggerate its dignity beyond measure
      (2) others claim prerogatives of the Holy Spirit are wrongly transferred to men
   b. points at issue:
      (1) passages in which God as the Author of preaching, joined His Spirit with it, and promises benefits from it
      (2) passages in which God, separating Himself from outward helps, claims for Himself alone both the beginnings of faith and its entire course
   c. those who present themselves teachably to ministers ordained by God shall realize why this way of teaching was pleasing to God and wisely imposed upon men for moderation's sake

The Visible Church: Its Membership and the Marks by Which It Is Recognized [*7–9*]

7. Invisible and visible church
   a. two meanings of "church" in Scripture:
      (1) the children of God by grace of adoption and true members of Christ by sanctification of the Holy Spirit;

e.g., present saints plus all the elect from the beginning of the world

(2) the whole multitude of men spread over the earth who profess to worship one God and Christ

b. while we recognize the church in the first sense, as invisible to us but visible to God, so we are commanded to revere and keep communion with the church in the second sense, called "church" in respect to men

8. The limitation of our judgment

a. ultimately the members of God's church are known to God alone, but He has pointed out to us by certain marks what we should know of the church

b. knowing, however, how useful it would be for us to be aware who were to be counted as His children, He accommodated Himself to our capacity in letting us recognize, by confession of faith, example of life, and partaking of the sacraments, the members of the church professing the same God and Christ with us

9. The marks of the church and our application of them to judgment

a. the two marks: a church of God undoubtedly exists

(1) wherever the Word of God is purely preached and heard

(2) wherever the sacraments are administered according to Christ's institution

b. the fundamentals of ecclesiology

(1) the church is a multitude gathered from all nations

(2) the church is divided and dispersed in separate places, but agreed on the one truth of divine doctrine, and bound by the same religion

(3) under it are included individual churches, disposed in towns and villages, according to human need, so that each rightly has the name and authority of the church

(4) individual men who, by their profession of religion, are reckoned within such churches, even though they may actually be strangers to the church, still in a sense belong to it until they have been rejected by public judgment

c. the church and the individual: sometimes, for the sake of the common agreement of the church, we have to tolerate persons unworthy of the fellowship: we are not thus approving such persons as members of the church, but leave them in their place among the people of God until it is lawfully taken from them

d. when does a church exist? if it has the ministry of the Word and honors it, and the administration of the sacraments

***A Church with These Marks, However Defective, Is Not to Be Forsaken: the Sin of Schism** [10–16]*

10. Marks and authority of the church
    a. where Word and sacraments are, there the church truly exists and we dare not break its unity
    b. additional Scriptural ground for maintaining the church inviolate: "pillar and ground of truth," "the house of God," etc.

11. The inviolable validity of the marks
    a. Satan plots to efface the marks of the church by an ever-varied strategy
    b. our attitude toward the church, whether of honor or shunning, should be determined by whether these marks are present

12. Heeding the marks guards against capricious separation
    a. even if these marks may be faultily administered, we ought not to leave the communion
    b. nonessential matters should never be a basis of schism among Christians, even though total agreement on all points would be preferable
    c. our task is to stay with the church as the place where piety and sacraments are guarded and to try out of duty to correct what displeases but not disturb its peace and discipline

13. Scandal in the church no occasion for leaving it
    a. there are two sorts of "perfectionists"
        (1) the "airy spirits," guilty of insane pride (e.g., Novationists, Donatists, Anabaptists)
        (2) ill-advised zealots for righteousness—who judge no church present where there is no complete correspondence between gospel and quality of life
    b. yes, the church of Christ is holy, but as the parables of Christ show, it is here mixed with good and bad men, until the day of judgment

14. Paul and the needs of his congregations
    a. they say: intolerable that these vices rage!
    b. Paul answers this in his analysis of the faults of the Corinthian church; yet despite these, the church abides among them (because Word and sacrament remain)

15. Fellowship with wicked persons
    a. they throw up at us Paul's barring of table fellowship with a man of shameful life
    b. yet, it is a pity that our churches let worthy and unworthy indiscriminately into the Lord's Supper, and we should try to keep discipline
    c. but such mingling is no ground for an individual to break from the fellowship
    d. even Paul's teaching on the Lord's Supper is more lenient than theirs, for he asserts that such men eat and drink to their condemnation

16. The false claim of perfection comes from distorted opinion
    a. pride and arrogance is the real source for such over-scrupulosity
    b. against this, Augustine's advice: "Mercifully to correct what they can; patiently to bear and lovingly to bewail and mourn what they cannot: until God either amends or corrects or in the harvest uproots the tares and winnows the chaff"
    c. let the over-scrupulous meditate on various mitigating facts in the life and discipline of the church, and accordingly temper their prideful impatience

The Imperfect Holiness of the Church Does Not Justify Schism, but Affords Occasion for the Exercise Within It of the Forgiveness of Sins [17–22]

17. The holiness of the church
    a. the church's holiness is not yet complete, for while given Christ to sanctify her, the Lord is daily at work cleansing her spots
    b. therefore the church is holy in that it is daily advancing but has not yet reached its goal
    c. the prophecies of Joel and Isaiah of a perfect Jerusalem and

temple, apply to a church, not yet perfect, but to which God out of kindness grants a growing sanctification

d. throughout human history, though all men have been in sin, God has never left Himself without a convenanted folk, however tiny

18. The example of the prophets
    a. the prophets repeatedly emphasize the imperfections of the church of Jerusalem
    b. yet they did not because of her impurity forsake her to found new churches, continuing to worship even among their corrupted brethren
    c. like the prophets, we must not break the unity by schism

19. The example of Christ and of the apostles
    a. in Christ's day despite the prevailing impiety, Christ and His apostles worshiped in the same temple
    b. Cyprian, too, teaches that unity should not be broken because of unclean persons in the church
    c. conclusion:
        (1) he who voluntarily deserts the outward communion of the church (where the Word of God is preached and the sacraments are administered) is without excuse
        (2) neither the vices of the few nor the vices of the many in any way prevent us from duly professing our faith there in ceremonies ordained by God

20. Forgiveness of sins and the church
    a. our adversaries refuse to recognize the church unless it is free of all blemishes, and reject upright teachers who urge men to take refuge in pardon
    b. yes, we should urge men to perfection, but we know that it cannot be fully attained in this life
    c. forgiveness of sins is the foundation of the covenant with God, as the prophets teach concerning God's reconciling mercy

21. Lasting forgiveness for the members of the church
    a. through forgiveness of sins the Lord receives us into the church and preserves us there

b. the work of reconciliation is not once for all, but is a daily reality for the believers

22. The power of the keys
    a. the keys have been given to impart this benefit to us, as Christ and Paul teach
    b. three things to be noted:
        (1) however great the holiness in which God's children excel, they still—so long as they dwell in mortal bodies—remain unable to stand before God without forgiveness of sins
        (2) this benefit so belongs to the church that we cannot enjoy it unless we abide in communion with the church
        (3) it is dispensed to us through the ministers and pastors of the church, either by the preaching of the gospel or by the administration of the sacraments: the chief power of the keys

***Incidents Illustrating Forgiveness Within the Community of Believers* [*23–29*]**

23. All believers are to seek forgiveness of their sins
    a. like the Novatianists of old, certain Anabaptists claim that through baptism people are reborn into an angelic life, from which if they fall away no further mercy is forthcoming from God
    b. refutation of this view from Scripture
        (1) Matt. 6:12: "Forgive us our debts": saints are to confess their sins and are assured of pardon
        (2) if we are asked to forgive our brother seventy times seven, is this not to emulate His mercy to us?

24. God's abundant grace to sinful believers under the Old Covenant
    a. some of the patriarchs, circumcised and taught righteousness, then turned to heinous crimes, e.g., Joseph's brothers, Simeon and Levi, Reuben, Judah
    b. David shed innocent blood
    c. yet divine mercy was forthcoming for all these

25. God's abundant grace to sinful believers under the Old Covenant: the prophets
    a. the prophets remind Israel of her rebellion and sin, yet hold out the hope of divine mercy, e.g., Jeremiah, Ezekiel

b. Solomon's prayer of dedication for the Temple indicates prayers would be made to obtain pardon of sins there
c. the Lord saw that His people would be hardened with sins—and so He provided a remedy

26. God's abundant grace to sinful believers under the New Covenant
 a. Christ's coming did not take away this pardon from His erring followers
 b. proofs:
  (1) Peter's denial forgiven
  (2) the Thessalonians are chastened and invited to repent
  (3) Simon the Magician is told to take refuge in prayer

27. God's abundant grace toward delinquent churches
 a. whole churches have sometimes been engulfed in heinous sins:
  (1) Galatians
  (2) Corinthians
 b. yet the Lord has shone mercy to them
 c. also the creed teaches that continual grace for sins remains in Christ's church

28. Are only unconscious sins forgivable?
 a. (Anabaptists) allow pardon only for sins involuntarily committed
 b. contrary evidence of Scripture
  (1) the Old Testament on the one hand provides one kind of sacrifice for one, another for the other
  (2) David, versed in the law, sinned voluntarily and was pardoned
  (3) Peter, duly warned, renounced his Master, and was pardoned

29. The quest of "second repentance" in the ancient church
 a. admittedly, ancient church writers divided sins into two classes, for practical purposes
  (1) slight errors
  (2) public crimes
 b. stern churchly correction was meted out upon the second class of offenders, not because divine forgiveness for them was harder to get, but to deter others from so sinning and having to be cut off from the church

CHAPTER 2
A Comparison of the False and the True Church

Departure from True Doctrine and Worship Invalidates the Roman Church's Claim to Be the True Church [*1–6*]

1. The basic distinction
   a. where the ministry remains whole, even where faults exist, there the church, with its two marks, exists
   b. but where falsehood breaks in and fundamental doctrine is overturned, sacraments destroyed; the church disappears—as Paul teaches in asserting the church as resting on Christ and the teaching of prophets and apostles

2. The Roman Church and its claim
   a. the papal "no-church":
      (1) ministry, Lord's Supper, worship deformed
      (2) to withdraw from this is not to break the unity of the church of Christ
   b. the Romanists falsely extol the antiquity and exclusiveness of their church and hold all who question it to be schismatics
   c. they claim an unbroken "succession" in Italy, France, Spain
      (1) but what of Africa, Egypt, and Asia—where the succession has lapsed?
      (2) also what of the Greeks, whose succession has remained unbroken—are they schismatics?

3. The false church, despite its high pretensions, shows that it does not hear God's Word
   a. parallel between the boasts of the ancient Jews and the modern Romanists: both claim their outward appearances as a church
      (1) Jeremiah and Ezekiel combat the stupid boast of Jews in their temple—devoid of God's Word
      (2) Paul also (Rom. 9—12) deals with claim of Jews to be God's people, while persecuting the Christians and rejecting Christ's teaching, through his allegory of Hagar and Sarah
      (3) Malachi also shows that God repudiated the corrupt priestly descendants of Levi, God's convenanted interpreter
   b. conclusion: the church does not exist merely in a succession of persons, to the exclusion of teaching

c. the church fathers (e.g., Augustine) were not trying to prove that the church exists where bishops succeed one another, but rather that doctrine through a succession of right teaching, kept the purity against new errors, from the apostles onward

4. The church is founded upon God's Word
   a. all the Romanist pomp should not put us off from insisting that the church exists only where God's Word is found
   b. summary: since the church is Christ's kingdom, and He reigns by His Word alone, it is a lie to imagine that the kingdom of Christ exists apart from His scepter (= His most holy Word)

5. Defense against the charge of schism and heresy
   a. they charge us with schism and heresy because we preach differently, do not obey their laws, and hold our separate religious assemblies
   b. distinction between schismatic and heretic:
      (1) heretics corrupt the sincerity of the faith with false dogmas
      (2) schismatics (sometimes of the same faith) break the bond of fellowship
   c. here church unity requires
      (1) unity of minds in Christ
      (2) unity of wills with mutual benevolence in Christ
   d. apart from the Lord's Word there is no agreement of believers, but factions of wicked men

6. Christ's headship the condition of unity
   a. Cyprian also asserts Christ's episcopate as the sole basis of church concord
   b. who have actually withdrawn from the church? like the apostles, we have been cast out of the synagogues, that we might come to Christ

The Roman Church Compared with Ancient Israel as to Worship and Jurisdiction [*7–11*]

7. The condition of the Roman Church resembles that of Israel under Jeroboam
   a. a comparision between the churches of the Romanists and the ancient church of Israel is instructive here

b. at first they had the true church under priests and prophets, and with proper sacramental rites
c. they then fell away into idolatry and superstition and partly lost the privilege of being a church

8. Despite the idolatry of the Jews, their church remained
   a. did no trace of the church remain after the Jews fell into idolatry?
   b. the history of Israel and Judah reviewed, to show the degrees of falling away
      (1) Jeroboam utterly corrupted religion
      (2) in Judah at last even the priests befouled God's Temple

9. The papal church corrupt and to be repudiated
   a. the papal church is even more debased than that under Jeroboam
   b. the papists demand two things of us:
      (1) participation by us in all their prayers, sacraments, ceremonies
      (2) granting their church every honor, power, and jurisdiction that Christ gives to His church
   c. Calvin's response:
      (1) true, the prophets at Jerusalem did not separate from the rest, but went along with the duly instituted but corrupt priesthood; yet they did not succumb to superstitious worship
      (2) the polluting of the papists is not to be compared with the Old Testament situation except that of Jeroboam, and what prophet ever sacrificed at Bethel in his reign?
   d. conclusion: among the godly, communion of the church ought not to mean precipitously following rites even after they have become profane and corrupted

10. Why we must separate from the corrupted church
    a. where we admit the church exists, we must revere it
    b. assuming a parallel between the Old Testament church and the present church of Rome is closer than can really be proved; nevertheless the prophets did not agree to their corrupt assemblies
    c. unbound to God's Word, the Church of Rome does not qualify as a true church

11. Vestiges of the church under the papacy
    a. God's covenant remained among the Jews in spite of their unfaithfulness as a witness to God's faithfulness
    b. analogously, He had established His covenant in France, Italy, Germany, Spain, England, and used two means there to keep it inviolable
        (1) maintained baptism as witness to covenant
        (2) caused other vestiges to remain, that the church might not utterly die

12. The sound elements do not make the corrupted church a true church
    a. even if the title "church" must be denied to the papists, we do not deny that churches exist among them
    b. being, however, under the evil domination of the Roman pontiff, these churches are choked with corruption
    c. yet, since a remnant of God's people remains in them, wonderfully preserved, they remain churches to this extent although their whole body, minus the marks, lacks the lawful form of the church

CHAPTER 3
The Doctors and Ministers of the Church, Their Election and Office

The Ministry Given by God: Its High and Necessary Functions [*1–3*]

1. Why does God need men's service?
    a. God alone should rule, and has power to do so
    b. but He does not dwell among men in visible presence
    c. therefore, He does His work through men's mouths
    d. He thus declares His regard for men
    e. He provides us with an exercise in humility
        (1) "For who would not dread the presence of his power?"
        (2) "When a puny man risen from the dust speaks in God's name, at this point we best evidence our piety and obedience toward God if we show ourselves teachable toward His minister, although he excels us in nothing."
    f. to bind men together as pastors and teachers; no man is self-sufficient [Eph. 4:4–7, 8, 10–16]

2. The significance of the ministry for the church
   a. Paul says [Eph. 4:4-7, 8, 10-16] the human ministry of the church is that which chiefly binds believers in one body
   b. through ministers Christ dispenses His gifts to the church
   c. through this institution Christ "shows Himself as present"
      (1) renewal of the saints is accomplished
      (2) the body of Christ is built up
      (3) we grow in Him and among ourselves
      (4) we are admitted into the unity of Christ
   d. to refuse the apostolic and pastoral order is to tear down the church

3. The prestige of the preaching office in Scripture
   a. God gives marks of approval [Isa. 52:7; Matt. 5:13-14]
   b. ministers represent God [Luke 10:16]
   c. Paul's testimony concerning the glory of the ministry of the gospel [II Cor. 4:6; 3:9]
   d. two historical examples
      (1) Cornelius was directed to Peter [Acts 10:3-6]
      (2) Paul was directed to Ananias [Acts 9:6ff.]

The Scriptural Offices of the Ministry Described [*4-9*]

4. The several sorts of offices according to Ephesians 4
   a. the temporary offices, established "only for that time during which churches were to be erected where none existed before, or where they were to be carried over from Moses to Christ," or called out later when needed (Luther, for example)
      (1) apostles, "sent out to lead the world back from rebellion to true obedience to God, and to establish his kingdom everywhere by the preaching of the gospel, or . . . as the first builders of the church, to lay its foundations in all the world" [I Cor. 3:10]
      (2) prophets, not all those who interpreted God's will, but those who "excelled in a particular revelation" [Eph. 4:11]
      (3) evangelists, second to the apostles (e.g. Luke, Timothy, Titus, or the seventy)
   b. The permanent offices, which the church can never go without
      (1) teachers: charged with interpretation of Scripture

(2) pastors: charged with interpretation of Scripture, but also with discipline, sacramental duties, warning, and exhortation, which teachers are not allowed

5. Temporary and permanent offices
   a. grouping evangelists and apostles together, two corresponding relationships occur
      (1) present-day teachers correspond to the ancient prophets: except for the singular revelation, the charge is the same
      (2) present-day pastors correspond to the apostles: though their ministries are limited to the churches to which they are assigned, pastors have the same charge as apostles who were sent over the world
   b. ambiguity of Scripture: all ministers can rightly be called apostles, having received a call from God; Scripture generally, though not consistently, uses "apostle" as a specific title for the twelve, plus Paul

6. Apostles and pastors
   a. preaching and administering the sacraments are the signs of an apostle [Matt. 28:19; Luke 22:19]
   b. the same signs apply for pastors [I Cor. 4:1; Titus 1:9, and elsewhere]
   c. teaching function includes public speech and private admonition
   d. pastors, by the doctrine of Christ:
      (1) instruct people to godliness
      (2) administer the sacred mysteries
      (3) keep discipline
   e. what apostles do in the world, pastors do for their own churches

7. The pastor is bound to his church
   a. "each person, content with his own limits, should not break over into another man's province"
      (1) to keep all from being in confusion
      (2) men would otherwise be more concerned about their own advantage than about the upbuilding of the church
   b. this is God's rule
      (1) Paul and Barnabas created presbyters [Acts 14:22-23]
      (2) Titus was told to create presbyters [Titus 1:5]

(3) the bishops of the Philippians [Phil. 1:1]
(4) Archippus the bishop of the Colossians [Col. 4:17]
(5) Paul's sermon to the presbyters of the church at Ephesus [Acts 20:18–19]

c. the rule binds all who would be ministers
d. this binding is not irrevocable; release is possible "on public authority" rather than by private whim

8. The designation of ministers of the Word: presbyters
   a. Scripture interchanges usage of the terms, "bishops," "presbyters," "pastors," and "ministers" for those who rule the churches [Titus 1:5, 7; Phil. 1:1; Acts 20:17, 28]
   b. other ministries not mentioned in Eph. 4, but in Rom. 12:7–8 and I Cor. 12:28
      (1) temporary ministries
         (a) powers
         (b) healing
         (c) interpretation
      (2) permanent ministries
         (a) government: church elders charged with the censure of morals and exercise of discipline, along with the bishop; each church from the beginning had a senate with jurisdiction over discipline
         (b) care of the poor: deacons

9. The deacons
   a. two kinds of deacon [Rom. 12:8]
      (1) deacons who distribute the alms, who serve the church in administering the affairs of the poor
      (2) deacons who care for the poor themselves

***The Calling, Authorization, and Ordination of Ministers** [**10–16**]*

10. Orderly calling is requisite
   a. "all things should be done decently and in order" [I Cor. 14:40], particularly as regards church government
   b. a minister must first be duly called
   c. he must respond to the call
   d. thus "noisy and troublesome men" will not be able to take it upon themselves to teach or rule

11. Outer and inner call
    a. consideration of the minister's call involves four points, to be discussed below
        (1) what sort of minister should be called
        (2) how he should be appointed
        (3) by whom he should be appointed
        (4) by what rite he should be installed
    b. the minister is called in secret by God; the church does not witness this, and it will be passed over in this treatise
    c. the minister is called in public by the church
        (1) "Yet, though one comes to it with an evil conscience, he is nonetheless duly called in the presence of the church, provided his wickedness is not open"
        (2) learning joined with piety: a preparation for the ministry
        (3) the Lord arms those whom He calls
    d. Paul reviews the gifts in which those who perform the offices ought to excel [I Cor. 12:7-11]

12. Who can become a minister of the church? How this takes place
    a. what sort of minister should be called
        (1) those of sound doctrine and holy life
        (2) those not having any fault which would disgrace the ministry or undermine authority
        (3) those instructed in the skills required by the office
    b. how he should be appointed
        (1) "how" refers to religious awe, which should be observed in the act of choosing
        (2) fasting and prayers involved
        (3) the Spirit of counsel and discretion should be sought

13. Who should chose ministers?
    a. the election of apostles provides no sure rule
        (1) apostleship was an extraordinary ministry sealed by a conspicuous calling
        (2) apostles were called and ordained by the mouth of the Lord himself
        (3) Paul was not created "an apostle by men or through a man, but through Christ and God the Father" [Gal. 1:1]
            (a) inasmuch as his ministry was not "by men," he had this in common with all godly ministers (i.e., his secret call)

(b) but his apostleship "through Christ and God the Father" was "proper and peculiar to him"—the "badge of his apostleship"

14. Human agency
    a. for men to appoint bishops is consonant with lawful calling, as is testified by Scripture
    b. Paul's statements [Gal. 1:1] refer to what is peculiar to an apostle, and do not contravene the appointment of bishops by men
    c. Luke testifies to a churchly call for Paul [Acts 13:2] and Matthias [Acts 1:23]

15. The vote of the people
    a. should the minister be chosen by
        (1) the whole church?
        (2) his colleagues and the elders charged with the censure of morals?
        (3) the authority of one person?
    b. the alleged evidence for the authority of one person [Titus 1:5; I Tim. 5:22] is discounted
    c. Saul and Barnabas appointed presbyters, but they were "presbyters elected by show of hands [*cheirotoneo*] in every church" [Acts 14:23]
    d. the same form of election would apply to Timothy and Titus, since Paul would not have given them more power than he himself assumed
    e. Cyprian favors the vote of the people
    f. Scriptural testimony
        (1) the Levitical priests [Lev. 8:4–6; Num. 20:26–27]
        (2) the appointment of Matthias [Acts 1:15ff.]
        (3) the seven deacons [Acts 6:27]
    g. therefore, a minister is lawfully called "when those who seemed fit are created by the consent and approval of the people; moreover, that other pastors ought to preside over the election in order that the multitude may not go wrong either through fickleness, through evil intentions, or through disorder"

16. Ordination: by what rite or ceremony should a minister be installed?
    a. apostles used the laying on of hands
        (1) the rite was derived from Hebrew custom

(2) it signified the offering to God of the new minister
(3) it was used also to confer the graces of the Spirit
(4) it was used in solemn rites for pastors, teachers, and deacons

b. there is no precept concerning the laying on of hands, but the careful observance of the primitive church should serve as a precept
c. the rite warns the minister he is no longer a law unto himself
d. pastors alone—not the whole church—performed the rite
e. there is uncertainty concerning the number of pastors involved in the ceremony

CHAPTER 4
The Condition of the Ancient Church, and the Kind of Government in Use Before the Papacy

Historical Development of the Ministry; Three Classes of Ministers: Teaching and Ruling Presbyters: One Presbyter Selected to Be Bishop: the Archbishop [*1–4*]

1. Fidelity of the ancient church to the Scriptural archetype
   a. the study of early church history will clarify the picture of the government of the early church
   b. even though early bishops promulgated many canons, they carefully conformed to the pattern of government set forth in God's Word
   c. Scripture tells us of three orders of ministers
   d. the early church also had three orders:
      (1) presbyters: some were pastors, some were teachers
      (2) presbyters: ruling elders, charged with the censure and correction of morals
      (3) deacons: charged with the care of the poor and the distribution of alms
   e. "readers" and "acolytes" were not titles of regular ministerial offices, but for those who were "clerics," i.e., preparing for the ministry
   f. Jerome lists five orders (bishops, presbyters, deacons, believers, and catechumens), but gives no place to the remaining clergy and monks

2. The position of the bishop
   a. all those entrusted with teaching were called "presbyters"
   b. in each city presbyters chose a "bishop" from among themselves
   c. bishops were created in order to prevent dissension
   d. the bishop acted as the consul in the senate
      (1) to report on business
      (2) to preside in counseling, admonishing, and exhorting
      (3) to govern the whole action by his authority
      (4) to carry out what was decreed by common decision
   e. testimony of the ancients indicates this was done "by human agreement to meet the needs of the times"
      (1) Jerome: "Bishop and presbyter are one and the same"
   f. "Just as the presbyters, therefore, know that they are, according to the custom of the church, subject to him who presides, so the bishops recognize that they are superior to the presbyters more according to the custom of the church than by the Lord's actual arrangement, and that they ought to govern the church in cooperation with them"
   g. Jerome again testifies to the early origins of this practice, dating it at least from the time of Mark
   h. conclusion:
      (1) each city had a college of presbyters, comprised of both pastors and teachers
      (2) presbyters in each city were drawn from a certain area which was considered to belong to the body of the church
      (3) each college chose one bishop to maintain organization and peace
      (4) "country bishops" were assigned to represent the bishop in cases where the episcopate was too large for one man adequately to serve

3. The chief duty of bishops and presbyters
   a. both bishops and presbyters dispensed the Word and sacraments
   b. at Alexandria alone (because of Arius) it was decreed that no presbyter should preach (and Jerome criticizes this fact)
   c. due to the "severity of the times," all ministers had to perform all the duties of their office
   d. even in Gregory's time, bishops were not tolerated if they did not preach

e. "therefore, it was a principle of long standing in the church that the primary duties of the bishop were to feed his people with the Word of God, or to build up the church publicly and privately with sound doctrine"

4. Archbishops and patriarchs
   a. the maintenance of discipline prompted
      (1) each province having one archbishop among the bishops
      (2) the decree of the Council of Nicea that patriarchs were ordained to be higher in rank than archbishops
   b. this practice, however, was rare
   c. if any incident in any church could not be settled even in discussion with the patriarchs and a synod, the next appeal had to be made to a general council
   d. "hierarchy" is an improper term for this form of government
   e. "but if, laying aside the word, we look at the thing itself, we shall find that the ancient bishops did not intend to fashion any other form of church rule than that which God has laid down in his Word"

Deacons and Archdeacons: the Administration of Property and Alms: Minor Clerics [*5–9*]

5. The office of deacon
   a. the diaconate remained as it had been under the apostles
      (1) deacons received the daily offerings and the yearly income of the church
      (2) some of this was distributed to the ministers; some to the poor
      (3) the distribution was made according to the wishes of the bishop, to whom the deacons had to make account
   b. canons giving the bishop charge over church possessions do not mean that he personally distributed them, but that he instructed the deacons
      (1) Apostolic Canons: "on his authority all things may be distributed to the poor through the presbyters and deacons, and be administered with fear and all carefulness"
      (2) the Council of Antioch called for restraint of bishops who act without the knowledge of the deacons and presbyters
      (3) letters of Gregory indicate the deacons were, under the bishop, the stewards of the poor

c. subdeacons were probably assigned to assist the deacons
d. archdeacons were created as the demands of the diaconate grew
    (1) archdeacons were known to Jerome
    (2) they were given charge of all revenues, possessions, equipment, and the daily offering
    (3) an archdeacon could, according to Gregory, be charged with fraud if the church property was mishandled
    (4) to enhance the office, archdeacons were allowed to read the gospel, to exhort the people to prayer, and to extend the cup in the Sacred Supper

6. The use of church possessions
    a. synods and ancient writers declare all church possessions to be the patrimony of the poor
    b. bishops and deacons frequently were exhorted to keep good faith and not to waste church property
    c. those who work for the church should be supported at public expense
    d. but those who did not need such support sinned if they took what belonged to the poor, as Jerome indicates

7. Fourfold division of revenues
    a. at first there were no laws concerning division of property, since this was done with "integrity of conscience" and "innocence of life"
    b. but greed and wicked examples necessitated a canonical rule on dividing property
        (1) one part to the clergy
        (2) one part to the poor
        (3) one part for the repair of churches
        (4) one part for the poor, foreign, and indigenous
    c. some canons designate the last part for the bishop
        (1) but this is not his private income
        (2) it may be used, according to Gregory and Gelasius, for the hospitality required of the rank
        (3) anyone found living in pomp or luxury was reprimanded or removed from office

8. Church treasure distributed to the poor
    a. at first little was used on the embellishment of sacred things

b. even as the church grew richer, moderation was the rule regarding this
c. funds remained intact for the poor
   (1) Cyril sold vestments and vessels to help those famishing in Jerusalem
   (2) Acacius of Amida melted sacred vessels to buy food and ransom for the poor: "Our God needs neither plates nor cups, for He neither eats nor drinks"
   (3) Jerome tells of Exuperius of Toulouse, who allowed no poor man to hunger
   (4) Ambrose melted down vessels, then told the Arians: "It were better for you to preserve vessels of living men than of metals"
d. Ambrose: "The bishop had nothing that did not belong to the poor"

9. The preparatory stages of the office
   a. writers mention certain exercises and preparations in addition to the regular ministries of the ancient church
   b. the ancients kept, protected, and instructed youths, called clerics, for preliminary training in the ministerial offices
   c. a better name than "clerics" would be preferred
   d. the institution is holy and profitable
      (1) those who wished to consecrate themselves to the church were brought up under the bishop's care
      (2) it insured that well-prepared ministers would be available
   e. instruction was given in certain rudiments
      (1) "doorkeepers" opened and closed the church
      (2) "acolytes" helped the bishop in household tasks
      (3) they were taught to read from the pulpit

History of Changes in the Election and Ordination of Ministers: Consent of the Magistrates, Clergy, and People in the Election of Bishops [*10–15*]

10. Paul's directions mainly followed: consent of the people
    a. in the first two considerations in calling ministers—what kind of man to choose, and how much care is involved in the choice—Paul was mainly followed by the ancient church
       (1) pastors were chosen with reverence and prayer
       (2) ministers were tested against the standard of Paul's life

(3) but they sinned somewhat by demanding more than Paul required, as in celibacy

b. in the third consideration—who should ordain ministers—no single procedure prevailed
   (1) but in the ancient church, no one was received into the clergy without consent of all the people, as Cyprian indicated when he broke this custom
   (2) popular consent ceased to be required, however, for the minor functions, because the candidates had been well prepared, and because the responsibilities were small

c. except for the episcopate, the people left it to the bishops and presbyters to select and recognize worthy candidates, with the assignment of presbyters to churches, however, still the prerogative of the people

d. yet this did not mean the people did not examine the candidates, because
   (1) to be ordained, one had to go through the ranks as cleric, subdeacon, deacon and presbyter
   (2) there were many canons to punish shortcomings
   (3) agreement of the people was always required for presbyters, according to the Apostolic Canons
   (4) ordination took place at specified times of the year, so that "no one might creep in secretly without the consent of the believers, or be too readily promoted without witnesses"

11. Consent in episcopal elections, to the time of Theodoret

a. freedom of the people to choose bishops was long preserved
   (1) Council of Antioch forbade admitting an unapproved bishop
   (2) in several places Leo I offers the same opinion
   (3) ordination of Nectarius required consent of the people

b. if a bishop named his own successor, he still needed popular consent
   (1) as when Augustine named Eraclius
   (2) Theodoret refers to the successor to Athanasius, Peter, who was approved by magistrates, leading citizens and all the people

12. Balance between people and clergy

a. the Council of Laodicea was justified in not leaving election to the multitude
   (1) unanimity is unlikely for large numbers

(2) generally, "the uncertain crowd is divided into contrary interests" [Vergil]

b. the council remedied this situation
   (1) the clergy alone made the choice
   (2) the magistrates and leading citizens considered the choice of the clergy
   (3) after approval, the candidate was presented to the people
   (4) sometimes the people's desires were first heard

c. Leo I: "The desires of the citizens, the testimonies of the people, the decision of the honorable, and the choice of the clergy must be looked for"

d. the decree of the Synod of Laodicea means that a balance of power is created between the clergy and people with regard to the election of clergy

13. Clergy and political rulers
   a. the method of the Council of Laodicea stayed in force until, and probably after, the time of Gregory, as his letters attest
      (1) even when he entrusts the election to some bishop, he still requires a decree signed by all
      (2) when Constantius was elected, Gregory thought he should be approved even by those Milanese who had fled to Genoa to escape the barbarians
   b. in 1049 Pope Nicholas established the college of cardinals to elect the popes: the decree of Leo was cited in this regard
   c. consent of the emperor was required only in Rome and Constantinople, the two imperial capitals; the experience of Ambrose at Milan contrasts with that of Gregory at Rome
   d. the custom was this: "when officials, clergy, and people had designated anyone, he would at once report to the emperor, who would confirm the election with his approval or abrogate it by his disapproval"
   e. decretals collected by Gratian indicate nothing else "than that a king must by no means be allowed to set aside a canonical election and appoint a bishop according to his whim, and that the metropolitans must not consecrate one thus promoted by violent powers"

14. The procedure in ordination
   a. the rite was called in Latin "ordination" or "consecration"
   b. in Greek it was called "raising of hands" or "laying on of hands," the former referring to the voting which took place

c. decree of the Council of Nicea:
   (1) the metropolitan and all bishops should meet to ordain the person elected
   (2) if this were not possible, at least three bishops should meet, the others consenting by letter
d. Cyprian indicates the bishops were also present at the elections
e. if speedy assembly were not possible at election time, the bishops could examine and ordain after the popular election took place

15. Consecration by the metropolitan
   a. gradually those elected began to seek ordination from the bishop of a metropolitan city
      (1) this was due to ambition, and the deterioration of the old order
      (2) there is no good reason for this practice
   b. soon Italian bishops sought ordination at Rome, as Gregory says
   c. Milan was an exception to this practice
   d. the ceremony used was the laying on of hands
      (1) bishops wore special dress
      (2) each bishop ordained his own presbyters
      (3) consequently, the ordination was called "his"
   e. "ancient writers often state that presbyter differs from bishop only in that the former does not have the power to ordain"

CHAPTER 5
The Ancient Form of Government Was Completely Overthrown by the Tyranny of the Papacy

Appointment of Unqualified Persons Without Vote of the People [*1–3*]

1. Scandalous neglect of requirements for the episcopate
   a. let us compare the present papal church with the ancient church to discern its nature; our plan, to begin with the call to ministry [1–7]; then deal with how they fulfill it [8–10]
   b. kind of bishops commonly chosen today
      (1) ignorant of sacred learning

(2) immoral
(3) often only children

2. The community deprived of the right to elect its bishop
   a. power to elect the bishops transferred from people to canons
   b. Leo and Cyprian cry out against this abuse
   c. Romanists' excuse for this:
      (1) corruption of the times demanded a remedy—what a remedy!
      (2) canons prescribed exactly how to elect—but the older church followed the rule laid down by God's Word
      (3) today even the best of laws lie buried in documents while riffraff are chosen
   d. should not the election of bishops be turned back to the people, away from "canons" who despise God's Word?

3. Neglect has led to the intervention of princes
   a. "canonical election" was not in fact devised as a remedy, for in the old days under popular elections when tumults occurred there were other ways of dealing with them
   b. this usurpation actually occurred when the people became more negligent in holding elections and let the presbyters do it, afterward confirming it
   c. later, princes took the right to nominate bishops away from the church

Abuses Associated with Collation to Clerical Benefices [4–7]

4. Abuses in the appointment of the presbyter ("priest") and deacon
   a. today, bishops usurp the right to appoint presbyters and deacons, but overlook their true duties
   b. contra: Council of Chalcedon required pastoral obligations to be attached to each office for two reasons;
      (1) not to burden the church with needless expense, diverting moneys from the poor to idle men
      (2) to impress the clergy that their office involves not an honor but an obligation
   c. this interpreted by the Romanists as meaning an income sufficient for their support
   d. further contemporary traffickings in priestly offices described

5. Ordination is travestied
   a. a presbyter should be appointed to a definite place, and not to perform sacrifice, but to govern a church; a deacon, to gather and distribute alms
   b. the travesty of an ordination examination of present day described

6. The nature of benefices
   a. the complexities of collation of benefices described—almost all livings involve simony today
   b. priestly livings conferred not to benefit churches but those men who receive them: "benefices" to these men mean largess
   c. how can one so appointed to office bear the name of "pastor"?

7. Monstrous abuses
   a. shameless pluralism described
   b. these abuses are utterly contrary to God, nature, and church government

Negligence and Idleness of Monks, Canons, and Others Holding Clerical Office [*8–10*]

8. Monks as "presbyters"
   a. our second topic: how faithfully these men exercise their office
   b. two kinds of priests: monks; seculars
   c. historical evidence cited to prove that monastic life and clerical office are incompatible and were so considered in the earlier church: therefore monks should not serve as clergy

9. Beneficed and hired priests
   a. beneficed priests
      (1) bishoprics and parishes have cure of souls
      (2) prebends, chaplaincies, etc.: in the pay of wealthy men
   b. hired priests, who perform masses for pay: a sorry lot!

10. Pretenses of the clerical orders
    a. all who are fed by idle benefices perform no ministry of the church

b. this is clearly shown by their negation of Christ's rule and by their failure to conform even to the pattern of the primitive church

***Corruption and Covetousness Prevail in the Ranks of Bishops, Pastors, and Deacons** [11–19]*

11. Bishops and parish priests
    a. bishops and parish rectors have a godly office, but only if they fulfill it, not turning their duties over to others
    b. the wide prevalence of absenteeism: how can one who has never seen a sheep of his flock be a shepherd of it?

12. Early stages of this evil: Gregory and Bernard
    a. already in Gregory the Great's day this evil had begun to creep in, and he spoke out against it
    b. by Bernard of Clairvaux's day things had gotten worse (but not as bad as today) and he inveighs against the abuse

13. Claim and actuality
    a. papal church government is a robber's den, clean contrary to Christ
    b. they claim to be successors of the apostles—but what do they have in common with the apostles?
    c. they claim the commendation of the church fathers for their church order—but their present church government bears no resemblance to what prevailed earlier

14. The priests' moral conduct
    a. far from Christ's demand is the immoral quality of their life
    b. if they were to be judged by the ancient canons, few would go unexcommunicated
    c. therefore their order is not from Christ, His apostles, the fathers, or the ancint church

15. The deacons
    a. deacons, who should collect and disperse alms, are by the Romanists assigned to the altars, etc.
    b. their diaconate is not the care of the poor, but a stepping stone to the priesthood

16. Distribution of church income
    a. in their misdistribution of church income, the city clergy have grown wealthy at others' expense
    b. the ancient canonical division of funds flaunted: the poor go without help
    c. their diaconate is sheer robbery

17. False and true splendor of the church
    a. they assert: funds used to keep the church's magnificence duly sustained
    b. Scriptural prophecies of splendor of Christ's kingdom not to be so fulfilled!
    c. the true riches of Christ's kingdom in the apostolic age, when men were physically poor, and in the early church, when emperors doffed their rich robes in penitence, and bishops like Ambrose loved modesty

18. Fraudulent and honest expenditure of church funds
    a. far from the ancient diaconate is the present church, which fails to follow and teach the practices of the ancient church
    b. how unlike Exuperius and Acacius and Ambrose are modern bishops!
    c. the enrichment of benefices with goods dedicated to Christ is not in accordance with His will!

19. Clerical possessions and power
    a. no real church order is to be seen in the peculations of bishops and abbots
    b. the intolerable contrast between the simplicity of the apostles and present day clerical capacity
    c. we have sufficiently proved the disappearance of the true diaconate from their midst

CHAPTER 6
The Primacy of the Roman See

Refutation of Assumption Regarding the Primacy of Peter [*1–7*]

1. The requirement of submission to Rome
    a. so far we have described the government of the ancient

church and its latter-day corruption to show how we are not guilty of schism, in "departing from the no-church"

b. we have until now not dealt with the papacy as of neither dominical nor apostolic origin

c. but for them the papacy is the very capstone of the church, through which it holds primacy over all others

2. The office of high priest of the Old Covenant cannot be cited as evidence for papal supremacy
    a. does the true form of the hierarchy require a visible human head? Answer: was this established by Christ?
    b. they rest their case of the high priesthood of the law at Jerusalem. Answer:
        (1) in Old Testament times, when the Jews were surrounded by idolaters, God centralized worship at the midpoint of the earth (Mt. Zion) to preserve unity
        (2) but now that Christianity is spread over the whole earth, it is absurd to put rule of east and west under one man
        (3) therefore we should not force what was useful in one nation and one time upon the whole earth
    c. they say that the high priesthood is a type of Christ: the priesthood being transferred, the right also is transferred. Answer: to whom is it transferred? not to the pope as vicar of Christ but to Christ Himself alone

3. Jesus' word to Peter did not establish this lordship of the church
    a. papists put forward two chief proof texts:
        (1) Matt. 16:18
        (2) John 21:15
    b. to claim these proofs they must demonstrate two things:
        (1) that power over all churches is committed to him who is ordered to feed Christ's flock
        (2) "bind and loose" = "rule the whole world"
    c. refutation:
        (1) Christ has given nothing to Peter above the other apostles
        (2) binding and loosing means to forgive and retain sins: this is the task of all ministers of the gospel equally

4. Perverse claim concerning the keys
    a. "keys" is an appropriate metaphor for the teaching of the gospel, which opens heaven's gates for those with faith, but closes them for those without faith

    (1) the pope, not prepared to bear the burden of the gospel, raises contention about the meaning of this verse
    (2) but "keys" means the dignity of the office of apostle, inseparable from its burden
  b. the "keys" is a common gift
    (1) because the preaching of the gospel was entrusted in common to all the apostles
    (2) what Christ promised to one (Peter) he conferred at the same time upon all (the disciples)
    (3) with Cyprian and Augustine, we see Christ's singling out of Peter as a commendation of unity to the church, a sort of "impersonation" of unity

5. Honor, not power, accorded to Peter
  a. Matt. 16:18 addressed to Peter and to no other person: it is unthinkable that Christ would say anything else about Peter than Peter or Paul would say about all Christians (I Peter 2:5f.; Eph. 2:20f.)
  b. we concede to Peter the honor of being first in the building of the church, but this is no warrant of a primacy of power

6. The one foundation
  a. it is pointless to quibble over their chief prooftext, Matt. 16:16, for others have treated it exhaustively and the meaning is clear
  b. the point is that Peter confessed (in his own and his brethren's name) that Christ was the Son of God: Christ (as Paul says) is the true foundation
  c. we will not prolong the argument with patristic quotations, e.g., Augustine

7. The place of Peter among the apostles according to the account of Scripture
  a. equality of Peter with rest of apostles seen in Acts, I Peter
  b. but especially in Galatians, where Paul contends his equality with Peter as apostle

Monarchy in the Church to Be Accorded to Christ Alone [*8–10*]

8. The church can have no human head
  a. granted that Peter was prince of the apostles—this was one man over a few, not over a great number

b. but do not apply the working arrangements for a small group to the whole earth:
   (1) the fallacy of the "cranes" and "bees" argument
   (2) classical statements commending monarchy not applicable

9. Christ's headship not transferable
   a. Christ the sole Head—which excludes the possibility of a centralized churchly monarchy for the whole world
   b. their answer—that Christ's power was transferred to a vicegerent—is not borne out by Scripture

10. Unity in Christ, not in a human monarch
   a. no evidence in Paul of any vicegerent
   b. Paul's view of church unity is in faith; not in a churchly monarchy, but in the varied offices for which we are divinely gifted

***Admission that Peter was Bishop of Rome Does Not Establish Rome's Perpetual Primacy* [*11–13*]**

11. If Peter himself had had supremacy, Rome could not claim it
   a. even if Christ had given the primacy to Peter to exist in unbroken succession from him, it could not be bound to a place
   b. neither Christ nor Moses conferred such an honor on the places where they ministered and died: Jerusalem and the desert!

12. Alleged transfer of the primacy from Antioch
   a. a letter (falsely) attributed to Pope Marcellus states that Antioch's primacy (based on Peter) was transferred to Rome when he moved there
   b. what legal ground for such a transfer of privilege? (Pandects)
      (1) if personal: then it does not belong to the place
      (2) if real: once given to a place, cannot be removed by departure of a person
      (3) if mixed: then not a simple consideration of place unless person corresponds
   c. therefore Rome cannot claim the primacy for itself

13. Ranking of the other patriarchates
   a. there is no apparent correlation between the importance of

various apostles and the order of importance attributed to the episcopal sees founded by them

b. this is seen in the high position of Alexandria (founded by Mark, a mere disciple) over other "apostolic" sees

Peter's Presence in Rome Unproved, while Paul's Is Beyond Doubt [***14–15***]

14. On the sojourn of Peter in Rome

a. chronology: against Eusebius' claim that Peter ruled twenty-five years over the Roman church

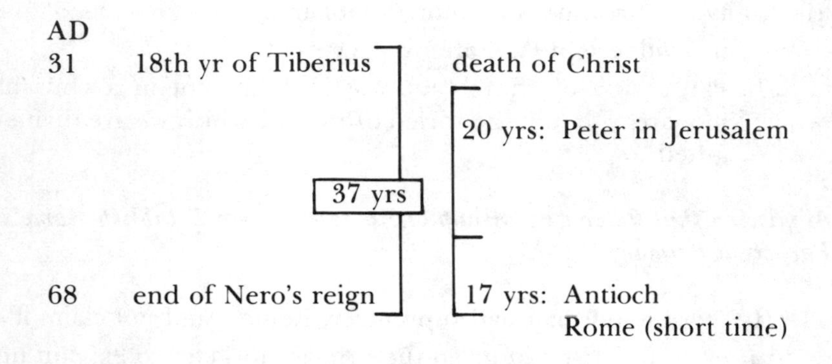

b. the Epistle to the Romans, written by Paul four years before he came to Rome, makes no mention of Peter, the supposed bishop of the church!

c. Peter absent from Paul's long list of the godly at Rome

15. Slender and inconclusive evidence

a. Paul, a prisoner at Rome, was writing to various churches, but without a mention of Peter

b. further, the claimed "succession" after Peter is not identically held, and the tradition of a conflict between Peter and Simon Magus doubted by Augustine

c. conclusions:

(1) Peter could have died at Rome; but not after a long sojourn there, and hardly as a bishop

(2) Peter's apostolate was to the Jews; Paul's to the Gentiles, and hence more important for us

d. thus there is very little foundation for Roman primacy in God's Word!

***Roman Church Honored but Not as Unifying Head** [16–17]*

16. The significance of the church at Rome during the earliest period
    a. Romanists' axiom
        (1) that the unity of the church can be maintained only if there is a supreme head on earth for all members to obey
        (2) and that the Lord accordingly gave the primacy to Peter and then by right of succession to the Roman see to reside therein even to the end
    b. yes, great honor was traditionally given to the Roman church, but for the following reasons:
        (1) called "apostolic see" because it was presumed to be founded and established by Peter's ministry
        (2) Rome as capital city of empire probably had on hand more men of experience, skill, etc.
        (3) when churches elsewhere experienced dissension, or when individual churchmen became disaffected, they would appeal to Rome

17. According to early church teaching, the unity of the church plainly required no universal bishop
    a. Romanists act wrongly in ascribing primacy and supreme power over other churches to Rome
    b. testimonies of unity of church in church fathers:
        (1) Jerome to Nepotianus: although a Roman presbyter, Jerome insists upon the autonomy of each church under its bishop and other officers
        (2) Cyprian's beautiful description of the unity of the church in Christ
    c. these citations adduced to show that the principle of unity of the hierarchy under an earthly head (held by Romanists today) was unknown to the ancient fathers

SUMMARY OF STEPS IN THE REFUTATION OF THE PETRINE SUPREMACY AND SUCCESSION

1. If primacy of Church was established in Peter, how thus at Rome, and permanently? [11]
2. If Peter's first see was at Antioch, how could it be transferred to Rome? [12]
3. If transferred to Rome, how then did Alexandria usurp Antioch's second place? [13]

4. How could Peter have come to Rome and have died there? [14]
5. If he did actually come to Rome and did die there, how could he have been bishop and for a long time there? [15]

CHAPTER 7
The Origin and Growth of the Roman Papacy Until It Raised Itself to Such a Height that the Freedom of the Church Was Oppressed, and All Restraint Overthrown

Modest Position of the Roman See in Early Times *[1–4]*

1. Position of the Roman see in the Councils of Nicea and Ephesus
   a. the primacy of the Roman see established not earlier than Nicea
   b. if Julius were recognized as head of the church, why were his delegates relegated to fourth place?
   c. question of the position of Cyril of Alexandria at the Council of Ephesus
   d. why did Dioscorus, patriarch of Alexandria, preside at the second Council of Ephesus as if by his own right?

2. In the Council of Chalcedon and the Fifth of Constantinople
   a. the representatives of the Roman Church occupied the first seat at the Council of Chalcedon only by concession of the Emperor, thus showing deviation from normal procedure
   b. later councils at which the legates of Rome did not preside

3. The proud titles of the later Roman bishops not yet known in the early period
   a. Cyprian speaks of the Roman bishop as "brother"
   b. Jerome cited to the effect that any bishop of any place is of the same merit as any other bishop

4. Gregory I refused the title "Universal [Ecumenical] Bishop" [see par. 16]
   a. Gregory, against John of Constantinople, protests that the appellation "universal" is profane, sacrilegious, the very precursor of Antichrist
   b. "if one bishop is called 'universal,' the universal church goes down when that universal bishop falls"

***Limitations of Its Authority in Relation to That of Emperors and Metropolitans** [5–10]*

5. Origin of Roman jurisdiction
   a. how the Roman church usurped some right over other churches
   b. following Athanasius in his fight with Arian factions, the pious willingly granted authority to Rome because they needed outside help
   c. authority of Rome increased when it became the seat of final appeal

6. The peculiar features of the Roman power of that time
   a. church power comprised under four headings
      (1) ordination of bishops
      (2) calling of councils
      (3) hearing of appeals or jurisdiction
      (4) motions of chastisement or censures
   b. bishops were originally ordained by their own metropolitans, not the Roman bishop
   c. when metropolitans were ordained, Rome sent a delegate to witness, not preside
   d. fellowship, not lordship, is indicated in the Roman bishop's subscribing to the holy and orthodox councils

7. Mutual admonition
   a. bishops could at first admonish and chastise the Roman prelate
   b. the Roman bishop was not yet endowed with a jurisdiction over those who were not of his province

8. Authority in the convening of synods
   a. each metropolitan summoned provincial synods
   b. only the emperor could call a universal council
   c. that decrees pertaining to the church universal should not be passed without the Roman pontiff indicates respect rather than dominion

9. Use of forged documents
   a. the Roman pontiff misrepresented his authority by fraudulent substitution of the Synod of Sardica for that of Nicea
   b. the majesty of the Roman see based on forged epistles

10. Constantine, Bishop Melchiades, and the Synod of Arles
    a. it was Constantine who gave the case of Donatus vs. Caecilian to Melchiades, Bishop of Rome
    b. the final right of appeal could not have been with Melchiades alone
    c. the case turned out such that the bishop of Arles was passing judgment on the bishop of Rome

***Attitude of Fifth- and Sixth-Century Popes: Rome vs. Constantinople** [**11–16**]*

11. Falsification and usurpation
    a. who today could believe that the interpretation which is referred to in Gratian under Anacletus's name belongs to Anacletus, namely, that Cephas is "head?"
    b. did the churches of Leo's day believe his talk of self-glorification?
    c. Leo's own declaration regarding the final authority of metropolitans, bishops, and councils in their respective provinces

12. Papal power at the time of Gregory I
    a. the prestige and power of the Roman pontiff increased under the conditions of a torn empire
    b. yet such power was not unbridled domination but equality in humility

13. Limitations of the office under Gregory I
    a. Gregory assumed no more power over others than he yielded to all over himself
    b. because of administrative burdens, Gregory was filling the office of pastor, but not fulfilling it

14. Rome and Constantinople in conflict over supremacy
    a. nothing did more to bestow the primacy upon Rome than the fact that the capital of the empire was first there
    b. cities which had been first in the civil government of each province were prime sees of bishops
    c. Innocent feared declining dignity for Rome with the rise of Constantinople

15. How Leo resented the recognition of Constantinople
    a. it was only sheer ambition which made Leo protest the au-

thority of the bishop of Constantinople after the authority of the Roman pontiff

b. it should have been the Eastern bishops who complained, not the Roman pontiff, when the honor given the see of Alexandria by the Council of Nicea was to be shifted to the see of Constantinople

16. Pride of John the Faster, and modesty of Gregory [see par. 4]
    a. John, calling himself the universal patriarch, wanted the boundaries of his bishopric to be the same as the boundaries of the empire
    b. Gregory calls such a title wicked, even when applied to himself

***Rome's Jurisdiction Enhanced Through Relations with the Usurpers Phocas and Pepin, and Thereafter Established to the Injury of the Church** [17–18]*

17. The eventual establishment of the papal supremacy
    a. Phocas granted to Boniface III that Rome should be head of all the churches, terminating the controversy
    b. the "cooperation" between Pepin and Pope Zacharias, by whose perfidy the pope received as his reward the Roman see's jurisdiction over the churches of Gaul and eventually headship over all bishops

18. The decay of the church until the time of Bernard of Clairvaux
    a. as things daily worsened, the tyranny of the Roman see increased
    b. this was partly due to the ignorance and sloth of bishops
    c. the church as pastures of devils rather than of sheep
    d. testimony of Bernard

***Later Papal Claims Contrary to the Principles of Gregory I and Bernard** [19–22]*

19. The present-day papacy in its claims to power
    a. today the supreme jurisdiction of all cases is in the possession of the Roman pontiff alone
    b. what is most unbearable is that they leave no jurisdiction on earth to control or restrain their lust if they abuse such power

20. New forgeries support extravagant claims
    a. forged letter of Anastasius (Athanasius) that nothing should be done which had not previously been referred to the Roman see
    b. the decretal epistles gathered by Gregory IX breathe out unrestrained fury
    c. the babble of such sayings as "the pope cannot err"

21. Gregory I condemned what popes now affirm
    a. the statement of Cyprian: "None of us says he is the bishop of bishops"
    b. popes now defend what was anathematized by Gregory I

22. The corruption of the present-day papacy
    a. should not the present day patrons of the Roman see be ashamed to defend the papacy?
    b. if the administration of the papacy in Gregory's time was a "sea," what is to be said of the present papacy?
    c. the times are as bad as those of Bernard

Arraignment of the Later Papacy [*23-30*]

23. Does there exist in Rome any church or bishopric at all?
    a. what is not a church cannot be the mother of churches; he who is not a bishop cannot be the prince of bishops
    b. how is the pope a bishop if he does not fill the function of bishop?

24. The apostasy
    a. if a king fails to fulfill his kingly responsibility, he retains his honor, but a bishop must fulfill the command of Christ
    b. how can the pontiff be chief of bishops when he is no bishop?
    c. the popes contend against reviving the doctrine of the gospel because this is the only way they can retain their power
    d. Rome, the mother of churches once, has ceased to be what it once was

25. The kingdom of Antichrist
    a. Paul's words which say that the Antichrist will sit in God's temple apply to the Roman pontiff
    b. the Antichrist, according to Paul, is he who deprives God of his honor in order to take it upon himself

26. The papacy far removed from a true church order
    a. the transfer of the church from Jerusalem to Pella demonstrates that primacy has nothing to do with a location
    b. the papacy itself is directly contrary to church order

27. The wicked behavior and the heretical teachings of the popes stand in stark contrast to their claims
    a. individual popes who have never grasped anything of Christ
    b. heretical teachings of the popes regarding God, Christ, and the resurrection

28. Apostasy of John XXII
    a. John openly asserted that souls are mortal and die along with bodies until the day of resurrection
    b. here a "pope that cannot err" fell fouly far from faith!

29. Moral abandonment of the popes
    a. the pontiffs no more become vicars of Christ because of the see which they occupy than an idol, when it is set in God's temple, is to be taken for God
    b. bishops do not tend to the morals of Roman citizens, or even to their own prostituted characters
    c. if Rome was once the head, today it is not worth being a toe

30. The cardinals
    a. a cardinal priest is nothing but a bishop
    b. cardinals were once less than bishops, while they now far exceed them
    c. summary statement: the Roman see as it exists today is very different from that ancient see

CHAPTER 8
The Power of the Church with Respect to Articles of Faith; and How in the Papacy, with Unbridled License, the Church Has Been Led to Corrupt All Purity of Doctrine

Ecclesiastical Power Limited by the Word of God [*1–9*]

1. Task and limits of the church's doctrinal authority
    a. the power of the church in

    (1) individual bishops
    (2) councils, provincial or general
  b. this power, which is spiritual, consists in
    (1) doctrine (chs. 8–9)
    (2) jurisdiction (ch. 11)
    (3) making laws (ch. 10)
  c. the doctrinal side has two parts
    (1) authority to lay down articles of faith
    (2) authority to explain them
  d. the power of the church has one purpose—upbuilding—and not destruction

2. The doctrinal authority of Moses and the priests
   a. authority given to priests and prophets not personally but to the ministry appointed them
   b. their authority lies in the Word they are to proclaim
   c. Moses was to be heard above all the rest, but he had been duly instructed

3. The doctrinal authority of the prophets
   a. is not he who is bidden to hear a Word from the Lord's mouth forbidden to invent anything of his own?
   b. when the prophets are set over nations and kingdoms to pluck up and root out . . . , the reason is He has put His word in their mouth

4. The doctrinal authority of the apostles
   a. their very name, "apostles," means those who do not prate whatever they please, but report the commands of their Sender
   b. the power of the church, therefore, is not infinite, but subject to the Lord's Word

5. Unity and multiplicity of revelation
   a. in the diversity of times there are diverse ways of learning this Word
   b. but holy men of old knew God only by beholding Him in His Son
   c. thus while such wisdom has been variously manifested, signs were given confirming that the message was from God

6. Scriptural foundation of the Word of God in the Old Covenant
   a. essential unity of doctrine from the law through the prophets and historical works

b. to this written standard, priests and teachers had to conform their teaching

7. The Word became flesh
   a. all that can be comprehended concerning the heavenly Father was at length revealed when the wisdom of God became flesh
   b. God has so fulfilled all functions of teaching in His Son that we must regard this as the final and eternal testimony from Him
   c. therefore, we fashion nothing new for ourselves, but remain content with the perfection of Christ's teaching

8. The apostles authorized to teach what Christ commanded
   a. what the church holds as the Word of God must conform to the law and prophets, and the writings of the apostles
   b. all authorized teaching in the church judged only by this standard

9. Not even the apostles were free to go beyond the Word: much less their successors
   a. speaking the Word in confidence, we reject at the same time all human inventions
   b. conformity to the Word is the power of pastors
   c. since the apostles were faithful to the Holy Spirit, their successors are to teach what is provided in Scripture
   d. even Paul denied dominion over the faith of the Corinthians

Rejection of Claims of Doctrinal Infallibility Apart from the Word [10–16]

10. The Roman claim
    a. Rome takes it for granted that a universal council is the true image of the church, and therefore, governed by the Holy Spirit, cannot err
    b. but bishops and prelates rule and even constitute the councils, claiming for themselves what is due the councils

11. The presence of Christ in His church does not annul its bond to the Word
    a. the promise of the presence of Christ was given to individual believers as well as to the whole church together

b. yet believers receive only the firstfruits and some taste of Christ's Spirit
c. therefore, both individuals and the whole church ought to keep themselves within the limits of God's Word

12. The church not infallible
    a. although what is given to one belongs to the whole, the riches of the church are always far from that supreme perfection of which our adversaries boast
    b. it is absurd and foolish to consider the church as already completely spotless when all its members are spotted
    c. the church is the "pillar and foundation of truth" only to the extent that the Word of the Lord is faithfully kept and preserved in its purity

13. Word and Spirit belong inseparably together
    a. claim of Rome: the church cannot err because it is governed by the Spirit of God and hence can ordain that which is beyond God's Word
    b. reply: the church cannot err if it forsakes its own wisdom and allows itself to be taught by the Holy Spirit through God's Word
    c. "The Spirit will lead you into all truth," because "the Spirit will recall all that I have said to you" (John 16:13, 14:26)
    d. as Christ spoke not from Himself but from the Spirit of the law and prophets, we speak from the Spirit of the gospel

14. Tradition subordinate to Scripture?
    a. claim: the church needed to add some things to the writings of the apostles; or, the apostles later supplied through a living voice what they had not clearly enough taught
    b. reply: were they so dull that they needed afterward to supply what they had omitted through ignorance?
    c. Augustine: "When the Lord said nothing, who of us may say, 'These things are or those things are'? Or if one dare say so, what proof does he provide?"

15. Contradiction in doctrinal decrees of the church
    a. in Matt. 18:17, Christ makes no mention of doctrine but of the correction of vices
    b. doctrinal decrees must not teach anything more than the Lord has revealed in His Word

16. Feebleness of our opponents' examples
    a. it would be a poor refuge if we had to defend infant baptism on the mere authority of the church
    b. the word "consubstantial" does not appear in Scripture, but in affirming it what else are the Nicene fathers doing than expounding the real meaning of Scripture?
    c. if Constantine at Nicea said in effect that disputations were to be resolved on the basis of Scripture, the fact that none of the bishops present rose to defend the idea that the church could go beyond Scripture demonstrates that such a dogma was then unknown

Appendix

Calvin's announced plan:

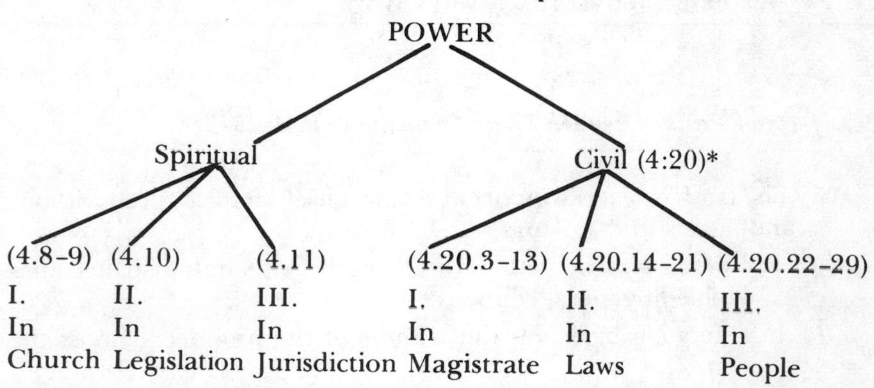

*Cf. the two kingdoms (3.19.15)

CHAPTER 9
Councils and Their Authority

True Authority of Church Councils [*1–2*]

1. Two prefatory remarks
   a. my severity toward the ancient councils does not mean that I esteem them less than I ought
   b. that I attribute less to the councils than do my opponents does not mean that I am afraid of them because they seemingly support my opponents

2. True and false councils
   a. Christ will be in the midst of a council only if it is gathered in His name
   b. criterion of "gathering in Christ's name": no decision must add or subtract from God's Word

Defects of Pastors Render Their Councils Fallible [*3–7*]

3. The truth can also support and assert itself in the church without and against the "pastors"
   a. Rome's assertion: the church itself exists only if it becomes visible in general councils
   b. refutation based on the witness of the prophets against the church

4. Defection of the pastors foretold
   a. the present age is equally susceptible to error as in the time of the Jews
   b. pastors pose the greatest dangers to the church

5. The need to judge them with discrimination
   a. I do not mean to undermine the authority of pastors, but discrimination is to be made among pastors themselves

b. as in the past, some pastors may be struck with blindness and dullness

6. The truth can also stand against councils
   a. the Jews had a true church under the prophets quite apart from councils
   b. if prophets upon whom the sun has gone down (Mic. 3:6) all got together, what spirit would have presided over their assembly?
   c. example of the council convened by Ahab (I Kings 22:6, 22)

7. Example from John 11:47
   a. the church was by no means embraced by the council of John 11:47, though the whole priestly order was there
   b. what assurance do we have that such a thing cannot happen to us?

Departing from Scripture, Councils Have Deteriorated, but Even Those of Nicea and Chalcedon Were Defective [*8–11*]

8. The validity of conciliar decisions
   a. circumstances of a council should be examined
   b. Augustine against Maximinus
   c. the councils such as Nicea, Constantinople, Ephesus I, and Chalcedon are to be embraced because they contain nothing but the pure exposition of Scripture

9. Councils against councils
   a. when council disagrees with council, we shall determine from Scripture which one is orthodox
   b. it is obvious that the decree of the Second Council of Nicea, restoring the use of images, emanated from Satan, since not only images themselves but also their worship was approved there
   c. now let the Romanists boast that the Holy Spirit is fastened and bound to their councils

10. Human failings in the councils
    a. even in the purer councils, men were present who were sometimes borne headlong with too much feeling
    b. example of Nicea, where the orthodox side turned against itself in dissension

11. Human fallibility in the councils
    a. the Council of Chalcedon charged with error by Pope Leo himself
    b. the Holy Spirit so governed the otherwise godly and holy councils as to allow something human to happen to them, lest we should put too much confidence in men

***We Must Not Obey Blind Guides; Decision of Later Councils Faulty in the Light of Scripture** [12–14]*

12. No blind obedience
    a. if we must accept the teaching of all pastors without doubting, what was the point of the Lord's frequent admonitions to us not to heed the talk of false prophets?
    b. titles should not blind us

13. The actual significance of councils for the interpretation of Scripture
    a. but if discussion arises over doctrine, the best remedy is for true bishops to be convened
    b. but I deny it to be always the case that an interpretation of Scripture adopted by vote of a council is true and certain

14. False evaluation of conciliar decisions on the part of the Roman Church
    a. everything ordained in councils is not interpretation of Scripture
    b. purgatory, intercession of saints, and auricular confession can hardly be called interpretation of Scripture
    c. the contrast between conciliar doctrine and "interpretation of Scripture" as seen in the communion cup, and marriage

d. according to Roman thought, Arius should not have allowed himself to be defeated by the testimony of the Gospel of John
e. at what council was the ancient list called "canon" approved?

CHAPTER 10
The Power of Making Laws, in Which the Pope, with His Supporters, Has Exercised upon Souls the Most Savage Tyranny and Butchery

Church Laws and Traditions, and the Christian's Conscience before God [*1-4*]

1. The basic question: whether the church may lawfully bind consciences by its laws
   a. the second part of church power is the making of laws (listed as the third part in IV.8.1)
   b. the concern here is not political order, but the worship of God and spiritual freedom
   c. by the laws of Rome, the freedom given by Christ to the consciences of believers is utterly oppressed

2. The Roman constitutions enslave consciences
   a. while Paul was cautious not to lay a restraint upon men, the number of the Roman constitutions is practically impossible to count
   b. the purpose here is to attack constitutions made to bind souls before God

3. The nature of conscience (=III.19.15)
   a. difficulty: men fail to distinguish sharply enough between the external forum and the forum of conscience
   b. resolution of difficulty: in understanding the nature of conscience
      (1) when men grasp the conception of things with the mind and the understanding, they are said "to know"
      (2) in like manner, when men have an awareness of divine judgment adjoined to them as a witness which does not

let them hide their sins but arraigns them as guilty before God's judgment-seat, this awareness is called "conscience"

4. Bondage and freedom of conscience (=III.19.16)
   a. works refer to men; conscience to God, i.e., inward uprightness of heart
   b. but sometimes conscience is extended to men (e.g., Acts 24:16): the fruit of a good conscience flows forth and comes even to men
   c. *adiaphora:* we should abstain from anything that might cause offense, but with a free conscience (e.g., meat offered to idols—I Cor. 10:28f.)

***Conscience in Relation to Human and Papal Laws: God the Only Lawgiver* [*5–8*]**

5. The meaning of human laws for the conscience
   a. our consciences do not have to do with human laws (earthly forum), but with God (forum of conscience)
   b. therefore man's conscience is higher than all human judgments
   c. question: if we obey rulers for conscience's sake, then do not rulers' laws have dominion over the conscience?
   d. reply: even though individual laws may not apply to the conscience, we are still held by God's general command commending to us the authority of magistrates

6. The church has no right to set up independent constitutions to bind consciences
   a. false bishops, thinking they are spiritual lawgivers, burden our consciences
   b. they have no right to command anything apart from God's Word
   c. such a right was even denied the apostles

7. All arbitrary lordship is an encroachment upon God's kingdom
   a. God claims one prerogative as His very own: to rule us by the authority and laws of His Word
   b. therefore the whole power of those who wish to command apart from God's Word is cut off

8. Directions to determine which human constitutions are inadmissible
   a. two reasons why the Lord is the sole lawgiver:
      (1) we should have in His will the perfect rule of all righteousness, thus possessing the perfect knowledge of the good life
      (2) God alone has authority over our souls
   b. therefore all human constitutions that pretend to relate to the true worship of God and that consciences are bound to keep are contrary to the Lord's Word
   c. examples of Paul

Ecclesiastical Constitutions Authorizing Ceremonies in Worship Are Tyrannous, Frivolous, and Contrary to Scripture [*9–18*]

9. The Roman constitutions are, according to the foregoing principles, to be rejected
   a. Roman "ecclesiastical" constitutions apply to ceremonies and rites, others more to discipline
   b. they subject the worship of God to their fictions and reduce it to men's decisions

10. The papal constitutions deny God's law
    a. castigations on auricular confession, meat on Friday, saints' days, celibacy, pilgrimages, pomp of the churches, idol worship, murmuring long senseless words in "prayer"
    b. according to our lawmakers, such observances are necessary rather than obedience to Scripture

11. Roman constitutions meaningless and useless
    a. two other great faults:
       (1) they prescribe observances which are useless and foolish
       (2) pious consciences are oppressed with an immense multitude of them by which they cannot reach Christ
    b. these constitutions keep men's minds pressed to the ground

12. Their mysteries are mockeries
    a. the "great mysteries" are pure mockeries
    b. ceremonies, extracted from ancient rites, are an ill-patched hodgepodge
    c. "canons" overturn rather than preserve discipline

13. The Roman Church constitutions, through their senseless accumulation, bring Jewish vexations upon the conscience
    a. the number of such traditions is unbearable
    b. testimony of Augustine to the effect that the condition of the Jews was more bearable

14. Ceremonies to show forth Christ, not to hide Him
    a. consciences tormented by the multitude and variety of rites
    b. the heaping up of ceremonies is of no help to the weak or untutored
    c. worship under Moses was wrapped in many ceremonies, but now, with fewer and more simple ceremonies, God is worshiped

15. Corruption of ceremonies regarded as expiatory sacrifices
    a. the ceremonies are not sacrifices by which God is appeased
    b. the value of ceremonies lies not in their own merit, but in our obedience

16. General application of common insights
    a. God strikes with blindness those of every age who worship Him with doctrines of men
    b. if, in any age, you wish to discover what human traditions should be repudiated, ask whether or not they are laws apart from God's Word

17. The Roman constitutions cannot, as they assume, count as church constitutions
    a. though Romanists claim their traditions are from God and come down through the apostles, they pass the bounds of God's Word in the framing of new laws
    b. they bring insult to the church by adding and mixing something of their own with God's teaching

18. The Roman constitutions do not reach back to the apostles, or even to the "apostolic tradition"
    a. the whole doctrine of the apostles has this intent: not to burden consciences with new observances, or contaminate the worship of God with our own inventions
    b. it is foolish for them to say that what was not committed to writing had been received in use and customary practice

***Accumulation of Useless Rites Falsely Called "Apostolic": Obligation to Weak Consciences** [19–22]*

19. Post-apostolic accumulation of useless rites
    a. the original simplicity of the apostolic Lord's Supper
    b. the idea that what was done by common consent in the church universal had come down from the apostles is refuted by Augustine

20. Augustine interpreted
    a. the idea of holy water does not come from the apostles
    b. while Augustine ascribes some things to the apostles, there is a great difference between an exercise which believers may use with free conscience, and making a law to trap consciences in bondage

21. The decree of Acts 15:20
    a. argument: if (according to Acts 15:20) the apostles and elders of the primitive church framed a decree outside the command of Christ, why should it not be allowed to their successors to follow the same practice?
    b. answer: the apostles brought nothing new of their own to God's eternal law, which forbids the offending of brethren

22. Obligation to weak brethren
    a. the apostles had no other intention than to urge the divine law concerning the avoiding of offense
    b. when the Romanists acknowledge that transgression of this law is nothing but the violation of love, they acknowledge that the law is no contrived addition to God's law

***Traditions and Human Inventions in Worship Condemned in Scripture and by Christ Himself** [23–26]*

23. The appeal to the authority of the church contradicts the evidence of Scripture
    a. the Roman ceremonies not only demand we endure some grave oppression in our body but also torment our consciences
    b. reverence to God consists simply in worshiping Him as He commands
    c. examples of foreign devices in Old Testament worship

24. Perverse worship an abomination to God
    a. even though those who obey human laws in the worship of God have some semblance of humility in this obedience, they are not humble in God's sight
    b. religion today is defiled with more senseless superstitions than ever any paganism was

25. Refutation of Romanist counterevidence
    a. the example of Samuel (I Sam. 7:17) was not to make any innovation in sacred rites
    b. the examples of Manoah (Judg. 13:19) and Gideon (Judg. 8:27)

26. Christ's warning against the leaven of the Pharisees
    a. the meaning of Matt. 23:3; 16:6; and 16:12, when not twisted, demonstrates that the Lord would not have the consciences of His people troubled by traditions peculiar to the Pharisees
    b. the argument supported by Augustine's words

Right Ordering of Church Government and Worship: Decency, Love, and a Free Conscience [*27–32*]

27. Necessity of church constitutions
    a. but the fact that men's consciences are bound by human traditions does not mean that all laws by which the order of the church is shaped are to be erased
    b. yet laws by which "all things can be done decently and in order" are not to be considered necessary for salvation or associated with the worship of God, thereby lodging piety in them

28. The problem of right church constitutions
    a. we may distinguish between impious constitutions and legitimate church observances if we keep two goals in view
        (1) in the sacred assembly of believers let all things be done decently and with becoming dignity
        (2) the human community must be kept in order with certain bonds of humanity and moderation
    b. there is a twofold purpose to the decorum which Paul commends
        (1) when rites are used which promote reverence toward sacred things, we are aroused to piety by such aids
        (2) that modesty and gravity greatly shine there

29. True decorum in worship, not theatrical show
    a. elegance and extravagance in worship is not equivalent to true decorum
    b. ceremonies, to be exercises of piety, ought to lead us straight to Christ
    c. examples from Paul

30. Bondage and freedom of church constitutions
    a. I approve only those human constitutions which are founded upon God's authority, drawn from Scripture, and, therefore, wholly divine
    b. the example of kneeling as both human and divine
    c. love will best judge what may hurt or edify

31. Bondage and freedom over against church constitutions
    a. this attitude toward the observance of rules maintains our freedom, while at the same time we voluntarily impose some necessity upon our freedom
    b. we occupy ourselves without superstition in the observance of these things, nor require it too fastidiously of others
    c. the entire use and purpose of observances is to be referred to the upbuilding of the church

32. Observances should be few and edifying
    a. we must strive to prevent error from creeping in
    b. principles to further this end:
        (1) keep freedom in worship practices, but with voluntary self-restraint upon our freedom as love requires
        (2) avoid superstition in observances and do not require such of others, lest we think ceremonies better the more they are piled up
        (3) make no perpetual law for ourselves, but refer the use and purpose of observances to the upbuilding of the church, with freedom to change as circumstances demand

CHAPTER 11
The Jurisdiction of the Church and Its Abuse as Seen in the Papacy

Jurisdiction and Discipline: the Power of the Keys and the Civil Magistracy [*1-5*]

1. The basis of church jurisdiction in the power of the keys
   a. the third part of ecclesiastical power now to be discussed, namely, jurisdiction
   b. the power of jurisdiction depends entirely upon the keys which Christ gave to the church (Matt. 18:15–18)
   c. the power of the keys is the preaching of the gospel; with regard to men it is not so much power as ministry (Matt. 16:19)

2. The power of binding and loosing
   a. the difference between the two passages
      (1) Matt. 18:17–18 is concerned with the preaching which the ministers of the Word execute
      (2) Matt. 16:19 is concerned with the discipline of excommunication which is entrusted to the church
   b. the church binds him whom it excommunicates; looses him whom it receives into communion
   c. the judgment by believers is nothing but the proclamation of the Lord's sentence

3. Civil and ecclesiastical jurisdiction
   a. while the function of the magistrate may produce punishment of the offender against his will, the function of the church is to elicit from the sinner repentance in a voluntary chastisement
   b. the argument that Christ entrusted these functions to the church only because there was no magistrate to carry them out is barren

4. The church and the Christian magistrate
   a. when emperors and magistrates began to accept Christ, the spiritual jurisdiction of the church was not at once annulled, but only so ordered that it should not detract from the civil jurisdiction

b. they who to honor the magistrate deprive the church of this power, corrupt Christ's utterance, and condemn all the holy bishops who have taken upon themselves the honor and office of magistrate on a false pretext

5. The spiritual character of ecclesiastical jurisdiction
   a. the aim of ecclesiastical jurisdiction: offenses resisted, and scandal wiped out
   b. two characteristics of ecclesiastical jurisdiction
      (1) that the spiritual power be completely separated from the right of the sword
      (2) that it be administered not by the decision of one man but by a lawful assembly
   c. joined with the ministry must be the right to admonish, correct, and excommunicate

***Abuses Caused by the Unwarranted Assumption of Power by the Bishops** [**6–10**]*

6. Administration of justice in the ancient church was not the function of an individual
   a. this power was in the hands of the assembly of the elders, which was to the church what the senate is to the city
   b. two kinds of presbyters: those ordained to teach, and others ordained to be censors of morals
   c. gradual degeneration from this original condition testified to by Ambrose

7. Deterioration of jurisdiction and discipline
   a. bishops, disdaining the business as something unworthy of their care, have delegated it to "officials"
   b. this business is nothing else than earthly matters, although under the guise of "spiritual jurisdiction"
   c. their admonitions and censure of vices are carried on in such a way that nothing is more contrary to the procedure instituted by Christ

8. The worldly power of the bishops contradicts the meaning of this office
   a. their new doctrines, wicked traditions and pretended ecclesiastical jurisdiction are a tyranny opposed to God's Word

b. the whole order, rather than the faults of individual men, is the plague
c. the functions of the civil government and the priesthood ought to be kept separate

9. Assumption of princely powers by the bishops
   a. bishops have gone so far as to usurp the right of the sword, involve themselves in judicial proceedings, and administer cities and provinces
   b. the contrasts between such passages as Matt. 20:25–26, Luke 17:14, Acts 6:2, and the involvement of bishops

10. How has this worldly power of the bishops come about?
    a. at various times they advanced themselves by craft and devious arts, through terror and threats, and the abuse of ill-advised generosity of princes
    b. bishops turned voluntary arbitration among the pious into ordinary jurisdiction, and the office of protector into the office of lord
    c. princes, though granted their generosity had some semblance of piety, corrupted the ancient discipline of the church

Inordinate and Fraudulent Claims of the Papacy and Its Usurpation of Worldly Powers [*11–16*]

11. The origin of papal world supremacy
    a. the Roman pontiff claims empire-wide domination on the basis of either divine right or the Donation of Constantine, or some other title
    b. the answer to this claim from Bernard: "Peter could not give what he did not have . . ."

12. The Donation of Constantine fraudulent and absurd
    a. Gregory, speaking of the emperor as "most serene Lord," and of himself as "unworthy servant," testifies to the absurdity of the claim of the Donation of Constantine
    b. Valla had roundly refuted the fable, only to have men like Augustinus Steuchus Eugubinus, hired by the Pope, attempt to defend it in the hope of gain

13. The relationship of Henry IV and Hildebrand
    a. five hundred years later the pontiffs were still in subjection to the princes

b. Hildebrand (Gregory VII) altered this arrangement in his dealings with Henry IV
c. result: the successors of Hildebrand were able to subject emperors to themselves

14. Appropriations anathematized under Gregory the Great
a. about 130 years ago the popes reduced the city itself to their control
b. but if long ago Gregory anathematized clerics who laid hands on estates which they reckoned as church property, what anathemas are strong enough to punish such examples?

15. Immunities of the Roman clergy
a. Roman clergy claim exemption from common courts and laws
b. but ancient bishops did not judge themselves harmed if they were under subjection
c. ecclesiastical cases were referred to the bishops' judgment
d. the example of Ambrose, who contended that a case involving religion ought not to be taken to a civil court

16. Bishops subject to secular courts
a. but holy men did not, however, disapprove of princes interposing their authority in ecclesiastical matters, provided it was done to preserve the order of the church and establish discipline
b. the relation between Emperor Maurice and Gregory

CHAPTER 12
The Discipline of the Church: Its Chief Use in Censures and Excommunication

Discussion of Power of the Keys in True Discipline: the Ends and Processes of Discipline [*1–7*]

1. Necessity and nature of church discipline
a. if society and even small families require discipline, how much more is it necessary in the church
b. as the saving doctrine of Christ is the soul of the church, discipline serves as its sinews

2. Stages of church discipline
   a. the first foundation of discipline is to provide a place for private admonition
   b. this is especially the duty of pastors and presbyters
   c. if anyone stubbornly rejects a second admonition, he should be called before the assembly of the elders

3. Concealed and open sins
   a. private sins are to be reproved privately; public sins are to be reproved publicly
   b. if the offense is public, let it be rebuked by the church

4. Light and grave sins
   a. of sins, some are faults; others, crimes or shameful acts
   b. for the latter, we must employ a severer remedy
   c. the judgment of the church by vote of believers is nothing but the publication of the Lord's own sentence

5. The purpose of church discipline
   a. the first end of church discipline: that they who lead a filthy and infamous life may not be called Christians, to the dishonor of God
   b. the second end: that the good be not corrupted by the constant company of the wicked
   c. the third end: that those overcome by shame for their baseness begin to repent

6. The handling of church discipline in the various cases
   a. in carrying out discipline, we remember that some sins are public, others private
   b. in the case of public sins, the offender ought to be summoned before the church, but the case of private sins does not come to the church unless the sinner becomes obstinate
   c. sins of severity should be treated by the sinner being deprived of the communion for a time
   d. solemn rites of repentance in the ancient church

7. In the ancient church, discipline applied to all offenders alike
   a. both princes and common people submitted to discipline
   b. excommunication enacted by the whole church, not the elders alone

***Moderation in Discipline Enjoined, and Rigorists Confuted** [8–13]*

8. Severity and mildness in church discipline
   a. we must always, as Paul bids us, take particular care that he who is punished be not overwhelmed with sorrow (II Cor. 2:7)
   b. we cannot excuse the excessive severity of the ancients
   c. examples of moderate discipline in Cyprian, Chrysostom, and Augustine

9. The limits of our judgment according to church discipline
   a. this gentleness is required in the whole body of the church
   b. we are to judge the character of each man's works by the law of the Lord, rather than condemn to death the very person who is in the hand and judgment of God alone

10. Excommunication is corrective
   a. the difference between excommunication and anathema
   b. while anathema ought rarely or never be used, excommunication strives only to forewarn the sinner of his future condemnation, and call him back to salvation
   c. unless gentleness is maintained, there is danger lest we slide down from discipline to butchery

11. Against willful excess in demanding church discipline
   a. necessity of moderation, so that laymen, seeing uncorrected vices, should not depart from the church
   b. pastors, unable to cleanse all that needs correction, should not resign their ministry
   c. Augustine on discipline

12. Disruptive severity: Donatists and Anabaptists
   a. Augustine counsels prudence because of the overscrupulousness of the Donatists and the angelic perfectionism of the Anabaptists
   b. "Satan transforms himself into an angel of light" (II Cor. 11:14) when, on occasion of just severity, he prompts men to merciless cruelty, seeking only to corrupt and break the bond of peace and unity

13. Augustine requires discrimination in discipline
   a. Augustine especially commends this one thing: if the contagion

of sin invades the multitude, the severe mercy of a vigorous discipline is necessary

b. he wishes the method of correction to be so tempered that, as far as possible, it may bring health rather than death to the body

The Use and Purpose of Fasting, Private and Public: Principles to Be Guarded in It [14–18]

14. Public and mutual practice of penance
    a. the remaining part of discipline, which is not properly contained within the power of the keys, is where pastors exhort the people to fasting and other acts of humility
    b. this observance was customary in the early church, which followed Old Testament practice

15. The purpose of fasting
    a. fasting has three objectives
        (1) to weaken the flesh that it may not act wantonly
        (2) that we may be better prepared for prayers and holy meditations
        (3) that it may be a testimony of our self-abasement before God when we wish to confess our guilt before him
    b. the first objective is more appropriate to private rather than public fasting
    c. the second and the third are common to both

16. Fasting and prayer
    a. whenever men are to pray to God concerning any great matter, it would be expedient to appoint fasting along with prayer
    b. biblical examples of fasting

17. Fasting and the practice of penance
    a. if either pestilence, or famine, or war begins to rage, the Lord's wrath may be averted through fasting
    b. it can readily be inferred from the words of Joel that this was the custom among the Israelites (Joel 2:15–16)
    c. fasting is not an external ceremony which ended in Christ, but is an excellent aid for believers today

18. The nature of fasting
    a. fasting is more than restraint and abstemiousness in food
    b. the whole life of the godly ought to bear some resemblance to a fast
    c. but in addition, there is another sort of fasting, temporary in character, when we withdraw something from the normal regimen of living
    d. this consists in three things: time, quality of foods, and in smallness of quantity

Danger of Superstition, Notions of Merit, and Hypocrisy in Fasting and the Observance of Lent [*19–21*]

19. Misconceptions of fasting; three errors:
    a. hypocritical fasting
    b. fasting as a work of merit or a form of divine worship
    c. extolling the nobility of fasting through too-rigid observance and too-immoderate praise of it

20. Degeneration of fasting in the history of the church; amazing diversity of practice
    a. the common people thought that in the superstitious observance of Lent they were doing some exceptional service to God
    b. the reason Christ fasted and the difference from the fast of Moses
    c. diversity in the manner of fasting related by Cassiodorus

21. Depraved indulgence in seasons of fasting
    a. worse times followed because of the incompetence and lust for mastery of bishops
    b. for them the highest worship of God is to abstain from meats, and in their place to abound in all sorts of delicacies
    c. in the present day papal practice, nothing remains deserving of praise

Requirement of Clerical Celibacy a Harmful Innovation [*22–28*]

22. The discipline of the clergy and its degeneration
    a. the second part of discipline applies particularly to the clergy
    b. the canons that the ancient bishops imposed upon themselves

c. admonition came from bishops and synods
d. how all this has fallen into disuse

23. Priestly celibacy and its contradiction of Scripture
 a. this prohibition has not only deprived the church of good and fit pastors, but has also brought in a sink of iniquities
 b. refutation of celibacy based on Scripture

24. Marriage enjoined and spiritually interpreted
 a. they object that the priest should be distinguished from the people by some mark
 b. while Paul lists marriage among the virtues of the bishop, the papists teach that it is an intolerable fault in the church order
 c. Christ deems marriage worthy of such honor that He wills it to be an image of His sacred union with the church (Eph. 5:23–24, 32)

25. Refutation of an opposing Scriptural argument
 a. the papists defend celibacy by citing the Levitical priests
 b. explanation of the reason Levitical priests had to sleep apart from their wives
 c. because the pastors of the church do not play this part today, it is pointless to compare them with the priests

26. The ancient church and celibacy
 a. what will they do with all the ancient fathers, who certainly not only tolerated marriage but also approved it for the order of bishops
 b. marriage remained sacred in the early church; and it caused no shame, nor was it thought to cast any spot upon the ministry

27. Late development of the requirement of celibacy
 a. the result was that the dignity of marriage was so weakened that a man who did not refrain from it seemed not to aspire to perfection with enough strength of purpose
 b. if my adversaries claim antiquity against me, my first answer is that this freedom of bishops to be married existed both under the apostles and for some centuries afterward
 c. the law of celibacy was imposed upon priests, not as a thing necessary in itself, but because a celibate was preferred to a married man

d. celibacy was not compelled of those unfit to keep continence, but only that, upon marriage, they give up their office

28. Abuses under the rule of celibacy
    a. what we would have to require of priests if the defenders of this new tyranny seek the pretext of antiquity
    b. of the remaining fathers, none, except Jerome, has so spitefully impugned the honorableness of marriage
    c. the tribute of Chrysostom

CHAPTER 13
Vows; and How Everyone Rashly Taking Them Has Miserably Entangled Himself

The Nature of Vows, and Prevalent Errors Concerning Them [*1–7*]

1. Degeneration and dangers
    a. the church, already oppressed by cruel tyranny and almost overwhelmed with a huge mass of traditions, now added vows, by which a greater and stricter obligation might be added to the common chains
    b. since what is required for piety is comprised in the law, and righteousness consists in simple obedience to His will, further inventions and feigned acts of worship are not looked upon by God with favor

2. God as the One to whom we make our vows
    a. in order to determine which vows are lawful and which objectionable, three things are to be considered:
        (1) who it is to whom the vow is made
        (2) who we are who make the vow
        (3) with what intention we make our vow
    b. the purpose of the first consideration is to make us realize that it is God with whom we have to deal, who declares all self-made religion, however splendid, accursed (Col. 2:23)
    c. our vows will attempt nothing rash if they have God going before them and dictating, as from His own Word, what is good or profitable to do

3. The man who makes the vow [the second consideration]
    a. second, we should measure our strength, keeping our calling

in mind, so as not to neglect the blessing of freedom which God has given us

b. he is a rash man who vows what is either not in his power or conflicts with his calling

c. celibacy holds the first place for insane boldness

4. Vows classified according to intention [the third consideration]

a. third, intention in making a vow is important because the same thing may at one time be pleasing to God and at another time displease Him, as the purpose in our mind may change

b. there are four ends to which our vows ought duly to be directed, two of which refer to past time [cf. 5a]

α (1) vows by which we attest our gratitude to God for benefits received (exercises of thanksgiving)

β (2) vows by which we punish ourselves for offenses committed, in order to avert God's wrath (exercises of repentance)

c. examples of the first sort

(1) tithes which Jacob vowed if the Lord should lead him back unharmed from exile to his homeland (Gen. 28:20–22)

(2) peace offerings which pious kings and leaders, about to undertake a righteous war, vowed to make if they should win the victory

d. example of the second sort: renouncing all dainty foods when, through the vice of gluttony, one falls into any misdeed

5. Vows of future reference

a. of the four ends to which our vows ought to be directed, two refer to future time [cf. 4b]

α (1) vows tending to make us more cautious

β (2) vows tending to arouse us, as by some stimulus, to our duty

b. example of the first sort: a man vowing to cut off the use of a thing for a time when, through the use of that which otherwise is not bad, he cannot prevent himself from falling directly into evil

c. example of the second sort: a man, forgetful or lazy toward the necessary duties of piety, making a vow to wake up his memory and shake off his laziness

d. thus, vows which look to one of these four ends are lawful, provided they are supported by God's approval, agree with our calling, and are limited to the endowment of grace given us by God

6. Lawful vows in general
   a. all believers have one common vow which, made in baptism, we confirm and, so to speak, sanction by catechism and receiving the Lord's Supper
   b. the common vow: renouncing Satan, we yield ourselves to God's service to obey His holy commandments but not to follow the wicked desires of our flesh (cf. Rom. 13:14)
   c. excess and repetition cheapen the whole religious character of vows

7. Perverse vows
   a. superstition surrounding such vows as abstinence, fasting, holy days, and pilgrimages
   b. judged by the rules given [above] they will be deemed not only empty and fleeting but full of manifest impiety
   c. hypocrites, when they have performed such follies, believe that they have procured for themselves exceptional righteousness

Monastic Vows and the Decline of Monastic Life [*8–10*]

8. The monasticism of the ancient church
   a. lest anyone should defend present-day monasticism on the grounds of its antiquity, we must note that a far different mode of living prevailed in monasteries
   b. the severity of monasteries attested by Gregory of Nazianzus, Basil, and Chrysostom
   c. Augustine shows that pious men customarily prepared themselves by monastic discipline to govern the church

9. Augustine's description of monasticism
   a. in the book, *On the Morals of the Catholic Church,* Augustine defends the holiness of the monastic profession against the slanders of the Manichees
   b. in another book, *On the Work of Monks,* Augustine inveighs against certain degenerate monks who were beginning to corrupt that institution
   c. summary of Augustine's teaching

10. Comparison of earlier with later monasticism
   a. Augustine, in sketching for us a holy and lawful monasticism, would dispense with all rigid requirement of those things left free to us by the Lord's Word
   b. yet today nothing is more sternly required!
   c. with respect to idleness and the purpose of brotherly love, the character of present-day monasticism is so different that you could scarcely find things more unlike, not to say contrary

The Erroneous Claim of Monastic Perfection [*11–14*]

11. Monasticism—a state of perfection?
   a. question: if they deny that they dream up some new sort of piety in addition to that piety to which Christ enjoins his followers to attend, then why do they dignify their order alone with the title of perfection, and take the same title away from all God's callings?
   b. their sophistical solution: monasticism is not to be called perfect because it contains perfection within itself, but because it is the best way of all to attain perfection
   c. reply:
      (1) monasticism is nowhere approved by even one syllable
      (2) calling their profession "a state of acquiring perfection" makes all other callings of God unworthy by comparison
      (3) a great injury is done to God when such a forgery is preferred to all the kinds of life ordained by him and praised by His own testimony

12. Christ's rule of life is for all Christians
   a. they openly teach that they shoulder a greater burden than Christ laid upon His people, seeing that they promise to keep the evangelical counsels to love one's enemies, not to seek vengeance, not to swear, etc. (Matt. 5:33ff.)—by which Christians are not commonly bound
   b. but all the ancients declare with one voice that men must of necessity obey every little word uttered by Christ
   c. the fundamental error of monasticism is the opinion that a more perfect rule of life can be devised than the common one committed by God to the whole church

13. The meaning of Matt. 19:21
   a. another argument for their perfection, which they regard as their strongest one, is the statement the Lord made to the

young man who inquired about perfect righteousness, "If you wish to be perfect, sell all you have and give to the poor" (Matt. 19:21)

b. if the sum of perfection lies in this, what does Paul mean when he teaches that he who gives all his goods to the poor is nothing unless he has love (I Cor. 13:3)?

c. the context and original import of the text examined

14. Monastic sectarianism

a. though this passage was misunderstood by some of the fathers, nothing was more remote from their thought than to set up a double Christianity

b. while Augustine says the ancient monks applied themselves wholly to love, it is completely foreign to this new profession

c. by erecting a private altar for themselves, what else have present-day monks done but broken the bond of unity, cutting themselves off from the lawful society of believers?

Differences of Ancient and Monastic Profession: New Testament Widows and Deaconesses Were Not Nuns [15–19]

15. The degeneration of the conduct of monks

a. until now we have been speaking of monasticism rather than monks, the fault of the order itself rather than the faults which inhere in the life of a few

b. but in fact, no order of men is more polluted by all sorts of foul vices

c. still, this charge does not apply to all with no exception whatever

16. Considerations against ancient monasticism

a. even in that ancient form which Augustine commends, monks were not without immoderate affectation and perverse zeal

b. rather than living without earthly care, God prefers devoted care in ruling a household

c. it is a beautiful thing to philosophize in retirement, but it is not the part of Christian meekness, as if in hatred of the human race, to flee to the desert and the wilderness and at the same time to forsake those duties which the Lord has especially commanded

17. Monastic vows, especially the vow of chastity
    a. because it is their intention to establish a new and forged worship to merit God's favor, whatever they vow is abominable in God's sight (cf. IV.10.17; IV.13.1)
    b. because they invent any mode of life they please without regard for God's call, this is a rash and therefore unlawful enterprise (cf. III.15.6; IV.13.2)
    c. because they bind themselves to many acts of worship at once perverted and impious, they are consecrated not to God but to an evil spirit
    d. "continence" is not that continence by which the body alone is kept pure from fornication but also that by which the mind keeps its chastity unsullied

18. The case of the widows in I Tim. 5:12
    a. it is true that the widows who pledged themselves and their services to the church took upon themselves the state of perpetual celibacy (I Tim. 5:11-12)
    b. but they did so not because they regarded it as something religious of itself but because they would not carry on their function without being their own masters and free of the marriage yoke
    c. they were not so bound that it was not better for them to marry than either to be troubled by the stings of the flesh or to fall into any uncleanness

19. Nuns are very different
    a. how can I Tim. 5:12 be applied to nuns?
    b. deaconesses were created not to appease God with songs or unintelligible mumbling, not to live the rest of the time in idleness, but to discharge the public ministry of the church toward the poor and to strive with all zeal, constancy, and diligence in the task of love

Unlawful and Superstitious Vows Are Not Binding [*20-21*]

20. Are inadmissible vows binding?
    a. all unlawful or improperly conceived vows, as they are of no value before God, should be invalid for us
    b. when Paul says "Whatever is not of faith is sin" (Rom. 14:23), he means that when a work is undertaken with doubt it is

faulty because the root of all good works is faith, by which we are sure they are acceptable to God

c. if men have undertaken anything rashly through the fault of ignorance, why should they not desist from it when once freed of error?

21. On the breaking of monastic vows
    a. there has been no bond where God abrogates what man confirms
    b. if the cross of Christ has such great power that it frees us from the curse of God's law, by which we were held bound (Gal. 3:13), how much more will it deliver us from those outward fetters which are nothing more than the deceptive nets of Satan!
    c. regarding those not fit for celibacy, what else but stubbornness will we call it when a man, warned that he needs marriage, and that it is given to him as a remedy by the Lord, not only despises it but also binds himself by an oath to despise it?

CHAPTER 14
The Sacraments

The Word "Sacrament" Explained: Sacraments Are Signs of God's Covenants [*1–6*]

1. Definition
    a. we have in the sacraments another aid to our faith related to the preaching of the gospel
    b. a sacrament is an outward sign by which the Lord seals on our consciences the promises of His good will toward us in order to sustain the weakness of our faith; and we in turn attest our piety toward Him in the presence of the Lord and of His angels and before men
    c. a shorter definition: a sacrament is a testimony of divine grace toward us, confirmed by an outward sign, with mutual attestation of our piety toward Him

2. The word "sacrament"
    a. the Latin rendering of the Greek word
    b. examples: Eph. 1:9, 3:2–3; Col. 1:26–27; I Tim. 3:16

c. the word "sacrament" preferred to the word "secret"
d. the Latin word "sacraments" and the Greek word "mysteries" are identical in meaning

3. Word and sign
   a. a sacrament is never without a preceding promise but is joined to it as a sort of appendix, with the purpose of confirming and sealing the promise itself, and of making it more evident to us and in a sense ratifying it
   b. a sacrament is not so much needed to confirm His sacred Word as to establish us in faith in it
   c. as Chrysostom says, if we were incorporeal, God would give us these very things naked and incorporeal, but because we have souls engrafted in bodies, He imparts spiritual things under visible ones

4. The Word must explain the sign
   a. our opponents say a sacrament consists of the Word and the outward sign
   b. but we ought to understand the Word not as one whispered without meaning and without faith—a mere noise like a magic incantation, which has the force to consecrate the element
   c. the Word should, when preached, make us understand what the visible sign means
   d. whenever God gave a sign to the holy patriarchs it was inseparably linked to doctrine, without which our senses would have been stunned in looking at the bare sign

5. The sacraments as seals
   a. as seals confirm what is written on a parchment, the sacraments confirm the Word of God preached preceding the sacraments
   b. this comparison was used by Paul (Rom. 4:11)
   c. the believer, when he sees the sacraments with his own eyes, does not halt at the physical sight of them, but rises up in devout contemplation to those lofty mysteries which lie hidden in the sacraments

6. The sacraments as signs of a covenant
   a. since the Lord calls His promises "covenants" (Gen. 6:18; 9:9;

17:2) and His sacraments "tokens" of the covenants, a simile can be taken from the covenants of men

b. for what can the slaughter of a sow accomplish unless words accompany the act, indeed, unless they precede it?

c. the sacraments, therefore, are exercises which make us more certain of the trustworthiness of God's Word

d. other comparisons: the sacraments as "pillars of our faith" or "mirrors"

They Confirm Faith, Not of Themselves, but as Agencies of the Holy Spirit and in Association with the Word; and They Are Distinguishing Marks of Our Profession of Faith Before Men [*7–13*]

7. The reception of the sacraments by the wicked is no evidence against their importance
   a. by the same argument, neither gospel nor Christ would be a testimony of God's grace, because Christ was seen and recognized by many but very few of them accepted Him
   b. the pledge of God's grace, offered in both Word and sacrament, is understood only by those who take Word and sacrament with sure faith
   c. those who say that our faith cannot be made better if it is already good would do well to pray with the apostles that the Lord increase their faith (Luke 17:5), rather than confidently to pretend such perfection of faith as no one of the children of men ever attained or ever will attain in this life

8. To what extent can we speak of a confirmation of faith through the sacraments?
   a. yet some say, Philip answers the eunuch that he was permitted to be baptized if he believed with all his heart (Acts 8:37); then they ask what place does confirmation of baptism have here, where faith fills the whole heart?
   b. but do they not feel a good portion of their heart devoid of faith, and daily acknowledge new increases?
   c. "to believe with all our heart" is not to believe Christ perfectly, but only to embrace Him from the heart and with a sincere mind; not to be sated with Him, but to hunger, thirst, and aspire to Him with fervent affection

9. The Holy Spirit in the sacraments
   a. the sacraments properly fulfill their office only when the Spirit, that inward teacher, comes to them, by whose power

alone hearts are penetrated and affections moved and our souls opened for the sacraments to enter in

b. what sight does in our eyes for seeing a light, and what hearing does in our ears for perceiving a voice, are analogous to the work of the Holy Spirit in our hearts, which is to conceive, sustain, nourish, and establish faith

10. Illustration from human persuasion

a. if we ascribe to creatures either the increase or the confirmation of faith, injustice is done to the Spirit of God, who should be recognized as its sole Author

b. as you may not be able to convince anyone by words to do something unless he is of a teachable disposition, so the Spirit softens the stubbornness of our hearts that the Word may not beat upon our ears in vain

c. finally, the Spirit transmits those outward words and sacraments from our ears to our soul

11. Word and sacrament work equally in the confirming of our faith

a. just as we say that from seed (cf. Matt. 13:3–23) grain is born, increases, and rises to maturity, why may we not say that from the Word faith takes its beginning, increase, and perfection?

b. but Paul concludes: "Neither he who plants nor he who waters is anything, but all things are to be ascribed to God who gives the growth" (I Cor. 3:7ff.)

c. thus the apostles express the power of the Spirit in their preaching, as far as God uses the instrument ordained by Himself for the unfolding of His spiritual grace

12. Sacramental elements have value only as God's instruments

a. sacraments, moreover, are so much confirmations of our faith that the Lord sometimes, when He would remove confidence in the very things that had been promised by Him in the sacraments, takes away the sacraments themselves

b. for instance, the removal of the fruit of life from Adam was a removal of the symbol of promise

c. therefore, our confidence ought not to inhere in the sacraments themselves, nor the glory of God be transferred to them

d. thus our faith and our confession ought to rise up to Him who is the author of the sacraments and of all things

13. The word *sacramentum*
    a. some say that the word *sacramentum* signifies the solemn oath that the soldier took to the commander when he entered military service
    b. thus, as recruits bind their fealty to their commander by this military oath and make profession of military service, so by our signs do we profess Christ our commander, and testify that we serve under His ensign
    c. but the ancients who applied the name *sacraments* to signs had given no attention to the use of this word by Latin writers
    d. what is secondary in the sacraments, the attestation of our confession before men, must not be placed before that which is primary, an aid and service to our faith

They Do Not of Themselves Impart Grace, but, Like the Word, Hold Forth Christ [*14–17*]

14. The error of a magical conception of the sacraments
    a. there are those who attach to the sacraments some sort of secret powers with which one nowhere reads that God has endowed them
    b. the schools of the Sophists have taught with remarkable agreement that the sacraments of the new law (those now used in the Christian church) justify and confer grace, provided we do not set up a barrier of mortal sin
    c. in promising a righteousness apart from faith, this teaching hurls souls headlong to destruction
    d. because the teaching draws the cause of righteousness from the sacraments, it binds men's pitiable minds in this superstition, so that they repose in the appearance of a physical thing rather than in God Himself
    e. from this it follows that assurance of salvation does not depend upon participation in the sacrament, as if justification consisted in it

15. Matter and sign to be distinguished
    a. the distinction between a sacrament and the matter of the sacrament signifies not only that the figure and the truth are contained in the sacrament, but that they are not so linked that they cannot be separated

b. Augustine speaks of this separation when he writes, "In the elect alone the sacraments effect what they represent"
c. further statements of Augustine on the subject

16. The sacraments have significance for us in faith in Christ
    a. Christ is the matter or (if you prefer) the substance of all the sacraments; for in Him they have all their firmness, and they do not promise anything apart from Him
    b. the force and truth of the sacrament do not depend upon the condition or choice of him who receives it
    c. two vices which, according to Augustine, are to be avoided
        (1) to receive the signs as though they had been given in vain, and by destroying or weakening their secret meanings through our antagonism, to cause them to be wholly fruitless to us
        (2) not to lift our minds beyond the visible sign, thus transferring to it the credit for those benefits which are conferred upon us by Christ alone

17. True office of the sacraments
    a. let it be a settled principle that the sacraments have the same office as the Word of God: to offer and set forth Christ to us, and in Him the treasures of heavenly grace
    b. God Himself is present in His institution by the very-present power of His Spirit
    c. nevertheless, the inner grace of the Spirit, as distinct from the outward ministry, ought to be considered and pondered separately
    d. the only question here is whether God acts by His own intrinsic power (as they say) or resigns His office to outward symbols
    e. God accomplishes within what the minister represents and attests by outward action, lest what God claims for Himself alone should be turned over to a mortal man

Wide Application of the Term to Scriptural Incidents and Its Restriction to the Ordinary Sacraments of the Church [*18–20*]

18. Sacraments in the wider sense
    a. the term *sacrament* embraces generally all those signs which God has ever enjoined upon men to render them more certain and confident of the truth of His promises

b. examples of sacraments presented in natural things
   (1) the tree of life given as a guarantee of immortality to Adam and Eve (Gen. 2:9; 3:22)
   (2) the rainbow, in which we may read the promise of God to Noah, even though it is but a reflection of the sun's rays upon the clouds opposite (Gen. 9:13–16)

c. examples of sacraments presented in miracles
   (1) light in a smoking fire pot (Gen. 15:17)
   (2) the fleece and the dew (Judg. 6:37–38)
   (3) the shadow of the sundial (II Kings 20:9–11; Isa. 38:7)

19. Ordinary sacraments of the church
   a. to use Augustine's words, "men cannot be welded together in any name of religion, whether true or false, unless they are bound in some partnership of signs or visible sacraments"
   b. since our most merciful Father foresaw this need, at the outset He instituted definite exercises of piety for His servants
   c. these however, were degraded and corrupted, because they were not grounded upon God's Word and they did not refer to that truth which all signs ought to set forth
   d. the ordinary sacraments, however, consist not of simple signs, but of ceremonies, or, if you prefer, the signs, here given are ceremonies

20. Christ promised in the Old Testament sacraments
   a. the sacraments themselves were also diverse, in keeping with the times, according to the dispensation by which the Lord was pleased to reveal Himself in various ways to men
   b. these ancient sacraments looked to the same purpose to which ours now tend: to direct and almost lead men by the hand to Christ, or rather, as images, to represent Him and show Him forth to be known

Sacraments of the Old Testament Closely Related to Those of the New as Foreshadowing the Full Manifestation of Christ [*21–26*]

21. Circumcision, purifications, sacrifices, point to Christ
   a. circumcision to the Jews was the symbol affirming that the whole nature of mankind is corrupt and needs pruning
   b. circumcision was a reminder to confirm them in the promise given to Abraham of the blessed seed in which all nations of the earth were to be blessed (Gen. 22:18), from whom they

were also to await their own blessing, and that saving seed, as we are taught by Paul, was Christ (Gal. 3:16)

c. thus, circumcision was to the Jews the same thing as in Paul's teaching it was to Abraham, namely, a sign of the righteousness of faith (Rom. 4:11)

d. while baptisms and purifications disclosed to the Jews their own uncleanness, these rites also promised another cleansing (Heb. 9:10, 14), which was Christ

e. sacrifices made them aware of their unrighteousness, taught them that some satisfaction must be paid to God's justice, and the necessity of a mediator, which was Christ (Heb. 4:14; 5:5; 9:11)

22. Christ more fully expressed in the Christian sacraments

a. as for our sacraments, baptism attests to us that we have been cleansed and washed; the Eucharistic Supper, that we have been redeemed

b. while water represents washing, and blood satisfaction, the Spirit is a third and primary witness, making us certain of this testimony

23. Similarity and dissimilarity of the old and new sacraments

a. we must utterly reject that Scholastic dogma which notes such a great difference between the sacraments of the old and new law, as if the former only foreshadowed God's grace, but the latter give it as a present reality

b. the fathers ate the same spiritual food as we, and that food was Christ (I Cor. 10:3)

24. Paul's teaching on the value of circumcision

a. some, by way of objection, quote what they read concerning "circumcision of the letter" in Paul (Rom. 2:29)

b. but the same thing could be said of our sacrament, for in baptism, God cares nothing about the outward washing unless the heart also be inwardly cleansed

c. in another place, some will say, Paul seems completely to despise the circumcision made with hands when he compares it with Christ's circumcision (Col. 2:11–12)

d. but in this passage Paul is disputing against those who require it as necessary although it has already been abolished

25. New Testament disparagement of Jewish ceremonies explained
    a. Paul does not make the Jewish ceremonies shadowed because they have no reality, but because their fulfillment had been, so to speak, held in suspense until the appearance of Christ
    b. all the pomp of ceremonies which was in the law of Moses, unless it be directed to Christ, is a fleeting and worthless thing (cf. 4.16.3–5)

26. Similarity and difference: Augustine's distinctions
    a. reading such statements of Augustine as, "The sacraments of the old law only promised the Savior; but ours give salvation," Sophists have failed to note that such figures of speech were exaggerated
    b. passages from Augustine demonstrating his conviction that while the visible appearance of sacraments from the time of Moses to our time has changed, still the inner signification remains the same
    c. yet there is some difference, for while both attest that God's Fatherly kindness and the graces of the Holy Spirit are offered us in Christ, ours are clearer and brighter
    d. whatever the Sophists have dreamed up concerning the *opus operatum* is not only false but contradicts the nature of the sacraments, which God so instituted that believers, poor and deprived of all goods, should bring nothing to it but begging

CHAPTER 15
Baptism

Baptism a Sign of Our Forgiveness, of Our Participation in Christ's Death and also in His Blessing [*1–6*]

1. The meaning of baptism
    a. definition: the sign of the initiation by which we are received into the society of the church, in order that, engrafted in Christ, we may be reckoned among God's children
    b. two ends
        (1) to serve our faith before Him
        (2) to serve our confession before men
    c. what baptism contributes to our faith: three benefits:
        (1) token and proof of our cleansing [1–4]

(2) token of mortification and renewal in Christ [5]
(3) token of our union with Christ [6]

d. rejection of Zwingli's view of sacrament as mere token or mark of our religion before men

2. Its virtue not in water without the Word
   a. Paul did not mean to signify (Eph. 5:26f.) that our cleansing and salvation are accomplished by water, or that water contains in itself the power to cleanse, regenerate, and renew; nor that here is the cause of salvation, but only that in this sacrament are received the knowledge and certainty of such gifts
   b. baptism promises us no other purification than through the sprinkling of Christ's blood, which is represented by means of water from the resemblance to cleansing and washing

3. Token of cleansing for the whole of life!
   a. baptism was not conferred upon us only for past time, so that for newly committed sins into which we fall after baptism we need not seek new remedies of expiation in some other sacraments
   b. we must realize that at whatever time we are baptized, we are once for all washed and purged for our whole life
   c. Christ's purity, offered us in baptism is defiled by no spots, but buries and cleanses away all our defilements
   d. this doctrine is given only to sinners who are oppressed by their own sins, and should not be an excuse to sin in the future

4. True relation of baptism and repentance
   a. some say that by the benefit of repentance and of the keys we obtain after baptism the forgiveness which in our first regeneration was given us through baptism alone
   b. but the power of the keys so depends upon baptism that it should by no means be severed from it
   c. this error has provided us with the fictitious sacrament of penance

5. Baptism as token of mortification and renewal in Christ (second benefit)
   a. when Paul talks of our being baptized into Christ's death (Rom. 6:3–4) he exhorts us to follow Christ by dying to our

own desires by an example of Christ's death and rising to righteousness by the example of His resurrection

b. Paul also takes hold of something far higher, namely, that through baptism Christ makes us sharers in His death, that we may be engrafted in it (Rom. 6:5)

6. Baptism as token of our union with Christ (third benefit)
   a. our faith receives from baptism the advantage of its sure testimony to us that we are not only engrafted into the death and life of Christ, but so united to Christ Himself that we become sharers in all His blessings
   b. Paul proves that we are children of God from the fact that we put on Christ in baptism (Gal. 3:26–27)
   c. being baptized in the name of the triune God, we obtain and, so to speak, clearly discern in the Father the cause, in the Son the matter, and in the Spirit the effect, of our purgation and our regeneration

The Baptism of John Not Different from That of the Apostles: Its Meaning Symbolized to the Israelites in the Exodus [*7–9*]

7. John's baptism and Christian baptism
   a. different hands that administer baptism do not make it different; but the same doctrine shows it to be the same baptism
   b. let no one be troubled by the attempt of ancient writers to differentiate the one thing from the other
   c. from God's Word this distinction alone may be made: John baptized in Him who was to come; but the apostles, in Him who had already revealed Himself (Luke 3:16; Acts 19:4)

8. Disparity in personality, not in baptism
   a. the fact that since Christ's resurrection richer graces of the Spirit have been poured out does not prove a diversity of baptism: baptism by the apostles also was Christ's baptism
   b. what is the meaning of John's statement that he baptizes with water but that Christ would come to baptize with the Holy Spirit and with fire (Matt. 3:11; Luke 3:16)?
   c. John did not mean to distinguish one sort of baptism from another, but he compared his person with that of Christ—that he was a minister of water, but Christ the giver of the Holy Spirit

d. Christ is the Author of the inward grace, both for the baptism of John and the baptism of ministers today

9. Prototype of baptism in the Old Covenant
   a. mortification and washing were foreshadowed in the people of Israel, who were on this account said to have been "baptized in the cloud and in the sea" (I Cor. 10:2)
   b. mortification was symbolized when the Lord made a way for them through the Red Sea (Exod. 14:21)
   c. in the cloud (Num. 9:15; Exod. 13:21) there was a symbol of cleansing

We Are Not by the Rite of Baptism Set Free from Original Sin, but by It We Make Confession of Faith Before Men [*10–13*]

10. Baptism, original sin, and new righteousness
    a. some falsely teach that through baptism we are released and made exempt from original sin, and from the corruption that descended from Adam into all his posterity; and are restored into that same righteousness and purity of nature which Adam would have obtained if he had remained upright as he was first created
    b. teachers of this type never understood that original sin is the depravity and corruption of our nature which first renders us liable to God's wrath, then also gives rise to what Scripture calls "works of the flesh" (Gal. 5:19)
    c. through baptism, believers are assured that this condemnation has been removed and withdrawn from them

11. We must strive to overcome persistent sin
    a. but this perversity never ceases in us, but continually bears new fruits
    b. but let no one cajole himself in his sinfulness when he hears that sin always dwells in us, for when we speak thus it is not that those who otherwise are all too prone to sin should slumber untroubled in their sins
    c. this doctrine should encourage those who are disturbed and pricked by their own flesh

12. Paul's inner struggle (Rom. 7)
    a. what is said here is the same thing that the apostle Paul very clearly explains in the seventh chapter of Romans
    b. all those who don Christ's righteousness are at the same time

regenerated by the Spirit, and have the pledge of this regeneration in baptism (Rom. 6:3ff.)

c. therefore believers ought not to let sin have lordship over their members (Rom. 6:12)

d. while there is always some weakness in believers, they are not under the law, but have been freed from it to cleave to Christ

e. the function of the law is that, convicted of our depravity, we may confess our weakness and misery

f. if Paul, as a regenerated man, cannot keep the law, his consolation is his engrafting into the communion of Christ and his adoption into the society of the church through baptism

13. Baptism as token of confession

a. baptism is the mark by which we publicly profess that we wish to be reckoned God's people

b. in baptism we testify that we agree in worshiping the same God, in one religion with all Christians, and finally openly affirm our faith

Baptism to Be Received with Trust in the Promise of Which It Is a Sign, and Not to Be Repeated [*14–18*]

14. Sign and thing

a. inasmuch as baptism is given for the arousing, nourishing, and confirming of our faith, it is to be received as from the hand of the Author Himself

b. all the graces which we see in baptism are not bound and enclosed in the sacrament so as to be conferred upon us by its power, but only because the Lord by this token attests His will toward us

15. Baptism as confirming faith

a. take as proof of this Cornelius the centurion, who, having already received forgiveness of sins and the visible graces of the Holy Spirit, was nevertheless baptized (Acts 10:48)

b. reality and truth are joined in the sign, insofar as God works through outward means, but from all sacraments we obtain only as much as we receive in faith

16. Baptism does not depend upon the merit of him who administers it

a. as it makes no difference who or of what sort the carrier of a letter is, provided the handwriting and seal are sufficiently recognized, so it ought to be enough for us to recognize the hand and seal of our Lord in His sacraments, whatever carrier may bring them

b. we are initiated by baptism not into the name of any man, but into the name of the Father and of the Son and of the Holy Spirit (Matt. 28:19)

c. baptism, like ancient circumcision, celebrated by impure priests, is not (as our opponents say) thereby defective and not a symbol of grace

17. Baptism not invalidated by the delay of repentance

a. in order to prove our baptism void, our opponents ask us what faith came to us during some years after our baptism, since it is not sanctified to us except when the Word of promise is accepted in faith

b. reply: we indeed, being blind and unbelieving, for a long time did not grasp the promise that had been given us in baptism; yet that promise, since it was of God, ever remained fixed and firm and trustworthy

c. for this reason, when the Lord invites the Jewish people to repentance, he enjoins no second circumcision upon those who were circumcised by an impious and sacrilegious hand

18. Paul did not rebaptize

a. some assert that Paul rebaptized those who had once been baptized with John's baptism (Acts 19:2–7)

b. the words "they were baptized in the name of Jesus" mean simply the visible graces of the Spirit given through the laying on of hands, and not a rebaptism

c. if ignorance vitiates a previous baptism so that it must be corrected by a second baptism, the apostles first of all would have had to be rebaptized, who for three whole years after their baptism had scarcely tasted a tiny fragment of purer doctrine

Objections to Ceremonial Accretions and to Baptism by Women [*19–21*]

19. Erroneous and correct baptismal usage

a. Christ's genuine institution should prevail in order to restrain the boldness of men

b. whether the person being baptized should be wholly immersed, and whether thrice or once, whether he should be sprinkled with poured water—these details are of no importance, but ought to be optional to churches according to the diversity of countries

c. yet the word "baptize" means to immerse, and it is clear that the rite of immersion was observed in the ancient church

20. Against "emergency" baptism

a. it is wrong for private individuals to assume the administration of baptism

b. baptism as well as the serving of the Supper is a function of the ecclesiastical ministry, for Christ did not command women, or men of every sort, to baptize, but gave this command to those whom He had appointed apostles

c. Augustine doubts whether laymen should baptize those in danger of death if a minister is not present

d. it is not true to say that those who die without baptism will be deprived of the grace of regeneration

21. Women not permitted to baptize

a. we learn from Tertullian that women were not allowed to speak in the church, nor teach, baptize, or offer, so that they might not claim the function of any man, much less that of a priest

b. since Epiphanius declares that it is a mockery to give women the right to baptize and makes no exception, it is clear enough that he condemns this corrupt practice as inexcusable under any pretext

22. Zipporah's circumcision of her son no precedent for baptism by women

a. nothing was farther from Zipporah's purpose than to perform some service to God (Exod. 4:25)

b. infants are not barred from the kingdom of heaven just because they happen to depart the present life before they have been immersed in water

c. yet serious injustice is done to God's covenant if we do not assent to it, since its effect depends neither upon baptism nor upon any additions

d. to the covenant there is added a sacrament, a sort of seal, not to confer efficacy upon God's promise as if it were invalid of itself, but only to confirm it to us

CHAPTER 16
Infant Baptism Best Accords with Christ's Institution and the Nature of the Sign

Infant Baptism, Considered in Relation to What it Typifies, Corresponds to Circumcision and Is Authorized in the Covenant with Abraham [*1–6*]

1. The attack on infant baptism
   a. this appendix added to silence those persons who stir up the church over infant baptism
   b. although this section may seem unduly long, it is worthwhile if it promotes
      (1) purity of doctrine
      (2) the peace of the church
   c. the question: is infant baptism ordained by the Lord?
      (1) if it is, it should be defended at all costs
      (2) if not, it should be set aside in favor of what God truly enjoins

2. The meaning of baptism determined
   a. the right understanding of sacramental signs rests
      (1) not so much on external rites
      (2) as on the promise and the spiritual mysteries for which God has ordained the sacrament
   b. hence we are not to become bogged down in contemplating the visible rite, but concentrate on the promise there set forth
   c. this is a commonplace in Scripture

3. Baptism and circumcision
   a. an examination of the differences and similarities of circumcision and baptism as set forth in Scripture will reveal their anagogic relationship; discussion of Scriptural texts
   b. widely taught in Scripture is the fact that the promise given to the patriarchs in circumcision is what is given us in baptism, for it represents:
      (1) forgiveness of sins
      (2) mortification of flesh

4. The difference is in externals only
   a. the similarity of the two signs consists in
      (1) the promise: God's favor, forgiveness of sins, eternal life
      (2) the thing represented: regeneration

b. the dissimilarity consists in the external ceremony, a matter of far less importance
c. Paul's rule of Scriptural interpretation, *analogia fidei,* leads us to the common core of both sacraments and to the conclusion that baptism does for us what circumcision did for the ancient Jews

5. Infants are participants in the covenant
   a. anyone penetrating beneath the outward observance to the spiritual mystery, will see that baptism is properly administered to infants as something owed to them
   b. if infants participate in the thing signified—provided thing and word are inseparably joined—how can they be denied the outward sign as well?

6. Difference in the mode of confirmation only
   a. the Lord's covenant with Abraham is as much in force for Christians as it once was for Jews: both, heirs of the covenant, and a holy seed
   b. common ground of Christians and ancient Jews
      (1) covenant, and reason for confirming it
      (2) only the mode of confirming it is different: baptism has supplanted circumcision

Christ Invited and Blessed Little Children; We Should Not Exclude Them from the Sign, and the Benefit, of Baptism [*7–9*]

7. Jesus and the children
   a. question: while Christ embraced little children (Matt. 19:13–15), He did not baptize them; what does baptism have in common with Christ's embracing the children?
   b. answer: if it is right for infants to be brought to Christ, and if the kingdom of heaven belongs to them, why should the sign be denied them?

8. The silence of Scripture on the practice of infant baptism
   a. objection: there is no evidence of a single infant ever being baptized by the hands of the apostles
   b. reply: because infants are not excluded when mention is made of a family being baptized, who in his senses can reason from that that they were not baptized?

9. The blessing of infant baptism
   a. the great benefit of baptism is the confirmation of the promise given to the pious parent that the Lord will be God to the infant and to his seed
   b. those who object that the promise ought to be enough do not understand that through the observance of baptism God deals tenderly with our weakness

Answer to the Anabaptist Argument that Baptism Is Not to Be Associated with Circumcision [*10–16*]

10. Differences falsely alleged
   a. objection: circumcision and baptism signify different things; the covenant in each is quite different; the calling of children under each is not the same
   b. when those who so object say circumcision was a figure of mortification and not of baptism, their claim is conceded, for it supports our argument
   c. since baptism and circumcision are signs of mortification, baptism is put in place of circumcision in order to represent to us what circumcision signified to the Jews of old
   d. therefore, if there were a difference in covenants, what else would be the result except that the Jewish nation was satiated for time with God's benefits (as men fatten a herd of swine in a sty), only to perish in eternal destruction?

11. The promises were spiritual
   a. when the apostle Paul speaks of "the circumcision of Christ" (Col. 2:11) and "burial with Christ" (Col. 2:12), what do these words mean except that the fulfillment and truth of baptism are also the truth and fulfillment of circumcision, since they signify one and the same thing?
   b. baptism is for the Christians what circumcision previously was for the Jews

12. Physical and spiritual infancy
   a. the physical infancy of the children of Abraham foreshadowed the spiritual infants of the New Testament, who were regenerated to immortal life by God's Word
   b. while there is a spark of truth in this, if some mean by it that God's spiritual blessing was never promised to Abraham's physical offspring, they are gravely mistaken

13. Abraham was father of all who believe
    a. circumcision was given in order to teach the Jews by its symbol that God is the Author of their salvation
    b. since Abraham was in uncircumcision justified by faith, and only afterward received the sign of circumcision, he is the father both of the circumcised and the uncircumcised

14. Covenant with the Jews not made void
    a. Paul's teaching (Rom. 9:7) that they are children of God who are children of the promise and not of the flesh does not mean physical descent amounts to nothing
    b. Paul is here warning the Jews not to boast in the covenant unless they keep the law of the covenant
    c. the covenant which God had made once for all with the descendants of Abraham could in no way be made void

15. The promise to be fulfilled not allegorically but literally
    a. it is utterly false to say that those infants who of old were circumcised merely prefigured that spiritual infancy which arises from the regeneration of God's Word
    b. the promise of the covenant is to be fulfilled literally for Abraham's physical offspring

16. Further apparent differences between baptism and circumcision
    a. the supposed differences between baptism and circumcision are mutually contradictory
    b. if baptism must be conformed to circumcision, then it would follow that women ought not to be baptized

Answer to the Argument that Infants Are Incapable of Faith [*17-20*]

17. Children should also have life in Christ
    a. some say children ought to be barred from baptism because they are not of an age to understand the mystery signified, namely, spiritual regeneration
    b. but if children are to be considered solely as children of Adam, they are left in death, since in Adam we die (Rom. 5:12ff.)
    c. if it is asked how infants, unendowed with knowledge of good or evil, are regenerated, the reply is that God's work, though beyond our understanding, is still not annulled

18. Argument from the infancy of Christ
    a. Christ was sanctified from earliest infancy
    b. infants can be regenerated by God's power, which is as easy and ready to Him as it is incomprehensible and wonderful to us

19. Objection: infants cannot understand preaching
    a. it may be objected that infants have not acquired faith, which comes by hearing (Rom. 10:17), nor are they capable of knowledge of God, since they are without the knowledge both of good and of evil (Deut. 1:39)
    b. but the apostle is describing only the ordinary arrangement and dispensation of the Lord, not an unvarying rule

20. Objection: infants are capable neither of repentance nor of faith
    a. if baptism of infants is not allowable on the grounds that it is a sacrament of repentance and faith, then why did God command circumcision of infants, which Scripture also calls a sign of repentance, and which Paul calls the seal of the righteousness of faith?
    b. infants are baptized into future repentance and faith, the seed of which lies hidden within them by the secret working of the Spirit

***Operation of the Spirit in Baptized Children** [21–22]*

21. The child grows into an understanding of his baptism
    a. in older persons the receiving of the sign ought to follow the understanding of the mystery, but infants must be regarded as following another order
    b. in infant baptism nothing more of present effectiveness must be required than to confirm and ratify the covenant made with them by the Lord

22. This thing is a comfort for children; hence, they must not be deprived of the sign
    a. objection: baptism is given for forgiveness of sins
    b. reply: since we are born sinners, we need forgiveness and pardon even from the time in our mother's womb
    c. another objection: the church has been cleansed by the Lord with the washing of water in the Word of life (Eph. 5:26)

d. reply: if such washing is attested by baptism, little ones should be baptized, since they are part of the church

Infant Baptism in the Beginning of the Church [*23–24*]

23. Scriptural statements which refer to adults should not without further evidence be applied to children
   a. some object that when those who had a mind to repent asked Peter what they should do, he advised them first to repent, then to be baptized for the forgiveness of sins (Acts 2:37–38)
   b. but those to whom these things were spoken were of fit age to think of repentance and to understand faith
   c. infants ought to be placed in another category

24. Abraham and Isaac exemplify the difference of adults and infants
   a. in Abraham's case the sacrament follows faith because it is fair that a grown man should learn the conditions of a covenant beforehand
   b. in Isaac's case the sacrament precedes all understanding for he by hereditary right is already included within the covenant from his mother's womb
   c. children of believers ought therefore not to be barred from the sign merely because they cannot swear to the provisions of the covenant

Certain Passages Adduced Against Infant Baptism Interpreted: Those Who Die Unbaptized Not All Condemned [*25–30*]

25. Reborn "of water and the Spirit"
   a. some object that according to John 3:5, "Unless a man be born again of water and the Spirit, he cannot enter into the kingdom of God," baptism is called regeneration
   b. simply because the word "water" is mentioned here, baptism is not necessarily implied
   c. to be reborn of water and the Spirit is but to receive that power of the Spirit which does in the soul what water does in the body

26. Not all the unbaptized are lost
   a. the fiction of those who consign all the unbaptized to eternal death is to be rejected

b. but this does not mean that baptism can be despised with impunity

27. Jesus' baptismal words
    a. the objection that Christ commanded the apostles first to teach them to baptize (Matt. 28:19)
    b. if the order of the words is so important, then in Christ's teaching that we must be reborn of "water and the Spirit" baptism would be prior to spiritual regeneration

28. Infants not referred to in Mark 16:16
    a. there is not one syllable about infants in the whole discourse
    b. the passage says only that the gospel must be preached to those who are capable of hearing, before they are baptized

29. Jesus as prototype of adult baptism
    a. should infants be denied food because the apostle allows only those who labor to eat (II Thess. 3:10)?
    b. that Jesus was baptized in His thirtieth year means only that baptism took its origin and beginning from the preaching of the gospel

30. Baptism and Lord's Supper
    a. some object that there is no more reason to administer baptism to infants than the Lord's Supper, which is not permitted them
    b. but baptism is an entrance and a sort of initiation into the church, while the Supper is given to older persons who, having passed tender infancy, can now take solid food
    c. the distinction clearly shown in Scripture (I Cor. 11:28)

Answers to Arguments of Servetus, and Conclusion *[31–32]*

31. Servetus' objections
    1. *Objection:* as the symbols instituted by Christ are perfect, they require perfect persons. Reply: the perfection of baptism is wrongly confined to one point of time
    2. *Objection:* Christ's symbols were instituted for remembrance, in order that everyone should remember that he was buried with Christ. Reply: what he applies to baptism rightly refers to the Sacred Supper
    3. *Objection:* since God's wrath remains on all who do not be-

lieve in the Son of God, infants lie in their own damnation. Reply: Christ speaks there (John 3:36) of those who despise the gospel, not infants

4. *Objection:* since what is physical comes first (I Cor. 15:46), we must await a mature time for baptism, which is spiritual. Reply: while all the offspring of Adam begotten of flesh bear their condemnation from the womb itself, this does not prevent God from providing an immediate remedy
5. *Objection:* an allegory that David, ascending into the stronghold of Zion, took neither blind nor lame men with him, but strong soldiers (II Sam. 5:8). Reply: the parable in which God invites the blind and lame to the heavenly banquet (Luke 14:21)
6. *Objection:* the apostles were fishers of men (Matt. 4:19), not of babes. Reply: the term ἀνθρώπους includes, without exception, the human race; why should Servetus deny that infants are human beings?
7. *Objection:* since spiritual things agree with spiritual (I Cor. 2:13–14), infants, who are not spiritual, are also not fit for baptism. Reply: Paul is dealing here with doctrine, rebuking the stupidity of the Corinthians who flattered themselves too much on their vain cleverness; Servetus has twisted Paul's meaning.
8. *Objection:* they must be fed spiritual food if they are new men. Reply: by baptism they are admitted into Christ's flock, and the symbol of their adoption suffices them until as adults they are able to bear solid food
9. *Objection:* Christ calls all His people to the Sacred Supper, therefore it is monstrous for a man, after being born, not to eat. Reply: souls are fed in another way than by the outward eating of the Supper.
10. *Objection:* a good steward distributes food to his household at the proper time (Matt. 24:45). Reply: by what rule will Servetus define the time of baptism for us, to prove that infancy is not the right time to give it?
11. *Objection:* in the first church Christians and disciples were identical (Acts 11:26). Reply: while it is true that those called disciples are men of full age, no one will rightly conclude from this that the infants, whom God attested to be of His own household, were strangers
12. *Objection:* all Christians are brothers, but to us, children are not of that number so long as we keep them away from the Supper. Reply: Christ's embrace was the true token of adop-

tion, by which infants are joined in common with adults; abstaining from the Supper for a time does not prevent them from belonging to the body of the church

13. *Objection:* no one can become our brother except through the Spirit of adoption (Rom. 8:15), which is conferred only through the hearing of faith (Gal. 3:2). Reply: Servetus preposterously applies to infants what was said concerning adults alone
14. *Objection:* Cornelius, having received the Holy Spirit, was baptized (Acts 10:44–48). Reply: Servetus wrongly draws a general rule from one example
15. *Objection:* we become gods by regeneration, but gods are those "to whom the Word of God came" (John 10:34–35; cf. Ps. 82:6), which is not possible for infant children. Reply: Christ says that kings and magistrates are called "gods" by the prophet because they bear an office divinely enjoined upon them, not because they have become divine
16. *Objection:* infants cannot be considered new men because they are not begotten through the Word. Reply: when we are not old enough to be taught, God keeps His own timetable of regeneration
17. *Objection:* in the law a sheep and a she-goat were not offered in sacrifice immediately at birth. Reply: all the firstborn, as they opened the womb, were sacred to God (Exod. 13:2)
18. *Objection:* only those prepared by John could come to Christ. Reply: the children whom Christ embraced and blessed did not have that preparation
19. *Objection:* according to Trismegistus and the sibyls, holy washings befit only adults. Reply: see how honorably Servetus thinks of the baptism of Christ, which he conforms to the profane rites of the heathen, that it may be administered only at the pleasure of Trismegistus!
20. *Objection:* if infants, without understanding, can be baptized, baptism can be administered by children at play as a farce and a mockery. Reply: circumcision was common to infants before they attained understanding

32. Gratitude due for God's care of our children
    a. through those who deny infant baptism, Satan is trying to take away from us the singular fruit of assurance and spiritual joy which is to be gathered from it, and also to diminish somewhat the glory of the divine goodness
    b. how sweet it is to godly minds to be assured, not only by word,

but by sight, that they obtain so much favor with the heavenly Father that their offspring are within his care

c. should we not, following David's example, rejoice with all our heart in thanksgiving, that His name may be hallowed by such an example of His goodnes (Ps. 48:10)?

CHAPTER 17
The Sacred Supper of Christ, and What It Brings to Us

The Lord's Supper, with the Signs of Bread and Wine, Provides Spiritual Food [*1–3*]

1. Sign and thing
   a. as sons of God, members of His family, we must needs be nourished by Him throughout life
      (1) to this end God assures us of His continuing liberality, by giving us His pledge
      (2) the pledge is the spiritual banquet wherein Christ attests Himself as the life-giving bread
   b. since Christians need to understand this high mystery, and Satan's confusions must be dissipated, a way must be found to make this doctrine intelligible to the unlearned, then to refute Satan's confusions
      (1) Christ is the only food of our soul, represented by the signs of bread and wine
      (2) since the mystery of Christ's secret union with the devout is incomprehensible, God shows it to us under signs adapted to our small capacity (accommodation)

2. Union with Christ as the special fruit of the Lord's Supper
   a. in the Supper we have joyous assurance of our growth into one body with Christ, and hence into eternal life and deliverance from our sins
   b. the wonderful exchange:
      (1) becoming Son of man with us/He has made us sons of God with Him
      (2) by His descent to earth/He has prepared an ascent to heaven for us
      (3) by taking our morality/He has conferred His immortality upon us

(4) accepting our weakness/He has strengthened us by His power
(5) receiving our poverty unto Himself/He has transferred his wealth to us
(6) taking the weight of our iniquity upon Himself/He has clothed us with His righteousness

3. The spiritual presence of Christ
   a. in the sacrament the witness of Christ is so full it is as if we actually have Christ physically present among us: take, eat, drink
   b. the great force of the sacrament is in the words: "which is shed for you": given once for all for our redemption, Christ's body and blood are represented under bread and wine for us to learn:
      (1) that they are ours
      (2) that they are destined as food for our spiritual life
   c. thus, from physical things in the sacrament, we are led by a sort of analogy to spiritual things: the physical benefits of bread and wine have their spiritual analogues

The Promise Sealed in the Supper as We Are Made Partakers of Christ's Flesh—a Mystery Felt Rather than Explained [*4–7*]

4. The meaning of the promise of the Lord's Supper
   a. the chief function of the sacrament is not simply to extend Christ's body to us, but to seal and confirm the promise that His flesh is food indeed and His blood is drink
   b. the sacrament sends us to the cross of Christ: in living experience we grasp the efficacy of His death
   c. "bread of life" not borrowed from the sacrament, but a symbol of His whole incarnation—from beginning to end

5. How we are partakers by faith
   a. how does all this apply to us? through the Supper in which He offers Himself and all His benefits to us and we receive Him in faith
   b. two dangers to be avoided:
      (1) by insufficient regard for the signs, to divorce them from their mysteries
      (2) by immoderately extolling them, to obscure the mysteries themselves

c. all believers agree that Christ is the bread of life by which we are nourished into eternal life; but disagree in the way we partake of Him
d. true nature of the eating
    (1) the life we receive from Him is by no mere knowledge
    (2) this "faith-eating" does not mean that eating = faith; but eating follows from faith—no mere quibble here:
    (3) as bread when eaten as food gives vigor to the body, so by true partaking of Christ, His life passes into us and is made ours

6. Augustine and Chrysostom on this
    a. Augustine taught that the eucharistic eating is of faith, not of mouth
    b. Chrysostom also taught that the faith with which we eat the Lord's Supper is no mere imagining
    c. sufficiently refuted are those who erroneously hold the Supper to be merely a mark of outward profession

7. Thought and words inadequate
    a. those holding communion with Christ to be of the spirit only, without flesh and blood, are wrong
    b. the opposite fault of the "extravagant doctors" will be refuted at greater length
    c. the impotence of language to encompass the sublime mystery of the Supper: wonder is the only proper response!
    d. however I will sum up my own views as true and useful to godly hearts

This Life-Giving Communion Is Brought About by the Holy Spirit [*8–10*]

8. Christ makes His abode in our flesh
    a. Christ is the source of life for all things created
    b. man, otherwise threatened by death for his sin, has to be received into communion with the Word to reach immortality
    c. when the source of life begins to abide in our flesh, we are enabled to partake of Him, be quickened and thus be fed unto heavenly immortal life

9. Sense in which Christ's body is life-giving
    a. Christ's flesh not life-giving, but possesses life through the Father's gift

b. Christ's flesh a fountain from which flows into us life springing forth from the Godhead itself, as many passages from Paul teach

10. The presence of Christ's body in the Lord's Supper
   a. summary: as bread and wine feed us physically, so flesh and blood of Christ feed our souls
   b. let our faith conceive what our mind cannot: that the Spirit truly unites things separated in space (Christ's flesh and ours)
   c. in the Supper Christ testifies and seals by no empty sign the sacred partaking of His flesh and blood by which He passes His life into us
   d. I Cor. 10:16 is more than an expression by which the name of the thing signified is given to the sign: by showing the symbol the thing itself is also shown
   e. a visible sign is given us to seal the gift of a thing invisible: let us then trust the body itself as also given to us

Relation of the Outward Sign and Invisible Reality Variously Misstated by the Schoolmen, and in the Doctrine of Transubstantiation [*11–15*]

11. Signification, matter, and effect of the sacrament
   a. common and accepted teaching of the church: the sacred mystery of Lord's Supper consists in two things:
      (1) physical signs (thrust before our eyes) represent to us (according to our feeble capacity) things invisible (accommodation)
      (2) spiritual truth, represented and displayed through the symbols themselves
   b. this truth, simply expounded, includes
      (1) signification: contained in the promises
      (2) matter that depends upon it: Christ with His death and resurrection
      (3) power or effect that follows from both: redemption, righteousness, sanctification, and eternal life, all other of Christ's benefits to us
   c. I teach a "true participation" in Christ, something more and deeper than by understanding and imagination alone
   d. Christ truly shows to us in the mystery of the Supper through the symbols of bread and wine, His very body and blood in which He has fulfilled all obedience to obtain righteousness for us:
      (1) that we may grow into one body with Him

(2) we are now partakers of His substance, that we may also feel His power in partaking of all His benefits

12. Spatial presence of Christ's body?
  a. Satan has taught through the Roman church that the body of Christ by a local presence is given to be touched, chewed, and swallowed
    (1) the monstrous folly of the *Ego Berengarius*
    (2) even Peter Lombard draws back somewhat from this
  b. Christ's body is limited by general characteristics of all human bodies, thus contained in heaven until His return in judgment
  c. thus we cannot
    (1) draw it back under corruptible elements
    (2) imagine it to be present everywhere
  d. we are bound to Christ through His spirit, in order to be made one with Him

13. Error of the Schoolmen: bread mistaken for God
  a. the Schoolmen, from Peter Lombard onward, avoid the barbarism of such a circumscriptive presence, but subtly talk about Christ being held under the "species" of bread, while at the same time He remains bodily in heaven
  b. the effect of their explanation is to ensnare unwary souls
    (1) no concern about true faith by which alone we attain fellowship with Christ
    (2) satisfied with a physical presence fabricated apart from God's Word

14. Transubstantiation
  a. this is the ground of transubstantiation which we will now discuss
  b. how can Christ's body be mixed up with substance of bread? their answer: by a conversion of bread into the body of Christ; in this they despise Scripture and ancient church practice
  c. are there any grounds for belief in "conversion"?
    (1) some old writers used the term, but only to teach that the bread dedicated to the mystery is far different from common bread, but not a physical conversion
    (2) transubstantiation is actually of recent origin, in a very corrupt age of the church
  d. we admit that a conversion in Lord's Supper is analogous to the change felt in baptism: but the water remains

CORPOREALIZATION AND SPIRITUALIZATION OF THE LORD'S SUPPER
to the Reformation

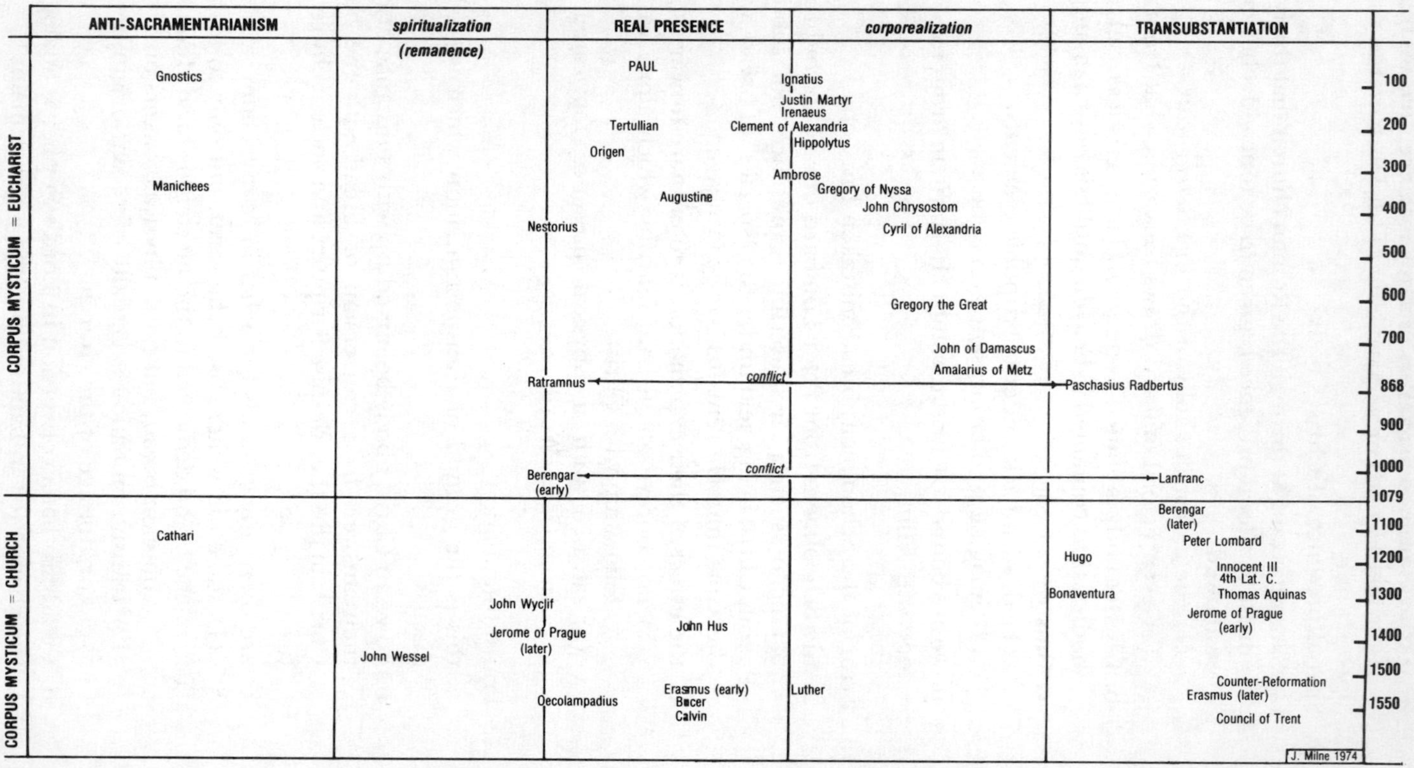

	ANTI-SACRAMENTARIANISM	*spiritualization* *(remanence)*	REAL PRESENCE	*corporealization*	TRANSUBSTANTIATION	
CORPUS MYSTICUM = EUCHARIST	Gnostics		PAUL	Ignatius		100
			Tertullian; Origen	Justin Martyr; Irenaeus; Clement of Alexandria; Hippolytus		200
	Manichees		Augustine	Ambrose; Gregory of Nyssa		300
		Nestorius		John Chrysostom; Cyril of Alexandria		400
						500
				Gregory the Great		600
				John of Damascus; Amalarius of Metz		700
			Ratramnus ← *conflict* →		→ Paschasius Radbertus	868
						900
			Berengar (early) ← *conflict* →		→ Lanfranc	1000
						1079
CORPUS MYSTICUM = CHURCH	Cathari				Berengar (later); Peter Lombard	1100
					Hugo; Innocent III; 4th Lat. C.	1200
		John Wyclif			Bonaventura; Thomas Aquinas	1300
		John Wessel; Jerome of Prague (later)	John Hus		Jerome of Prague (early)	1400
					Counter-Reformation	1500
			Oecolampadius; Erasmus (early); Bucer; Calvin	Luther	Erasmus (later); Council of Trent	1550

J. Milne 1974

e. if true bread did not remain throughout the sacrament, there could be no true witness by outward symbol of His flesh as food: only real bread could so serve

15. The actual basis of the doctrine of transubstantiation and the arguments adduced for it
    a. underlying their view of "theophagy" is a crude idea of magical incantation
    b. an Old Testament parallel to the wine of the Lord's Supper is in the water gushing from the rock (Exod. 17:6): earthly elements applied to a spiritual use undergo no other conversion than to become (still remaining physical) seals of divine promises
    c. God plans to lift us to Himself by appropriate means; we cannot mentally leap the infinite space between us and Christ; thus they transmute Christ's body to a local presence to make Christ physically near
    d. even in Bernard of Clairvaux's day transubstantiation was not yet recognized
    e. Old Testament passages adduced as proofs by them refuted
        (1) Moses' rod into serpent (Exod. 7:12)
        (2) Jeremiah's "wood-bread": no relation to Christ's cross (Jer. 11:19)

***Arguments for Rejection of the Doctrine of the Ubiquity of the Body as Narrowly Literal, Together with Exposition of the Spiritual View of Communion with Christ in Heaven* [*16–31*]**

16. The opposing statement
    a. others accept the view that bread and wine remain earthly and corruptible elements in the Lord's Supper, but hold that the body of Christ is enclosed underneath
    b. we object here to assigning ubiquity to Christ's body, thus making it invisible and immeasurable
    c. this view shows their misunderstanding of descent by which He lifts us up to Himself
    d. thus they can think only of local contact

17. The doctrine of our opponents cancels the true corporeality of Christ
    a. some assert Christ's flesh was always infinite in dimensions; being enclosed by a "certain dispensation" during His incar-

nation to carry out His earthly mission: a mere Marcionite apparition!

b. some assert the body given in the sacrament to be glorious and immortal—therefore not absurd if it is unconfined by space or form

c. refutation:
   (1) Christ the day before He suffered gave His disciples the very mortal body which He was shortly to give up
   (2) in the transfiguration, Christ by showing His splendor to three disciples, gave them a foretaste of immortality
   (3) there, then, is no twofold body, but Christ's own body, adorned with new glory (to hold to such a double body view would be to turn Marcionite)

18. The presence is known when our minds are lifted up to heaven
   a. in the Lord's Supper body and blood are separate: how can the Lord's body be dividedly attached to itself?—the absurdity of the doctrine of concomitance
   b. we are lifted up to heaven with our eyes and minds to seek Christ in the glory of His kingdom
   c. deprived of Christ's physical presence, we know His power, exerted wherever He pleases in heaven and on earth, and preeminently upon His own people, as if He were with them in the flesh

19. How is the presence of Christ in the Lord's Supper to be thought of?
   a. no circumscribing presence of Christ can be accepted, as it would depart from His heavenly glory
   b. two limits to anything we say about Christ's eucharistic presence:
      (1) withdraw nothing from Christ's heavenly glory
      (2) ascribe nothing inappropriate to human nature, to His body
   c. with these limitations in mind, I accept any expression of a true and substantial partaking of the blood and body of the Lord in the Supper
   d. this doctrine commended as Scriptural, clear, unambiguous: why should Satan stir up opposition to it then?

20. The words of institution
   a. our foes claim we depart from Christ's own words of institu-

tion: thus we must examine and interpret Christ's words of institution as they are reported in the Synoptics and Paul

b. the transubstantiationalists
   (1) "this" = form of bread, because the consecration is effected by the whole content of the utterance, and there is no substance that can be pointed to
       answer: Christ took bread in His hands and declared it to be His body, but the bread was still shown; it is absurd to transfer to the form what is predicated of the bread
   (2) "is" = is transubstantiated, a violently distorted gloss!
       answer: it is something unheard of in all nations and languages that the word "is" should be taken to mean "to be converted into something else"

c. the "classic" Lutheran
   (1) realized that bread = body was untenable
   (2) but then asserted that body of Christ is with, in, and under the bread, shunning any metaphorical interpretation, and leapt from Christ's simple designation to widely divergent phrases of their own

d. "Westphalians"
   (1) assert literally that bread = Christ's body, and that whole Christ is offered in the Supper, but draw back from identifying Christ, and consequently God, with bread
   (2) we respond, with Scripture, that bread is not body, but the testament of body

e. I am not attempting to lessen the communicating of Christ's body, but rather, on Paul and Luke's authority, to refute foolish stubbornness

f. the nature of this testament in Christ's body and blood: a covenant ratified by the sacrifice of His death would not benefit us unless there were joined to it that secret communication by which we grow into one with Christ

21. The figurative interpretation of the decisive words

a. the expression must be interpreted figuratively, yet the analogy is most fitting

b. metonymy
   (1) many other instances in Scripture
   (2) though the symbol differs in essence from the thing signified (in that the latter is spiritual and heavenly, while the former is physical and visible), still, because it not only symbolizes the thing that it has been consecrated to

represent as a bare and empty token, but also truly exhibits it, why may its name not rightly belong to the thing?

c. we reject the sobriquet "tropist"
   (1) because our view is commonly attested in Scripture
   (2) also mention metonymy in connection with the sacrament of the Supper

22. The word "is"
   a. objection: the substantive (= copulative) "is" does not allow a figurative interpretation
      (1) Scriptural usage of "is" to refute this
      (2) especially Paul's expression: Christ is the church (a literal interpretation could hardly serve here!)
   b. it is not our opponents (who claim we discredit Christ's words) but we who more obediently and reverently follow Christ's words
   c. we claim the right to investigate the true sense of Christ's words, against their claim that human reason gets in the way of true belief

23. The impossibility of a purely literal interpretation
   a. like the ancient Anthropomorphites, these literalists forbid even the slightest departure from the letter
   b. their objection: Christ in preparing a singular comfort for His disciples in adversity, spoke clearly and not in an enigma
      (1) this contention actually supports my view rather than my opponents' for obviously the disciples took the utterance in the same figurative way
      (2) for the disciples, as for us, the name of the thing signified is transferred to the sign, a common occurrence in sacraments
      (3) also, a literal interpretation of Christ's words—calling bread body, and wine blood—would infer confusion of utterance or a division between body and blood: this would be absurd!
   c. thus, far from discrediting Christ's words of institution, we are faithfully and rightly expounding them, while our opponents are madly perverting and confounding them

24. Defense against the reproach that our interpretation is dictated by reason
   a. their objection: that we are so bound to human reason as to

attribute no more to the power of God than the order of nature allows and common sense dictates

b. on the contrary, our doctrine is not measured with the measure of human reason, or subjected to the laws of nature
   (1) Christ feeds our souls from heaven with His flesh, while our bodies are nourished by bread and wine: is this a doctrine learned from physics?
   (2) human reason would be more satisfied to believe that Christ's flesh enters us to be our food, than to accept this faith in God's secret power: that Christ descends to us both by the outward symbol and by His Spirit, in order that He may truly quicken our souls by the substance of His flesh and of His blood
   (3) nothing is in fact more incredible than that things severed and removed from one another by the whole space between heaven and earth should not only be connected across such a great distance but also be united, so that souls may receive nourishment from Christ's flesh

c. not a question of what God could do, but what He willed to do: flesh remained flesh; spirit, spirit; thus Christ took flesh, giving to it incorruption and glory, and not taking away from it nature and truth

25. The word requires understanding and interpretation
   a. agreed—
      (1) they have the Word by which the will of God has been made plain—if the gift of interpretation (which sheds light upon the Word) is banished from the church
      (2) they have the Word—but a carnal word like that of the Anthropomorphites who made God corporeal; or as Marcionites and Manichees, who gave Christ a heavenly or spectral body
   b. these persons claim that to give Christ's body in the Supper they must infer that the body of Christ is visible in heaven but lies invisible on earth under crumbs of bread—clearly contrary to Scripture!
   c. do I as they claim diminish anything of God's power? certainly not!
   d. unreason vs. reason
      (1) to them, "This is my body" means a miracle which they irrationally and unscripturally claim for God's omnipotence
      (2) I, on the other hand, study to obtain a sound under-

standing of this passage, and embrace the meaning which the Holy Spirit offers

26. The body of Christ is in heaven
    a. our doctrine—that Christ's body is finite and now located in heaven—derived not from Aristotle but from Scripture
        (1) Christ announces His departure and coming of Holy Spirit
        (2) also: "I will not be with you always": their false exegesis of this refuted
        (3) other Scriptural passages adduced in support also
    b. according to Augustine:
        (1) Christ is present among us in three ways:
            (a) in majesty
            (b) in providence
            (c) in ineffable grace (marvelous communion of Christ's body and blood, through the power of the Holy Spirit)
        (2) "departing" and "ascending" not apparent but actual acts
            (a) objection: assign to Christ a definite region of heaven?
            (b) answer: with Augustine—a prying and superfluous question—it is enough to believers that Christ is in heaven

27. The meaning of the ascension for the above-mentioned question
    a. ascension: moving from one place to another? or merely signifying the majesty of Christ's rule?
    b. Scriptural witness to His ascension proves Christ no longer abides on earth, but in heaven
    c. opponents claim that Christ never really left the earth but remains invisible among His own, and will one day come in visible form:
    d. but the angels warned the disciples not to gaze in vain to heaven, but to wait patiently until He comes to gather His own people to Himself there

28. The witness of Augustine
    a. because the opponents claim that witness of Augustine, it is necessary to quote him in support of my view

b. opponents wrongly infer from Augustine's teaching with their refutation:
   (1) in the Supper Christ's flesh and blood (the sacrificial victim once for all offered on the cross) are distributed refutation: the sacrament of the body is the body in the sense that sacraments take their names from their likeness to the things they signify
   (2) Christ's body falls to earth and enters the mouth
   (3) when Christ proffered the mystical bread to His disciples, He in a manner bore Himself in His own hands refutation: Augustine, by inserting the adverb of likeness, teaches that Christ was not truly or really enclosed under the bread; also he teaches that bodies deprived of location in space will not be anywhere, and hence will not exist

c. for Augustine there is an antithesis between presence of majesty and presence of flesh
   (1) seen in the contrast: I am with you always/You will not always have me
   (2) also: Christ withdrew His bodily presence from His disciples in order to be with them in spiritual presence

29. On the reality of Christ's body
   a. their teaching about Christ's invisible presence has no Scriptural warrant
   b. this forces them to a double-body view of Christ: visible in itself in heaven, yet in the Supper invisible by a special mode of dispensation
   c. they teach that Christ is everywhere in space but without form, holding it wrong for the nature of the glorious body to submit to the laws of common nature
   d. this is to infer that Christ's body is swallowed up by His divinity, tantamount to what Servetus teaches
   e. Christ's multiform body is visible in one place but invisible in another: this denies the very nature of a body, which has its dimensions and its unity
   f. they take refuge in their "dispensation," self-devised, but Christ is no specter, being visible in the flesh; to square with their view would entail a new definition of body
   g. New Testament passages adduced by them in proof of their view of Christ's body

(1) appearance to Stephen (Acts 7:55); also to Paul (Acts 9:4):
answer: Christ did not need to change His place, but gave His servants a clarity of visions to pierce the heavens

(2) passage through the sepulcher stone and through closed doors (Matt. 28:6; John 20:19)
answer: the hardness of the stone yielded at Christ's approach; or the stone was removed at His command and replaced after He left; the passage through closed doors means opening an entrance through them by divine power

(3) sudden vanishing of Christ from the disciples on the Emmaus road (Luke 24:31)
answer: Christ did not make Himself invisible, but only disappeared

h. conclusion: opponents make a spirit out of Christ's flesh, endowing it with utterly contrary qualities, hence postulating a double body for Him

30. The ubiquity of Christ's body rejected

a. how can an "immeasurable" Christ be confined, hidden under bread? they answer with the monstrous notion of ubiquity

b. already proved that Christ's body was circumscribed by the measure of a human body: when it passes to another place, it leaves the previous one

c. "I am with you," etc., not to be applied to Christ's body, but rather to the help promised His disciples, to sustain them against Satan and the world

d. worse than the papists (whose doctrine is more modest) are the views of the "neo-Eutychians" (Servetus) who postulate a flesh inseparable from His soul, so that wherever Christ's divinity is, there is His flesh also

(1) against this we assert that the one person of Christ so consists of two natures that each nevertheless retains unimpaired its own distinctive character

(2) supporting Scripture adduced by them refuted

e. in the sacrament the whole Christ is present, but not in His wholeness—until the last judgment His flesh will remain in heaven

31. Christ not brought down to us; we are lifted up to Him
    a. our opponents cannot conceive of a union with Christ unless He comes down to us
    b. for us, He lifts us to Himself, for here is a heavenly mystery

***The True Nature of the Corporeal Presence in which Believers Partake Through the Spirit** [32–34]*

32. Involved solutions of the mystery rejected
    a. how does this ascent take place?
        (1) too lofty a mystery to explain in words
        (2) something experienced rather than understood
    b. we stand with Scripture, rejecting only things
        (1) unworthy of Christ's heavenly majesty
        (2) incompatible with His human nature
    c. all persons carried beyond this are obscuring truth
    d. their teaching concerning the mixture of Christ's flesh with our own rejected:
        (1) Christ pours His very own life into us from the substance of His flesh though His actual flesh does not enter into us
        (2) Paul's "analogy of faith" supports this

33. Spiritual and, hence, actual partaking of Christ; partaking of the Lord's Supper by unbelievers
    a. 400 years of wrong teaching—that participation involves actual swallowing of Christ's flesh—lamented
    b. difference as to the fundamental question:
        (1) Romanists: how does Christ's body lie hidden under the bread, or under the form of bread?
        (2) Calvin: how body of Christ given once for us, is made ours, and how we become partakers in the blood once shed
    c. two objections:
        (1) "spiritual eating" does not do justice to the carnal mode of eating expressed by them in "enclosing Christ in bread"
        (2) our teaching concerned only with benefits believers receive from eating Christ's flesh
        (3) here they are erroneously following Peter Lombard who confused the sacrament with the eating of Christ's flesh

d. do the wicked, though estranged from Christ, still eat His body in the sacrament?
   (1) opponents—yes
   (2) Calvin—no (with refutation of their proof texts)
e. conclusion: it is not so much eating or not eating the Supper, but trampling Christ's promise of sacred union with God

34. Partaking of the Lord's Supper by unbelievers, according to Augustine
   a. Augustine, of ancient writers, has especially clearly distinguished between real and sacramental eating of the flesh of Christ
      (1) sacramental, outward eating of visible elements, shared by all, but unbelievers go no further
      (2) real eating, inward eating of invisible body and power of Christ, confined to believers who hunger spiritually and are spiritually filled (Old Testament parallel: the manna)
   b. many passages from Augustine cited which make his antithesis between sacramental and real eating: these refute Calvin's opponents, who confuse unbelievers' eating as real and actual

Superstitious Adoration of the Elements Excluded [*35–37*]

35. Adoration of the elements rejected
   a. some opponents, in refusing to separate Christ's soul and divinity from His body, worship Christ in bread
   b. the true way, enjoined by Scripture: receive the sacrament without adoration but in mutual breaking of bread

36. Superstition and idolatry in such adoration
   a. as we have already taught, for pious souls to apprehend Christ in the Supper, they must be raised up to heaven; the Supper's task is to help man's weak mind to do this
   b. superstitious adoration of Christ in bread forbidden by Scripture and by Canon 20 of Nicea
   c. worship of Christ in bread is also a form of idolatry
      (1) honor taken from God and transferred to creature
      (2) God's holy gift turned into an idol

37. Superstitious rites with the consecrated host
   a. new and unwarranted rites now devised by them to adore Christ in the sign, not Christ seated in heaven

b. the "consecrated host" carried in procession to be seen and worshiped
   (1) their justification: "This is my body"
   (2) rejoinder: to which is added, "Take and eat": a promise joined to a command, then separated from it, ceases to be a promise
c. the second use of the sacrament: "to declare the Lord's death till He come" means: by the confession of our mouth before men, we should declare what our faith recognizes in the sacrament: that the death of Christ is our life

Points of Special Emphasis: Mutual Love; the Accompaniment of Preaching; Medicine for Sick Souls; Worthy Partaking; Suitable Form and the Frequency of Administration [*38–46*]

38. The Lord's Supper implies mutual love
   a. the third use of the sacrament: exhortation to
      (1) purity and holiness of life
      (2) love, peace, and concord
   b. Christ has but one body; therefore we must become one body with Him
      (1) if we injure a brother, we injure Christ
      (2) in this sacrament Christ by His own example of self-giving bids us give ourselves to one another

39. The Lord's Supper cannot exist apart from the Word
   a. Word and sacrament must go together
   b. away, then, with the papists' "silent action"
      (1) depending solely on the intention of the priest
      (2) promises in which consecration is accomplished they direct to the elements themselves, not to the worshipers who are to receive the elements
      (3) the priests' words are a sort of mumbled incantation addressed to the elements, not to the people
   c. consequently, the reservation of the sacrament for distribution to the sick is useless, for it is a sacrament divorced from the Word

40. Of unworthy partaking of the sacrament
   a. depending upon the worshipers' intention, the Supper can be
      (1) healthful, life-producing and arousing to thanksgiving, or
      (2) poisonous for those without faith who take it

b. in their unbelief, the latter befoul the symbol of Christ's body in taking it, and therefore bring condemnation upon themselves
c. this is why Paul enjoins self-examination before taking the Supper; questions the worshiper is to ask himself:
    (1) do I rest with inward assurance of heart upon the salvation purchased by Christ?
    (2) do I acknowledge it by confession of mouth?
    (3) do I aspire to the imitation of Christ with the zeal of innocence and holiness?
    (4) am I, after Christ's example, prepared to give myself for my brethren, and to communicate myself to those with whom I share Christ in common?
    (5) as I am counted a member by Christ, do I in turn so hold all my brethren as members of His body?
    (6) do I desire to cherish, protect, and help them as my own members?

41. Who is "worthy"?
    a. Romanists teach that all "in a state of grace" (= pure and purged of all sin) eat the Supper worthily: a veritable torture of conscience, this!
    b. their method of acquiring worthiness—through threefold confession by contrition, confession, and satisfaction—has already been exposed as a feeble, yet burdensome form of expiation
    c. if only the truly innocent are to be admitted to the Lord's Supper, who can partake? for we cannot assure ourselves of our righteousness

42. Faith and love requisite, but not perfection
    a. the Romanists' doctrine, derived from Satan, deprives sinners of the consolation of this sacrament (in which all the delights of the gospel are set before them)
    b. remember: this sacrament is a medicine for sick souls; the perfect would not need it!
    c. the right attitude in preparing to receive the Supper:
        (1) poor, we come to a kindly Giver
        (2) sick, we come to a Physician
        (3) sinners, we come to the Author of righteousness
        (4) dead, we come to the Lifegiver
    d. by a different demand—that of perfect faith and love—the

Anabaptists fall into the same trap as the Romanists: of denying sinners access to the Supper

e. conclusion: it is a sacrament ordained not for the perfect, but for the weak and feeble, to awaken, arouse, stimulate, and exercise the feeling of faith and love, and to correct the defect of both

43. On the proper celebration of the Lord's Supper
    a. outward details of the ceremony are *adiaphoric;* at the discretion of the church
    b. but the simplicity of the ancient church's practice contrasted with the theatrical trifling of contemporary Romanism: away with the pile of ceremonies, and back to frequent communion!
    c. a proposed order for weekly communion:
        (1) public prayers
        (2) sermon
        (3) when the bread and wine are placed on the table, the minister repeats the words of institution
        (4) recital of the promises; excommunication of all those barred from the Supper by the Lord's prohibition
        (5) prayer that the Lord, with the kindness shown in giving us this sacred food, may also teach and form us to receive it with faith and thankfulness of heart; and by His mercy make us worthy of such a feast
        (6) psalm or reading
        (7) partaking of the holy banquet: ministers breaking the bread and giving the cup
        (8) after the Supper, an exhortation to sincere faith and confession of faith, to love and behavior worthy of Christians
        (9) thanksgiving, and praises sung to God
        (10) church dismissed in peace

44. The Lord's Supper should be celebrated frequently
    a. the Lord's Supper is ordained to be used among Christians frequently—not just once a year as the Romanists do
        (1) returning frequently in memory to Christ's passion we
            (a) sustain and strengthen our faith
            (b) urge ourselves to sing thanksgiving to God and proclaim His goodness
            (c) nourish mutual love, giving witness to this love, and discerning its bond in the unity of Christ's body

(2) whenever we partake of the symbol of the Lord's body, we bind one another in love to protect and help one another

b. in the apostolic church (Acts 2:42) each meeting of the church included the Word, prayers, Supper, and almsgiving

c. this is the basis of the ancient canons that enjoined worshipers to stay to the end and partake

45. Augustine and Chrysostom on the duty of participation

a. as time passed, the people grew more lax, and took communion less frequently

b. this laxity was sharply rebuked by such writers as Augustine and Chrysostom, who urged frequent communion

46. Communicating only once a year condemned

a. compulsory annual communion an invention of the devil

b. the Romanists claim Zephyrinus was the author of the decree enjoining yearly communion

(1) in his form it was probably a good thing, as in that era communion was set at every service, but few took it together

(2) thus he was trying to insure that all together take communion at least once a year

(3) this is a far cry from the later canon (Fourth Lateran Council) which encourages sloth the rest of the year

(4) against this abuse of attending but not partaking (creeping in in the fourth and fifth centuries) Chrysostom spoke out

Withdrawal of the Cup from the Lay People Condemned [*47–50*]

47. Refutation of "communion in one kind"

a. another evil regulation: denial of cup to laity on the ground of the danger if the cup were offered to all, and on basis of concomitance

b. their false doctrine of concomitance

(1) claim the body contains the blood also

(2) but Christ gave both to us to show that He is for us both food and drink

(3) therefore they are defrauding pious souls of the confirmation of faith, deemed necessary by Christ

48. False arguments adduced by the Romanists
    a. from a simple act, one cannot adduce a general rule
       answer: they lie in claiming "Drink ye all from this cup" to be merely a simple act!
    b. the apostles, as "sacrificers" were admitted by Christ to full participation in the Lord's Supper
    c. our answer: five questions for them to respond to:
       i. what oracle has revealed this solution to them—so foreign to God's Word?
       ii. why for a thousand years after that better, apostolic age, did all partake of both symbols? Evidence from the fathers [questions continue, 50]

49. Reception by laymen maintained to a late date; evidence:
    (1) Cyprian's insistence on full participation by all
    (2) Gregory the Great
    (3) Gelasius

    thus restriction of Gelasius' decree to the priests alone a mere quibble

50. The words of Scripture plainly accord the cup to all
    iii. why did Christ say "you" concerning the bread, but "you all" concerning the cup? (Mark 14:22f.; Matt. 26:26f.)
    iv. if the Lord honored only "sacrificers," who would ever have dared call strangers excluded by the Lord to partake of the Supper?
    v. was Paul lying when he said to the Corinthians that he had received from the Lord what he delivered to them?

CHAPTER 18
The Papal Mass, a Sacrilege by which Christ's Supper Was Not Only Profaned but Annihilated

Rejection of the Mass as Sacrilegious and as a Nullification of the Lord's Supper [*1–7*]

1. The Romanist doctrine
   a. Satan's supreme effort to obscure and defile Christ's Supper is the Mass, which teaches that it is a sacrifice and offering to obtain forgiveness of sins

b. the Roman Church teaches that the Mass
   (1) is a work by which the priest who offers up Christ, and the others participating, merit God's favor or
   (2) is an expiatory victim, by which they reconcile God to themselves

c. only the Word of God itself can expose this pernicious doctrine and its frightful consequences in the world

[FIVE "FUNCTIONS" OF THE MASS]

2. The Mass as a blasphemy against Christ [first function]
   a. unlike the Old Testament priests who were consecrated for a time and hence required successors, Christ was consecrated priest and pontiff for eternity, thus requiring no vicar to replace Himself
   b. but the Romanists put priests in Christ's place as successors and vicars, thus depriving Christ of His priesthood, and also misinterpreting the Melchizedek passages [Gen. 14 and Heb. 7] to buttress their usurpation of Christ's priesthood

3. The Mass as suppression of Christ's passion [second function]
   a. in setting up an altar for daily sacrifice of Christ, the cross's once-for-all event is set aside and its everlasting power to cleanse is abrogated
   b. thus fundamental texts of the New Testament are negated by their invention, but Scripture boldly unmasks this plot of Satan to obscure the truth
   c. the proponents of the Mass try by various shifts to circumvent the clear words of Scripture—as that the priestly act is not a repetition but an "application"
   d. all such arguments are answered by the fact that Christ's sacrifice benefits man by the preaching of the gospel and the administration of the Sacred Supper, to be received in true faith

4. The argument from Malachi 1:11
   a. "the time will come when incense and a pure offering shall be offered to the Lord's name throughout all the earth"
   b. here the prophets are not foretelling the papal mass, but are describing through the types of their own time the truth revealed by the gospel: the calling of the Gentiles to the spiritual worship of God

  c. the Mass is not the true sacrifice, the pure oblation of worshipers (see sect. 16, below)

5. The Mass brings forgetfulness of Christ's death [third function]
  a. a testament is confirmed by the death of the testator: by His death Christ has willed to us forgiveness of sins and everlasting righteousness [Heb. 9:5–17]
  b. the Mass, in altering and adding to this testament, becomes a wholly new and different testament, thus setting aside the old
  c. consequently, this new testament requires new deaths of the testator, performed daily in thousands of masses: thus obscuring the once-for-all death of Christ on Calvary
  d. their shift that this is an "unbloody sacrifice" does not get them off the hook: the shedding of blood is required for any cleansing [Heb. 9:22]

6. The Mass robs us of the benefit of Christ's death [fourth function]
  a. because the Mass offers new redemption, new forgiveness of sins, it sets aside the benefits of Christ's death
  b. their reply, that we obtain forgiveness of sins in the Mass solely because it has already been purchased by Christ's death, is but to boast that we have been redeemed by Christ on condition that we redeem ourselves
  c. we must understand not only that Christ is the sole victim: there is also but one sacrifice, lashing our faith to His cross

7. The Mass nullifies the Lord's Supper [fifth function]
  a. contrast between the true and the false, the latter marking man's ungratefulness
    (1) the Supper is a gift of God, to be received with thanksgiving
    (2) the Mass, conversely, is the paying of a price to God for Him to receive as satisfaction
  b. in the true Supper, restoration to life and continual revivification versus in the Mass, a daily sacrifice required to benefit us
  c. the Supper teaches a communion of believers bound together in Christ: the Mass tears the community apart
    (1) by letting the priests perform the sacrifice
    (2) in opening up the possibility of private Masses

Early Practice and the Rise of Misconceptions [8–11]

8. Private masses a repudiation of communion
   a. origin of the term "Mass" uncertain unless it refers to offerings given in early church
   b. the Lord's Supper is a sharing among the worshipers of Christ's body and blood; hence private Masses are an utter denial of its purpose, in fact a false imitation of it and hence its corruption
   c. private Masses led to other abuses: Mass without communion and idolatrous worship of the Host

9. The Mass not Scriptural and not primitive
   a. any study of the ancient church and the early fathers will disclose no basis for the Mass
   b. since obedience to God is stronger than sacrificial victims, seeing that Scripture provides no command of Mass-sacrifice, how can God be pleased with this human invention of the Mass-doctors?
   c. they must either show God to be its author, or they must abandon it forthwith

10. Did the church fathers look upon the Mass as a sacrifice?
    a. quoting isolated passages from the fathers which mention "sacrifice" does not prove the antiquity of the Mass, for by sacrifice the fathers mean nothing more than the remembrance of Christ's one true sacrifice
    b. this is clear, for example, from Augustine, who emphasizes the Old Testament sacrifices as but prefiguring the final, culminating sacrifice of Christ
    c. Chrysostom, too, would deny that any bishop can be an intercessor between God and man

11. Church fathers deviate from the divine institution
    a. yet the fathers sometimes erred in describing the Supper too much in terms of repeated or at least renewed sacrifice
    b. this was due to excessive emphasis upon an anagogical interpretation of Old Testament sacrifice, but was not meant in any way to detract from the Lord's unique sacrifice

c. it is better for pious hearts to rely solely on God's simple and pure ordinance

The Idea of Sacrifice in the Eucharist, and Scriptural Use of the Word "Sacrifice"; the Mass a Sacrilege [12–18]

12. The oblation of the Old Covenant and the Lord's Supper
    a. the Mosaic sacrifices were intended to set forth to the Jewish people the same effectiveness of Christ's death as the Supper today shows to us
    b. the mode of representation was different
        (1) Old Testament: Christ's death prefigured to the people, at the altar
        (2) New Testament: the benefits of Christ's death imparted to us, at the Table, as at a feast
    c. hence this loftiest mystery of all bids us lay aside all effort at human understanding, and to cleave solely to what Scripture teaches

13. The nature of sacrifice
    a. at this point some definition of the terms "sacrifice" and "priest" should be given for clarity's sake
    b. the Greek counterpart of the Scriptural term "sacrifice"—*thusia, prosphora, telete*—in a general sense means anything offered to God
    c. in Mosaic sacrifices there were two types, to be anagogically interpreted as foreshadowing the universal truth of sacrifices for God's people
        (1) offering of satisfaction for sin to redeem guilt before God
        (2) offering of supplication for God's favor:
            (a) thanksgiving for benefits received
            (b) exercise of simple piety to renew the confirmation of the covenant
    d. following this classification, our sacrifices fall into two classes:
        (1) a "sacrifice of praise and reverence" (or of "thanksgiving")
        (2) a "sacrifice of propitiation or expiation," to appease God's wrath, purge the sinner of filth, that he may return to God's favor
    e. in the Mosaic sacrifices, the victims did not actually atone for

sins but prefigured the true sacrifice of Christ alone, perfect and once-for-all

14. The sale of Masses
    a. to suppose that by repeating the oblation one obtains pardon for sins is a blasphemy against Christ and His cross
    b. the application of the Mass to particular persons, and for money, makes this an even greater abomination, worse than Judas' betrayal of Christ for money
    c. these priests by their oblation do not obtain atonement for sins; only Christ Himself can do this, by His eternal priesthood, supplanter of all old priesthoods

15. Plato's remarks on similar pretense and delusion
    a. Plato's description of the old propitiatory offerings in the second book of the *Republic* is very apropos regarding the falsities of the Mass
    b. the ancients laughed at by Plato thought that by money payments they could lighten their punishment in the afterlife, even though in the present life they were scoundrels
    c. what difference is there between these and men today who think that thus they will get off easily in purgatory?

16. The "thank offering" of the Christian church
    a. under the "sacrifice of thanksgiving" are included the love we show to our fellow members, our prayers, and our worship, not mere outward acts, but total dedication of ourselves to the Lord
    b. this kind of sacrifice is not concerned with appeasing God's wrath but with magnifying His holy name; it is utterly necessary for the life and health of the church

17. Scriptural phrases illustrate the sacrifices of praise
    a. a common truth for Christian church and Jewish nation underlay those carnal sacrifices
    b. this seen in the Old Testament, e.g., in the prayers of David and Hosea's "calves of lips"
    c. this seen in the New Testament: we are a royal priesthood as, in confessing His name, and through Christ as our sole intercessor, we offer the "fruit of our lips" (Heb. 13:15, Vulgate)

18. The Mass itself, apart from its profanation, is sacrilege
    a. the holiest holiness of the Mass is an utter abomination to Satan's means of subverting whole nations
    b. there is no need to elaborate, then, on the manifold abuses of the Mass itself

***Conclusion of Chapters 14 to 17 and Transition to Chapter 19: Two Christian Sacraments Only** [19-20]*

19. Baptism and the Lord's Supper are the only sacraments
    a. the summary of what should be known about the two true sacraments
        (1) baptism should be an entry into the church, an initiation into faith: one baptism only
        (2) the Supper should be a sort of continual food on which Christ spiritually feeds the household of his believers: repeatedly distributed
    b. only God, not man, can institute a sacrament: there are but two sacraments appointed by God
        (1) to instruct us concerning His promise
        (2) to attest His good will toward us

20. The addition of sacraments not permitted
    a. let the church be content, even to the end of time, with but these two
    b. God gave the Jews different "sacraments" in accordance with changing conditions, but with the intent (by their very impermanence) to point to something better yet to come
    c. the conditions under which we live, however, are far different: under the sacraments given us, without further addition, we are to look to the great day when the Lord will fully manifest the glory of His kingdom
    d. just as men are denied the right to coin new sacraments, they are not to trick out the dominical sacraments with newfangled human inventions
        (1) today the sacraments are cluttered with processions, ceremonies, and mimes, not authorized by God's Word
        (2) yet God's Word goes unmentioned

CHAPTER 19
The Five Other Ceremonies, Falsely Termed Sacraments; Although Commonly Considered Sacraments Hitherto, They Are Proved Not to Be Such and Their Real Nature Is Shown

***Five Alleged Sacraments, Not Authorized by God's Word or Used in the Early Church** [1–3]*

1. It is not merely a matter of the term "sacrament"
   a. were it not for the fact that the notion of seven sacraments is deeply ingrained in people today, our exposition of the two truly dominical sacraments would be sufficient
   b. our motive in attacking the false sacraments: not a mere desire to quarrel, but the intent is to expose opponents' indiscriminate definition of all seven as visible forms of an invisible grace, thus making all vessels of the Holy Spirit means to righteousness and grace
   c. the term wrongly applied to the five because to them is not attached the command or promise of the Lord

2. God alone can establish a sacrament
   a. as Augustine says, the Word of God must precede to make a sacrament a sacrament; men are incapable of concealing the very mysteries of God under humble, physical things
   b. a useful distinction made in Scripture: between sacraments and other ceremonies

3. That the sacraments are seven in number was unknown in the ancient church
   a. the early church used the term "sacrament" in two ways
      (1) to refer to all ceremonies, outward rites, exercises of piety
      (2) specifically to refer to Baptism and Eucharist, sole testimonies to us of divine grace
   b. this fact demonstrated from Augustine's usage

***Confirmation Not a Sacrament: Early Practice of Reception after Instruction Should Be Restored** [4–13]*

4. Custom of the ancient church
   a. to afford those baptized as infants the same opportunity to

confess their faith before the church as was given to adult catechumens, there grew up the practice of bringing them at the onset of adolescence before the bishop and people, with catechetical examination, public confession, and solemn blessing with laying on of hands

b. this practice remarked by Leo I and Jerome (although the latter wrongly claimed apostolic origin for it)

c. we have no quarrel with the practice of such blessing, provided it be restored to pure use

5. Full development and meaning of confirmation according to Romanist teaching
   a. later generations, however, have wrongly erected this rite into a full sacrament, conferring the Holy Spirit for an increase of grace, with anointing and an impressive formula
   b. but where is the word, the command to ministers to perform this as a sacrament? the burden of proof rests with its proponents

6. Appeal to apostolic laying on of hands is unfounded
   a. instances of the laying on of hands by the apostles rehearsed: we interpret their practice as signifying thereby that those on whom they laid their hands were commended to God and offered to Him
   b. contrast between the apostolic age and our own
      (1) God worked mighty miracles in the early years of the church to establish it
      (2) once established and disclosed, the church has not been forsaken by the Holy Spirit, but no longer is it marked by such unheard-of miracles
   c. hence, present practitioners of laying on of hands falsely claim they are using the rite in the same manner as the apostles

7. Anointing with oil is a counterfeit sacrament
   a. who taught our opponents to seek salvation in oil, a physical, perishable element?
   b. opponents' reply: in baptism, water and in Eucharist, bread and wine
   c. rejoinder:
      (1) two things are to be noted in dominical sacraments
         (a) substance of the physical thing set forth to us

(b) form impressed on it by God's Word, wherein its whole force lies

(2) as physical things they will pass away (I Cor. 7:31) but as sanctified by God's Word as sacraments, they transcend the flesh and truly teach us spiritually

8. Confirmation as the devaluation of baptism
   a. contention of opponents: the Holy Spirit given in baptism for innocence; in confirmation, for increase of grace; hence confirmation completes the incomplete impartation of the Holy Spirit in baptism
   b. this notion is false as proved by
      (1) Canon 3, Synod of Milevis (AD 416)
      (2) New Testament passages

9. The doctrine of the necessity of confirmation for salvation is nonsense
   a. the notion that confirmation makes incomplete Christians complete is clearly counter to the teaching of the Scripture and contends that apostles and martyrs (not having had this sacrament) never attained the status of real Christians
   b. its proponents refute themselves by letting so many "half-Christians" in their churches go unconfirmed

10. The papists would put confirmation above baptism
    a. their reasons
       (1) baptism can be administered by a simple priest, but confirmation only by a bishop
       (2) or: confirmation is given by those more worthy; confirmation is imparted to the worthier part of the body, the forehead
       (3) or: confirmation provides a greater increase of virtues, although baptism avails more for forgiveness of sins
    b. first reason refuted by a *reductio ad absurdum*

11. Frivolous arguments for esteeming confirmation above baptism
    a. second reason—that confirmation (in which the forehead is smeared with oil) is superior to baptism (in which oil is poured on the top of the head)—promotes oil beyond water as the means of baptism: a sheer corruption of the sacrament of baptism!
    b. third reason refuted: no comparison between the apostles' laying on of hands and these men's grease!

12. Confirmation cannot be upheld by the practice of the ancient church
    a. denied Scriptural foundation for their claimed sacrament, the papists have recourse to "ancient traditions"
    b. but here, too, the fathers are on our side: when they speak expressly of sacraments, they count only two
    c. this point confirmed from Augustine

13. True confirmation is catechesis
    a. true confirmation is not this false sacrament but a proper catechesis
    b. plan: a catechetical discipline for children with a simple summary of the articles of our religion, duly studied by children who would present themselves at age ten before the church to confess their faith
    c. values of such a procedure
        (1) slothful parents would be aroused by the threat of public disgrace to desist from their negligence
        (2) there would be more agreement in faith among Christian people
        (3) not so many would go untaught and ignorant or be carried away into new and strange doctrines

Penance Fails to Answer the Definition of a Sacrament [*14–17*]

14. The practice of penance in the ancient church
    a. since the Scriptural doctrine of repentance has been discussed already, this section will be confined to dealing with the notion that penance is a sacrament
    b. however, it is useful to review the rite of the ancient church from which the papists falsely claim an origin for their so-called sacrament
        (1) originally after public confession and satisfaction for sin, the penitent was reconciled by a solemn laying on of hands
        (2) to avoid excessive leniency, the responsibility came to be laid upon the bishops, although usually in concert with the other clergy
        (3) after the rite of reconciliation the person was restored to communion
        (4) later this practice deteriorated and the rite also came to be used for private absolutions as well

c. our opinion
   (1) the ancient rite should be restored
   (2) the present form is less necessary
   (3) the important thing: this is a ceremony ordained by men, not by God—having a lower place, therefore, than those commended by God's Word

15. Penance is no sacrament
   a. confused scholastic opinions concerning sign (outward penance?) and matter (inner repentance?) or double sacrament (inner plus outer repentance?)
   b. in the conflict over the definition of sacrament, Augustine is on our side ("an outward ceremony instituted by the Lord to confirm our faith") against the schools

16. Why not make absolution the sacrament?
   a. priestly absolution has more right to be called a sacrament than does penance, if one says absolution is a ceremony to confirm our faith in forgiveness of sins and has the promise of the keys
   b. even Augustine would support such a view; their claim that penance is a sacrament is far more confused

17. Baptism the sacrament of repentance
   a. ground for denying penance to be a sacrament
      (1) there is no special promise of God to this effect
      (2) the rites connected with penance are man-made; ceremonies of true sacraments are ordained by God alone
   b. Jerome's improper statement about "the second plank after shipwreck" is misapplied to penance by the Romanists
   c. the true sacrament of penance is baptism itself
      (1) see [pseudo] Augustine's *De fide ad Petrum* 30.73
      (2) or more to the point: Mark 1:4; Luke 3:3

***Extreme Unction Rests Upon a Misuse of James 5:14–15 and Is No Sacrament** [18–21]*

18. Alleged Scripture on extreme unction rejected
   a. rite of extreme unction described, with its two claimed powers
      (1) forgiveness of sins
      (2) easing of bodily sickness or salvation of the soul
   b. Scriptural teaching
      (1) James 5:14, their proof text, wrongly applied

(2) use of oil, spittle, mud, etc., in healing miracles of New Testament incidental, or rather, significatory of the Lord's power, which really accomplished the miracles, rather than human agency [oil—Holy Spirit]

c. what applied in the apostolic age to miracles was subsequently replaced by marvellous power of the preaching of the gospel: hence those apostolic arrangements have nothing to do with us

19. Extreme unction is no sacrament

a. other miraculous acts of the apostles could, on their reasoning, just as well be sacraments

b. James was talking about a direct blessing to the church of that time; the Lord, present with His people in every age, gave a temporary gift of healing to the apostles: today His healing is not dispensed through apostolic hands

20. Unction has no divine authorization or promise

a. oil used in contrary ways by the apostles and by the Romanists

(1) for apostles: not their power but the Holy Spirit's

(2) for Romanists: putrid oil identified with power of the Holy Spirit

b. anointing not a sacrament because

(1) not instituted by God, nor delivered to us

(2) without a promise, nor applied to us

c. in the case of circumcision the rite was at least of divine institution and promise, although not for us

21. The papists do not proceed at all according to James' "words of institution"

a. even if we allowed that this rite applies now, as it did in apostolic times, the Romanists' procedure does not follow James

b. differences:

	James	*papal rite*
(1) applies to	all sick persons	half-dead corpses
(2) administered by	elders of the church	priest only
(3) employs	common oil	holy oil consecrated by a bishop
(4) absolves	through prayers of faithful	through application of oil itself

c. also Innocent I at Rome established the practice that all Christians (not just priests) should use oil for anointing as needed

The Alleged Sacrament of Holy Orders Complicated by the Seven Ranks of Clergy; the Ceremonies of Institution and Functions of These Criticized [22-23]

22. One sacrament—or seven?
   a. confusion among ecclesiastical authorities over the actual composition of the "sacrament" of order
      (1) are the seven grades of the priesthood because of their different graces actually in themselves seven separate sacraments?
      (2) false derivation from the seven (actually, six) gifts of the Holy Spirit
      (3) or are there really nine orders (symbolic of the church triumphant?)
   b. Peter Lombard says "seven" but the most enlightened doctors (yet disagreeing among themselves) say otherwise

23. Christ must have occupied all seven offices; nonsensical exegesis:
   a. doorkeeping (John 2:15; Matt. 21:12; John 10:7)
   b. reader (Luke 4:17)
   c. exorcist (Matt. 7:32f.)
   d. acolyte (John 8:12)
   e. subdeacon (John 13:4f.)
   f. deacon (Matt. 26:26)
   g. priest (Matt. 27:50; Eph. 5:2)

24. The holders of the lower orders do not practice their office at all
   a. function of readers, psalmists, doorkeepers, acolytes actually performed today by boys or hired laymen; persons in these minor orders never peform these duties
   b. in the perversity of this age their failure to follow their own regulations leaves them under anathema
   c. the exorcists especially illustrate the disuse of functions
   d. the only source for such regulations is the Sorbonnists and Canonists

25. The ceremonies of consecration, especially the tonsure
   a. the shaving of the head supposed to represent the crown of the "royal priesthood"

b. this is a false exegesis of I Peter 1:15–16, which really refers to the whole people of God

26. To cite the Nazarites and Paul is beside the point
    a. their claim to imitate the purifications of the Nazarites is a reintroduction of Judaism into Christianity
    b. in Acts 18:18 the shaving of Priscilla is not recorded, that of Aquila is doubtful, and Paul's was done not for piety's sake but out of love for the weaker brethren
    c. stupid custom of the coronal or circular tonsure

27. Historical interpretation of the tonsure
    a. in the earliest period clerical tonsure was instituted to distinguish the clergy from effeminate men who let their hair grow long
    b. as fashions changed, the clergy tended to take the opposite tack, to distinguish themselves from the worldly style
    c. as things grew more and more corrupt, the justification of tonsure was sought in religious mystery, rather than practical necessity
    d. each of these orders receives symbolic objects and formulas—supposedly marking them as sacraments
    e. the claim of the Schoolmen and Canonists that these are minor orders is absurd, for they were devised centuries after the primitive church

28. "Priest" and "presbyter"
    a. the three top levels they call "major orders" and especially consider them "holy"
    b. because the "priest" according to them is to perform the sacrifice of Christ's body and blood in the altar, frame prayers, and bless God's gifts, he receives paten and host and anointing of hands—rites unsupported by the Word of God
    c. this wrongs Christ the sole priest who offered Himself once for all
    d. the true office of presbyter
        (1) not a sacrament because it is not common to all believers but only to those chosen
        (2) has to do with the gospel and sacraments, not with sacrificing

29. The ceremonies in ordaining priests
    a. their insufflation and other ordination rites are false and

wanton imitations of the acts of Jesus and of the apostles, which acts were not intended for ritual repetition by their followers

b. we are here primarily condemning the ordination rites which are really unscriptural

30. Christ's priesthood supersedes that of Aaron
   a. the Roman order claims the Aaronic priesthood as the source of their anointing, while we assert, with the New Testament, that the Old Testament priesthood foreshadowed and prefigured the priesthood of Christ, in whom they ceased and were fulfilled
   b. if the Romanists so delight in Jewish worship why do they not take over the sacrifice of calves and oxen to make their imitation complete?
   c. yet in emulating the Levites, the Romanists are not really authentic, and what's more, they are apostates to Christ

31. Signs claimed for this supposed sacrament
   a. oil?
      (1) how can oil (which can be washed off the skin) imprint an indelible character?
      (2) ah, but it is spiritual
      (3) well, then, where is the Word that makes it a sacrament?
      (4) God's commands through Moses to Aaron
      (5) but this is nothing but shaping one religion out of Christianity and Judaism and paganism by sewing patches together—all of which lacks the Word of God
   b. but what about laying on of hands?
      (1) in lawful ordinations a sacrament, yes
      (2) but in these false rites, sans command and promise, no!

32. The deacons
   a. the claimed office of deacon (assistant to the priest) not in accord with the true gospel ministry of deacons
   b. how the ordination rites for the deacons imitate the ordination of Christ's apostles
   c. why not call them "Levites" instead of deacons, as they actually admit them to be?

33. Subdeacons
   a. in the ancient church the subdeacons cared for the poor; today they perform trifling functions in the Mass

b. their rite of consecration illustrates the familiar pattern of claiming the Holy Spirit to be enclosed in unscriptural, man-made ceremonies

c. summary: no sacrament here because to this ceremony no promise is joined

Erroneous Claim that Marriage Is a Sacrament from Misunderstanding of Eph. 5:28, and Other Passages: Abuses Connected with Marriage [*34–37*]

34. Marriage is no sacrament
    a. a lawful ordinance of God as other human activities are, marriage was never admininstered as a sacrament until the time of Gregory VII (AD 1073–1085)
    b. is this the sign of a sacred thing, that is, of the spiritual joining of Christ with the church?
    c. no! this is mistaking a similitude (of which there are many in Scripture not so interpreted!) for a sacrament

35. They misapply Eph. 5:28
    a. they base their claim that marriage is a sacrament upon Paul's words
    b. here, however, Paul is trying to show married men with what kind of love they ought to embrace their wives, using Christ's boundless love of the church as the measure

36. This confusion arises from the translation of the word "mystery" and their low view of marriage
    a. the Vulgate version wrongly translates *mysterion* as *sacramentum*
    b. suppose, however, this were a sacrament—what a low view they have of it in barring priests from it
        (1) they answer they are only barring them from the lust of copulation
        (2) yet copulation is a part of the sacrament, and that alone is the figure of the union we have with Christ
        (3) if grace of the Holy Spirit is conferred in the sacrament and copulation is a sacrament, how can they deny that the Holy Spirit is ever present in copulation?

37. Oppressive consequences of the Roman doctrine
    a. by making marriage a sacrament, the Roman Church initiated a whole series of abominations

b. they set up special marriage courts and hedged marriage round with innumerable rules and regulations which are a tyranny to the human spirit

CHAPTER 20
Civil Government

How Civil and Spiritual Government Are Related [*1–2*]

1. Differences between spiritual and civil government
   a. having already dealt with spiritual government, it is now necessary to discuss civil, which has to do with civil practice and outward morality
   b. this discussion is made necessary by two extreme parties that endanger purity of faith
      (1) some try violently to overthrow this divinely established twofold government [Anabaptists]
      (2) others, in flattering their earthly princes, well nigh set aside God's own rule [Machiavelli?]
   c. false ideas of freedom
      (1) some Christian revolutionaries think freedom is possible only if courts, laws, magistrates, etc. be abolished
      (2) this foolish attitude is marked by a failure to understand that Christ's spiritual kingdom and civil jurisdiction are completely distinct, as Paul's teaching repeatedly shows: "it is a Jewish vanity to seek and enclose Christ's kingdom within the elements of this world"

2. The two "governments" are not antithetical
   a. certain fanatics (of antinomian bent) reject earthly responsibility and government as unclean and beneath their heavenly condition
   b. but earthly and heavenly kingdoms while distinct are not at variance
      (1) spiritual government here and now gives us a forecast of immortal and incorruptible blessedness
      (2) civil government, while we live among men has the following ends:
         (a) to cherish and protect the outward worship of God
         (b) to defend sound doctrine of piety and the position of the church
         (c) to adjust our life to the society of men

(d) to form our social behavior to civil righteousness
(e) to reconcile us with one another
(f) to promote general peace and tranquillity
c. our opponents' views based on a false idea of perfection

Necessity and Divine Sanction of Civil Government [*3–7*]

3. The chief tasks and burdens of civil government
   a. civil government, far from deserving abolition, is as necessary to men as bread, water, sun, air; it provides that
      (1) humanity be maintained among men
      (2) public manifestation of religion exist among Christians
   b. there is no contradiction between giving civil government the task of rightly establishing religion and asserting the independence of Christian faith and worship from civil authority
   c. the three parts of civil government here to be discussed separately:
      (1) magistrate
         (a) lawful calling approved of God?
         (b) nature of the office
         (c) extent of its power
      (2) laws: with what laws a Christian government ought to be governed
      (3) people
         (a) how the laws benefit the people
         (b) what obedience they owe to the magistrate

4. The magistracy is ordained by God
   a. Scripture gives magistrates lofty titles and functions:
      (1) "Gods" = vicegerents of God
      (2) their reign is God's doing = divine providence and holy ordinance
      (3) "ruling" a gift of God
      (4) power divinely ordained
      (5) "ministers of God"
   b. Scriptural examples:
      (1) kings: David, Josiah, Hezekiah
      (2) lordships: Joseph, Daniel
      (3) civil rulers of a free people: Moses, Joshua, Judges
   c. civil authority the most honorable of all callings in the whole life of mortal men

5. Against the "Christian" denial or rejection of magistracy
   a. it is wrong to assert an evangelical perfection in today's en-

lightenment that repudiates as outmoded the rule of ancient kings and judges over ignorant folk

b. on the contrary, both Old Testament and New Testament assert the continuing validity and necessity of civil government even under the dispensation of Christ

6. Magistrates should be faithful deputies
   a. if magistrates remember they are vicars of God, they must needs strive to represent in themselves to men some image of divine providence, protection, goodness, benevolence and justice
   b. as many Scriptural references show, magistrates are to remember they will be called to account by God for their administration

7. The coercive character of magistracy does not hinder its recognition
   a. opponents (Anabaptists) falsely draw an analogy between kings and disciples Luke 22:25–26: all this proves is that apostles and magistrates hold two different offices
   b. Scripture teaches the providential character of magistrates' power and rule

***Forms of Government, and Duties of Magistrates: Issues of War and Taxation** [8–13]*

8. The diversity of forms of government
   a. each of the basic forms of government has its own usefulness and arises out of particular circumstances
   b. but, other things being equal, an aristocracy bordering on democracy (as in pre-Davidic Israel) is desirable because it affords checks and balances against human wilfulness not found in absolute monarchies
   c. in the world as a whole we see divine providence work in the diversity of governments tailored to the distinctive condition of each region

9. Concern for both tables of the law
   a. first table: both in Scripture and in secular writings, political theory begins with the establishment and support of religion
      (1) Scripture praises kings who restored the fallen worship of God and decries anarchy

(2) folly of those who neglect religion and concentrate on human justice alone as the end of government

b. second table:

(1) instances from Scripture of call upon rulers to execute human justice

(2) to carry out this duty, rulers have two instruments:

	Scriptural		*Classical*
(a)	Justice	~	Reward
(b)		~	Punishment (cf. Solon)

10. The magistrates' exercise of force is compatible with piety

a. question: "thou shalt not kill" versus "pious shedding of blood by magistrates"?

b. answer: the magistrate is not acting for himself but for God when he administers punishment

(1) Scriptural teaching and examples

(2) clemency in executing judgment: the need for a mean between excessive severity and the affectation of clemency

11. On the right of the government to wage war

a. wars undertaken to execute public vengeance against those who disrupt tranquillity and perpetrate sedition are lawful

b. there is no difference between a robber who harms a few and those who invade a country wherein they have no right

c. hence princes are to protect the dominions under their care if they are attacked, just as they restrain private persons' misdeeds by judicial punishment

12. Restraint and humanity in war

a. why is there no express testimony in the New Testament that war is lawful for Christians?

(1) ancient reasons for waging war and for defending peoples still pertain today

(2) the apostles, whose task was to establish the spiritual kingdom of Christ—not a civil government—had no reason to provide such teaching

(3) Christ did not tell soldiers, asking about salvation, to throw away their arms, but to be content with their wages (i.e., to continue bearing arms) Luke 3:14—*Aug. Ep.* 138; *Serm.* 13

b. magistrates must avoid hatred and practice restraint in going to war

(1) take pity on the common nature of him whose fault they are punishing
(2) undertake war only in great necessity, and after all means short of war have been tried
(3) be guided by concern for the people alone; otherwise magistrates will be wickedly abusing their power

c. the same basis applied to establishment of:
(1) garrisons; troops stationed to defend boundaries of a country from invasion
(2) leagues: pacts of mutual assistance
(3) civil defense: things used in the art of war

13. Concerning the right of the government to levy tribute
a. tributes and taxes lawful revenues for princes, both for public expenses of their office and for the magnificence of a household befitting their dignity; Scriptural examples
b. yet all such expenditures are to be used with the understanding that these are not so much private chests as treasuries of the entire people; imposts to be laid only for public necessity, not without cause
c. princes must therefore avoid waste and needless luxury, keeping a pure conscience before God; private citizens are not to complain about such due expenses of princes

***Public Law and Judicial Procedures, as Related to Christian Duty* [*14-21*]**

14. Old Testament law and the laws of nations
a. the laws and the magistrate stand together in the state: "the laws are a silent magistrate; the magistrate is a living law"
b. by what laws ought a Christian state be governed?
(1) only a brief summary will be given here
(2) a theocracy based upon the judicial laws of the Old Testament, advocated by some, is foolish, for
(3) the Mosaic law is divided into moral, ceremonial, and judicial
(a) only the moral laws remain unchanged
(b) the other two classes, while containing some moral aspects, can and have been changed and abrogated

15. Moral, ceremonial, and judicial law distinguished
a. scope of the three "layers" of the Mosaic law
(1) moral law

(a) two heads: worship God with pure faith and piety; embrace men with sincere affection

(b) this eternal rule of worship and fraternal love enjoined upon all times and nations

(2) ceremonial law: tutelage of the Jews for their training unto Christ when the divine wisdom would be fully revealed to all nations; kept the church of the Jews reverent to God; but it is distinct from piety itself

(3) judicial law: basis of the civil government of the Jews, for a blameless and peaceable life; intended to preserve the love enjoined by God's eternal law, but distinct from that precept of love

(4) therefore, ceremonial and judicial laws could be abrogated, yet the precepts of love still remained

b. all nations, then, free to make laws profitable to themselves—but in conformity to the perpetual rule of love

16. Unity and diversity of laws

a. all laws have two elements

(1) the constitution: the variable, dependent on the circumstances of promulgation

(2) the equity: the constant, goal of all laws, and foundation of their constitution

b. law of God = moral law = testimony of natural law and of conscience engraved by God on men's minds

c. laws of other nations vary tremendously in detail from the Mosaic law—due to differences of times and places, but tend to the same end; to punish the crimes condemned by God's eternal law: murder, theft, adultery, false witness

d. it is foolish, then, to complain that God's law is contravened when new laws replace the transient elements in the Mosaic law

17. Christians may use the law courts, but without hatred and revenge

a. two questions to examine

(1) usefulness for the common society of Christians of laws, judgments and magistrate

(2) extent of the obedience of the private citizen to the magistrate

b. two extremes of men with respect to use of law courts:

(1) those who reject recourse to law as forbidden in New Testament; this is a wrong attitude, for the magistrate is

God's minister (Rom. 13:4) for our protection (I Tim. 2:2) and we are therefore to avail ourselves of his help when necessary
(2) those of a litigious and vengeful spirit who enter lawsuits in a vindictive spirit: these two are wrong, for they fail to maintain Christian charity

18. The Christian's motives in litigation
   a. what constitutes right use of a lawsuit?
      (1) the accused defends himself without bitterness, seeking only to defend what is his by right
      (2) the plaintiff, in the magistrate's care, seeks what is fair and good
   b. unless free of contention and malice, court actions of even the justest cause are impious
   c. the principle: treat one's adversary with the same love and good will as if the whole matter were already amicably settled
   d. admittedly such "ideal" lawsuits are rare in these times; but this is the way Christians should conduct them

19. Against the rejection of the judicial process
   a. the second class of persons reject all legal contention, thus repudiating God's holy ordinance
   b. yet, in using the law courts, all Christians are forbidden to desire revenge—to return evil for evil; the right motive is, without vengeful mind to seek to prevent harm being done to society
   c. but should we not wait for the Lord to do the avenging as He promised? no, for the magistrate's revenge is God's not man's

20. The Christian endures insults, but with amity and equity defends the public interest
   a. in using the law courts, Christians do not run counter to Christ's precepts on love of enemies, etc.
   b. they enjoy the magistrate's help in preserving their own possessions, while friendly toward enemies and zealous for public welfare
   c. Augustine's interpretation of the precepts:
      (1) bear the malice of those one desires to become good, to increase the number of good men, not to add oneself to the number of the bad by a like malice
      (2) pertains more to the inner intention which is the secret basis for our outward well doing

21. Paul condemns a litigious spirit, but not all litigation
    a. Paul does not totally condemn lawsuits: he was coping with the excessive litigiousness of the Corinthians
        (1) the gospel disgraced by their intemperate quarrels
        (2) disruption of brotherly love and outbreak of greed among men also rebuked
    b. only lawsuits undertaken apart from, and going beyond, love run counter to Paul's advice

Obedience, with Reverence, Due Even Unjust Rulers [22-29]

22. Deference
    a. to honor magistrates means more than to tolerate them as a necessary evil; we must then respect and reverence them as God's ministers
    b. we should obey the magistrate out of love of God (the source of his office) rather than fear of the magistrate himself
    c. therefore we respect the magistrate for the dignity of his office, not because a mask of dignity covers a wicked person

23. Obedience
    a. we should show our willing obedience to our rulers by obeying their proclamations, paying taxes, shouldering public offices and defense tasks, etc.: teaching of Paul and Peter on this
    b. resistance of the magistrate tantamount to resisting God Himself, and subject to the same vengeance
    c. this obedience includes private citizens' refraining from public political action unless invested with political authority by the ruler himself

24. Obedience is also due the unjust magistrate
    a. our teaching applies, of course, to good rulers
    b. but in most times there have been "lords of misrule": need these be obeyed? some ask—an attitude of great antiquity toward all tyrants

25. The wicked ruler a judgment of God
    a. God's Word teaches that the magistrate's office has its authority from Him:
        (1) the good magistrate for public benefit
        (2) the unjust and incompetent ones are for the punishment of public wickedness

b. before giving Scriptural evidence for this, we must assert that the same plenitude of divinely-given power rests in the wicked as upon the good ruler, and this demands our obedience to both

26. Obedience to bad kings required in Scripture: the special operation of God's providence in kingdoms and kings
    a. in Daniel the divine determination of all kingship
    b. Samuel's warning upon the inauguration of the kingdom concerning the coming oppression of the people in Israel: the subjects are not to complain but to obey

27. The case of Nebuchadnezzar in Jeremiah 27
    a. Jeremiah teaches the subjection, for a time, of the nations to Nebuchadnezzar
    b. we must never harbor the seditious thought that a king should be treated according to his merits

28. General testimonies of Scripture on the sanctity of the royal person
    a. the command to obey princes regardless of their merits but solely on the basis of the divine appointment of their office not confined to Israel
    b. Scriptural testimonies of this

29. It is not the part of subjects but of God to vindicate the right
    a. reverence owed to rulers not because they are just and good but because of their divinely imprinted and inviolable majesty (whether they be bad or good)
    b. argument from analogy of families: the wickedness or undutifulness of parents toward children or wives toward husbands does not abrogate the requirement of obedience
    c. let us look to our own duties and our own misdeeds, rather than another's
        (1) this will humble and restrain our impatience
        (2) and lead us to implore the Lord's help, in whose hand are all kings and kingdoms, as Scripture teaches

Constitutional Magistrates, However, Ought to Check the Tyranny of Kings; Obedience to God Comes First [*30–31*]

30. As Scripture shows, God intervenes to bring relief from tyrannous rulers

a. sometimes by open avengers to punish and deliver at His express command (a lawful act)
b. sometimes by unwitting agents whose original intentions and final results are different (unlawful and evil act, but directed by God to a good end)

31. Constitutional defenders of the people's freedom
 a. this means of relief from tyranny through divinely ordained human action is not to be jumped at lightly, and never to be usurped by private individuals
 b. in ancient times (and today?) there were special magistrates for the restraint of magistrates; they must do their divinely-appointed duty of protecting the people against misrule
  (1) ephors versus Spartan Kings
  (2) tribunes of the people versus Roman consuls
  (3) demarch versus Athenian senate
  (4) three estates versus the French king

32. Obedience to man must not become disobedience to God
 a. no human command is ever to be obeyed that contravenes God's will
 b. this principle amply illustrated in both Old Testament and New Testament: Daniel, Hosea, Peter, Paul: "We must obey God rather than men" Acts 5:29

GOD BE PRAISED